PASSTRAK

SERIES 6

INVESTMENT COMPANY/VARIABLE CONTRACTS LIMITED REPRESENTATIVE

LICENSE EXAM MANUAL

19TH EDITION

DEARBORN™
A **Kaplan Professional** Company

At press time, this 19th edition of PASSTRAK® Series 6 contains the most complete and accurate information currently available for the NASD Series 6 license examination. Owing to the nature of securities license examinations, however, information may have been added recently to the actual test that does not appear in this edition.

This publication is designed to provide accurate and authoritative information in regard to the subject matter covered. It is sold with the understanding that the publisher is not engaged in rendering legal, accounting, or other professional service. If legal advice or other expert assistance is required, the services of a competent professional person should be sought.

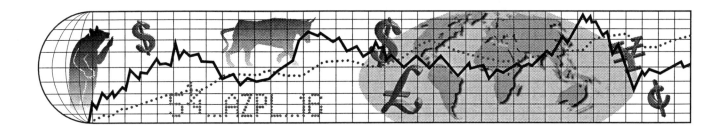

Table of Contents

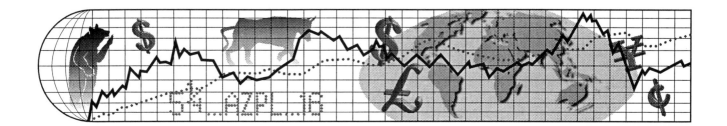

Acknowledgments

My thanks to the many Dearborn students, instructors and customers who contributed to the 19th edition of the *Series 6 License Exam Manual*. Special thanks to Marc Katz, Rock Sytsma, Lynn Nessa, Carla Gordon and Phil Keener, for their valuable time and expertise . I would also like to thank Kelley Prosser, Lucy Jenkins and Gail Chandler, whose amazing effort and skill brought this project to completion.

Marcia Burak
Publisher

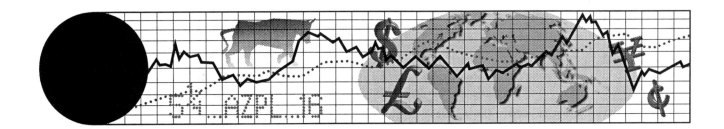

Series 6 Introduction

Welcome to Dearborn's *Series 6 License Exam Manual*. Because you probably have a lot of questions about the course and the exam, we have tried to anticipate some of them and provide you with answers to help you on your way.

How is the License Exam Manual *organized?*

Dearborn's *Series 6 License Exam Manual* consists of lessons, lesson exams and practice finals.

In addition to the regular text, each lesson also has some unique features to help with your quick understanding of the material. When an additional point will be valuable to your comprehension, special notes are embedded in the text. These two types of notes have a specific purpose and are denoted with different text markers:

✓ *Take Note:* Have you ever felt after you finished reading a paragraph that a little extra insight would make the subject more clear? These extra notes give you tips and examples that help make the important test points stand out.

 **Test Topic Alert!**　　Have you ever worked hard to prepare for an exam, only to find out that the questions you encountered weren't what you expected? Here the content is related to what you are likely to see on your Series 6 exam.

As you read each Lesson, you will also see Quick Quizzes that will ensure that you have understood and retained the material covered in that particular section. The Quick Quizzes aren't intended to be difficult—just a quick interactive review of what you just read.

In addition to the Quick Quizzes, the Lesson Hotsheets at the end of each lesson summarize the key points in an easy-to-use format. These Hotsheets are reprinted at the end of the License Exam Manual on perforated pages for your convenience. Use these Hotsheets as review notes when you are on the go but still want to keep the material fresh in your mind.

The book is made up of four lessons outlined the same way the NASD has outlined the material for the exam.

- **Lesson One** defines equity and debt instruments and introduces securities markets, investor strategies and risks, and economic fundamentals.
- **Lesson Two** introduces investment companies and explains characteristics of and regulations relevant to the sale of mutual funds.
- **Lesson Three** focuses on the features of variable annuities, variable life and retirement plans.
- **Lesson Four** concludes with a review of securities industry regulation, with particular emphasis on regulations that pertain to the sale of mutual funds, variable annuities and variable life.

The enclosed Drill and Practice CD ROM includes a large bank of questions that are similar in style and content to those you will encounter on the Series 6 exam. You may use it to generate exams by specific topic or to create 100-question practice finals that are similar in difficulty and proportionate mixture to your actual Series 6 examination. You should devote a significant amount of your study time to the completion of practice questions and review of rationales.

How much time should I spend studying?

You should plan to spend approximately 40 to 60 hours reading the material and working through the questions. Your actual time, of course, may vary from this figure depending on your reading rate, comprehension, professional background and study environment.

Spread your study time over the three or four weeks before the date on which you are scheduled to take the Series 6 exam. Select a time and place for studying that will allow you to concentrate your full attention on the material at hand. You have a lot of information to learn and a lot of ground to cover. Be sure to give yourself enough time to learn the material.

What is the best way to structure my study time?

The following schedule is suggested to help you obtain maximum retention from your study efforts. Remember, this is a guideline only, because each individual may require more or less time to complete the steps included. Think of this plan as your *10-Step Program to Series 6 Success!*

Step 1: Read Lesson 1 and complete the lesson exam. Review rationales for all questions whether you got them right or wrong. (7–11 hours)

Step 2: On the Drill and Practice CD-ROM, create and complete an exam for each topic included under the Lesson 1 heading. For best results, select the maximum number of questions within each topic. Carefully review all rationales. Do an additional exam on any topic on which you score under 60 percent. After completion of all topic exams, create a 50-question exam comprised of all Lesson 1 topics. Repeat this 50-question exam until you score at least 70 percent. (5–10 hours)

Do not be overly concerned with your score on the first attempt at any of these exams. Instead, take the opportunity to learn from your mistakes and increase your knowledge.

Step 3: Read Lesson 2 and complete the lesson exam. Review rationales for all questions whether you got them right or wrong. (6–10 hours)

Step 4: On the Drill and Practice CD-ROM, create and complete an exam for each topic included under the Lesson 2 heading. For best results, select the maximum number of questions within each topic. Carefully review all rationales. Do an additional exam on any topic on which you score under 60 percent . After completion of all topic exams, create a 50-question exam comprised of all Lesson 2 topics. Repeat this 50-question exam until you score at least 70 percent. (5–10 hours)

Step 5: Read Lesson 3 and complete the lesson exam. Review rationales for all questions whether you got them right or wrong. (3–5 hours)

Step 6: On the Drill and Practice CD-ROM, create and complete an exam for each topic included under the Lesson 3 heading. For best results, select the maximum number of questions within each topic. Carefully review all rationales. Do an additional exam on any topic on which you score under 60 percent. After completion of all topic exams, create a 30-question exam comprised of all Lesson 3 topics. Repeat this 30-question exam until you score at least 70 percent. (3–6 hours)

Step 7: Read Lesson 4 and complete the lesson exam. Review rationales for all questions whether you got them right or wrong. (3-5 hours)

Step 8: On the Drill and Practice CD-ROM, create and complete an exam for each topic included under the Lesson 4 heading. For best results, select the maximum number of questions within each topic. Carefully review all rationales. Do an additional exam on any topic on which you score under 60 percent. After completion of all topic exams, create a 50-question exam comprised of all Lesson 4 topics. Repeat this 50-question exam until you score at least 70 percent. (3–6 hours)

Step 9: On the Drill and Practice CD-ROM, complete at least five of the 100-question practice final exams. Complete more exams as necessary to achieve

xii   Series 6 Introduction

a score of at least 80–90 percent. Create and complete additional topic exams as necessary to correct problem areas. (10–20 hours)

Step 10: Pass the test!

Do I need to take all of the exams?

The exams test the same knowledge you will need in order to answer the questions on the NASD Series 6 exam. By completing all the exams and checking your answers against the rationales, you should be able to pinpoint any areas with which you are still having difficulty. Review any questions you miss, paying particular attention to the rationale for those questions. If any subjects still seem troublesome, go back and review the section(s) covering those topics. At the end of each rationale, you will find a page reference that directs you to the page in the text portion where the information is covered.

Is there someone I can contact if I have questions as I study?

Dearborn is here to help you with every step of your study process. If you have any questions about your study materials, please contact Dearborn's **AnswerPhone** at

1-800-621-9621, ext. 3598

between the hours of 8 A.M. and 6:00 P.M. CT, Monday through Friday. **AnswerPhone's** staff of content experts will answer your questions and clarify the material as needed.

Also, Dearborn offers numerous exam preparation classes throughout the country. For scheduling information, contact Dearborn Customer Service at 1-800-621-9621.

Why do I need to pass the Series 6 exam?

The NASD requires individuals to pass a qualification exam in order to become registered to sell investment company and variable products. This exam qualifies representatives for the sale of mutual funds, unit investment trusts, variable products and primary offerings of closed-end company shares.

Note that almost all states require representatives to pass the Series 63 exam (Blue-sky test) in addition to the Series 6 for state registration.

What is the Series 6 exam like?

The Series 6 is a two-hour and 15-minute, 100-question exam administered by the NASD. It is offered as a computer-based test at various testing sites around the country. A pencil-and-paper exam is available to those candidates who apply to and obtain permission from the NASD to take a written exam.

What topics will I see covered on the exam?

This course covers the wide range of topics that the National Association of Securities Dealers (NASD) has outlined as essential to the Series 6 Limited Representative. The Series 6 exam is divided into four broad topic areas:

Securities and Markets, Investment Risks and Policies—23%
Investment Companies, Taxation and Customer Accounts—36%
Variable Contracts and Retirement Plans—16%
Securities Industry Regulation—25%

What score must I achieve in order to pass?

You must answer correctly at least 70 percent of the questions on the Series 6 exam in order to pass and become eligible for registration as a Limited Representative.

How long does the exam take?

You will be allowed two hours and 15 minutes in which to finish the exam. If you are taking the computerized version of the exam, you will be given additional time before the test to become familiar with the computer terminal.

How do I enroll for the exam?

To obtain an admission ticket to the Series 6 exam, your firm must file the proper application form with the NASD, along with the appropriate processing fees. The NASD will then send you a directory of Sylvan Learning Centers and a enrollment valid for a stated number of days. To take the exam during this period, you must make an appointment with a Sylvan Learning Center as far in advance as possible of the date on which you would like to sit for the test.

You may contact Sylvan Learning Centers at 1-800-578-6273.

What should I take to the exam?

Take one form of personal identification that bears your signature and your photograph as issued by a government agency. You are not allowed to take reference materials or anything else into the testing area. Calculators are available upon request; you will not be allowed to use your personal calculator.

Scratch paper and pencils will be provided by the testing center, although you will not be permitted to take them with you when you leave.

How well can I expect to do on the exam?

The examinations administered by the NASD are not easy. You will be required to display considerable understanding and knowledge of the topics presented in this course in order to pass the Series 6 exam and qualify for registration. If you study and complete all of the sections of the course, and consistently score at least 80 percent on the exams, you should be well prepared to pass the Series 6 exam.

Successful Test-Taking Tips

Passing any NASD Series exam depends not only on how well you learn the subject matter but also on how well you take tests. You can develop your test-taking skills, and thus improve your score, by learning a few simple test-taking techniques:

- Read the full question.
- Avoid jumping to conclusions—watch for hedge clauses.
- Interpret the unfamiliar question.
- Look for key words and phrases.
- Identify the intent of the question.
- Recognize synonymous terms.
- Eliminate/short-list Roman numeral choices.
- Use a calculator.
- Beware of changing answers.
- Pace yourself.

Each of these pointers is explained below, including examples that show how to use them to improve performance on the NASD exams.

Note that the examples below are not specific to the Series 6 exam.

Read the Full Question

You cannot expect to answer a question correctly if you do not know what it is asking. If you see a question that seems familiar and easy, you might anticipate the answer, mark it and move on before you finish reading it. This is a serious mistake and can result in errors. Be sure to read the full question before answering it—the questions are often written to trap people who assume too much. Here is an example of a question in which an assumption could produce a wrong answer.

What is the term for a divided underwriting of municipal securities that is priced through a bidding process involving more than one investment banking firm?

A. Eastern
B. Western
C. Negotiated
D. Competitive

The answer is D — the question describes a situation in which competitive bidding determines the offering price. This is an easy question to answer only for someone who has read the full question, because the point is made in the second half. If you read the question too quickly, you might get to the word "divided" and assume that you are being asked to remember whether a divided underwriting is also called an Eastern underwriting or a Western underwriting.

Avoid Jumping to Conclusions—Watch for Hedge Clauses

The questions on NASD exams are often embellished with deceptive distractors as choices. To avoid being taken in by seemingly obvious answers, make it a practice to read each question and each answer twice before selecting your choice. Doing so will provide you with a much better chance of doing well on the test. Watch out for hedge clauses embedded in the question. (Examples of hedge clauses include the terms *if, not, all, none* and *except.*) In the case of *if* statements, the question can be answered correctly only by taking into account the qualifier. If you ignore the qualifier, you will not answer correctly. Qualifiers are sometimes combined in a question. Some that you will frequently see together are *all* with *except* and *none* with *except*. In general, when a question starts with *all* or *none* and ends with *except*, you are looking for an answer that is opposite to what the question appears to be asking. For example:

All of the following are characteristics of Treasury bills EXCEPT that they

I. mature in more than one year
II. are sold at a discount
III. pay interest semiannually
IV. are very safe investments

A. I and II
B. I and III
C. II and III
D. II and IV

If you neglect to read the *except*, you will look for the choices that are characteristics of T bills. In fact, the question asks which choices are *not* characteristics of T bills (that is, the exceptions). T bills mature in one year or less and do not pay periodic interest; therefore, choices I and III are incorrect and the answer is B.

Interpret the Unfamiliar Question

Do not be surprised if some questions on the test seem unfamiliar at first. If you have studied your material, you will have the information to answer all the questions correctly. The challenge may be a matter of understanding what the question is asking.

Very often, questions present information indirectly. You may have to interpret the meaning of certain elements before you can answer the question. The following two examples concerning bond yields and prices highlight this point.

> *What is the effect of a decline in purchasing power on the current yields of outstanding bonds?*
>
> A. The yields decrease.
> B. The yields increase.
> C. The yields stay the same.
> D. This cannot be determined with the information given.

This question is asking you to apply knowledge of economics, investment recommendations and the relationship between bond prices and yields. Consumer purchasing power declines during periods of inflation. Inflation causes interest rates to rise, and this in turn causes prices of outstanding bonds to decrease. When a bond declines in price or sells at a discount, the current yield increases (answer B).

This same content could have been tested in a different way, as illustrated by the next example.

> *What is the effect of tight money on bond prices?*
>
> A. Bond prices decrease.
> B. Bond prices increase.
> C. Bond prices stay the same.
> D. This cannot be determined with the information given.

Tight money is closely related to high interest rates. When money is scarce (tight), interest rates rise. When interest rates rise, prices of outstanding bonds decrease (answer A).

At first glance, the two questions appear very different, but in fact they test the same relationship — the relationship between a bond's price and its yield. Be aware that the exam will approach a concept from different angles.

Look for Key Words and Phrases

Look for words that are tip-offs to the situation presented. For example, if you see the word "prospectus" in the question stem, you know the question is about a new issue. Sometimes a question will even supply you with the answer if you can recognize the key words it contains. The following is an example of how a key word can help you answer correctly.

Whose Social Security number must appear on an account under the Uniform Gifts to Minors Act?

A. Minor
B. Donor
C. Legal guardian
D. Parent

Looking at the answers, answer A is a likely candidate. Under UGMA, the minor is the owner of the securities. As the owner, the minor's Social Security number must be listed on the account. Few questions provide clues as blatant as this one, but many do offer key words that can guide you to selecting the correct answer if you pay attention. Be sure to read all instructional phrases carefully, as illustrated in the next example.

Rank the following persons in descending order of their claims against a corporation's assets when the corporation is forced into liquidation.

  I. General creditors
 II. Preferred stockholders
III. Bondholders
 IV. Common stockholders

A. I, II, III, IV
B. I, III, II, IV
C. III, I, II, IV
D. III, II, IV, I

The most important aspect of this question is identifying the key word—*descending*. A descending order ranks a list from highest to lowest—in this question, the highest claim on assets to the lowest claim on assets. (The answer is C: bondholders, general creditors, preferred stockholders, common stockholders.) The question could have asked for the ascending order—lowest to highest. Or it could have asked you to rank the choices from junior claim to senior claim or vice versa. Take time to identify the key words to answer this type of question correctly.

Identify the Intent of the Question

Many questions on NASD exams supply so much information that you lose track of what is being asked. This is often the case in story problems. Learn to separate the "story" from the question. For example:

You have decided to buy 100 shares of ArGood Mutual Fund, which prices its shares at 5:00 P.M. every business day. You turn in your order at 3:00 P.M. when the shares are priced at $10 NAV, $10.86 POP. The sales load is 7.9 percent. What will your 100 shares cost?

A. $1,000
B. $1,079
C. $1,086
D. 100 times the offering price that will be calculated at 5:00 P.M.

A clue to the answer is presented in the first sentence — the fund price at 5:00 P.M. Orders for mutual funds are executed based on the next price calculated (forward pricing); therefore, the answer to this question is D. You do not need to calculate anything.

Take the time to identify what the question is asking. Of course, your ability to do so assumes you have studied sufficiently. There is no magic method for answering questions if you don't know the material.

Recognize Synonymous Terms

The securities industry has a tendency to abbreviate terms and use acronyms. Several terms may be used interchangeably throughout the test, and you should be able to recognize them. Examples include:

Industry Term	Synonyms or Acronym
Effective date	release date
Self Regulatory Organization	SRO
long	buy, own
short	sell, owe
registered representative (RR), account executive (AE)	agent
tax-sheltered annuity (TSA)	tax-deferred annuity (TDA)
Uniform Gifts to Minors Act (UGMA)	Uniform Transfers to Minors Act (UTMA)
VLI	variable life insurance
Fidelity bond	Surety bond
Registration by filing	notification

Eliminate/Short-List Roman Numeral Choices

Roman numeral (or multiple-multiple) questions are common on NASD exams; they require you to distinguish between several likely answers. When you are confronted with Roman numeral choices, try to eliminate one or two of them. Doing so helps to narrow your choices. For example, if you can eliminate choice II in a Roman numeral question, and three of the four answers contain choice II, you have successfully narrowed down your options to the correct answer by the process of elimination. For example:

An owner of common stock has which of the following rights?

I. Right to determine when dividends will be issued
II. Right to vote at stockholders' meetings or by proxy
III. Right to determine the amount of any dividends issued
IV. Right to buy redeemed shares before they are offered to the public

A. I, III and IV
B. II
C. II, III and IV
D. II and IV

The answer to this question is B. Stockholders have the right to vote on certain corporate matters and the right to dividends if and when declared. Stockholders do not vote on when a dividend is to be paid, nor on the amount of dividend to be paid. Knowing this, you can eliminate answers A and C. You are now left with only two answers from which to choose.

Use a Calculator

For the most part, the NASD exams will not require the use of a calculator. Most of the questions are written so that any math required is simple. However, if you have become accustomed to using a calculator for math, you will be provided with one by the testing center staff.

Beware of Changing Answers

If you are unsure of an answer, your first hunch is the one most likely to be correct. **Do not** change answers on the exam without good reason. In general, change an answer only if you:

- discover that you did not read the question correctly or
- find new or additional helpful information in another question.

Pace Yourself

Some people will finish the exam early; some will use the entire time allowed; and some do not have time to finish all the questions. Watch the time carefully (your time remaining will be displayed on your computer screen) and pace yourself through the exam.

Do not waste time by dwelling on a question if you simply do not know the answer. Make the best guess you can, mark the question for "Record for Review," and return to the question if time allows. Make sure that you have time to read all the questions so that you can record the answers you do know.

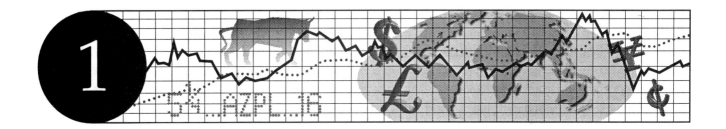

Securities and Markets, Investment Risks and Policies

Introduction

Welcome to your first lesson in preparation for your Series 6 examination. This lesson encompasses a wide discussion of different securities, the markets in which securities trade, basic economics and investment risks and rewards. This lesson will account for 23 questions on your Series 6 test. The securities industry fundamentals that you learn in this lesson will lay the groundwork for your success in future sections.

After you complete this lesson you should be able to:

- Describe the basic features of equity and debt
- Name five types of preferred stock and the unique features of each
- Discuss the inverse relationship between bond prices and yields
- Compare the different types of marketable government securities
- List and describe common money-market instruments
- Identify the different markets in the secondary marketplace
- Define trade date, settlement date, and ex-dates
- Describe the various roles of a broker-dealer
- Describe the four phases and key characteristics of the business cycle
- List and describe common investor objectives
- List and describe at least seven types of investment risk

Equity Securities

Owning equity in a company is perhaps the most visible and widely accessible means by which wealth is created. Individual investors become owners of a publicly traded company by purchasing stock in that company. In so doing, they can participate in the company's growth over time.

In this section, we will cover:

- common stock;
- preferred stock; and
- related equity securities.

What Is a Security?

In the simplest terms, a **security** is an investment that represents either an ownership stake or a debt stake in a company. An investor becomes part owner in a company by buying shares of the company's stock. A debt security is usually acquired by buying a company's bonds. A debt investment is a loan to a company in exchange for interest income and the promise to repay the loan at a future **maturity date**.

Stocks and bonds are normally purchased and sold on a stock exchange or in the over-the-counter (OTC) market. A stock exchange, such as the New York Stock Exchange (NYSE), is an auction market where buyers and sellers are matched by a specialist who maintains a fair and orderly market for a particular stock. The NYSE is located on Wall Street in New York City. The OTC market is an interdealer market linked by computer terminals to National Association of Securities Dealers (NASD) member firms across the country. The OTC market has no physical location. Traders do not transact business face to face as they do on stock exchange floors.

Equity and Debt   Stock represents equity or ownership in a company, and bonds are a loan to a company. A company discloses the composition of its total capitalization—debt and equity—by publishing a balance sheet. The balance sheet summarizes the company's:

- assets—what the company owns: cash in the bank, accounts receivable (money it is owed), investments, property, inventory, etc.;
- liabilities—what the company owes: accounts payable (current bills it must pay), short-term and long-term debt and other obligations; and
- equity—the excess of the value of assets over the value of liabilities—that is, the company's net worth.

A company's net worth is computed by subtracting all liabilities from the value of total assets. This computation is summarized by the basic balance sheet equation:

$$Assets - Liabilities = Net\ Worth$$

Common Stock

A company issues stock as its primary means of raising business capital. Investors who buy the stock buy a share of ownership in the company's net worth. Whatever a business owns (its assets) less its creditors' claims (its liabilities) belongs to the business owners (its stockholders).

Each share of stock entitles its owner to a portion of the company's profits and dividends and an equal vote on directors and other important matters. Most corporations are organized in such a way that their stockholders regularly vote for and elect candidates to a board of directors to oversee the company's business. By electing a board of directors, stockholders have some say in the company's management but are not involved with the day-to-day details of its operations.

✓ **Take Note:** An individual's stock ownership represents his or her proportionate interest in a company. If a company issues 100 shares of stock, each share represents an identical 1/100—or 1 percent—ownership position in the company. A person who owns 10 shares of stock owns 10 percent of the company; a person who owns 50 shares of stock owns 50 percent of the company.

Types of Stock Corporations may issue two types of stock: common stock and preferred stock. When speaking of stocks, people generally refer to common stock, as our discussion does. Preferred stock represents equity ownership in a corporation, but it usually does not have the same voting rights or appreciation potential as common stock. Preferred stock normally pays a fixed quarterly dividend and has priority claims over common stock; that is, the preferred is paid first if a company declares bankruptcy. Common stock can be classified in four ways.

Authorized Stock

As part of its original charter, a corporation receives authorization from the state to issue, or sell, a specific number of shares of stock. Often, a company sells only a portion of the authorized shares, raising enough capital for its foreseeable needs. The company may sell the remaining authorized shares in the future or use them for other purposes. Should the company decide to sell more shares than are authorized, it must amend its charter through a stockholder vote that approves more shares.

Issued Stock

Issued stock has been authorized and distributed to investors. When a corporation issues or sells fewer shares than the total number authorized, it normally reserves the **unissued** shares for future needs, such as:

- raising new capital for expansion;
- paying stock dividends;
- providing stock purchase plans for employees or stock options for corporate officers;
- exchanging common stock for outstanding convertible bonds or preferred stock; or
- satisfying the exercise of outstanding stock purchase warrants.

Authorized but unissued stock does not carry the rights and privileges of issued shares and is not considered in determining a company's total capitalization.

Outstanding Stock

Outstanding stock includes any shares that a company has issued, but has not repurchased—that is, investor-owned stock.

Treasury Stock

Treasury stock is stock a corporation has issued and subsequently repurchased from the public. The corporation can hold this stock indefinitely or can reissue or retire it. A corporation could reissue its treasury stock to fund employee bonus plans, distribute it to stockholders as a stock dividend or, under certain circumstances, redistribute it to the public in an additional offering. Treasury stock does not carry the rights of outstanding common shares, such as voting rights and the right to receive dividends.

 **Test Topic Alert!**   The testable features of treasury stock are the following:

- It was outstanding stock before it was repurchased by the issuer.
- It has no voting rights.
- It does not receive dividends.
- It can be reissued or retired.

By buying its own shares in the open market, the corporation reduces the number of shares outstanding. If fewer shares are outstanding and operating income remains the same, earnings per share increase.

A corporation buys back its stock for a number of reasons, such as to:

- increase earnings per share;
- have an inventory of stock available to distribute as stock options, fund an employee pension plan and so on; or

- use for future acquisitions.

Expect to see a question about outstanding stock that will be similar to the following:

ABC company has authorized 1 million shares of common stock. It issued 800,000 shares one year ago. It then purchased 200,000 shares for its treasury. How many shares of ABC stock are outstanding?

The solution requires that you know a basic formula:

Issued stock – Treasury stock = Outstanding stock

In applying this formula to our sample question, the solution is as follows:

800,000 – 200,000 = 600,000. ABC company has 600,000 shares of common stock outstanding.

This question illustrates another point about NASD exams. The question provided you information about the number of shares of authorized stock, but this information is actually unnecessary. Get used to questions that give you more information than you need! The Series 6 exam wants you to know concepts so well that you can determine both what is and what is not essential to the solution of a problem!

Common Stock Values

The laws of supply and demand, which are based largely on the perception of a company's profitability and business prospects, determine the company's stock price in the market. Although a stock's market price is the most meaningful measure of its value, other measures include par value and book value.

Par Value

For investors, a common stock's par value is meaningless. It is an arbitrary value the company gives the stock in its articles of incorporation, and it has no effect on the stock's market price. If a stock has been assigned a par value for accounting purposes, such as $1 or $.01, it is usually printed on the face of the stock certificate.

When the corporation sells stock, the money received exceeding par value is recorded on the corporate balance sheet as capital in excess of par, also known as paid-in surplus, capital surplus or paid-in capital.

Book Value

A stock's book value per share is a measure of how much a common stockholder could expect to receive for each share if the corporation were liquidated. Most commonly used by analysts, the book value per share is the difference between the value of a corporation's tangible assets and its liabilities, divided by the number of shares outstanding. The book value per share can—and usually does—differ substantially from a stock's market value.

Market Value

The most familiar measure of a stock's value is its market price, the price investors must pay to buy the stock. Market value is influenced by a company's business prospects and the consequent effect on supply (the number of shares available to investors) and demand (the number of shares investors want to buy).

✓ *Take Note:* For your exam, remember that the three methods of common stock valuation do not result in the same amount. Think of the following:

- Par value = an accounting estimate
- Book value = current liquidation value of a share
- Market value = supply and demand price

The market value is most meaningful and familiar to the typical investor.

🖉 **Quick Quiz 1.1** Match the following items to the appropriate description below

　　　A.　outstanding stock
　　　B.　authorized stock
　　　C.　book value
　　　D.　par value

___　1.　Number of shares that a corporation is permitted to issue

___　2.　Dollar amount assigned to a security by its issuer

___　3.　Net worth of each share of common stock

___　4.　Equity securities in the hands of the public

See page 327 for answers.

The Rights of Stock Ownership　Because stockholders are owners of a company, they have certain rights that protect their ownership interests.

Voting Rights

Common stockholders exercise control of a corporation by electing a board of directors and by voting on important corporate policy matters at annual meetings, such as:

- issuance of convertible securities (dilutive to current stockholders) or additional common stock; and
- substantial changes in the corporation's business, such as mergers or acquisitions.

Stockholders have the right to vote on the issuance of convertible bonds because they will dilute current stockholders' proportionate ownership when converted (changed into shares of common).

Calculating the Number of Votes

A stockholder can cast one vote for each share of stock owned. Depending on the company's bylaws and applicable state laws, a stockholder may have a statutory or cumulative vote.

Statutory Voting. Statutory voting allows a stockholder to cast one vote per share owned for each item on a ballot, such as candidates for the board of directors. A board candidate needs a simple majority to be elected.

Cumulative Voting. Cumulative voting allows stockholders to allocate their votes in any manner they choose.

 Take Note: Let's review the difference between statutory and cumulative voting. First, remember that shares vote, not people. A shareholder has one vote for each share he owns.

Now, consider the following example: ABC Company will elect three directors to its board.

Shareholder, Mr. X, owns 100 shares.

Mr. X 100 Shares			
Example One: Statutory Voting	100	100	100
Example Two: Cumulative Voting	175	50 or 0	75
	300	0	0

Example one illustrates statutory voting. Mr. X has up to 100 votes per seat on the board.

Example two illustrates cumulative voting. Mr. X may take the total number of his votes (100 x 3 = 300) and allocate them as he chooses.

Cumulative voting may be advantageous for small shareholders. It gives them a greater opportunity to offset the votes of large shareholders by combining all their shares on a single seat.

One more point on voting: Shareholders do not vote on anything that has to do with dividends, such as when they are declared and how much they will be. Shareholders do vote on stock splits, Board members, and issuance of additional securities like common stock, preferred stock and convertible bonds.

Proxies

Stockholders often find it difficult to attend the annual stockholders' meeting, so most vote on company matters by means of a proxy, a form of absentee ballot. Once it has been returned to the company, a proxy can be canceled automatically if the stockholder attends the meeting, authorizes a subsequent proxy or dies.

Preemptive Rights

When a corporation raises capital through the sale of additional common stock, it may be required by law or its corporate charter to offer the securities to its common stockholders before the general public; this is known as an antidilution provision. Stockholders then have a preemptive right to purchase enough newly issued shares to maintain their proportionate ownership in the corporation.

✓ **Take Note:** Remember that *preemptive* rights give investors the right to maintain a *proportionate* interest in a company's stock.

As an example, assume that ABC has 1,000,000 shares of common stock outstanding. Mr. X owns 100,000 shares of ABC common stock, or 10 percent. If ABC issues an additional 500,000 shares, Mr. X will have the opportunity to purchase 50,000 of those shares.

	Original		New		
ABC:	1,000,000 shares	+	500,000	=	1,500,000 shares
Mr. X:	100,000 shares	+	50,000	=	150,000 shares
	10%		10%		10%

Limited Liability

Stockholders cannot lose more than the amount they have paid for a corporation's stock. Limited liability protects stockholders from having to pay a corporation's debts in bankruptcy.

 Take Note: Limited liability means that a shareholder of common stock cannot lose more than was invested. A shareholder can lose the full value of his stock only.

Inspection of Corporate Books

Stockholders have the right to receive annual financial statements and obtain lists of stockholders. Inspection rights do not include the right to examine detailed financial records or the minutes of directors' meetings.

Residual Claims to Assets

If a corporation is liquidated, the common stockholder, as owner, has a residual right to claim corporate assets after all debts and other security holders have been satisfied. The common stockholder is at the bottom of the liquidation priority list.

Benefits and Risks of Owning Common Stock

Generally, and throughout this course, we assume an investor buys or owns shares of stock with the intent of selling them at a higher price at some point in the future—buy low, sell high later. An investor who buys shares is considered *long* the stock.

An investor may also sell shares before he owns them, with the intent of buying them back at a lower price in the future—sell high, buy low later. Such a transaction, known as a *short sale*, involves borrowing shares to sell that the investor must eventually replace. An investor who sells borrowed shares is considered *short* the stock until he or she buys and returns the shares to the lender.

Benefits of Owning Stock

People generally expect to receive financial growth, income or both from common stock investments.

Growth. An increase in the market price of shares is known as capital appreciation. Historically, owning common stock has provided investors with high real returns.

Income. Many corporations pay regular quarterly cash dividends to stockholders. A company's dividends may increase over time as profitability increases. Dividends, which can be a significant source of income for investors, are a major reason many people invest in stocks.

✓ *Take Note:* Buying low and selling high is one of the main objectives of stock investors. When this is accomplished, investors experience capital gains. If the investor sells the stock at the higher price, the investor has a *realized gain*, and will be responsible for taxes on the gain. If the investor does not sell the stock, the investor has an *unrealized gain,* which is not taxed. Stock gains are taxable only when they are realized.

Another reason people buy stock is to generate income from the dividends paid. Investors who receive dividends must generally pay ordinary income taxes on them. The IRS makes no exceptions for individuals; corporations, however, receive a 70 percent exclusion on dividend income.

Risks of Owning Stock

Regardless of their expectations, investors have no assurances that they will receive the returns they expect from their investments.

Market Risk. The chance that a stock will decline in price at a time the investor needs her money is one risk of owning common stock. A stock's price fluctuates daily as perceptions of the company's business prospects change and affect the actions of buyers and sellers. An investor has no assurance whatsoever that she will be able to recoup her investment in a stock at any point in time.

A long investor's losses are limited to his total investment in a stock. A short seller's losses are theoretically unlimited because there is no limit to how high a stock's price may climb.

Decreased or No Income. Another risk of stock ownership is the possibility of dividend income decreasing or ceasing entirely if the company loses money.

Low Priority at Dissolution. If a company declares bankruptcy, the holders of its bonds and preferred stock have priority over common stockholders. Therefore, a company's debt and preferred shares are considered senior securities. Common stockholders have only residual rights to corporate assets upon dissolution.

 Take Note: Because common shareholders are last in line when a corporation' assets are liquidated, common stock is sometimes called a *junior* security.

Quick Quiz 1.2

1. Which of the following represent(s) ownership (equity) in a company?

    I. Corporate bonds
    II. Common stock
    III. Preferred stock
    IV. Mortgage bonds

    A. I and IV only
    B. II only
    C. II and III only
    D. I, II, III and IV

2. Which of the following statements describe treasury stock?

    I. It has voting rights and is entitled to a dividend when declared.
    II. It has no voting rights and no dividend entitlement.
    III. It has been issued and repurchased by the company.
    IV. It is authorized but unissued stock.

    A. I and III
    B. I and IV
    C. II and III
    D. II and IV

3. Stockholders' preemptive rights include which of the following rights?

    A. Right to serve as an officer on the board of directors
    B. Right to maintain proportionate ownership interest in the corporation
    C. Right to purchase treasury stock
    D. Right to a subscription price on stock

4. At the annual meeting of Huron Corporation, five directors are to be elected. Under the cumulative voting system, an investor with 100 shares of Huron would have a total of

    A. 100 votes to be cast for each of five directors
    B. 500 votes to be cast in any way the investor chooses for five directors
    C. 500 votes to be cast for each of five directors
    D. 100 votes to be cast for only one director

5. Which of the following statements is true of cumulative voting rights?

    A. They benefit the large investor.
    B. They aid the corporation's best customers.
    C. They give preferred stockholders an advantage over common stockholders.
    D. They benefit the small investor.

6. Stockholders must approve

    A. declaration of a stock dividend
    B. a 3-for-1 stock split
    C. repurchase of 100,000 shares for the treasury
    D. declaration of a 15% stock dividend

7. What is the basic formula of the balance sheet?

    A. Assets = Liabilities – Net Worth
    B. Assets + Liabilities = Net Worth
    C. Assets = Net Worth
    D. Net Worth = Assets - Liabilities

See page 327 for answers and rationale.

Preferred Stock

Preferred stock has features of both equity and debt securities. Preferred stock is an equity security because it represents ownership in the corporation. However, it does not normally offer the appreciation potential associated with common stock. Like a bond, preferred stock is usually issued as a fixed-income security with a fixed dividend. Its price tends to fluctuate with changes in interest rates rather than with the issuing company's business prospects unless, of course, dramatic changes occur in the company's credit quality. Unlike common stock, most preferred stock is nonvoting.

Although preferred stock does not typically have the same growth potential as common stock, preferred stockholders generally have two advantages over common stockholders:

1. When the board of directors declares dividends, owners of preferred stock receive their dividends before common stockholders.
2. If a corporation goes bankrupt, preferred stockholders have a priority claim over common stockholders on the assets remaining after creditors have been paid.

Because of these features, preferred stock appeals to investors seeking income and safety.

✓ **Take Note:** Preferred stock has preference over common stock in payment of dividends and in claim to assets in the event the issuing corporation goes bankrupt.

 **Test Topic Alert!**   Be sure to remember that preferred stock represents ownership in a company like common stock. However, it reacts to the market more like a bond because its price is sensitive to interest rates.

Fixed Rate of Return

A preferred stock's fixed dividend is a key attraction for income-oriented investors. Normally, a preferred stock is identified by its annual dividend payment stated as a percentage of its par value, which is usually $100. (A preferred stock's par value is meaningful, unlike that of a common stock.) A preferred stock with a par value of $100 that pays $6 in annual dividends is known as a 6 percent preferred. The dividend of preferred stock with no par value is stated in a dollar amount, such as a $6 no-par preferred.

✔ *Take Note:* The stated rate of dividend payment causes the price of preferred stock to act like the price of a bond.

Consider a 6 percent preferred. If interest rates are currently 8 percent and you want to sell your preferred, you will have to sell at a discounted price. Who would be willing to pay full value for an investment that is not paying a competitive market rate?

But if interest rates fall to 5 percent, the 6 percent preferred will trade at a premium. Because it is offering a stream of income above the current market rate, it will command a higher price.

We have just stated that when interest rates rise, the preferred price falls. Conversely, when interest rates fall, the preferred stock's price rises. This exact relationship occurs in bonds, and is known as the *inverse relationship* between price and interest rates.

The test will expect you to know that the price of preferred stock is affected by interest rates just like the price of a bond.

Adjustable-Rate Preferred

Some preferred stocks are issued with adjustable, or variable, dividend rates. Such dividends are usually tied to the rates of other interest rate benchmarks, such as Treasury bill and money-market rates, and can be adjusted as often as quarterly.

Limited Ownership Privileges

Except for rare instances, preferred stock does not have voting or preemptive rights.

No Maturity Date or Set Maturity Value

Although a fixed-income investment, preferred stock, unlike bonds, has no preset date at which it matures and no scheduled redemption date.

Categories of Preferred Stock

Separate categories of preferred may differ in the dividend rate, in profit participation privileges or in other ways. All, however, maintain a degree of preference over common stock. Preferred stock may have one or more of the following characteristics.

Straight (Noncumulative)

Straight preferred has no special features beyond the stated dividend payment. Missed dividends are not paid to the holder. The year's stated dividend must be paid on straight preferred if any dividend is to be paid to common shareholders.

 Take Note: Preferred stock with no special features is known as straight preferred. One or several of the features described below may characterize issues of preferred stock

Cumulative Preferred

Buyers of preferred stock expect fixed quarterly dividend payments. The directors of a company in financial difficulty can reduce or suspend dividend payments to both common and preferred stockholders. Most likely, the corporation will never make up any dividends common stockholders miss. All dividends due cumulative preferred stock accumulate on the company's books until the corporation can pay them. When the company can resume full payment of dividends, cumulative preferred stockholders receive their current dividends plus the total accumulated dividends—dividends in arrears—before any dividends may be distributed to common stockholders. Therefore, cumulative preferred stock is safer than straight preferred stock.

Test Topic Alert!

The Series 6 exam is likely to include a question on cumulative preferred stock similar to the following:

RST Corporation has both common stock and cumulative preferred stock outstanding. Its preferred stock has a stated dividend rate of 5 percent (par value $100). Because of financial difficulties, no dividend was paid on the preferred stock in 1998 and 1999. If RST wished to declare a common stock dividend in 2000, RST is required to first pay how much in dividends to the cumulative preferred shareholders?

RST must pay missed dividends to cumulative preferred before dividends are paid on common stock. RST must pay $5 for 1998, $5 for 1999 and $5 for 2000, for a total of $15.

If RST had noncumulative preferred stock outstanding instead, the answer would have been $5. Only the current year dividend would need payment before common, because noncumulative preferred is not entitled to dividends in arrears.

✓ **Take Note:** Any special feature attached to preferred, such as a cumulative feature, has a price. The cost for such a benefit is less dividend income. Cumulative preferred typically has a lower stated dividend than straight preferred.

Another way to think of this is: Less risk, less reward.

Convertible Preferred

A preferred stock is convertible if the owner can exchange each preferred share for shares of common stock.

The price at which the investor can convert is a preset amount and is noted on the stock certificate. Because the value of a convertible preferred stock is linked to the value of the issuer's common stock, the convertible preferred's price fluctuates in line with the common.

Convertible preferred is often issued with a lower stated dividend rate than nonconvertible preferred because the investor may have the opportunity to convert to common shares and enjoy capital gains. In addition, the conversion of preferred stock into shares of common increases the total number of common shares outstanding, which decreases earnings per common share and may decrease the common stock's market value.

Participating Preferred

In addition to fixed dividends, participating preferred stock offers its owners a share of corporate profits that remain after all dividends and interest due other securities are paid. The percentage to which participating preferred stock participates is noted on the stock certificate. If a preferred stock is described as "XYZ 6 percent preferred participating to 9 percent," the company pays its holders up to 3 percent in additional dividends in profitable years if the board declares so.

Callable Preferred

Corporations often issue callable, or redeemable, preferred, which a company can buy back from investors at a stated price after a specified date. The right to call the stock allows the company to replace a relatively high fixed dividend obligation with a lower one.

When a corporation calls a preferred stock, dividend payments and conversion rights generally cease on the call date. In return for the call privilege, the corporation usually pays a premium exceeding the stock's par value at the call, such as $103 for a $100 par value stock.

✓ **Take Note:** Callable preferred stock is unique because of the risk that the issuer may buy it back and end dividend payments. Because of this risk, callable preferred has a higher stated rate of dividend payment than straight, non-callable preferred.

Issuers are likely to call securities when interest rates are falling. Like anyone, an issuer would prefer to pay a lower rate for money. Issuers call securities with high rates and replace them with securities that have lower fixed rate obligations.

Test Topic Alert!

Below are several test points on preferred stock:

1. Which of the following types of preferred stock typically has the highest stated rate of dividend (all other factors being equal)?

   A. Participating
   B. Straight
   C. Cumulative
   D. Callable

   D. Callable preferred. When the stock is called, dividend payments are no longer made. To compensate for that possibility, the issuer must pay a higher dividend.

2. Of straight and cumulative preferred, which would you expect to have the higher stated rate?

   The answer: Straight preferred. Cumulative preferred is safer, and there is always a risk-reward trade-off. Because straight preferred has no special features, it will pay a higher stated rate of dividend.

3. Which of the following types of preferred stock is most influenced by the price of an issuer's common stock?

   A. Participating
   B. Straight
   C. Convertible
   D. Callable

   C. Because convertible can be exchanged for common shares, its price is closed linked to the price of the issuer's common.

   Finally, remember that although preferred stock is an equity instrument, it will fluctuate in price more like a debt interest. The stated rate of dividend payment causes the price of preferred stock to act like the price of a bond.

Return on Investment

An investment's total return is a combination of the dividend income and price appreciation or decline over a given period of time. You will need to know how to calculate current return, or yield, for the exam.

Dividends

Dividends are distributions of a company's profits to its stockholders. Investors who buy stock are entitled to dividends only when the company's Board of Directors votes to make such distributions. Stockholders are automatically sent any dividends to which their shares entitle them.

 Take Note: Dividends are never guaranteed to shareholders. This distribution of corporate profits is made only when declared by the Board of Directors.

Cash Dividends. Cash dividends are normally distributed by check if an investor holds the stock certificate or are automatically deposited to a brokerage account if the shares are held in street name—that is, held in a brokerage account in the firm's name to facilitate payments and delivery. Dividends are usually paid quarterly and taxed as ordinary income in the year they are received.

Stock Dividends. If a company uses its cash for business purposes rather than to pay cash dividends, its Board of Directors may declare a stock dividend. This is typical of many growth companies that invest their cash resources in research and development. Under these circumstances, the company issues shares of its common stock as a dividend to its current stockholders. A stock's market price declines after a stock dividend, as with a stock split, but the company's total market value remains the same.

Calculating Dividend Yield

The dividend yield is the annual dividend (normally four times the quarterly dividend) divided by the current price of the stock.

 Take Note: You will probably be asked to calculate dividend yield on your exam. As you've read, the calculation is as follows:

$$\frac{\text{Annual Dividend}}{\text{Current Market Value of the Stock}}$$

Assume RST stock has a current market value of $50. Total dividends paid during the year were $5. What is the dividend yield?

The solution is found by dividing $5 by $50. The yield is 10 percent.

Be alert for a slightly "tricky" approach to this question. The question might state that RST has a current market value of $50. The most recent quarterly dividend paid was $1.25. What is the dividend yield?

The solution is found by annualizing the dividend (multiplying by 4) first. $1.25 × 4 = $5. $5 ÷ $50 = a 10 percent dividend yield. Remember to use *annual* dividends in calculating yield!

 **Test Topic Alert!**   You may see a question that asks about the priority of dividend payments made by a corporation. The order of payment is as follows:

1. Dividends in arrears paid to cumulative shares

2. Stated dividends paid to all preferred shares

3. Common dividend and participating excess dividend paid

Transferability of Ownership   The ease with which stocks and other securities can be bought and sold contributes to the smooth operation of the securities markets. When an investor buys or sells a security, the exchange of money and ownership requires little or no additional action on his part.

The Stock Certificate

A stock certificate is a receipt for the shares of a corporation a person owns. The vast majority of stock transactions are for round lot numbers of shares—that is, share amounts evenly divisible by 100. Odd lot transactions are share amounts of fewer than 100 shares, such as 4 or 99. Individual stock certificates may be issued for any number of shares. For example, an investor who buys 100 shares of General Gizmonics receives one certificate for 100 shares.

Stock certificates identify the company's name, number of shares and investor's name, among other things. In addition, each certificate is printed with the security's CUSIP number.

Negotiability

Shares of stock are negotiable; that is, a stockholder can give, transfer, assign or sell shares he owns with few or no restrictions.

Quick Quiz 1.3   Match the following items to the appropriate description below.

A. 100
B. Preemptive right
C. Current yield
D. Quarterly

___ 1. Typical frequency of dividend payment

___ 2. Number of shares in a standard trading unit of stock

___ 3. Stockholders may maintain proportionate ownership by purchasing newly issued shares before they are offered to the public

_____ 4. Annualized dividend divided by current market price

See page 328 for answers.

American Depositary Receipts

American depositary receipts (ADRs), also known as American depositary shares (ADSs), facilitate the trading of foreign stocks in U.S. markets. An ADR is a negotiable security that represents a receipt for shares of stock in a non-U.S. corporation, usually from 1 to 10 shares. ADRs are bought and sold in the U.S. securities markets like stock.

 ✓ *Take Note:* ADRs make it easy for domestic investors to purchase shares in foreign companies. Many investors like to include foreign issues in their portfolios for diversification.

Rights of ADR Owners

ADR owners have most of the rights common stockholders normally hold. These include voting rights and the right to receive dividends when declared. ADR holders do not normally have preemptive rights.

Delivery of Foreign Security. ADR owners have the right to exchange their ADR certificates for the foreign shares they represent. They can do this by returning the ADRs to the depository banks, which cancel the ADRs and deliver the underlying stock.

Currency Risk. In addition to the normal risks associated with stock ownership, ADR investors are subject to currency risk. Currency risk is the possibility that an investment denominated in one currency, such as the Mexican peso, could decline if the value of that currency declines in its exchange rate with the U.S. dollar. Because ADRs represent shares of stock in companies located in foreign countries, currency exchange rates are an important consideration.

 **Test Topic Alert!**   The following question identifies nearly all of the testable points on ADRs:

Which of the following statements about ADRS is true?

A. Owners of ADRs do not have voting rights
B. ADRs allow foreign investors to purchase domestic issues of stock
C. Owners of ADRs receive dividends in foreign currency
D. ADR owners are subject to currency risk

D. Owners of ADRs face currency risk. The exchange rate between the foreign currency of the ADR issuer and the U.S. dollar causes the dividend payment to rise and fall. Owners of ADRs have voting rights but not preemptive rights. ADRs allow domestic investors to purchase foreign issues, not the reverse. ADR owners receive dividends in dollars.

Quick Quiz 1.4

1. ADRs are used to facilitate the

   A. foreign trading of domestic securities
   B. foreign trading of U.S. government securities
   C. domestic trading of U.S. government securities
   D. domestic trading of foreign securities

2. The owner of an ADR is likely to receive which of the following?

   A. Dividends
   B. Capital gains or losses
   C. Both dividends and capital gains or losses
   D. Neither dividends nor capital gains or losses

See page 328 for answers and rationale.

Tracking Equity Securities

Common and preferred stock prices are listed in the financial sections of daily newspapers and in other financial publications. A stock's market price is quoted in whole dollars, also known as points, plus fractions of a dollar.

✓ **Take Note:** The test will probably require you to determine the cost of a round lot of stock in whole dollars from its quoted price. For example, if ABC stock is quoted at 83 1/8, how much does the investor pay for 100 shares?

To express the fraction in cents, simply divide the upper number by the lower number on your calculator. In this situation, 1 divided by 8 will result in .125. The price for one share of ABC is $83.125. To determine the price of a round lot, simply multiply by 100 (move the decimal point two places to the right). The investor will pay $8,312.50 for a round lot of ABC stock.

Calculators will be available to you at the test center. However, don't expect many math questions. Typically the entire test includes fewer than five calculations.

FIGURE 1.3 NYSE Composite Transactions

New York Stock Exchange Composite Transactions

Tuesday, September 13, 1999

Quotations include trades on the Chicago, Pacific, Philadelphia, Boston and Cincinnati Stock Exchanges and reported by the National Association of Securities Dealers and INSTINET.

52 Weeks High	Low	Stock	Div	Yld %	PE Ratio	Sales 100s	High	Low	Close	Net Chg.
80	40	ABCorp	.75	.1	12	3329	78	71	73	- 1 1/2
n 8 3/8	6 1/2	ACM IncFd	1.01	12.4	...	178	8 1/4	8 1/8	8 1/8	- 1/8
42 5/8	26 7/8	ALFA	2.40	5.6	12	x 1265	42 5/8	41 1/4	42 5/8	+1 1/4
35	24 5/8	Anchor	1.48	4.9	36	1960	30	29 3/4	30	+ 1/4
27 1/4	25	ANR pf	2.67	10.3	...	6	26	26	26	...
6	1 7/8	ATT Cap wt	...	...	...	20	5 7/8	5 3/4	5 3/4	- 1/4
s 22 3/4	14	AVEMCO	.40	1.9	17	6	21 1/2	21 3/8	21 1/2	...
84 1/4	40	BrlNth	2.20	3.7	13	2701	59 3/8	58 1/4	58 3/4	+ 1/2
4 3/4	1/2	Brooke rt	...	...	...	26	4 5/8	4 5/8	4 5/8	...
7	2 1/2	CV REIT	.25	4.0	...	10	6 3/8	6 1/4	6 1/4	...
3 1/8	2 1/4	CalifREIT	.40	13.9	...	3	2 7/8	2 7/8	2 7/8	...
39 3/8	17 7/8	Circus wi	...	...	...	14	39 1/4	38 7/8	39 1/4	+ 5/8
82 1/2	39 5/8	Dsny	.32	.6	17	6211	53 3/4	52	53 1/4	+1 1/4
38 3/8	19 1/2	Fubar	.24	.9	13	z 1454	28	26 7/8	27 3/8	+ 1/4
8 3/4	3 5/8	Navistr	...	...	...	6484	4 1/2	4 1/8	4 1/4	...

EXPLANATORY NOTES

The following explanations apply to New York and American Exchange listed issues and the National Association of Securities Dealers Automated Quotations system's over-the-counter securities.
The 52-week high and low columns show the highest and lowest price of the issue during the preceding 52 weeks. Dividend rates, unless noted, are annual disbursements. Yield is the dividends paid by a company on its securities, expressed as a percentage of price. The PE ratio is determined by dividing the price of a share of stock by its company's earnings. Sales figures are quoted in 100s (00 omitted). a-Extra dividend. b-Annual rate of the cash dividend and a stock dividend was paid. n-Newly issued in the past 52 weeks. pf-Preferred. rt-Rights. s-Stock split or dividend greater than 25% in the past 52 weeks. vi-In bankruptcy or receivership. wd-When distributed. wi-When issued. wt-Warrants. ww-With warrants. x-Ex-dividend or ex-rights. xw-Without warrants. z-Sales in full, not in hundreds.

Exchange-Listed Stocks

The illustration above is an example of an NYSE composite transactions listing as it might be printed in *The Wall Street Journal*. These consolidated stock tables, which present the most complete information available, report activity for the previous business day. The information presented on the table is defined in Figure 1.4.

Nasdaq National Market Stocks

Over-the-counter (OTC) stocks with very high national interest are listed on the Nasdaq National Market (NNM). Although these securities may be eligible for listing on an exchange, the companies have chosen to trade OTC instead. Intel is an example of a well-known company that does not list its stock on an exchange. NNM listings contain similar information as is supplied for exchange-listed securities

FIGURE 1.4 Information on a Stock Table

52 Week					PE	Sales				
High	**Low**	**Stock**	**Div.**	**Yld.**	**Ratio**	**100s**	**High**	**Low**	**Close**	**Net Chg.**
80	40	ABCCo.	.75	.1	12	3329	78	71	73	−1 1/2
❶		❷	❸	❹	❺	❻	❼	❽	❾	❿

❶ The stock's highest and lowest prices over the past 52 weeks
❷ The issuer's abbreviated name
❸ The annual cash dividend
❹ The annual dividend divided by the closing price
❺ The price earnings ratio is the stock's price divided by its earnings per share
❻ The number of lots of 100 shares that traded on the day of the report
❼ The highest price for which the stock sold during the day
❽ The lowest price for which the stock sold during the day
❾ The final price for the day
❿ The difference between the closing price on the trading day and previous day's closing price

FIGURE 1.5 NNM Transactions

Nasdaq National Market Issues

Quotations as of 4 pm Eastern Time
Tuesday, September 13, 1998

52 Weeks High	Low	Stock	Symbol	Div	Yld %	PE Ratio	Sales 100s	High	Low	Close	Net Chg.
37 3/4	20	A&W Brands	SODA	.40	1.1	26	237	36 3/4	35 3/4	36	- 1/2
8 1/2	5 1/8	Acme Steel	ACME	.32	5.1	20	3	6 1/4	6	6 1/4	+ 1/4
s 13 1/2	4 1/8	Adobe Sys	ADBE	.16	1.6	20	59	10 1/4	9 3/4	10 1/4	+ 1/2
43 1/2	15 1/4	AdvMktg	ADMS	...	...	21	226	41 1/4	40 1/4	40 1/4	- 1/4
30	7 5/8	AffBkshCo	AFBK	t	...	3	x 3764	11 1/2	9 1/8	10 7/8	+1 7/8
7 1/4	4	Aldus	ALDS	...	...	18	3211	6 1/2	6 1/8	6 1/2	...
41 1/2	26 5/8	AmGreetgs	AGREA	.70	2.1	13	1511	34 1/2	33 3/8	33 3/8	- 1

Nasdaq Symbol Explanation

Securities in the Nasdaq system are identified by a four or five letter symbol. The fifth letter, as described below, indicates issues that aren't common stock, or which are subject to restrictions or special conditions. A-Class A. B-Class B. C-Exempt from Nasdaq listing qualifications for a limited period. D-New issue. E-Delinquent J-Voting. K-Nonvoting. L-Miscellaneous. M-Fourth preferred. N-Third preferred. O-Second preferred. P-First preferred. Q-In bankruptcy. R-Rights. S-Shares of beneficial interest. T-With warrants or rights. U-Units. V-When issued or when in required SEC filings. F-Foreign. G-First convertible bond. H-Second convertible bond. I-Third convertible bond. distributed. W-Warrants. Y-American Depositary Receipt. Z-Miscellaneous situations.

Nasdaq Small Cap Issues

OTC stocks that have national interest are listed on the National Association of Securities Dealers Automated Quotation System (Nasdaq). Quotes for these securities can be found on a quote machine, a computer that facilitates OTC trading.

Listings for more frequently traded Nasdaq securities may appear in *The Wall Street Journal*. The listing shows the stock name, its dividend, its sales volume in round lots, the execution price of the day's last transaction and the net change from the previous day's last transaction.

FIGURE 1.6   Nasdaq Small Cap Transactions

Nasdaq Small Cap Issues

Quotations as of 4 pm Eastern Time
Tuesday, September 13, 1998

Stock & Div	Sales 100s	Last	Net Chg.	Stock & Div	Sales 100s	Last	Net Chg.
A&A Fd g	29	4 5/8	- 1/16	FtnPh un	5	15	...
ACS En	12	1 3/8	...	Frnchtx .03e	118	5 1/2	+ 1/8
ACTV	14	1 7/8	...	FrntAd .04e	20	2 1/2	...
ACTV wt	86	3/4	...	FutCm	472	6 3/4	- 1/16
AFN s	390	1 7/8	...	BG Fds	209	4 1/2	+ 1/16
AGBag	162	4 5/8	...	GTEC 56pf .90	6	10 1/2	...
APA	40	4 1/2	...	GTEC 5pf 1.00	z65	11 1/2	...

Over-the-Counter (Non-Nasdaq) Stocks

Thousands of securities trade in the OTC market. Daily transactions for these securities and the names of market makers who trade each of them are found in the *Pink Sheets*. These are interdealer quotations subject to change.

Rights and Warrants

In addition to issuing stock, a company can issue securities that allow the owner to buy its stock under certain conditions. A company can issue rights to existing stockholders that allow the owner to buy stock at a favorable price for a short period of time. A company can issue warrants, normally in conjunction with another security, that allow the holder to buy the stock at a set, higher price for a long period of time.

Rights   Preemptive rights allow existing stockholders to maintain their proportionate ownership in a company by buying newly issued shares before the company offers them to the general public. A rights offering allows stockholders to purchase common stock below the current market price. The rights are valued separately from the stock and trade in the secondary market during the subscription period. A stockholder who receives rights may:

- exercise the rights to buy stock by sending the rights certificates and a check for the required amount to the rights agent;
- sell the rights and profit from their market value (rights certificates are negotiable securities); or
- let the rights expire and lose their value.

Approval of Additional Stock. The board of directors must approve decisions to issue additional stock through a rights offering. If the additional shares will increase the stock outstanding beyond the amount authorized in the company charter, the stockholders must vote to amend the charter.

Characteristics of Rights

Once a rights offering has been issued, the rights may be bought or sold in the secondary market just as stocks are bought and sold. If the holder of a right does not sell it, he or she may exercise it to buy the stock specified in the right or let it expire.

Subscription Right Certificate. A subscription right is a certificate representing a short-term (typically 30 to 45 days) privilege to buy additional shares of a corporation. One right is issued for each common stock share.

Terms of the Offering. The terms of a rights offering are stipulated on the subscription right certificates mailed to stockholders on the payable date. The terms describe how many new shares a stockholder may buy, the price, the date the new stock will be issued and the final date for exercising the rights.

Standby Underwriting. If the current stockholders do not subscribe to all the additional stock, the issuer may offer unsold rights to a broker-dealer in a standby underwriting. A standby underwriting is done on a firm commitment basis, meaning the broker-dealer buys all unsold shares from the issuer then resells them to the general public.

Warrants   A **warrant** is a certificate granting its owner the right to purchase securities from the issuer at a specified price, normally higher than the current market price. Unlike a right, a warrant is usually a long-term instrument, giving the investor the choice of buying shares at a later date at the exercise price.

Origination of Warrants

Warrants are usually offered to the public as "sweeteners" (inducements) in connection with other securities, such as debentures or preferred stock, to make those securities more attractive. Such offerings are often bundled as **units**.

Warrants may be detachable or nondetachable from other securities. If detachable, they trade in the secondary market in line with the common stock's price. When first issued, a warrant's exercise price is set well above the stock's market price. As the stock's price increases, the owner can exercise the warrant and buy the stock below the market price or sell the warrant in the market.

TABLE 1.1   Comparison of Rights and Warrants

Rights	Warrants
Short-term	Long-term
Exercisable below market value	Exercisable above market value
May trade with or separate from the common stock	May trade with or separate from the units
Offered to existing shareholders with preemptive rights	Offered as a sweetener for another security(ies)
One right issued per each share outstanding	Number issued is determined by corporation

 **Test Topic Alert!**

Here are some key test points to remember about rights and warrants:

Rights: Short-term instruments, exercise price is *below* market price; issued to current shareholders only.

Warrants: Long-term instruments; exercise price is *above* market price; used as sweeteners with issues of more speculative corporate bonds.

Both rights and warrants are traded in the secondary market.

1. Which of the following statements is true of warrants?

    A. Warrants are offered to current shareholders only.
    B. Warrants have longer terms than rights.
    C. Warrants do not trade in the secondary market.
    D. At the time of issuance, the exercise price of a warrant is typically below the market value of the underlying stock.

2. Which of the following statements about rights is true?

    A. Common stockholders do not have the right to subscribe to rights offerings.
    B. Preferred stockholders do not have the right to subscribe to rights offerings.
    C. Both common and preferred stockholders have the right to subscribe to rights offerings.
    D. Neither common nor preferred stockholders have the right to subscribe to rights offerings.

See page 328 for answers and rationale.

Introduction to Options

An option is simply a contract that establishes a price and time frame for the purchase or sale of a particular investment instrument. Two parties are involved in the contract: One party receives the right to exercise the contract to buy or sell the underlying security; the other is obligated to fulfill the terms of the contract.

Calls and Puts   Listed option contracts are issued in standardized formats by the Options Clearing Corporation (OCC) and traded on the Chicago Board Options Exchange (CBOE) or another exchange. Because the CBOE and other exchanges provide forums to trade, and the OCC stands behind option contracts in the event of a firm's failure, options are easily tradable.

Two types of option contracts exist: calls and puts.

- A call option gives the buyer the right to call (buy) a security away from someone. You can buy that right for yourself, or you can sell that right to someone else.
- A put option gives the buyer the right to put (sell) a security to someone. You can buy that right for yourself, or you can sell that right to someone else.

Each stock option contract covers 100 shares (a round lot) of stock at a specific price within a specific time frame. An option's cost is called the premium. Premiums are quoted in dollars per share. Because each contract covers 100 shares, a premium of $3 means $3 for each share times 100 shares, or $300.

Exercise Prices

An option's **exercise** or **strike price** is the price at which the option owner is entitled to buy or sell the underlying security and the price at which the option seller has agreed to sell or buy the security.

Leverage. Option contracts provide investors with leverage: a relatively small cash outlay allows an investor to "control" an investment that would otherwise require a much larger sum.

 Take Note: Options are a game of opposites. Buyers always do the opposite of sellers. If you can remember what the buyer of an option does, you can always figure out what the seller does. For example, in a call:

The *buyer* of the call has the *right to buy*; the *seller* of the call has the *obligation to sell.*

In a put:

The *buyer* of the put has the *right to sell*; the *seller* of the put has the *obligation to buy.*

 **Test Topic Alert!**

Your test will have very few questions that ask about options. Don't overwork this section!

You will be well prepared if you know information in Figures 1.7 and 1.8. Figure 1.8 helps identify the market attitude of each option position. You may wish to learn it and draw it on scratch paper when you take your exam.

Note that the upward pointing arrow denotes a "bullish" investor who profits when the market goes up, and a downward pointing arrow denotes a "bearish" investor who profits when the market goes down.

FIGURE 1.7   Buyer vs. Seller in an option contract

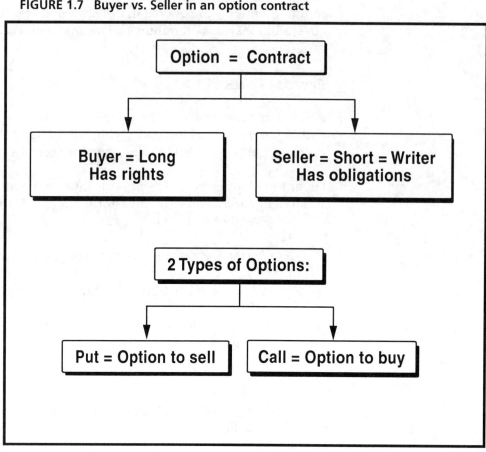

FIGURE 1.8   Buy vs. Sell and Call vs. Put

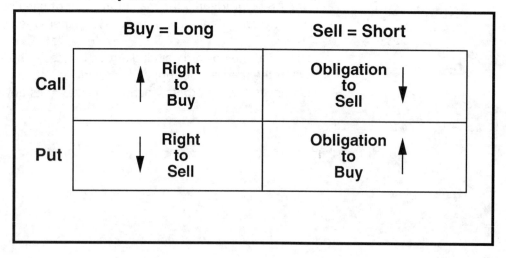

Each quadrant of Figure 1.8 identifies an option position. Here's how to read the chart:

The upper left quadrant depicts buying a call (long call position).

- An investor who is long a call is bullish and has the right to buy stock

The upper right quadrant depicts selling a call (short call position or call writer).

- An investor who is short a call is bearish and has the obligation to sell stock

The lower left quadrant depicts buying a put (long put position).

- An investor who is long a put is bearish and has the right to sell stock

The lower right quadrate depicts selling a put (short put position or put writer).

- An investor who is short a put is bullish and has the obligation to buy stock

Be prepared to answer the following questions:

Which options position are bearish?	Long put, short call
Which options position are bullish?	Long call, short put
Which positions buy stock at exercise?	Long call, short put
Which positions sell stock at exercise?	Long put, short call
Which positions have rights?	Long call, long put
Which positions have obligations?	Short call, short put

The chart can make these questions easy if you use it!

Debt Securities

Bonds, whether issued by corporations, municipalities, the U.S. government or its agencies are **debt securities**; that is, they represent an investor's loan to an issuer. As a borrower, the issuer promises to repay the debt on a specified date and to pay interest on the loan amount. Because the interest rate the investor receives is set when the bond is issued, it is a *fixed-income security*. Individual bonds usually have a face (or par) value of $1,000.

Take Note: An investor who buys stock in a company is an owner, or has equity in the company. An investor who buys bonds is owed money by the company. Bondholders are *creditors* of the corporation. Like any other borrower the bond issuer pays interest for the use of the money to the lender.

Characteristics of Bonds

Unlike stockholders, bondholders have no ownership interest in the issuing corporation or voice in management. As creditors, bondholders receive preferential treatment over common and preferred stockholders if a corporation files for bankruptcy. Because creditor claims are settled before the claims of stockholders, bonds are considered senior securities. Therefore, stockholders' interests are subordinate to those of bondholders.

Issuers   Corporations issue bonds to raise working capital or funds for capital expenditures such as plant construction or equipment and other major purchases. Corporate bonds are commonly referred to as funded debt. Funded debt is any long-term debt payable in five years or more.

The federal government is the nation's largest borrower and the most secure credit risk. Treasury bills (maturities of one year or less), notes (1- to 10-year maturities) and bonds (10- to 30-year maturities) are backed by the full faith and credit of the government and its unlimited taxing powers.

Municipal securities are the debt obligations of state and local governments and their agencies. Most are issued to raise capital to finance public works or construction projects that benefit the general public.

 Take Note: In general, you can assume that bonds issued by the federal government are the safest, followed by municipal bonds, followed by corporate bonds. Because corporate bonds are the most risky, they provide the highest potential income to investors.

Interest   Both the interest rate an issuer pays its bondholders and the timing of payments are set when a bond is issued. The interest rate, or coupon, is calculated from the bond's par value. Par value, also known as face value, is normally $1,000 per bond, meaning each bond will be redeemed for $1,000 when it matures. Interest on a bond accrues daily and is paid in semiannual installments over the life of the bond.

The final interest payment is made when the bond matures, and it is normally combined with repayment of the principal amount. If a bondholder has been receiving semiannual payments of $350 from 10 bonds, he or she will receive a check for $10,350 when the bonds mature.

 Take Note: Be prepared to solve a question on the test that is similar to the following:

An investor purchases an ABC J&J 8s of '09. What will the investor receive at maturity of the bond?

In order to solve the problem, you need to decode the bond quote first!

ABC: The issuer of the bond; it is a corporate bond because of its three-letter name (Corporate stock and bond symbols are from one to five letters).

J & J: The bond pays semiannual interest on January and July 1 each year. The interest dates are six months apart. (An M & S bond would pay interest on March and September 1.)

8s: The bond pays a stated rate of interest of 8 percent annually. This is known as the coupon or nominal or stated rate of interest.

'09: The investor will receive the principal at the bond's maturity in 2009.

Now back to the original question. The investor will receive the full principal plus the last semiannual interest payment when the bond matures.

Bond Principal:	$1,000	
Semiannual interest:	40	(Annual interest is $80 per thousand; the
Total at Maturity:	$1,040	semiannual interest is $40.)

Maturities On the maturity date, the loan principal is repaid to the investor. Each bond has its own maturity date. The most common maturities fall in the 5- to 30-year range.

Bond Certificates All bond certificates contain basic information including the following:

- Name of issuer;
- Interest rate and payment date;
- Maturity date;
- Call features;
- Principal amount;
- CUSIP number for identification;
- Dated date—the date that interest starts accruing; and
- Reference to the bond indenture.

Registration of Bonds Bonds are registered, in varying degrees, to record ownership should a certificate be lost or stolen. Tracking a bond's ownership through its registration has been common in the United States only since the early 1970s.

Coupon (Bearer) Bonds

Though rare today, in past years most bonds were issued in coupon, or bearer, form. Issuers kept no records of purchasers, and securities were issued without an investor's name printed on the certificate. Because coupon bonds are not registered, whoever possesses them can collect interest on, sell or redeem the bonds.

Interest coupons are attached to bearer bonds, and holders collect interest by clipping the coupons and delivering them to an issuer's paying agent. Individual coupons are payable to the bearer. When a bond matures, the bearer delivers it to the paying agent and receives his or her principal.

No proof of ownership is needed to sell a bearer bond. Even through bearer bonds are rarely issued today, the term *coupon* is still used to describe interest payments received by bondholders.

Registered Bonds

The most common form of bond currently issued is the registered bond. When a registered bond is issued, the issuer's transfer agent records the bondholder's name. The buyer's name appears on the bond certificate's face.

Fully Registered. When bonds are registered as to both principal and interest, the transfer agent maintains a list of bondholders and updates this list as bond ownership changes. Interest payments are automatically sent to bondholders of record. The transfer agent transfers a registered bond whenever a bond is sold by canceling the seller's certificate and issuing a new one in the buyer's name. Most corporate bonds are issued in fully registered form.

Registered as to Principal Only. Principal-only registered bonds have the owner's name printed on the certificate, but the coupons are in bearer form.

When bonds registered as to principal only are sold, the names of the new owners are recorded (in order) on the bond certificates and on the issuer's registration record. Like bearer bonds, bonds registered as to principal only are no longer issued.

Book-Entry Bonds

Book-entry bond owners do not receive certificates. Rather, the transfer agent maintains the security's ownership records. While the names of buyers of both registered and book-entry bonds are recorded (registered), the book-entry bond owner does not receive a certificate—the registered bond owner does. The trade confirmation serves as evidence of book-entry bond ownership. Most U.S. government bonds are available only in book-entry form.

✓ **Take Note:** The test might ask you in what form a bond must be for an investor to receive interest and principal payments by mail. Bonds must be fully registered – the issuer must have the name of the investor entitled to both principal and interest payments on his or her ownership list.

New bonds are only issued in registered form.

Pricing   Once issued, bonds are bought and sold in the secondary market at prices determined by conditions unique to the issuer or common to all debt securities.

Par, Premium and Discount

Bonds are issued with a face, or par, value of $1,000. Par represents the dollar amount of the investor's loan to the issuer, and it is the amount repaid when the bond matures.

✓ **Take Note:** Note that the par value of *bonds* is $1,000. The par value of *preferred stock* is $100.

When a bond's price is above $1,000 it is trading at a premium. When a bond's price is below $1,000 it is trading at a discount.

In the secondary market, bonds can sell for any price—at par, below par (at a discount) or above par (at a premium). The two primary factors affecting a bond's market price are the issuer's financial stability and overall trends in interest rates. If an issuer's credit rating remains constant, interest rates are the only factor that affect the market price.

✓ **Take Note:** Just like preferred stock, bonds prices are directly influenced by interest rates. As interest rates fall, bond prices rise; as interest rates rise, bond prices fall. As we learned before, this is known as an inverse relationship and affects any fixed income security.

FIGURE 1.10 Bond Price/Yield Relationship

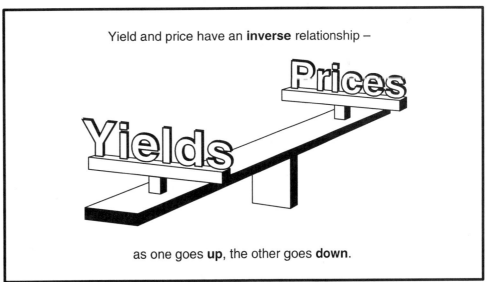

Yield and price have an **inverse** relationship –

as one goes **up**, the other goes **down**.

Bond quotes are commonly stated as percentages of par. A bid of 100 means 100 percent of par, or $1,000. A bond quote of 98⅛, means 98 and ⅛ percent (98.125 percent) of $1,000, or $981.25. Bond price changes are quoted in news-

papers in points. One point is 1 percent of $1,000, or $10; ¼ point equals $2.50.
The minimum variation for most corporate and municipal bond quotes is ⅛
(.125 percent, or $1.25).

TABLE 1.2   Example of Corporate Bond Pricing

A Price of . . .	Means . . .	Or . . .
92	92% of $1,000	$920.00
93⅛	93⅛% of $1,000	$931.25
94¼	94¼% of $1,000	$942.50
95⅜	95⅜% of $1,000	$953.75
96½	96½% of $1,000	$965.00
97⅝	97⅝% of $1,000	$976.25
98¾	98¾% of $1,000	$987.50
99⅞	99⅞% of $1,000	$998.75
100	100% of $1,000	$1,000.00
105	105% of $1,000	$1,050.00

Rating and Analyzing Bonds

Rating services, such as Standard & Poor's and Moody's, evaluate the credit
quality of bond issues and publish their ratings. Standard & Poor's and
Moody's rate both corporate and municipal bonds. Both base their bond ratings primarily on an issuer's creditworthiness—that is, the issuer's ability to
pay interest and principal as they come due.

The rating organizations rate those issues that either pay to be rated or have
enough bonds outstanding to generate constant investor interest. The fact
that a bond is not rated does not indicate its quality; many issues are too
small to justify the expense of a bond rating.

Basis for Bond Ratings

Bond ratings are based on an issuer's financial stability. The rating services
apply a series of financial tests to assess a corporation's financial strength.

Specific criteria used to rate corporate and municipal bonds include:

- the amount and composition of existing debt;
- the stability of the issuer's cash flow;
- the issuer's ability to meet scheduled payments of interest and principal on its debt;
- obligations;

- asset protection; and
- management capability.

A bond's rating may change over time as the issuer's ability to make interest and principal payments changes.

Investment Grade. The Comptroller of the Currency, the Federal Deposit Insurance Corporation (FDIC), the Federal Reserve and state banking authorities have established policies determining which securities banks can purchase. A municipal bond must be investment grade (a rating of BBB/Baa or higher) to be suitable for purchase by banks. Investment-grade bonds are also known as bank-grade bonds.

TABLE 1.3   Bond Ratings

Standard & Poor's	Moody's	Interpretation
Bank grade (investment grade) bonds		
AAA	Aaa	Highest rating. Capacity to repay principal and interest judged high.
AA	Aa	Very strong. Only slightly less secure than the highest rating.
A	A	Judged to be slightly more susceptible to adverse economic conditions.
BBB	Baa	Adequate capacity to repay principal and interest. Slightly speculative.
Speculative (non-investment grade) bonds		
BB	Ba	Speculative. Significant chance that issuer could miss an interest payment.
B	B	Issuer has missed one or more interest or principal payments.
C	Caa	No interest is being paid on bond at this time.
D	D	Issuer is in default. Payment of interest or principal is in arrears.

 **Test Topic Alert!**   A test question may ask you to choose the bond with the highest rating. Remember that ratings are like reports cards: the more A's the better. For example:

Which of the following bonds is considered to be the safest?

A. A rated Mortgage Bond
B. Baa rated Equipment Trust Certificate
C. AA rated Unsecured Debenture
D. B rated Funded Debt

    C. The safest of the bonds listed is the AA rated Unsecured Debenture. You do not need to be concerned with the type of bond; the rating takes into account all features of the security when rating the credit risk.

Relationship of Rating to Yield

Generally, the higher a bond's rating, the lower its yield. Investors will accept lower returns on their investments if their principal and interest payments are safe. Bonds with low ratings due to the issuer's instability pay higher rates because of the risks to principal and interest associated with such uncertainties.

Qualitative Analysis. In addition to financial statistics, qualitative factors such as an industry's stability, the issuer's quality of management and the regulatory climate may be considered when bonds are rated.

Comparative Safety of Debt Securities

Investors will normally accept a lower return for a higher degree of safety. Although there are exceptions to the rule, a hierarchy exists in the degree of safety associated with different categories of debt securities. Normally, the higher the degree of safety, the lower the yield relative to other investments at the same point in time.

U.S. Government Securities. The highest degree of safety is in securities backed by the full faith and credit of the U.S. government. These securities include:

- U.S. Treasury bills, notes and bonds, as well as Series EE and HH bonds;
- Government National Mortgage Association (GNMA or Ginnie Mae); and
- New Housing Authority bonds (NHAs).

Government Agency Issues. The second highest degree of safety is in securities issued by government agencies and government-sponsored corporations, although the U.S. government does not back the securities. These organizations include:

- Federal Farm Credit Banks (FFCBs)
- Federal Home Loan Mortgage (Freddie Mac); and
- Federal National Mortgage Association (FNMA or Fannie Mae).

Municipal Issues. Generally, the next level of safety is in securities issued by municipalities. General obligation bonds (GOs), backed by the taxing power of the issuer, are usually safer than revenue bonds. Revenue bonds are backed by revenues from the facility financed by the bond issue.

Corporate Debt. Corporate debt securities cover the safety spectrum, from very safe (AAA corporates) to very risky (junk bonds). Corporate bonds are backed, in varying degrees, by the issuing corporation. Usually, these securities are ranked from safe to risky, as follows:

1. Secured bonds
2. Debentures
3. Subordinated debentures
4. Income bonds

However, these rankings serve only as a rough guideline.

Liquidity   Liquidity is the ease with which a bond or any other security can be sold. Many factors determine a bond's liquidity, including:

- quality;
- rating;
- maturity;
- call features;
- coupon rate and current market value;
- issuer; and
- existence of a sinking fund.

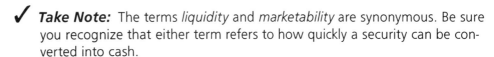 **Take Note:** The terms *liquidity* and *marketability* are synonymous. Be sure you recognize that either term refers to how quickly a security can be converted into cash.

Maturity   The longer the term to maturity, the greater the risk to bondholders. Bonds with longer terms to maturity experience greater fluctuation in price, or *volatility*, than short-term bonds. Short-term interest rates, however, fluctuate more than long-term interest rates.

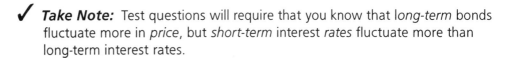 **Take Note:** Test questions will require that you know that *long-term* bonds fluctuate more in *price*, but *short-term* interest *rates* fluctuate more than long-term interest rates.

Debt Retirement   The schedule of interest and principal payments due on a bond issue is known as the debt service.

Redemption

When a bond's principal is repaid, the bond is redeemed. Redemption usually occurs on the maturity date.

Sinking Fund. To facilitate the retirement of its bonds, a corporate or municipal issuer establishes a sinking fund operated by the bonds' trustee. The trust indenture often requires a sinking fund, which can be used to call bonds, redeem bonds at maturity or buy back bonds in the open market.

To establish a sinking fund, the issuer deposits cash in an account with the trustee. Because a sinking fund makes money available for redeeming bonds, it can aid the bonds' price stability.

Calling Bonds

Bonds are often issued with a call feature, or call option. A call feature allows the issuer to redeem a bond issue before its maturity date, either in whole or in part (in-whole or partial calls).

The issuer does this by notifying bondholders that it will redeem the bonds at a particular price on a certain date.

Call Premium. The right to call bonds for early redemption gives issuers flexibility in their financial management. In return, an issuer usually pays bondholders a premium, a price higher than par, known as a call premium. Various municipal bonds, corporate bonds and preferred stocks are callable at some point over their terms, although many are not.

Advantages of a Call to the Issuer. Callable bonds can benefit the issuer in numerous ways:

- If general interest rates decline, the issuer can redeem bonds with a high interest rate and replace them with bonds with a lower rate.
- The issuer can call bonds to reduce its debt any time after the initial call date.
- The issuer can replace short-term debt issues with long-term issues, and vice versa.
- The issuer can call bonds as a means of forcing the conversion of convertible corporate securities.

Term bonds are generally called by random drawing. Serial bonds, on the other hand, are usually called in inverse order of their maturities because longer maturities tend to have higher interest rates. Calling the long maturities lowers the issuer's interest expense by the largest amount.

If a bond issue's trust indenture does not include a call provision, the issuer normally can buy bonds in the open market, known as tendering, to retire a portion of its debt.

Call Protection. Bonds are called when general interest rates are lower than they were when the bonds were issued. Investors, therefore, are faced with having to replace a relatively high fixed-income investment with one that pays less; this is known as call risk. A newly issued bond normally has a non-callable period of 5 or 10 years to provide some protection to investors. During this period, the issuer cannot call any of its bonds. When the call protection period expires, the issuer may call any or all of the bonds, usually at a premium. A call protection feature can be an advantage to bondholders in periods of declining interest rates.

Effects of a Call on Trading. After a call notice is issued, but before the call date, called bonds continue to trade in the open market. When bonds are called, a bondholder can turn in the bonds to the issuer immediately or sell them in the open market. The bonds will trade at a slight discount to the call price during this period. By selling at the small discount, the investor doesn't have to wait until the call date to get her money.

Test Topic Alert!

Here are three test points pertaining to bond call features:

1. Under what economic circumstances do issuers call bonds?

   Bonds are typically called when interest rates are declining. Put yourself in the issuer's shoes. Would you want to pay more interest for the use of money than you need to?

2. Investors who purchase callable bonds face what type(s) of investment risk?

   Call risk is the risk that the bonds will be called and the investor will lose the stream of income from the bond. Remember that bonds don't pay interest after they have been called. The call feature also causes *reinvestment risk.* If interest rates are down when the call takes place, what likelihood does the investor have of investing the principal received at a comparable rate?

   Both call risk and reinvestment risk apply to callable preferred stock.

3. Which of the following would an investor prefer?

   A. A long call protection period when interest rates are high
   B. A long call protection period when interest rates are low
   C. A short call protection period when interest rates are high
   D. A short call protection period when interest rates are low

   The best answer is A. Investors want to lock in the highest possible rate of interest for the longest period of time. Remember, during the call protection period the issuer cannot call the bonds away.

Refunding Bonds

Refunding is the practice of raising money to call a bond. Specifically, the issuer sells a new bond issue to buy back the old bond issue. Refunding, like a call, can occur in full or in part. Generally, an entire issue is refunded at once.

Refunding is common for bonds approaching maturity. An issuer may not have enough cash to pay off the entire issue, or it may choose to use its cash for other needs.

 Take Note: Refunding can be thought of as issuer *refinancing*. Homeowners know all about this: when interest rates drop, it makes sense to replace a high interest mortgage with a new mortgage at a more competitive rate. An issuer can accomplish the same thing by refunding.

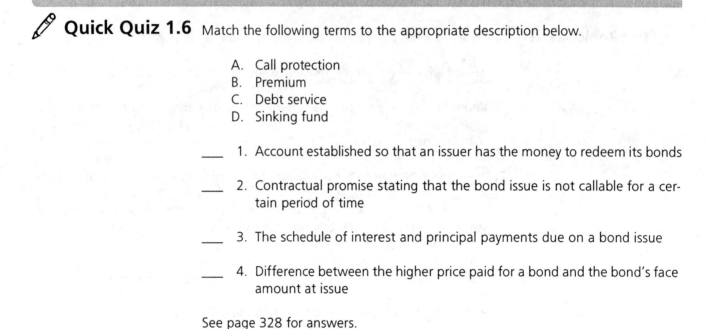

Quick Quiz 1.6 Match the following terms to the appropriate description below.

A. Call protection
B. Premium
C. Debt service
D. Sinking fund

____ 1. Account established so that an issuer has the money to redeem its bonds

____ 2. Contractual promise stating that the bond issue is not callable for a certain period of time

____ 3. The schedule of interest and principal payments due on a bond issue

____ 4. Difference between the higher price paid for a bond and the bond's face amount at issue

See page 328 for answers.

Bond Yields

A bond's yield expresses the cash interest payments in relation to the bond's value. Yield is determined by the issuer's credit quality, prevailing interest rates, time to maturity and call features. Bonds can be quoted and traded in terms of their yield as well as a percentage of par dollar amount.

Comparing Yields   Because bonds most frequently trade for prices other than par, the price discount or premium from par is taken into consideration when calculating a bond's overall yield. You can look at a bond's yield in several ways.

Nominal Yield

A bond's coupon yield, or nominal yield, is set at issuance and printed on the face of the bond. The nominal yield is a fixed percentage of the bond's par value. A coupon of 6 percent, for instance, indicates the bondholder is paid $60 in interest annually until the bond matures.

✓ **Take Note:** Be sure to recognize the different names for a bond's nominal yield. It can be called the coupon rate, the fixed rate or the stated rate of the bond. The nominal rate of interest will always be paid to the bondholder, regardless of whether the bond's price changes.

Current Yield

Current yield (CY) measures a bond's annual interest relative to its market price, as shown in the following equation:

$$\text{Annual Interest} \div \text{Market price} = \text{Current yield}$$

Bond prices and yields move in opposite directions: as a bond's price rises, its yield declines, and vice versa. When a bond trades at a discount, its current yield increases; when it trades at a premium, its current yield decreases.

Yield to Maturity

A bond's yield to maturity (YTM) reflects the annualized return of the bond if held to maturity. In calculating yield to maturity, the bondholder takes into account the difference between the price paid for a bond and par value. If the bond's price is less than par, the discount amount increases the return. If the bond's price is greater than par, the premium amount decreases the return.

FIGURE 1.11   Relationship Between Bond Prices and Current Yields

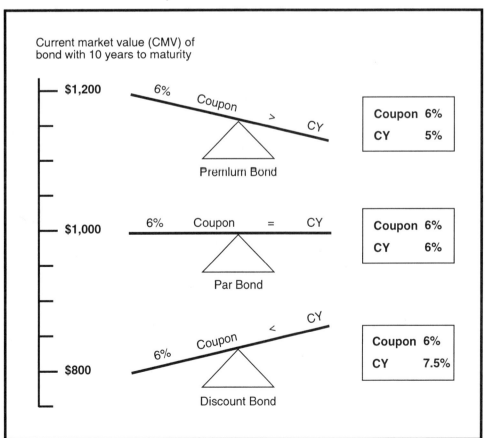

FIGURE 1.12   Relationship Between Bond Prices and Yields to Maturity

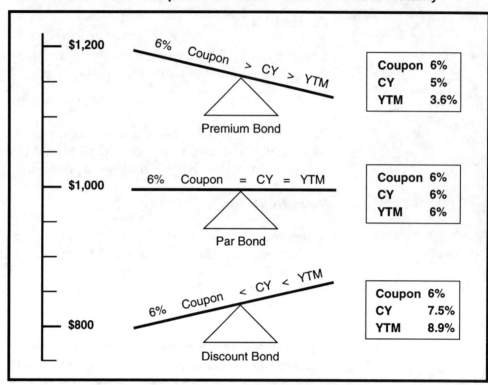

✔ **_Take Note:_** What is the current yield of a 6 percent bond that is trading for $800?

Current yield (CY) = Annual Interest ÷ Current Market Price.

Find the solution as follows: $60 ÷ $800 = 7.5 percent. Note that this bond is trading at a discount. When prices fall, yields rise. The current yield (7.5 percent) is greater than the nominal yield (6 percent) when bonds are trading at a discount.

What is the current yield of a 6 percent bond that is trading for $1,200?

Find the solution as follows: $60/$1200 = 5 percent. This bond is trading at a premium. Price is up, so the yield is down. The current yield (5 percent) is less than the nominal yield (6 percent) when bonds are trading at a premium.

The teeter-totter diagram below is effective in helping you master the relationships in bond yields. It is critical that you understand this inverse relationship between price and yield.

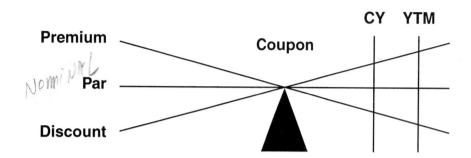

Follow the lines on the chart to identify these concepts:

1. When bonds are at par, coupon and current yield are equal. (The point of intersection on the CY line is neither higher or lower than the coupon on the line that represents *par.*)
2. When bonds are at a premium, the CY is less than the coupon. (The point of intersection on the CY line is below the coupon on the line that represents *premium.*)
3. When bonds are at a discount, the CY is greater than the nominal yield. (The point of intersection on the CY line is above the coupon on the line that represents *discount.*)

When you are comfortable with the chart, you can also compare the bond's yield to maturity to its coupon and current yield. For example, when a bond is trading at a premium, its YTM is less than its current yield. You can see that the point of intersection on the YTM line is below the current yield on the line that represents *premium.*

These are important relationships to remember. Use the chart to keep this in mind. When you take your Series 6 exam, draw this chart for your reference on a piece of scratch paper. You'll answer your yield questions without even thinking! Be sure to practice drawing it (it appears on the Hotsheet at the end of this lesson).

Use the teeter-totter diagram to answer the following questions.

/ **Quick Quiz 1.7** Match the following terms to the appropriate description below.

    A. Premium
    B. Discount
    C. Par

___ 1. YTM is greater the CY.

___ 2. CY is less than coupon.

___ 3. YTM is greater than CY.

___ 4. YTM is equal to nominal.

___ 5. CY is less than YTM.

___ 6. YTM is less than coupon.

___ 7. YTM is equal to CY.

Match each of the following terms with the appropriate description below.

   A. Nominal yield
   B. Investment grade
   C. Book entry
   D. Current yield
   E. Yield to maturity

___ 8. Percentage return reflecting the annualized return of the bond if held to maturity

___ 9. Stated on the face of the bond certificate

___ 10. Annual interest divided by today's market price

___ 11. Bondowner's name is stored in records kept by the issuer or a transfer agent

___ 12. Bonds rated BBB/Baa or above

See page 328 for answers and rationale.

✎ Quick Quiz 1.8

1. A new bond contains a provision that it cannot be called for five years after the date of issuance. This call protection would be most valuable to a recent purchaser of the bond if interest rates are

   A. falling
   B. rising
   C. stable
   D. fluctuating

2. What is the calculation for determining the current yield on a bond?

   A. Annual interest ÷ Par value
   B. Annual interest ÷ Current market price
   C. Yield to maturity ÷ Par value
   D. Yield to maturity ÷ Current market price

3. A customer purchased a 5 percent U.S. government bond yielding 6 percent. A year before the bond matures, new U.S. government bonds are being issued at 4 percent, and the customer sells the 5 percent bond. The customer probably

   I. bought it at a discount
   II. bought it at a premium
   III. sold it at a discount
   IV. sold it at a premium

   A. I and III
   B. I and IV
   C. II and III
   D. II and IV

4. Which yield to maturity would be higher?

   A. 10 percent nominal yield bond with a premium price
   B. 10 percent nominal yield bond with a discount price
   C. 10 percent nominal yield bond with a price at par

5. In a comparison of long-term bonds with short-term bonds, all of the following are characteristics of long-term bonds EXCEPT that they

   A. usually have higher yields than short-term bonds
   B. usually provide greater liquidity than short-term bonds
   C. are more likely to be callable
   D. will fluctuate in price more than short-term bonds in response to interest rate changes

6. When interest rates are falling or rising, the price fluctuations of which of the following will be the greatest?

   A. Short-term bonds
   B. Long-term bonds
   C. Money-market instruments
   D. Common stock

See page 328 for answers and rationale.

Corporate Bonds

Corporate bonds are issued to raise working capital or capital for expenditures such as plant construction and equipment purchases.

Types of Corporate Bonds The two primary types of corporate bonds are secured and unsecured. Others are discussed in this section, as well.

Secured Bonds

A bond is secured when the issuer has identified specific assets as collateral for interest and principal payments. The trustee holds the title to the assets that secure the bond. In a default, the bondholder can lay claim to the collateral.

Mortgage Bonds. Mortgage bonds have the highest priority among all claims on assets pledged as collateral. While mortgage bonds, in general, are considered relatively safe, individual bonds are only as secure as the assets that secure them and are rated accordingly.

Collateral Trust Bonds. Collateral trust bonds are usually issued by corporations that own securities of other companies as investments. A corporation issues bonds secured by a pledge of those securities as collateral. The trust indenture usually contains a covenant requiring that a trustee hold the pledged securities.

Collateral trust bonds may be backed by one or more of the following securities:

- stocks and bonds of partially or wholly owned subsidiaries;
- another company's stocks and bonds; or
- installment payments or other obligations of the corporation's clients.

Equipment Trust Certificates. Railroads, airlines, trucking companies and oil companies use equipment trust certificates (or equipment notes and bonds) to finance the purchase of capital equipment.

Title to the newly acquired equipment is held in trust, usually by a bank, until all certificates have been paid in full. Because the certificates normally mature before the equipment wears out, the amount borrowed is generally less than the full value of the property securing the certificates.

Unsecured Bonds

Unsecured bonds have no specific collateral backing and are classified as either debentures or subordinated debentures.

Debentures. Debentures are backed by the general credit of the issuing corporation, and a debenture owner is considered a general creditor of the company. Debentures are below secured bonds and above subordinated debentures and preferred and common stock in the priority of claims on corporate assets.

Subordinated Debentures. The claims of subordinated debenture owners are junior to the claims of other general creditors. Subordinated debentures generally offer higher income than either straight debentures or secured bonds due to their subordinate, therefore riskier, status, and they often have conversion features.

Guaranteed Bonds

Guaranteed bonds are backed by a company other than the issuer, such as a subsidiary's parent company. This effectively increases the issue's safety.

Income Bonds

Income bonds, also known as adjustment bonds, are used when a company is reorganizing and coming out of bankruptcy. Income bonds pay interest only if the corporation has enough income to meet the interest payment and the Board of Directors declares a payment.

Because missed interest payments do not accumulate for future payment, these bonds are not suitable investments for customers seeking income.

 Take Note: *Unsecured bonds* and *debentures* are interchangeable terms. Both refer to bonds that have specific collateral backing. Subordinated debentures are designated as junior in claim to other debentures. As a result of this higher risk, subordinated debentures pay higher interest.

Zero-Coupon Bonds

Bonds are normally issued as fixed-income securities. Zero-coupon bonds are an issuer's debt obligations that do not make regular interest payments.

Instead, zeros are issued at a deep discount from their face value and mature at par. The difference between the discounted purchase price and the full face value at maturity is the return (accreted interest) the investor receives.

The price of a zero-coupon bond reflects the general interest rate climate for similar maturities.

Zero-coupon bonds are issued by corporations, municipalities and the U.S. Treasury and may be created by broker-dealers from other types of securities.

Advantages and Disadvantages of Zero-Coupon Bonds. A zero-coupon bond requires a relatively small investment—perhaps $100 to $200 per bond—and matures at $1,000.

Zero-coupon bonds offer investors a way to speculate on interest rate moves. Because they sell at deep discounts and offer no cash interest payments to the holder, zeros are substantially more volatile than traditional bonds; their prices fluctuate wildly with changes in market rates. Moreover, the longer the time to maturity, the greater the volatility. When interest rates change, a zero's price changes much more as a percentage of its market value than an ordinary bond's price.

Taxation of Zero-Coupon Bonds. Although zeros pay no regular interest income, an investor who owns taxable (government or corporate) zeros owes income tax each year on the amount by which the bonds have accreted, just as if the investor had received it in cash. The income tax is due regardless of the direction of the market price. Because the annual interest is not prorated in equal amounts, the bond issuer must send each investor an Internal Revenue Service (IRS) Form 1099 annually showing the amount of interest subject to taxation.

 **Test Topic Alert!**

Here are two test points on zeros to be prepared for:

If asked which of the following securities has no reinvestment risk, the answer to look for is a zero.

If given a suitability question that asks what you would recommend to a couple who wishes to have $100,000 available in a college education fund in 10 years, choose a zero coupon. Any time a test question asks you to select an investment that provides for a certain dollar amount in the future, zeros are a good choice. An investor knows they will receive the face amount at maturity.

Liquidation

In the event a company goes bankrupt, the hierarchy of claims on the company's assets are as follows:

1. unpaid wages;
2. IRS (taxes);
3. secured debt (bonds and mortgages);
4. unsecured liabilities (debentures) and general creditors;
5. subordinated debt;
6. preferred stockholders;
7. common stockholders.

 **Test Topic Alert!**

Be ready for a question on liquidation priority. The hardest part to remember is the order of debt. Secured is safest, followed by unsecured or general creditors, then subordinated. Common stock is always last in line. Bonds are frequently called *senior* securities because of their priority in this hierarchy.

The Trust Indenture   The Trust Indenture Act of 1939 requires corporate bonds to be issued under a trust indenture, a legal contract between the bond issuer and a trustee representing bondholders. Although the face of a bond certificate mentions the trust indenture, it is not automatically supplied to bondholders.

The trust indenture specifies the issuer's obligation and bondholders' rights, and it identifies the trustee.

The Trustee

The Trust Indenture Act of 1939 requires a corporation to appoint a trustee—usually a commercial bank or trust company—for its bonds. The trustee ensures compliance with the covenants of the indenture and acts on behalf of the bondholders if the issuer defaults.

Exemptions. Federal and municipal governments are exempt from the Trust Indenture Act provisions, although municipal revenue bonds are typically issued with a trust indenture to make them more marketable.

Convertible Bonds   Convertible bonds are corporate bonds that may be exchanged for a fixed number of shares of the issuing company's common stock. Because they are convertible into common stock, convertible bonds pay lower interest rates than nonconvertible bonds and generally trade in line with the common stock. Because they are bonds with fixed interest payments and maturity dates, convertible bonds are less volatile than common stock. Issuers add convertible features to bonds or preferred stock to make these issues more marketable.

Investor Considerations

Convertible bonds offer the safety of the fixed-income market and the potential appreciation of the equity market. This provides investors with several advantages:

- As a debt security, a convertible debenture pays interest at a fixed rate and is redeemable for its face value at maturity, provided the debenture is not converted. As a rule, interest income is higher and surer than dividend income on the underlying common stock. Similarly, convertible preferred stock usually pays a higher dividend than does common stock.
- If a corporation experiences financial difficulties, convertible bondholders have priority over common stockholders in the event of a corporate liquidation.
- In theory, a convertible debenture's market price tends to be more stable during market declines than the underlying common stock's price.

Current yields of other competitive debt securities support the debenture's value in the marketplace.

- Because convertibles can be exchanged for common stock, their market price tends to move upward if the stock price moves up. For this reason, convertible securities are more volatile in price during times of steady interest rates than are other fixed-income securities.

Conversion of a senior security into common stock is not considered a purchase and a sale for tax purposes. Thus, the investor incurs no tax liability on the conversion transaction.

Conversion Price and Conversion Ratio

The conversion price is the stock price at which a convertible bond can be exchanged for shares of common stock.

The conversion ratio, also called conversion rate, expresses the number of shares of stock a bond may be converted into. A bond with a conversion price of $40, for instance, has a conversion ratio of 25-to-1 ($1,000 ÷ $40 = 25). Conversion terms are stated in the indenture agreement, either as a conversion ratio or as a conversion price.

✓ **Take Note:** The conversion ratio of a bond is always stated on the bond certificate and the investor's confirmation. However it isn't stated directly in the number of shares but rather in terms of the price at which a conversion can take place. For example, if a bond has a conversion price of $40 per share you can determine that an investor is entitled to convert it into 25 shares. Always start with the par value of the instrument: Par of $1000 divided by conversion price of $40 results in a conversion ratio of 25 shares.

The same concept applies to convertible preferred stock. Assume an investor has purchased a share of preferred that converts at $20. By starting with the assumed par of $100 you can derive that the investor is entitled to five shares of common ($100 divided by the conversion price of $20 equals conversion rate of five shares).

Calculating Conversion Parity

Parity means that two securities, in this case a convertible bond and the common stock into which it can be converted, are of equal dollar value. If a corporation issues a bond that is convertible at $50, the conversion ratio is 20-to-1.

If a bond selling for 104 ($1,040) is convertible into 20 shares of common, the common stock price would have to be $52 to be at parity with, or equal to, the convertible bond price ($1,040 ÷ 20 = $52). If the common stock is selling below 52, the convertible bond is worth more than the stock. If the stock is selling above 52, the investor can make more money by acquiring the bond, converting to common and selling the shares.

✔ ***Take Note:*** On the Series 6 exam, there will most likely be a question on the parity concept. Here are two methods to help you solve the problem:

RST bond is convertible to common at $25. If RST is currently trading for $1,200, what is the parity price of the common?

Method One

Remember, *parity* means "equal." We are solving for equal circumstances at the new price. First solve for the conversion ratio by setting up as follows:

Bond price:	$1,000
Conversion price:	25
Conversion ratio:	40

Next, determine the stock price equivalent based on the new bond price. The conversion ratio *does not change*, so we set up as follows:

Bond price:	$1,000	$1,200
Conversion price:	25	
Conversion ratio:	40	40

The parity stock price is found by dividing $1,200 by 40. The parity price of the common is $30.

Don't be afraid to take the time to write down information and be organized. This helps prevent stupid errors we all make when trying to do things in our head!

Method Two

If you prefer to think in percentages, you can simply identify that the new bond price of $1,200 is 20 percent greater than the original $1,000 price. To be at equivalence, the stock price must also increase by 20 percent. So add 20 percent to 25 and your problem is solved—20 percent of 25 is 5; 5 + 25 = parity price of $30.

In a rising market, the convertible's value rises with the common stock's value. In a declining market, the convertible's market price tends to level off when its yield becomes competitive with the yield on nonconvertible bonds, and it may not decline in price as far as the common stock.

Convertible bonds normally sell at a premium above parity, which is why they are not constantly exchanged for common stock when the stock price is rising.

Quick Quiz 1.9 Match each of the following items with the best definition or description.

A. Zero-coupon bonds
B. Parity
C. Guaranteed bonds
D. Subordinated debenture

____ 1. Claims are junior to those of other creditors

____ 2. Party other than the issuing corporation promises to maintain payments of principal and interest

____ 3. Dollar amount at which a convertible security is equal in value to its corresponding stock

____ 4. Investor receives Form 1099 and reports interest for taxation even though no interest income has been received

Match each of the following items with the best definition or description.

A. Collateral trust bond
B. Income bond
C. Mortgage bond
D. Convertible bond

____ 5. Debt obligation secured as a property pledge

____ 6. Debenture that can be exchanged for common stock at specified prices or rates

____ 7. Secured bond backed by stocks or bonds of another issuer

____ 8. Interest payment must be declared by issuer's board of directors

See 329 for answers and rationale.

Quick Quiz 1.10

1. Consolidated Codfish, Inc. has filed for bankruptcy. Interested parties will be paid off in which of the following orders?

   I. Holders of secured debt
   II. Holders of subordinated debentures
   III. General creditors
   IV. Preferred stockholders

   A. I, III, II, IV
   B. III, I, II, IV
   C. I, II, III, IV
   D. IV, I, II, III

2. Moody's Bond Page lists the following:

   GMAC ZR '12 54 ¼
   Ogden 5s '93 78 7/8
   The annual interest on 50 Ogden bonds is

   A. $93
   B. $500
   C. $930
   D. $2,500

3. Which of the following is NOT true concerning convertible bonds?

   A. Coupon rates are usually higher than nonconvertible bond rates of the same issuer.
   B. Convertible bondholders are creditors of the corporation.
   C. Coupon rates are usually lower than nonconvertible bond rates of the same issuer.
   D. If the underlying common stock should decline to the point where there is no advantage to convert the bonds into common stock, the bonds will sell at a price based on their inherent value as bonds, disregarding the convertible feature.

4. A bond is convertible to common stock at $20 per share. If the market value of the bond falls to $800, what is the new parity price of the stock?

   A. $12
   B. $16
   C. $25
   D. $40

5. A convertible bond is purchased at its face value and convertible at $125. What is the conversion ratio?

A. 2
B. 8
C. 12
D. 20

See page 329 for answers and rationale.

Tracking Corporate Bonds

Bonds are listed in newspapers and other financial publications such as *Barron's* and *The Wall Street Journal*. Figure 1.14 is an example of a New York Stock Exchange bond table as it might appear in a financial publication. Take, for example, Alabama Power 9s 2000 (AlaP). The description of its 9s 2000 bond indicates that the bond pays 9 percent interest and matures in the year 2000. The current yield is given as 8.9 percent, which indicates that the bond is selling at a premium. The "Vol" (volume, or sales) column states how many bonds traded the previous day (the day being reported). In this case, 18 bonds, or $18,000 par value, were traded in Alabama Power 9s 2000.

.The next three columns explain the high, low and closing prices for the day.

FIGURE 1.14   Corporate Bond Quotations

New York Exchange Bonds
Quotations as of 4 pm Eastern Time
Friday, July 16, 1999
Corporation Bonds
Volume $45,198,000

Bonds	Cur Yld	Vol	High	Low	Close	Net Chg
AForP 5s 30r	9.6	50	52 1/4	51 7/8	52	+3/4
AbbtL 7 5/8s 96	7.6	21	99 3/4	99 3/4	99 3/4	...
Advst 9s 08	cv	72	103 1/2	103	103	...
AetnLf 8 1/8s 07	8.5	15	95 3/4	95 3/4	95 3/4	– 1
AirbF 7 1/2s 11	cv	32	114	112	114	+1
AlaP 9s 2000	8.9	18	100 3/4	100 5/8	100 3/4	+1/4
AlaP 8 1/2s 01	8.6	13	98 3/8	98 3/8	98 3/8	– 3/8
AlaP 8 7/8s 03	8.5	65	102 7/8	102 1/2	102 1/2	– 3/8
AlldC zr 12	...	10	91 1/2	91 1/8	91 1/2	– 1/8
viAmes 7 1/2s 14f	cv	79	15 1/2	14 3/4	15	+1
Ancp 13 7/8s 02f	cv	10	91	89 3/8	91	+2

EXPLANATORY NOTES

Yield is current yield. cld–Called. cv–Convertible bond. dc–Deep discount. f–Dealt in flat. m–Matured bonds, negotiability impaired by maturity. na–No accrual. r–Registered. zr–Zero coupon. vi–In bankruptcy or receivership or being reorganized.

For AlaP, the high was 100¾, the low was 100⅝ and the bonds closed at (last trade) 100¾. Net change (the last column) refers to how much the bond's closing price was up or down from the previous day's close. Alabama Power 9s of 2000 closed up ¼ of a point, or $2.50. AlaP closed yesterday at 100½ (100¾ − ¼).

Note that the Allied Chemical (AlldC) zr bonds have "..." in the current yield column; these are zero-coupon bonds that do not pay interest

✓ **Take Note:** A test question may ask you to determine the price of a bond from a bond quote. You must remember that 1 bond point = $10. If the bond's quote is 105, its price is $1,050.

If a bond is quoted at 97⅝, find its price in three easy steps:

1. 97 × 10 = $970
2. ⅝ = .625 × 10 = $6.25
3. $970 + $6.25 = $976.25

U.S. Government and Agency Securities

The U.S. Treasury Department determines the quantity and types of government securities it must issue to meet federal budget needs. The marketplace determines the interest rates those securities will pay. In general, the interest government securities pay is exempt from state and municipal taxation, but subject to federal taxation.

The federal government is the nation's largest borrower as well as the best credit risk. Securities issued by the U.S. government are backed by its full faith and credit, which is based on its power to tax.

Most government securities are issued in book-entry form, meaning no physical certificates exist.

Marketable Government Securities

Treasury securities are classified as bills, notes and bonds to distinguish an issue's term to maturity.

Treasury Bills

T bills are short-term obligations issued at a discount from par in competitive bid auctions. Large U.S. government securities dealers submit bids, or tenders, for large blocks of T bills at weekly and monthly auctions held on Mondays. Each competitive tender is submitted for a price that reflects the interest rate the bidder wishes to receive. The Treasury awards the bills to the highest bidders (those that bid the lowest interest rates) beginning at the top of the list and working down. Not all bids are filled. Those bids that are filled settle in federal funds, as do all U.S. government securities. (Federal funds are reserves that held by banks that exceed the Federal Reserve Board's prescribed reserve requirement.)

T bills may be purchased by submitting a noncompetitive bid as well. The investor who submits a noncompetitive bid agrees to pay the average of the competitive bids accepted at that auction and is guaranteed to have his or her order filled. Noncompetitive bids are limited to a maximum of $500,000.

Rather than making regular cash interest payments, bills trade at a discount from par value; the return on a T bill is the difference between the price the investor pays and the par value at which the bill matures.

Maturities and Denominations. Treasury bills issued in denominations of $1,000 to $1 million mature in 13, 26 or 52 weeks. (The minimum denomination was formerly $10,000, but this was changed in September 1998.) T bills with 13-week and 26-week maturities are auctioned weekly, while 52-week maturities are auctioned every four weeks.

Pricing. T bills are quoted and sold at a discount from par. Note the following quote:

U.S. Treasury Bills

Mat. Date	Bid	Ask	Yield
-2002-			
12/15	5.00	4.75	4.81

The bid and ask quotes are discounts from the par value. For example, if a 6-month T bill had a bid of 5.00, an investor would receive 10,000 – 5%(10,000) or $9,500. The ask of 4.75 means that the investor would pay $10,000 – 4.75%(10,000), or $9,525.

Treasury Notes

Unlike Treasury bills, T notes pay interest every six months.

Maturities and Denominations. Issued in denominations of $1,000 to $1 million, T notes are intermediate-term bonds maturing in 1 to 10 years. T notes mature at par, or they can be refunded. If a T note is refunded, the government offers the investor a new security with a new interest rate and maturity date as an alternative to a cash payment for the maturing note. Bondholders may always request their principal in cash.

Pricing. T notes are issued, quoted and traded in $\frac{1}{32}$ of a percentage of par. A quote of 98.24, which can also be expressed as 98-24 or 98:24, on a $1,000 note means that the note is selling for $98\frac{24}{32}$ percent of its $1,000 par value.

In this instance, .24 designates ²⁴⁄₃₂ of 1 percent, not a decimal. A quote of 98.24 equals 98.75 percent of $1,000, or $987.50.

Other examples follow.

A bid of ...	*Means ...*	*Or...*
98.01	98¹⁄₃₂% of $1,000	$980.3125
98.02	98²⁄₃₂% of $1,000	$980.6250
98.03	98³⁄₃₂% of $1,000	$980.9375
98.10	98¹⁰⁄₃₂% of $1,000	$983.1250
98.11	98¹¹⁄₃₂% of $1,000	$983.4375
98.12	98¹²⁄₃₂% of $1,000	$983.7500

Treasury Bonds

Treasury bonds are long-term securities that pay interest every six months.

Maturities and Denominations. Treasury bonds are issued in denominations of $1,000 to $1 million and mature in 10 to 30 years.

Pricing. T bonds are quoted exactly like T notes.

Callable. Some Treasury bonds have optional call dates, ranging from three to five years before maturity. U.S. government securities are always called at par. The Treasury department must give bondholders four months' notice before calling the bonds.

Table 1.4 highlights the testable features of T-bills, T-notes and T-bonds.

TABLE 1.4   Marketable Government Securities

Type	Maturity	Pricing	Form
Treasury Bills	90 days to one year (short-term)	Issued at a discount; priced on discount basis	Book entry
Treasury Notes	One to 10 years (intermediate-term)	Priced at percentage of par	Book entry
Treasury bonds	Usually 10 to 30 years (long-term)	Priced at percentage of par	Book entry

Treasury Receipts

Brokerage firms can create Treasury receipts from U.S. Treasury notes and bonds. Broker-dealers buy Treasury securities, place them in trust at a bank and sell separate receipts against the principal and coupon payments. The Treasury securities held in trust collateralize the Treasury receipts. Unlike Treasury securities, Treasury receipts are not backed by the full faith and credit of the U.S. government.

To illustrate how Treasury receipts are created, think of a $1,000 10-year Treasury note with a 6 percent coupon as 21 separate payment obligations. The first 20 are the semiannual $30 interest payment obligations until maturity. The 21st is the obligation to repay the $1,000 principal at maturity. An investor may purchase a Treasury receipt for any of the 20 interest payments or the principal repayment. Each Treasury receipt is priced at a discount from the payment amount, like a zero-coupon bond.

STRIPS. In 1984, the Treasury department entered the zero-coupon bond market by designating certain Treasury issues as suitable for stripping into interest and principal components. These securities became known as STRIPS, which stands for Separate Trading of Registered Interest and Principal of Securities.

While the securities underlying Treasury STRIPS are the U.S. government's direct obligation, major banks and dealers perform the actual separation and trading.

 Take Note: An important test point to remember is that STRIPS are backed in full by the U.S. government. Receipts are not. Both are zero-coupon instruments.

Nonmarketable Government Securities

Nonmarketable government securities include Series EE and Series HH bonds. These bonds are nontransferable; that is, they are not bought and sold between investors. They are purchased from the Treasury Department and can be redeemed only by the purchaser or a beneficiary. Series EE and Series HH bonds are exempt from state and municipal taxation, but are subject to federal taxation.

Series EE bonds are bought at a discount and can be redeemed for the face value at maturity. Series EE bonds are issued at 50 percent of their face value in denominations from $50 to $10,000. The bonds can be redeemed before maturity, but will receive a lower rate of return. The tax on accrued interest can be paid annually or deferred until the bonds mature. Tax can be deferred further by trading EE bonds for HH bonds.

Series HH bonds can be purchased only by trading in matured Series EE bonds. Series HH bonds pay semiannual interest, come in denominations of $500 to $10,000 and mature in 10 years, although the investor can redeem them at face value at any time.

✔ ***Take Note:*** For the test, remember the EE bonds pay no current interest, but HH bonds pay interest semiannually. There is no secondary market trading of either of these issues.

Agency Issues   Congress authorizes agencies of the federal government to issue debt securities:

Yields and Maturities. Agency issues have higher yields than direct obligations of the federal government, but lower yields than corporate debt securities. Their maturities range from short to long term. Agency issues are quoted as percentages of par and trade actively in the secondary market.

Backing. Agency issues are backed by revenues from taxes, fees or interest income from lending activities. They may also be backed by collateral, such as cash or U.S. Treasury securities, by a U.S. Treasury guarantee or by the full faith and credit of the government.

Taxation. Interest on government agency issues is sometimes exempt from state and local income taxes, but is always subject to federal income tax. Interest from Fannie Mae, Freddie Mac and Ginnie Mae securities, for instance, is taxed at the federal, state and local levels.

Government National Mortgage Association (Ginnie Mae)

The Government National Mortgage Association is a government-owned corporation that supports the Department of Housing and Urban Development. Ginnie Maes are backed by the full faith and credit of the government.

Types of Issues. GNMA buys Federal Housing Administration (FHA) and Department of Veteran Affairs (VA) mortgages and auctions them to private lenders, which pool the mortgages to create pass-through certificates for sale to investors. Thus, monthly principal and interest payments from the pool of mortgages pass through to investors. Like the principal on a single mortgage, the principal represented by a GNMA certificate constantly decreases as the mortgages are paid down.

GNMA pass-throughs pay higher interest rates than comparable Treasury securities, yet are guaranteed by the federal government. GNMA also guarantees timely payment of interest and principal. Because GNMAs are backed directly by the government, risk of default is nearly zero. Prices, yields and maturities fluctuate in line with general interest rate trends. If interest rates fall, homeowners tend to pay off their mortgages early, which accelerates the certificates' maturities. If interest rates rise, certificates may mature more slowly.

GNMAs are issued in minimum denominations of $25,000. Because few mortgages last the full term, yield quotes are based on a 12-year prepayment assumption; that is, a mortgage balance should be prepaid in full after 12 years of normally scheduled payments.

Taxation. Interest earned on GNMA certificates is taxable at the federal, state and local levels.

 Test Topic Alert!   Of agency securities, GNMAs are the most testable. Prepare yourself by learning the following points:

- Ginnie Maes are the only agency security that is backed in full by the U.S. government
- Investors receive interest on a monthly basis; investors buy them to satisfy income objectives
- Yields on Ginnie Maes are slightly higher than treasuries
- Ginnie Mae issues pass-through certificates

Federal Home Loan Mortgage Corporation (Freddie Mac)

The Federal Home Loan Mortgage Corporation is a public corporation whose stock trades on the NYSE. It was created to promote the development of a nationwide secondary market in mortgages by purchasing residential mortgages from financial institutions and packaging them into mortgage-backed securities for sale to investors.

Federal National Mortgage Association (Fannie Mae)

The Federal National Mortgage Association is a publicly held corporation that provides mortgage capital. FNMA purchases conventional and insured mortgages from agencies such as the FHA and the VA. The securities it creates are backed by FNMA's general credit, not by the U.S. government. FNMA stock also trades on the NYSE.

✓ **Take Note:** Ginnie Mae is the only agency that is backed by the U.S. government. Freddie Mac, Fannie Mae and other agencies are backed by their own issuing authority. Freddie Mac and Fannie Mae are *publicly* owned and traded, but Ginnie Mae is fully owned by the U.S. government.

Collateralized Mortgage Obligations   Collateralized mortgage obligations (CMOs) are mortgage-backed securities like the pass-through obligations Ginnie Mae and Fannie Mae issue. CMOs pool a large number of mortgages, usually on single-family residences. A pool of mortgages is structured into maturity classes called tranches. CMOs are issued by private sector financing corporations and by government-sponsored corporations such as FNMA and FHLMC.

A CMO pays principal and interest from the mortgage pool monthly; however, it repays principal to only one tranche at a time. In addition to interest payments, investors in a short-term tranche must receive all of their principal before the next tranche begins to receive principal repayments. Principal payments are made in $1,000 increments to randomly selected bonds within a tranche. Changes in interest rates affect the rate of mortgage prepayments, and this, in turn, affects the flow of interest payment and principal repayment to the CMO investor.

A CMO's yield and maturity are estimates based on historical data or projections of mortgage prepayments from the Public Securities Association (PSA). The particular tranche an investor owns determines the priority of his principal repayment. The time to maturity, amount of interest received and amount of principal returned are not guaranteed.

CMO Characteristics

Because mortgages back CMOs, they are considered relatively safe. However, their susceptibility to interest rate movements and the resulting changes in the mortgage repayment rate mean CMOs carry several risks.

The rate of principal repayment varies.

- If interest rates fall and homeowner refinancing increases, principal is received sooner than anticipated.
- If interest rates rise and refinancing declines, the CMO investor may have to hold his investment longer than anticipated.

Yields. CMOs yield more than Treasury securities and normally pay investors interest and principal monthly. Principal repayments are made in $1,000 increments to investors in one tranche before any principal is repaid to the next tranche.

Taxation. Interest from CMOs is subject to federal, state and local taxes.

Liquidity. An active secondary market exists for CMOs. However, the market for CMOs with more complex characteristics may be limited or nonexistent.

Certain tranches of a given CMO may be riskier than others. Some CMOs or certain tranches carry the risk that repayment of principal may take longer than anticipated.

Denominations. CMOs are issued in $1,000 denominations.

Suitability. Some varieties of CMOs, such as Planned Amortization Class (PAC) companion tranches, may be particularly unsuitable for small or unsophisticated investors because of their complexity and risks. The customer may be required to sign a suitability statement before buying high-risk classes.

✓ *Take Note:* CMOs are mortgage-backed corporate securities. Recognize that the term *tranche* is associated with CMOs.

🖉 **Quick Quiz 1.11** Match the items below with the best definition or description:

A. Treasury bill
B. GNMA Pass-Through Certificate
C. Collateralized Mortgage Obligation
D. Separate Trading of Registered Interest and Principal of Securities (STRIPS)

_____ 1. Zero-coupon bond issued and backed by the Treasury Department

_____ 2. Marketable U.S. government debt with a maturity of one year or less

_____ 3. Security representing an interest in a pool of mortgages that is guaranteed by the full faith and credit of the U.S. government

_____ 4. Mortgage-backed corporate security that attempts to return interest and principal at a predetermined rate

5. CMOs are backed by which of the following?

A. Mortgages
B. Real estate
C. Municipal taxes
D. Full faith and credit of U.S. government

6. The term *tranche* is associated with which of the following investments?

A. FNMA
B. CMO
C. GNMA
D. SLMA

See page 329 for answers and rationale.

Municipal Bonds

Municipal securities are considered second only to U.S. government and U.S. government agency securities in terms of safety. The degree of safety, of course, varies from issue to issue and municipality to municipality. The safety of a municipal issue is generally based on the municipality's viability.

Interest Payments. Municipal bonds pay interest semiannually. The interest payment schedule is set when the bonds are issued.

Tax Benefits

The federal government does not tax the interest from debt obligations of municipalities. However, any capital gains from municipal transactions are taxable. This tax-advantaged status of municipal bonds allows municipalities to pay lower interest rates on their bond issues. Municipal securities are more appropriate for investors in high tax brackets than investors in low tax brackets because the amount of tax savings for high tax-bracket investors is larger.

Calculating Tax Benefits

An investor considering the purchase of a tax-exempt bond should compare its yield carefully with the yields of taxable securities. Because of the tax savings, the tax-free bond may be more attractive than a taxable bond with a higher interest rate. This depends, in part, on the investor's tax bracket: the higher the tax bracket, the greater the tax exemption's value.

To determine the tax benefit of a municipal bond investment, an investor must calculate the tax-equivalent yield. To do so, divide the tax-free yield by 100 percent less the investor's tax rate.

 Take Note: Let's practice the calculation of tax-equivalent yield with the following example:

Assume that two investors, one in a 15 percent tax bracket and one in a 30 percent tax bracket, consider purchasing $10,000 worth of a new municipal bond with a 7 percent coupon. Comparable corporate bonds are currently being issued at 8.5 percent.

The investor in the 15 percent tax bracket would receive a tax-equivalent yield of 8.2 percent. To calculate this, divide 7 percent by 100 percent minus his tax rate of 15 percent, or 7 percent divided by 85 percent (.85), which equals 8.2 percent. The municipal bond would not be a good choice for this investor because he could get a higher rate of return by investing in corporates.

The investor in the 30 percent tax bracket would receive a tax-equivalent yield of 10 percent (7 percent divided by 100 percent minus his 30 percent tax rate, or 7 percent divided by 70 percent, which equals 10 percent). Therefore, he would receive a higher after-tax yield from the municipal bond.

 Test Topic Alert!

The most important point to remember about municipal debt for test questions is that interest earned on these securities is generally exempt from federal taxation. It is most suitable for high tax-bracket investors. It is generally not suitable for investors in low tax brackets or within retirement plans.

General Obligation Bonds

General Obligation Bonds (GOs) are also known as full faith and credit bonds because the interest and principal payments are backed by the full faith and credit of the issuer. GOs are used to raise funds for municipal capital improvements that benefit the entire community—road repairs, for instance. These facilities typically do not produce revenues.

Sources of Funds

GOs are backed by the municipality's taxing power. Bonds issued by states are backed by income taxes, license fees and sales taxes. Bonds issued by towns, cities and counties are backed by property taxes, license fees, fines and all other sources of revenue to a municipality. School, road and park districts may also issue municipal bonds backed by property taxes.

Revenue Bonds

Revenue bonds can be used to finance any municipal facility that generates enough income.

Sources of Revenue

The interest and principal payments of revenue bonds are payable to bondholders only from the specific earnings and net lease payments of revenue-producing facilities such as:

- utility (water, sewer, electric);
- housing;
- transportation (airports, toll roads);
- education (college dorms, student loans);
- health (hospitals, retirement centers); and
- industrial (industrial development, pollution control).

Debt service payments do not come from general or real estate taxes and are not backed by the full faith and credit of the municipality.

Special Revenue Bonds

A municipality issues industrial development revenue bonds (IDRs or IDBs) to construct facilities or purchase equipment, which is then leased to a corporation. The municipality uses the money from lease payments to pay the principal and interest on the bonds. The ultimate responsibility for the payment of principal and interest rests with the corporation; therefore, the bonds carry the corporation's debt rating.

Technically, industrial revenue bonds are issued for the benefit of a corporation. Under the Tax Reform Act of 1986, the interest on these bonds is usually taxable because the act reserves tax exemption for public purposes. Some

IDRs remain exempt from taxation because of how their proceeds are used or because of their size.

Legal Opinion Attached to every bond certificate (unless the bond is specifically stamped "ex-legal") is a legal opinion written and signed by the bond counsel, an attorney specializing in tax-exempt bond offerings. The legal opinion states that the issue conforms with applicable laws, the state constitution and established procedures. If interest from the bond is tax exempt, that too is stated in the legal opinion.

Quick Quiz 1.12   True or False?

___ 1. Municipal issues are issued by federal and state governments.

___ 2. Capital gains from the profitable sale of municipal securities are *not* exempt from taxation.

___ 3. Municipal revenue bond are generally backed by taxes collected by the municipality.

___ 4. The interest on IDRs is typically taxable at the federal level.

___ 5. Bonds issued by school, road and park districts are examples of GOs.

___ 6. Municipals generally pay less interest than corporate issuers.

See page 330 for answers and rationale

The Money Market

In the financial marketplace, a distinction is made between the capital market and the money market. The capital market serves as a source of intermediate-term to long-term financing usually in the form of equity or debt securities with maturities of more than one year.

The money market, on the other hand, provides very short-term funds to corporations, municipalities and the U.S. government. Money-market securities are debt issues with maturities of one year or less.

✔ *Take Note:* Know that the money market is the source for short-term financing, while the capital market is the source for medium-term to long-term financing. Money market funds are short-term, liquid *debt* obligations.

Money Market Instruments   Money-market instruments provide businesses, financial institutions and governments a means to finance their short-term cash requirements.

Liquidity and Safety. Money-market instruments are fixed-income securities with short-term maturities—typically one year or less. Because they are short-term instruments, money-market securities are highly liquid. Money-market securities also provide a relatively high degree of safety because most issuers have high credit ratings.

Money-market securities issued by the U.S. government and its agencies include:

- Treasury bills that trade in the secondary market;
- Treasury and agency securities with remaining maturities of less than one year;
- Federal National Mortgage Association short-term discount notes; and
- short-term discount notes issued by various smaller agencies.

Money-market portfolios that include municipal securities are considered tax-exempt money market instruments.

Corporations and banks have a number of ways to raise short-term funds in the money market, such as:

- bankers' acceptances (time drafts);
- commercial paper (prime paper);
- negotiable certificates of deposit;
- federal funds; and
- brokers' and dealers' loans.

Bankers' Acceptances

A banker's acceptance (BA) is a short-term time draft with a specified payment date drawn on a bank—essentially a postdated check or line of credit. The payment date of a banker's acceptance is normally between 1 and 270 days.

American corporations use bankers' acceptances extensively to finance international trade—that is, a banker's acceptance typically pays for goods and services in a foreign country.

Commercial Paper

Corporations issue short-term, unsecured commercial paper, or promissory notes, to raise cash to finance accounts receivable and seasonal inventory gluts. Commercial paper interest rates are lower than bank loan rates.

Commercial paper maturities range from 1 to 270 days, although most mature within 90 days. Commercial paper normally is issued in bearer form at a discount from face value.

Typically, companies with excellent credit ratings issue commercial paper. The primary buyers of commercial paper are money-market funds, commercial banks, pension funds, insurance companies, corporations and nongovernmental agencies.

Certificates of Deposit

Banks issue and guarantee certificates of deposit (CDs) with fixed interest rates and minimum face values of $100,000, although face values of $1 million and up are more common. Some can be traded in the secondary market.

Nonnegotiable CDs. Most investors are familiar with the CD time deposits having set maturities and fixed interest rates and offered by banks and savings and loans. Banks offer nonnegotiable CDs with maturities ranging from 30 days to 10 years or more. Banks may issue nonnegotiable CDs for small or large amounts, which are insured by the Federal Deposit Insurance Corporation (FDIC) for up to $100,000. Nonnegotiable CDs are not traded in the secondary market and are not money-market securities.

Negotiable CDs. Negotiable CDs are time deposits banks offer. They have minimum face values of $100,000, but most are issued for $1 million or more.

A negotiable CD is an unsecured promissory note guaranteed by the issuing bank. Most negotiable CDs mature in one year or less, with the maturity date often set to suit a buyer's needs. Because the CDs are negotiable, they can be traded in the secondary market before their maturity.

 **Test Topic Alert!**

Learn the features of each of the money market instruments listed below for test questions.

Bankers' Acceptances
- time draft or letter of credit for foreign trade
- maximum maturity of 270 days

Commercial Paper
- Issued by corporations
- Unsecured promissory note
- Maximum maturity of 270 days

Negotiable CDs
- Issued by banks
- Minimum face value of $100,000
- Mature in one year or less

Interest Rates

The cost of doing business is closely linked to the cost of money; the cost of money is called interest rates. The money supply and inflation levels within the economy determine the level of general interest rates. The level of a specific interest rate can be tied to one or more benchmark rates, such as those described below.

Federal Funds Rate

The federal funds rate is the rate federal banks charge each other for overnight loans of $1 million or more. It is considered a barometer of the direction of short-term interest rates, which fluctuate constantly. The federal funds rate is listed in daily newspapers.

Prime Rate

The prime rate is the interest rate that large U.S. money center commercial banks charge their most creditworthy corporate borrowers for unsecured loans. Each bank sets its own prime rate, with larger banks generally setting a rate other banks use.

Banks lower their prime rates when the Fed eases the money supply, and they raise rates when the Fed contracts the money supply.

Discount Rate

The discount rate is the rate the New York Federal Reserve Bank (FRB) charges for short-term loans to member banks. The discount rate also indicates the direction of FRB monetary policy: a decreasing rate indicates an easing of FRB policy; an increasing rate indicates a tightening of FRB policy.

Broker Loan Rate

The broker loan rate is the interest rate banks charge broker-dealers on money they borrow to lend to margin account customers. The broker loan rate is also known as the call loan rate or call money rate. The broker loan rate usually is a percentage point or so above other short-term rates. Broker call loans are callable on 24 hours' notice.

Interest Rate Summary

Interest rates reflect the cost of money and, therefore, the cost of doing business. The key interest rates people monitor include the following:

- Federal funds rate. The interest rate charged on reserves traded among member banks for overnight use in amounts of $1 million or more. The federal funds rate changes daily in response to the borrowing banks' needs.
- CD rate. Bank rate offered on nonnegotiable CDs. It is considered the least volatile of the rates listed

- Prime rate. The base rate on corporate loans at large U.S. money center commercial banks. The prime rate changes when banks react to changes in FRB policy.
- Discount rate. The charge on loans to depository institutions by the New York Federal Reserve Bank (FRB)
- Call money rate. The charge on loans to brokers of stock exchange collateral
- Commercial paper. The rate on commercial paper placed directly by finance companies or the rate on high-grade unsecured notes that major corporations sell through dealers

✐ **Quick Quiz 1.13** 1. All of the following are money-market instruments EXCEPT

   A. Treasury bills
   B. municipal notes
   C. commercial paper
   D. newly issued Treasury bonds

2. The maximum maturity of commercial paper is how many days?

   A. 90
   B. 180
   C. 270
   D. 360

3. Which of the following statements are true of negotiable certificates of deposit?

   I. The issuing bank guarantees them.
   II. They are callable.
   III. Minimum denominations are $1,000.
   IV. They can be traded in the secondary market.

   A. I, II and III only
   B. I and IV only
   C. II and III only
   D. I, II, III and IV

4. Commercial paper is

   A. a secured note issued by a corporation
   B. a guaranteed note issued by a corporation
   C. a promissory note issued by a corporation
   D. None of the above

5. Which of the following money-market instruments finances imports and exports?

    A. Eurodollars
    B. Bankers' acceptances
    C. ADRs
    D. Commercial paper

6. The federal funds rate is calculated from the

    A. daily average rate charged by the largest money center banks
    B. daily average rate charged by the national Federal Reserve member banks
    C. weekly average rate charged by the largest money center banks
    D. weekly average rate charged by the national Federal Reserve member banks

7. Which of the following interest rates is considered the MOST volatile?

    A. Discount rate
    B. Federal funds rate
    C. Prime rate
    D. LIBOR

See page 330 for answers and rationale.

Issuing Securities

In general, securities are bought either as new issues from a corporation, municipality or federal government or in the secondary market as trades between investors. This section introduces the market for newly issued securities and the role an investment banker plays in various types of offerings.

Investment Banking

A business or municipal government that plans to issue securities usually works with an investment bank, a securities broker-dealer that may also specialize in underwriting new issues.

An investment bank's functions may include:

- advising corporations on the best ways to raise long-term capital;
- raising capital for issuers by distributing new securities;
- buying securities from issuers and reselling them to the public;

- distributing large blocks of stock to the public and to institutions; and
- helping issuers comply with securities laws.

 Take Note: Investment bankers help issuers raise money through the sale of securities. They do not loan money. They are sometimes also called underwriters. All underwriters of corporate securities must be NASD member firms.

Participants in a Corporate New Issue

The main participants in a new issue are the company selling the securities and the broker-dealer acting as the underwriter.

The Issuer. The issuer, the party selling the securities to raise money, is responsible for:

- filing the registration statement with the SEC;
- filing a registration statement with the states in which it intends to sell securities (also known as *blue-skying* the issue); and
- negotiating the securities' price and the amount of the spread with the underwriter.

The Underwriter. The underwriter assists with the registration and distribution of the new security and may advise the corporate issuer on the best way to raise capital.

Underwriting Compensation

The price at which underwriters buy stock from issuers always differs from the price at which they offer the shares to the public. The price the issuer receives is known as the underwriting proceeds, and the price investors pay is the public offering price. The underwriting spread, the difference between the two prices, consists of the:

- manager's fee, for negotiating the deal and managing the underwriting and distribution process;
- underwriting fee, for assuming the risk of buying securities from the issuer without assurance that the securities can be resold; and
- selling concession, for placing the securities with investors.

 Take Note: The largest part of the underwriting spread is the selling concession, which is paid for the sale of the securities to investors.

Types of Offerings

A new stock offering is identified by who is selling the securities as well as by whether or not the company is already publicly traded.

New Issues

The new issue market is composed of companies going public by selling common stock to the public for the first time in an initial public offering (IPO).

Additional Issues

The additional issues market is made up of new securities issued by companies that are already publicly owned. These companies increase their equity capitalization by issuing more stock and having an underwriter either distribute the stock in a public offering or arrange for the shares to be sold in a private placement. In addition to being classified as new or additional issues of stock, offerings can be classified by the final distribution of their proceeds.

Primary Offering

In a primary offering, the underwriting proceeds go to the issuing corporation. The corporation increases its capitalization by selling stock, in either a new or an additional issue. It may do this at any time and in any amount, provided the total stock outstanding does not exceed the amount authorized in the corporation's bylaws.

Secondary Offering

In a secondary offering, one or more major stockholders in the corporation sell all or a major portion of their holdings. The underwriting proceeds are paid to the stockholders rather than to the corporation itself.

Split Offering (or Combined Distribution)

A split offering simply combines a primary and a secondary offering. The corporation issues some of the stock offered; present corporation stockholders offer the rest.

TABLE 1.5   Offerings and Markets

	New Issue (IPO) Market	Additional Issue Market
Primary Offering	Company is going public; underwriting proceeds go to the company.	Company is already public; underwriting proceeds go to the company.
Secondary Offering	Company is going public; underwriting proceeds go to the selling stockholders.	Company is public; underwriting proceeds go to the selling stockholders.

Types of Underwriting Commitments

Different types of underwriting agreements require different levels of commitment from underwriters. This results in different levels of risk.

Firm Commitment

The firm commitment is the most widely used type of underwriting contract. Under its terms, the underwriter contracts with the issuing corporation, selling stockholders or both to buy the securities at a specified price and quantity range, on or about a given date. The underwriter commits to buy securities from the issuer and pay the underwriting proceeds to the company. Under a firm commitment contract, any losses incurred due to unsold shares are prorated among the underwriting firms according to their participation.

Negotiated Underwriting. In a negotiated underwriting, the issuer and the investment banker negotiate the offering terms, including the amount of securities to be offered, the offering price and the underwriting fees.

Negotiated underwritings are standard in underwriting corporate securities because of close business relationships between issuing corporations and investment banking firms.

Competitive Bid. Competitive bid arrangements are the standard for underwriting most municipal securities and are often required by state law. In a competitive bid, a state or municipal government invites investment bankers to bid for a new issue of bonds. The issuer awards the securities to the underwriter(s) whose bid results in the lowest net interest cost to the issuer.

Best Efforts

In a best efforts arrangement, the underwriter acts as agent for the issuing corporation, contingent on the underwriter's ability to sell shares in either a public offering or a private placement.

Standby

When a company's current stockholders do not exercise their preemptive rights in an additional offering, a corporation usually has an underwriter standing by to purchase the unused rights, exercise them and sell the shares.

Firm Commitment. The standby underwriter unconditionally agrees to buy all shares current stockholders do not subscribe to at the subscription price.

Underwriter Exercises Rights. At the end of the subscription period, the standby underwriter uses the rights acquired in the open market and any rights abandoned by stockholders to buy the unsubscribed portion of the offering at the subscription price minus an underwriting fee.

Public Offering. The standby underwriter then offers the stock to the general public at the original subscription price, which now becomes the public offering price.

✓ *Take Note:* In a *firm commitment* underwriting, the underwriter takes on the financial risk because the securities are purchased from the issuer. Because of this risk, the underwriter is acting in a *principal capacity*.

In a *best efforts* underwriting, the underwriter sells as much as possible, without liability for what cannot be sold. The underwriter is acting in an *agent capacity* with no financial risk. For example, if a corporation plans to sell 100,000 shares of common stock, but after exerting "best efforts" the underwriter can only sell 80,000 shares, the underwriter has no liability for the remaining 20,000 shares.

> **Firm commitment** = *principal capacity, underwriter has risk*

> **Best efforts** = *agency capacity, underwriter has no risk*

Finally, remember that a standby offering is a firm commitment offering involving unexercised preemptive rights.

🖉 **Quick Quiz 1.14**   Match the items below with the best definition or description:

A. best efforts
B. investment banker
C. standby
D. firm commitment
E. spread

____ 1. Assists an issuer in determining what securities to issue

____ 2. Underwriter acts as an agent for the issuer and attempts to sell as many shares as possible

____ 3. Compensation paid to underwriters in a new issue

____ 4. Underwriter acts as principal and takes liability for unsold shares

____ 5. A firm commitment offering involving rights

See page 331 for answers.

Trading Securities

Stock and bond trades take place on exchanges and through a nationwide network of broker-dealers known as the over-the-counter market. The terminology of trading securities is introduced below.

Securities Markets

A market is the exchange on which securities are traded. The market in which securities are bought and sold is also known as the secondary market, as opposed to the primary market for new issues. All securities transactions take place in one of four trading markets.

Exchange Market

The exchange market is composed of the NYSE and other exchanges on which listed securities are traded. The term *listed security* refers to any security listed for trading on an exchange.

Over-the-Counter Market

The OTC market is an interdealer market in which unlisted securities—that is, securities not listed on any exchange—trade.

In the OTC market, securities dealers across the country are connected by computer and telephone. Tens of thousands of securities are traded OTC, including stocks, bonds and all municipal and U.S. government securities.

Third Market (OTC-Listed)

The third market is a trading market in which exchange-listed securities are traded in the OTC market. Broker-dealers registered as OTC **market makers** in listed securities arrange third market transactions.

All securities listed on the NYSE and AMEX and most securities listed on the regional exchanges are eligible for OTC trading.

Fourth Market

The fourth market is a market for institutional investors in which large blocks of stock, both listed and unlisted, trade in privately negotiated transactions unassisted by broker-dealers. Most of these transactions take place through the **INSTINET** service.

Registered with the SEC as a broker-dealer, INSTINET includes a large number of mutual funds and other institutional investors among its subscribers. All INSTINET members are linked by computer terminals.

Listed and OTC Markets

Differences between the listed and OTC markets affect a transaction's cost and execution. As computers play an increasingly critical role in executing transactions on all markets, however, the differences should diminish.

Listed Markets

Each stock exchange requires companies to meet certain criteria before it will allow their stock to be listed for trading on the exchange.

Location. Listed markets, such as the NYSE or AMEX, have central marketplaces and trading floor facilities.

Pricing System. Listed markets operate as double-auction markets. Floor brokers compete among themselves to execute trades at prices most favorable to the public.

Price Dynamics. When a floor broker representing a buyer executes a trade by taking stock at a current offer price higher than the last sale, a plus tick occurs (market up); when a selling broker accepts a current bid price below the last sale price, a minus tick occurs (market down).

Major Force in the Market. The specialist maintains an orderly market and provides price continuity. He fills limit and market orders for the public and trades for his own account to either stabilize or facilitate trading when imbalances in supply and demand occur.

OTC Markets

Historically, the criteria a company was required to meet to have its stock traded in the OTC market were rather loose. In recent years, however, the quality of companies that trade OTC has improved substantially.

Location. No central marketplace facilitates OTC trading. Trading takes place over the phone, over computer networks and in trading rooms across the country.

Pricing System. The OTC market works through an interdealer network. Registered market makers compete among themselves to post the best bid and ask prices. The OTC market is a negotiated market.

Price Dynamics. When a market maker raises its bid price to attract sellers, the stock price rises; when a market maker lowers its ask price to attract buyers, the stock price declines.

Major Force in the Market. Market makers post the current bid and ask prices. The best price at which the public can buy (best ask) and the best price at which the public can sell (best bid) are called the inside market.

 **Test Topic Alert!**   The test will ask about basic terminology in the securities marketplace. You need to know the following:

Exchange = *Listed* securities = prices determined by auction

OTC = *Unlisted* securities = prices determined by negotiation

Government and municipal bonds and unlisted corporate stocks and bonds trade in the OTC market.

Role of the Broker-Dealer

Firms engaged in buying and selling securities for the public must register as broker-dealers. Most firms act both as brokers and dealers, but not in the same transaction.

Brokers. Brokers are agents that arrange trades for clients and charge commissions. Brokers do not buy shares, but simply arrange trades between buyers and sellers.

Dealers. Dealers, or principals, buy and sell securities for their own accounts, often called **position trading**. When selling from their inventories, dealers charge their clients markups rather than commissions. A markup is the difference between the current interdealer offering price and the actual price charged the client. When a price to a client includes a dealer's markup, it is called the *net price*.

 Take Note: If you're a little uncertain about the role of "dealers" in the securities market place, try thinking of them like a car dealer. If you were a car dealer, you would maintain an inventory, or lot, of cars. If someone bought a car from you, you wouldn't sell it at the wholesale price. Instead, you would *mark up* the price to make a profit.

If someone wished to sell you his used car, you wouldn't offer him top dollar. Instead, you would *mark down* the price to make a profit.

Securities dealers hold inventories of securities and buy and sell from inventory. They profit on transactions by charging markups and markdowns.

TABLE 1.6   Comparison of Brokers vs. Dealers

Broker	Dealer
Acts as an agent, transacting orders on the clients behalf	Acts as a principal, dealing in securities for its own account and at its own risk
Charges a commission	Charges a markup or markdown
Is not a market maker	Makes markets and takes positions (long or short) in securities
Must disclose its role to the client and the amount of its commission	Must disclose its role to the client, but not necessarily the amount or source of the markup or markdown.

Filling an Order. A broker-dealer may fill a customer's order to buy securities in any of the following ways:

- The *broker* may act as the client's agent by finding a seller of the securities and arranging a trade.
- The *dealer* may buy the securities from a market maker, mark up the price and resell them to the client.
- If it has the securities in its own inventory, the *dealer* may sell the shares to the client from that inventory.

Broker-Dealer Role in Transactions. A firm cannot act as both a broker and a dealer in the same transaction.

Table 1.6 compares the important features of brokers and dealers.

✓ *Take Note:* All firms can act in one of two capacities in a customer transaction. If the firm acts as agent, it is the broker *between* the buying and selling parties. Agents receive commissions for transactions they perform, and commissions must be disclosed on confirmations. If the firm acts as a dealer and transacts business for/from its inventory, it acts in a principal capacity and it is compensated by a markup or markdown. Confirmations do not disclose markups or markdowns. A firm is never allowed to act as both agent and principal in a single transaction.

An easy way to remember the roles of broker-dealers is to memorize the letters **ABC** and **DPP**.

ABC = Agents are brokers, and are paid commission

DPP = Dealers act as principals for profit

Brokerage Office Procedures

Transactions and Trade Settlement

When a representative accepts a buy or sell order from a customer, the rep must be assured that the customer can pay for or deliver the securities. If the customer claims the securities are being held in street name at another firm, the rep must verify this before executing a sale for the customer.

Trade Confirmations

A confirmation is a printed document that confirms a trade, its settlement date and the amount of money due from or owed to the customer. For each transaction, a customer must be sent or given a written confirmation of the trade *at or before the completion of the transaction*, the **settlement date**. An exception to this rule is made for wire order purchases of mutual funds, for which selling agents may send confirmation as late as the day after the settlement date. A registered rep receives a copy of a customer's confirmation and checks its accuracy against the order ticket.

 **Test Topic Alert!**

The test may ask when a customer must receive a confirmation. Confirmations must be sent to customers no later than the settlement date of a transaction.

FIGURE 1.15 Customer Confirmation

Confirmation of your order:

Order	No.	Description	Price	Amount	Inter. or Tax	Reg. Fee	Commission
BOT	100	G. Heileman	28 7/8	2887.50	.00	.10	87.20

Trade Date 5/13/99		Account No.	AE No.	AE Name	**Odd-lot Diff.** 00.00
Settlement 5/16/99		453-01243-1	27	Walker	**Net Amount** 2974.80

Customer Name/Address:

Ms. Jaxson Pollac
5047 W. Kenneth Ave.
Chicago, IL 60699-3287

PLEASE NOTE: On odd-lot orders (orders for other than 100-share lots) on all exchanges purchases are executed at the round-lot price plus a premium (odd-lot differential). Sales are executed at the round-lot price less a discount.

Payment for securities bought and delivery of securities sold are due promptly and in any event on or before the end of payment period in order to comply with federal Regulation T and to avoid interest or premium charges.

ALFA Financial Services, Inc.   **Please keep a copy of this confirmation for your records.**

Transaction Settlement Dates and Terms

Settlement date is the date on which ownership changes between buyer and seller. It is the date on which broker-dealers are required to exchange the securities and funds involved in a transaction and the date on which customers are requested to pay for securities bought and deliver securities sold. The Uniform Practice Code (UPC) standardizes the dates and times for each type of settlement.

Regular Way Settlement. Regular way settlement for most securities transactions is the third business day following the trade date, also known as T+3. As an example, if a trade occurs on a Tuesday (trade date), it would settle regular way on Friday. If a trade takes place on a Thursday, it would settle the following Tuesday.

If the seller delivers before the settlement date, the buyer may either accept the security or refuse it without prejudice.

U.S. government note and bond transactions settle regular way the next business day. Money-market securities transactions settle the same day.

Cash Settlement. Cash settlement, or same day settlement, requires delivery of securities from the seller and payment from the buyer on the same day a trade is executed. Stock or bonds sold for cash settlement must be available on the spot for delivery to the buyer.

Cash trade settlement occurs no later than 2:30 P.M. EST if the trade is executed before 2:00 P.M. If the trade occurs after 2:00 P.M., settlement is due within 30 minutes.

Regulation T Payment. Regulation T specifies the date customers are required to pay for purchase transactions. Under Reg T, payment is due two business days after regular way settlement. Customer payment is due one calendar week after the trade date.

Extensions. If a buyer cannot pay for a trade within five business days from the trade date, the broker-dealer may request an extension from its designated examining authority (DEA) before the fifth business day. The broker-dealer has the option of ignoring amounts of less than $1,000 without violating Reg T requirements. If the customer cannot pay by the end of the extension, the broker-dealer sells the securities in a close-out transaction. After the close-out, the account is restricted for 90 days. A restricted account must have sufficient cash before a buy transaction may be executed.

Frozen Accounts. If a customer buys securities in a cash account and sells them before paying for the buy side by the fifth business day, the account is frozen. Any additional buy transactions require full payment in the account, and sell transactions need securities on deposit. Frozen account status continues for 90 calendar days.

TABLE 1.7   Summary of Contracts and Settlement Dates

Type of Security	Delivery Contract	Delivery Time
Corporate and Municipal Securities	Cash	By 2:30 pm on the same day as the trade.
	Regular way	On the third business day after the trade date.
	Seller's/buyer's option	No sooner than the fourth business day after the trade date but no later than 60 calendar days after the trade date.
	When issued	Exempt from regular way settlement; normally settle three business days after the securities are ready for delivery.
	COD/DVP	No sooner than regular way settlement but no later than 35 calendar days.
Government Securities	Cash	By 2:30 pm on the same day as the trade.
	Regular way	On the first business day following the trade date.
	Seller's/buyer's option	No sooner than the second business day after the trade date but no later than 60 calendar days after the trade date.
	When issued	One business day after the securities are ready for delivery.
	COD/DVP	No sooner than regular way settlement but no later than 35 calendar days.

✔ *Take Note:* If you are confused about the relationship between regular way and Reg T settlement, think of it this way: brokerage firms request customers to settle trades within three business days, because the Act of 1934, through Reg T, *requires* final settlement within five business days. If customer settlement does not take place as planned, the firm has two days to correct the problem before it is out of compliance with Reg T. Customer settlement is regular way; firm settlement is Reg T.

Always assume the question is asking about the normal customer settlement terms, regular way, unless the question specifically mentions Reg T.

Quick Quiz 1.15

Match the items below with the best descriptions which follow:

A. $1,000
B. third business day after the trade
C. T + 5
D. 90 days

___ 1. Regular way settlement for corporate securities

___ 2. Amount that can be ignored by a B-D without violating Reg T settlement

___ 3. The length of time for which frozen account status is imposed

___ 4. Reg T settlement

See page 331 for answers

Dividend Department

The dividend department collects and distributes cash dividends for stocks held in street name. In addition to processing cash dividends, the department handles registered bonds' interest payments, stock dividends, stock splits, rights offerings, warrants and any special distributions to a corporation's stockholders or bondholders.

Dividend Disbursing Agent

Stockholders are sent cash, property or stock dividends, or new shares after a split or a reverse split. If the broker-dealer holds the securities in street name, the dividend disbursing agent (DDA, in the case of dividends) or the transfer agent (in the case of stock splits) makes the appropriate distributions or transfers directly to the broker-dealer. The broker-dealer's dividend department then distributes the dividends or additional shares to the appropriate accounts.

If a stockholder has possession of the shares, the DDA or the transfer agent contacts him or her directly.

Dividend Disbursing Process

Declaration Date. When a company's board of directors approves a dividend payment, it also designates the payment date and the dividend record date. The SEC requires any corporation that intends to pay cash dividends or make other distributions to notify the NASD or the appropriate exchange at least 10 business days before the record date. This enables the NASD or exchange to establish the ex-date.

Ex-Dividend Date. Based on the dividend record date, the NASD Uniform Practice Committee or the exchange, if the stock is listed, posts an ex-date. The ex-date is two business days before the record date. Because most trades settle regular way—three business days after the trade date—a customer must purchase the stock three business days before the record date to qualify for the dividend.

On the ex-date, the stock's opening price drops to compensate for the fact that customers who buy the stock that day or later do not qualify for the dividend. Trades executed regular way on or after the ex-date do not settle until after the record date.

The customer who buys the stock before the ex-date receives the dividend, but pays a higher price for the stock. The customer who buys the stock after the ex-date does not receive the dividend, but pays a lower price for the stock.

Dividend Record Date. The stockholders of record on the record date receive the dividend distribution.

Payable Date. Two or three weeks after the record date, the dividend disbursing agent sends dividend checks to all stockholders whose names appeared on the books as of the record date.

✓ *Take Note:* The imaginary word **DERP** will help you remember the order in which the dates involving dividend distributions occur.

The **D**eclaration takes place first; the **P**ayment of the dividend is actually the last step in the process. The dividend is paid to owners on the date of **R**ecord.

The corporation's board of directors determines the declaration, record and payable dates. The **ex**-date is determined by NASD rules.

✓ *Take Note:* Let's work through some scenarios involving the ex-date to ensure that you fully understand the concept. The calendar shown here assumes a record date of June 21:

June

Sun	Mon	Tue	Wed	Thu	Fri	Sat
				1	2	3
4	5	6	7	8	9	10
11	12	13	14	15	16	17
18	19	20	21	22	23	24
25	26	27	28	29	30	

Record date

If an investor purchases the stock on Friday, June 16, will he receive the dividend?

In this situation, the investor would receive the dividend because regular way settlement takes place three business days after the trade. Monday, Tuesday and Wednesday are the three business days that must be counted. The investor settles on Wednesday, June 21, which means he owns the stock on the record date, and *is* entitled to the dividend.

But, what if the transaction had taken place on Monday, June 19, instead? Counting the three business days required, regular way settlement would take place on Thursday, June 22. The investor would own the stock on the business day after the record date – too late to receive the dividend. This example illustrates that the 19th is the first day the investor buys the stock *without* the dividend (the ex-date) when the record date is June 21. An investor must buy the stock *before* the ex-date to get the dividend. The seller receives the dividend if the transaction takes place on or after the ex-date.

June

	Sun	Mon	Tue	Wed	Thu	Fri	Sat
Declaration date					1	2	3
	4	5	6	7	8	9	10
Ex-date	11	12	13	14	15	16	17
	18	19	20	21	22	23	24
Record date	25	26	27	28	29	30	Payable date

The ex-date is *two business days before the record date* in transactions executed with regular way settlement.

Another possible question on ex-dates: referring to the calendar again, assume the investor purchased the stock on Wednesday, June 21, in a cash settlement transaction. Because the settlement takes place the same day, the investor receives the dividend, and he owns the stock on the record date of the 21st. The ex-date in this circumstance is the *business day after the record date*.

As you will learn in the next lesson, mutual fund ex-dates are typically the business day after the record date like cash settlement.

TABLE 1.8   Summary of Ex-dates

Event	Definition	Duration/Expiration
Trade date	Date on which the transaction occurs.	Initiation date for all types of payment contracts. Due date for cash settlement.
Settlement date	Date on which payment must be received under NASD, NYSE or MSRB rules.	Varies according to type of delivery contract: same day for cash; three business days for regular way; 60 days for seller's or buyer's option.
Record date	Date that determines who is eligible to receive dividends or rights distributions. Fixed by the issuing corporation.	The investor must have settled the transaction to be considered the stockholder of record on the record date.
Ex-date (Ex-dividend date)	Date set by the Uniform Practice Committee after being informed of the distribution declaration by the issuer. Stock is sold without (ex-) the right to receive the dividend.	One-day period dictated by the record date for distributions. Normally two business days before the record date. Stock trades without (ex-) rights or dividends.

Quick Quiz 1.16   Match the items below with the best definitions or descriptions which follow:

A. trade date
B. settlement date
C. ex-date
D. frozen account

____ 1. Account requiring cash in advance before a buy order is executed because the account holder has violated Regulation T

____ 2. The day that obligates the parties to the terms of the trade

____ 3. First date on which a security trades without entitling the buyer to receive a previously declared distribution

____ 4. Date on which ownership changes between buyer and seller

True or False?

_____ 5. In order to receive a dividend, a shareholder must own the stock on the ex-date.

_____ 6. The ex-date is two business days following the record date.

_____ 7. The buyer gets the dividend if the sale takes place on the ex-date.

_____ 8. The payable date is usually before the record date.

_____ 9. The ex-date for a cash settlement transaction is the business day after the record date.

See page 331 for answers and rationale.

Rules of Good Delivery

A security must be in good delivery form before it can be delivered to a buyer. It is the registered rep's responsibility to ensure that a security is in good delivery when a customer sells it.

"Good delivery" describes the physical condition of, signatures on, attachments to and denomination of the certificates involved in a securities transaction. Good delivery is normally a back-office consideration between buying and selling brokers. In any broker-to-broker transaction, the delivered securities must be accompanied by a properly executed uniform delivery ticket. The transfer agent is the final arbiter of whether a security meets the requirements of good delivery.

Economics

Economic activity reflects the overall health of a country's economy. In particular, economists attempt to measure and predict the economy's cycles and the effect on various industries and corporations.

Economics is the study of supply and demand. When people want to buy an item that is in short supply, the item's price rises. When people do not want to buy an item that is in plentiful supply, the price declines. This simple notion, the foundation of all economic study, is true for bread, shoes, cars, clothes, stocks, bonds and money.

Introduction to Economics

The economic climate has an enormous effect on the condition of individual companies and, therefore, the securities markets. In addition to a company's earnings and business prospects, business cycles, changes in the money supply, Federal Reserve Board (FRB) actions and a host of complex international monetary factors affect securities prices and trading.

Business Cycles   Throughout history, periods of economic expansion have been followed by periods of economic contraction in a pattern called the business cycle. Business cycles go through four stages:

1. expansion;
2. peak;
3. contraction (decline); and
4. trough.

Expansion is characterized by increased business activity—increasing sales, manufacturing and wages—throughout the economy. For a variety of reasons, an expanding economy can grow for only so long; when it reaches its upper limit, it has reached its peak. When business activity declines from its peak, the economy is contracting. Economists consider the economy to be in a recession if declining Gross Domestic Product (GDP) continues for six months. Depressions occur when the GDP declines for six consecutive quarters, or 18 months. When business activity stops declining and levels off, it is known as a trough. Figure 1.17 illustrates the four stages of the business cycle.

According to the U.S. Commerce Department, the economy is in a recession when a decline in real output of goods and services (the GDP) lasts for six

FIGURE 1.17   The Four Stages of the Business Cycle

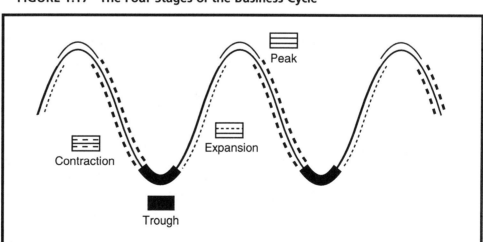

months or more. It defines a depression as a severe downturn lasting for several years, with unemployment rates greater than 15 percent.

In the normal course of events, some industries or corporations prosper as others fail. So to determine the economy's overall direction, economists consider many aspects of business activity. Expansions are characterized by:

- increases in industrial production;
- bullish (rising) stock markets;
- rising property values;
- increased consumer demand for goods and services; and
- increasing GDP.

Downturns in the business cycle tend to be characterized by:

- rising numbers of bankruptcies and bond defaults;
- higher consumer debt;
- bearish (falling) stock markets;
- rising inventories (a sign of slackening consumer demand in hard times); and
- decreasing GDP.

Gross Domestic Product

A nation's annual economic output, all of the goods and services produced within it, is known as its gross domestic product. The United States' GDP includes personal consumption, government spending, gross private investment, foreign investment and the total value of exports.

Price Levels

When comparing the economic output of one period with that of another, analysts must account for changes in the relative prices of products that have occurred during the intervening time. Economists adjust GDP figures to constant dollars, rather than compare actual dollars. This allows economists and others who use GDP figures to compare the actual purchasing power of the dollars, instead of the dollars themselves.

Consumer Price Index. The most prominent measure of general price changes is the Consumer Price Index (CPI). The CPI measures the rate of increase or decrease in a broad range of consumer prices, such as food, housing, transportation, medical care, clothing, electricity, entertainment and services.

Inflation. Inflation is a general increase in prices. Mild inflation can encourage economic growth because gradually increasing prices tend to stimulate business investments. High inflation reduces the buying power of a dollar, which hurts the economy.

Gold prices usually rise during periods of high inflation. Increased inflation drives up interest rates of fixed-income securities, which drives down bond prices. Decreases in the inflation rate have the opposite effect: as inflation declines, bond yields decline and prices rise.

Deflation. Though rare, deflation is a general decline in prices. Deflation usually occurs during severe recessions when unemployment is on the rise.

☼ Test Topic Alert!

Know the order in which the four phases of the business cycle occur for the test.

The correct order is: expansion, peak, contraction, trough.

Also, be sure to know that inflation causes purchasing power risk. Today's dollars can buy fewer goods tomorrow. A *constant dollar adjustment* must be made to compare dollars from year to year that have been affected by inflation.

Economics Policy

The Federal Reserve Board (the Fed) conducts its monetary policy by influencing the money supply, which in turn affects interest rates and the economy. The government conducts its fiscal policy by influencing the economy through its powers to tax and spend.

Monetary Policy Most people think of money as cash in their pockets. An economist takes a much broader view and includes loans, credit and an assortment of other liquid instruments. To a monetarist, the rate of expansion or contraction of the money supply is the most important element in determining economic health. The Federal Reserve Board determines monetary policy.

The Federal Reserve Board The Federal Reserve consists of 12 regional Federal Reserve Banks and hundreds of national and state banks. To determine monetary policy, the FRB:

- acts as an agent of the U.S. Treasury;
- regulates the U.S. money supply;
- sets reserve requirements for members;
- supervises the printing of currency;
- clears fund transfers throughout the system;
- examines members to ensure compliance with federal regulations.

Because the FRB determines how much money is available for businesses and consumers to spend, its decisions are critical to the U.S. economy. The FRB affects the money supply through its use of three policy tools:

1. changes in reserve requirements;
2. changes in the discount rate (on loans to member banks); and
3. open-market operations (buying and selling Treasury bills).

Reserve Requirements

Commercial banks must deposit a certain percentage of their depositors' money with the Federal Reserve. This is known as the reserve requirement. All money deposited by commercial banks at Federal Reserve Banks, including money exceeding the reserve requirement, is called federal funds.

When the Fed raises the reserve requirement, banks must deposit more funds with the Fed and, thus, have less money to lend. Reducing the reserve requirement has the opposite effect.

To compensate for shortfalls in its reserve requirement, a bank may borrow money directly from the Fed at its discount rate, or it may borrow the excess reserves (federal funds) from another member bank. The interest rate that banks charge each other for such loans is called the federal funds rate.

The federal funds rate fluctuates daily and is among the most volatile interest rates. A rising rate usually indicates that member banks are more reluctant to lend their funds and, therefore, want a higher rate of interest in return. A higher rate usually results from a shortage of funds to lend and probably indicates that deposits, in general, are shrinking. A falling federal funds rate usually means that the lending banks are in competition to loan money and are trying to make their own loans more attractive by lowering their rates. A lower rate often results from an excess of deposits.

Discount Rate. The Fed can also adjust the money supply by raising or lowering the discount rate—the interest rate the Fed charges its members for short-term loans.

Lowering the discount rate reduces the cost of money to banks, which increases the demand for loans. Raising the discount rate increases the cost of money and reduces the demand for loans.

Open-Market Operations

The Fed buys and sells U.S. government securities in the open market to expand and contract the money supply. The Federal Open Market Committee (FOMC) meets monthly to direct the government's open-market operations.

When the FOMC buys securities, it increases the supply of money in the banking system, and when it sells securities, it decreases the supply of money in the banking system.

When the Fed wants to expand (or loosen) the money supply, it buys securities from banks. The banks receive direct credit in their reserve accounts. The increase of reserves allows banks to make more loans and effectively lowers interest rates. Thus, by buying securities, the Fed pumps money into the banking system, expanding the money supply.

When the Fed wants to contract (or tighten) the money supply, it sells securities to banks. Each sale is charged against a bank's reserve balance. This reduces the bank's ability to lend money, which tightens credit and effectively raises interest rates. By selling securities, the Fed pulls money out of the system, contracting the money supply.

When the Fed buys securities, bank excess reserves go up; when the Fed sells securities, bank excess reserves go down. When the Fed buys, it expands the money supply; when the Fed sells, it contracts the money supply. Because most of these transactions involve next-day payment, the effects on the money supply are immediate, making open-market operations the Fed's most efficient tool.

Fiscal Policy   Fiscal policy refers to governmental budget decisions, which can include increases or decreases in:

- federal spending;
- money raised through taxation; and
- federal budget deficits or surpluses.

Fiscal policy is based on the assumption that the government can control the levels of unemployment and inflation by adjusting overall demand for goods and services.

Through its fiscal policies, increasing or decreasing taxes, and spending, the government can

- reduce the rate of inflation by reducing aggregate demand for goods and services if price levels are excessive; or
- increase the rate of inflation by increasing aggregate demand if low inflation is causing unemployment and economic stagnation.

Economic Policy and the Stock Market   Fiscal and monetary policies have considerable influence on the market. If the FRB eases interest rates, the money supply increases, making credit easier to obtain. This increases overall liquidity.

Similarly, lower tax rates can stimulate spending because they leave more spendable dollars in the hands of individuals and businesses. Like easier credit, lower tax rates are bullish for the stock market. Raising taxes has the opposite effect; it reduces the amount of money available to businesses and consumers for spending and investment.

The political process determines fiscal policy. Therefore, it takes time for conditions and solutions to be identified and implemented. Because of the time and negotiations involved, fiscal policy is an inefficient means to solve short-term economic problems.

Interest Rates

A loan's interest rate is the cost of the money. The rate of interest is determined in large measure by the supply and demand of money. When the money supply exceeds demand, interest rates fall. When the FRB tightens the money supply, interest rates rise. The Fed influences the money supply in several ways, which directly or indirectly affect interest rate levels.

High interest rates reflect inflation due to insufficient liquidity in the system; they lead to economic contraction. When interest rates decline, overall liquidity increases, which encourages economic expansion.

Disintermediation

When people deposit money with a bank, they earn interest on their funds. The bank, in turn, acts as an intermediary by lending the money at a higher interest rate that allows it to pay the depositor and earn a profit. Disintermediation is the flow of money from traditional, low-yielding savings accounts to higher yielding investments in the marketplace without the bank acting as an intermediary or a middleman. Disintermediation often takes place when the FRB tightens the money supply and interest rates rise.

International Monetary Factors

Fiscal and monetary policy are not the only influences on the economy. In today's global marketplace, international monetary factors include the balance of payments and currency exchange rates.

Balance of Payments

The flow of money between the United States and other countries is known as the balance of payments.

The balance of payments may be a surplus (more money flowing into the country than out) or a deficit (more money flowing out of the country than in). A deficit may occur when interest rates in another country are high as money flows to where it will earn the highest return.

The largest component of the balance of payments is the balance of trade—the export and import of merchandise. On the U.S. credit side are sales of American products to foreign countries. On the debit side are American purchases of foreign goods that cause American dollars to flow out of the country. When debits exceed credits, a deficit in the balance of payments occurs; when credits exceed debits, a surplus exists.

 **Test Topic Alert!**

The exam requires that you know fundamental features of fiscal and monetary policy. The most critical points are:

Fiscal Policy:
- Actions of Congress and the President
- Government spending and taxation

Monetary Policy:
- Policy of the Federal Reserve Board (FRB)
- Discount rate
- Reserve requirement (most drastic)
- Open market operations (most frequently used)

Note the following key points:
- The FRB sets the discount rate, *not* the federal funds rate.
- A change in the reserve requirement has a *multiplier* effect on the money supply.
- Open market operations are the most frequently used tool of the FRB.

Quick Quiz 1.17 1. When the FOMC purchases T bills in the open market, which two of the following scenarios are likely to occur?

  I.   Secondary bond prices will rise.
  II. Secondary bond prices will fall.
  III. Interest rates will rise.
  IV. Interest rates will fall.

  A. I and III
  B. I and IV
  C. II and III
  D. II and IV

2. Which of the following situations could cause a fall in the value of the U S dollar in relation to the Japanese yen?

  I.   Japanese investors buying U.S. Treasury securities
  II. U.S. investors buying Japanese corporations
  III. Increase in Japan's trade surplus over that of the United States
  IV. General decrease in U.S. interest rates

  A. I, II and III
  B. I and IV
  C. II and III
  D. II, III and IV

3. Disintermediation is MOST likely to occur when

    A. money is tight
    B. interest rates are low
    C. margin requirements are high
    D. the interest ceilings on certificates of deposit have been raised

4. To tighten credit during inflationary periods, the Federal Reserve Board can take any of the following actions EXCEPT

    A. raise reserve requirements
    B. change the amount of U.S. government debt held by institutions
    C. sell securities in the open market
    D. lower taxes

See page 331 for answers and rationale.

Know Your Customer

The more you know about your customer's income, current investment portfolio, retirement plans and net worth, as well as other aspects of his current financial situation, the better your recommendations will be. The more your customer knows about the risks and rewards associated with each type of investment, the better will be his investment decisions.

Financial Profile

Before you enter the first trade for a new customer, it is important to find out as much about that person's financial status as you can.

Customer's Balance Sheet
An individual, like a business, has a financial balance sheet—a snapshot of his or her financial condition at a point in time. A customer's net worth is determined by subtracting liabilities from assets (Assets – liabilities = net worth). You can determine the status of your customer's personal balance sheet by asking questions similar to the following:

- What kinds of assets do you own? Do you own your home? A car? Collectibles? A second home?
- What are your liabilities? Do you make mortgage payments on your home? Do you make car payments? Do you have any other outstanding loans or regular financial commitments?
- Do you own any marketable securities? What types of investments do you currently hold?

- Have you established any long-term investment accounts? Do you have an IRA, a Keogh or a corporate pension or profit-sharing plan? Are you contributing to any annuities? What is the cash value of your life insurance?

Customer's Income Statement

To make appropriate investment recommendations, you need to know your customer's income situation.

To gather information about your customer's marital status, financial responsibilities, projected inheritances and pending job changes, ask the following questions:

- What is your total gross income? What is your total family income? How stable is this income? Do you see major changes taking place over the next few years?
- How much do you pay in expenses each month? Is this a relatively stable figure? Do you anticipate any change in this amount over the next few years?
- What is your net spendable income after expenses? How much of this is available for investment?
- What is your net worth? How much of it is liquid?

Other Financial Elements

After you have gathered information about your customer's personal balance sheet and income, you will want to know:

- whether the person owns his own home;
- how much and what type of insurance he has;
- what his tax bracket is and what changes may occur in it over the next few years; and
- whether he has experienced any credit problems.

Nonfinancial Investment Considerations

Once you have an idea of your customer's financial status, gather information on his nonfinancial status. Nonfinancial considerations often carry more weight than the financial information.

Some of the items you will want to ask your customer about include:

- age;
- marital status;
- number and ages of dependents;
- employment;
- employment of family members;
- current and future family educational needs; and
- current and future family health care needs.

Finally, no matter how much an analysis of a person's financial status tells you about his ability to invest, it is the customer's emotional acceptance of investing and his motivation to invest that mold his portfolio. To understand a customer's aptitude for investment, ask questions similar to the following:

- What kind of risks can you afford to take?
- How liquid must your investments be?
- How important are tax considerations?
- Are you seeking long-term or short-term investments?
- What is your investment experience?
- What types of investments do you currently hold?
- How would you react to a loss of 5 percent of your principal? 10 percent? 50 percent?
- What level of return do you consider good? Poor? Excellent?
- What combination of risks and returns would you feel comfortable with?
- What is your investment temperament?
- Do you get bored with stable investments?
- Can you tolerate market fluctuations?

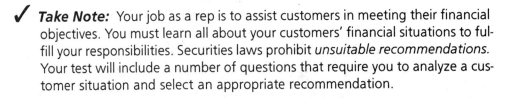 ✓ ***Take Note:*** Your job as a rep is to assist customers in meeting their financial objectives. You must learn all about your customers' financial situations to fulfill your responsibilities. Securities laws prohibit *unsuitable recommendations.* Your test will include a number of questions that require you to analyze a customer situation and select an appropriate recommendation.

Customer Investment Outlook

People have many reasons for investing. Most customers will claim that they invest so that their money will grow. By careful questioning, however, you may learn that because of tax status, income or other events, some growth investments are appropriate, while others are not.

Some of the basic financial objectives customers may have are discussed in the following sections.

Preservation of Capital. For many people, the most important investment objective is to preserve their capital. In general, when clients speak of safety, they usually mean preservation of capital from losses.

Current Income. Many investors, particularly those on fixed incomes, want to generate additional current income from their investments. Corporate bonds, municipal bonds, government and agency securities, income-oriented mutual funds, some stocks (including utilities and real estate investment trusts—REITs), money-market funds, annuities and some direct participation programs (DPPs) are among the investments that can contribute current income through dividend or interest payments.

Capital Growth. Growth refers to an increase in an investment's value over time. This can come from increases in the security's value, the reinvestment

FIGURE 1.18 The Investment Pyramid

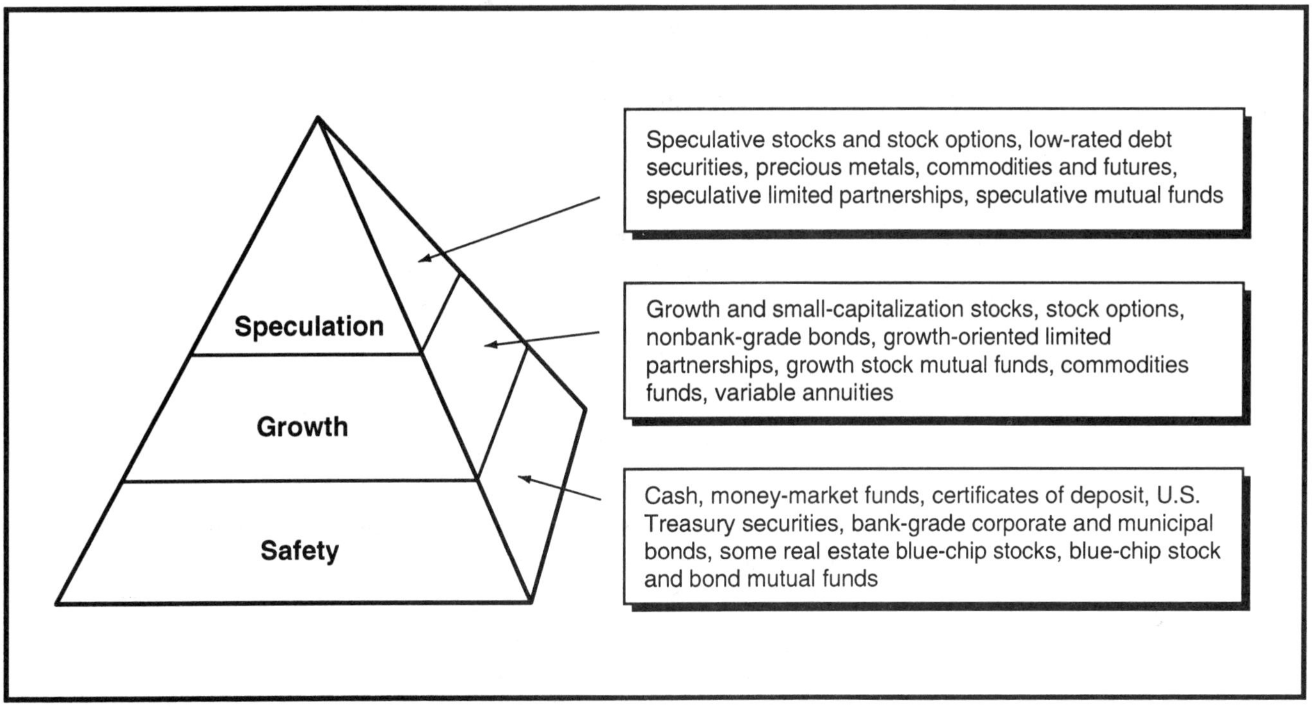

of dividends and income, or both. The most common growth-oriented investments are common stock and stock mutual funds.

Defensive and Cyclical stocks. Certain stocks are likely to perform consistently regardless of changes in the economic cycle. These include utilities, food, clothing and other products that have consistent demand. They are relatively resistant to economic downturns. Cyclical stocks are those that are very susceptible to changes in the economy. Increased sales and earnings are likely in periods of economic expansion while sales and earnings are likely to decrease in periods of economic contraction. Examples of cyclical stocks include durable goods like refrigerators, cars and heavy equipment.

Tax Advantages. Investors often seek ways to reduce their taxes. Some products, like individual retirement accounts (IRAs) and annuities, allow interest to accumulate tax deferred; that is, an investor pays no taxes until she withdraws money from the account. Other products, like municipal bonds, offer tax-free interest income.

Portfolio. Investors with portfolios concentrated in only one or a few securities or investments are exposed to much higher risks. For them, portfolio diversification can be an important objective. Typical of these customers are retirees with large profit-sharing distributions of one company's stock, or investors with all of their money in CDs or U.S. government bonds.

Figure 1.18 illustrates the categories used in portfolio diversification.

Liquidity. Some people want immediate access to their money at all times. A product is liquid if a customer can sell it quickly at face amount (or very close to it) or at a fair market price without losing significant principal. Stock, for instance, has varying degrees of liquidity, while DPPs, annuities and bank CDs generally are considered illiquid. Real estate is the classic example of an illiquid product because of the time and money it takes to convert it into cash.

Speculation. A customer may want to speculate—that is, try to earn much higher than average returns in exchange for higher than average risks. Such investors may be interested in technology stocks, cyclical stocks and "growth stocks," which are expected to appreciate rapidly

 Take Note: You may see several questions about recommendations based on a customer's investment objectives. Below is a quick and easy guide of key words to help you with these questions.

TABLE 1.9   Recommendations Based On Customer Objectives

Investor Objective	Recommendation
Preservation of capital; safety	Government securities or Ginnie Maes
Growth	Common stock or common stock mutual funds
"balanced" or "moderate" growth	"blue chip" stocks, defensive stocks
"aggressive" growth	technology stocks or sector funds cyclical stocks
Income	Bonds – but not *zero-coupons*
Tax free income	Municipal Bonds or muni bond funds
High yield income	Corporate bonds or corporate bond funds
From a stock portfolio	Preferred stock and utility stocks
Liquidity	Money market funds (DPPs, CDs, real estate and annuities are not considered liquid)

Quick Quiz 1.18

1. Which of the following characteristics best define(s) the term *growth*?

   A. Increase in the value of an investment over time
   B. Increase in principal and accumulating interest and dividends over time
   C. Investments that appreciate tax deferred
   D. All of the above

2. Which of the following investments is LEAST appropriate for a client who is primarily concerned with liquidity?

   A. Preferred stock
   B. Municipal bond mutual funds
   C. Bank savings accounts
   D. Direct participation programs

3. Which of the following securities generates the greatest current income with moderate risk?

   A. Common stock of a new company
   B. Security convertible into the common stock of a company
   C. Fixed-income security
   D. Income bond

4. Which of the following investments is MOST suitable for an investor seeking monthly income?

   A. Zero-coupon bond
   B. Growth stock
   C. Mutual fund investing in small-cap issues
   D. GNMA mutual fund

See page 332 for answers and rationale.

Analyzing Financial Risks and Rewards

Because all investments involve trade-offs, the investment adviser's task is to select securities that will provide the right balance between investor characteristics and investment capabilities.

Suitability

Selecting suitable investments to meet investor needs is both an art and a science.

Occasionally, a customer asks a registered rep to enter a trade that the rep feels is unsuitable. It is the rep's responsibility to explain why the trade might not be right for the customer. If the customer insists on entering the transaction, the registered rep should have the customer sign a statement acknowledging that the rep recommended against the trade, and the rep should mark the order ticket "unsolicited."

Investment Risks

In general terms, the greater the risk the investor assumes, the greater the potential for reward. Consider several risks in determining the suitability of various types of investments:

Inflation Risk

Also known as purchasing power risk, inflation risk is the effect of continually rising prices on investments. If a bond's yield is lower than the rate of inflation, a client's money will have less purchasing power as time goes on. A client who buys a bond or a fixed annuity may be able to purchase far less with his or her money when the investment matures.

Capital Risk

Capital risk is the potential for an investor to lose all of his money, his invested capital, under circumstances unrelated to an issuer's financial strength.

Timing Risk

Timing can be everything. Even an investment in the soundest company with the most profit potential might do poorly simply because the investment was timed wrong. The risk to an investor of buying or selling at the wrong time and incurring losses or lower gains is known as timing risk.

Interest Rate Risk

Interest rate risk refers to the sensitivity of an investment's price or value to fluctuations in interest rates. The term is generally associated with bonds because bond prices change with shifts in interest rates.

Reinvestment Risk

When interest rates decline, it is difficult for bond investors to invest the proceeds from maturities and calls to maintain the same level of income without increasing their credit or market risks.

Market Risk

Both stocks and bonds involve some degree of market risk—that is, the risk that investors may lose some of their principal due to price volatility in the overall market. This is also known as systematic risk.

Bond prices fluctuate with changing interest rates. An inverse relationship between bond prices and bond yields exists: as bond yields go up, bond prices go down, and vice versa.

The longer a bond's maturity, the more volatile it is in response to interest rate changes compared with similar short-term bonds. For bonds with short maturities, the opposite is true. Their prices remain fairly stable because investors generally will not sell them at deep discounts or buy them at high premiums. A client's income from short maturities, however, varies with prevailing interest rates.

Credit Risk

Credit risk, also called financial risk or default risk, involves the danger of losing all or part of one's invested principal through an issuer's failure. Credit risk varies with the investment product. Bonds backed by the federal government or municipalities tend to be very secure and have low credit risk. Long-term bonds involve more credit risk than short-term bonds because of the increased uncertainty that results from holding bonds for many years. Preferred stocks generally are safer than common stocks. Mutual funds offer increased safety through diversification. On the other hand, penny stocks, nonbank-grade bonds and some option positions can be risky, yet right for some customers.

Bond investors concerned about credit risks should pay attention to the ratings. Two of the best known rating services that analyze the financial strength of thousands of corporate and municipal issuers are Moody's Investors Service and Standard & Poor's Corporation. To a great extent, a bond's value depends on how much credit risk investors take. The higher the rating, the less likely the bond is to default and, therefore, the lower the coupon rate. Clients seeking the highest possible yields from bonds might want to buy bonds with lower ratings. The higher yields reward investors for taking more credit risk.

Liquidity Risk

The risk that a client might not be able to sell her investment is known as liquidity risk. The marketability of the securities you recommend must be consistent with the client's liquidity needs. Government bonds, for instance, are sold easily; DPPs, on the other hand, are illiquid and extremely difficult to sell. Municipal securities have regional rather than national markets; therefore, they may be less marketable than more widely held securities.

Legislative Risk

Congress has the power to change laws affecting securities. The risk that such a change in law might affect an investment adversely is known as legislative risk or political risk. When you recommend suitable investments, warn clients of any pending changes in the law that may affect those investments.

Call Risk

Related to reinvestment risk, call risk is the risk that a bond might be called before maturity and investors cannot reinvest their principal at the same or a higher rate of return. When interest rates are falling, bonds with higher coupon rates are most likely to be called. Investors concerned about call risk should look for call protection—a period of time during which a bond cannot be called. Corporate and municipal issuers generally provide some years of call protection.

✓ **Take Note:** Be sure to review the risk analysis information just presented very thoroughly. Between various types of risks and suitability of recommendations, you are likely to see 10–15 questions on your exam!

🖉 **Quick Quiz 1.19**   Sharpen your memory of investment risk definitions with this matching exercise.

    A. Market Risk
    B. Credit Risk
    C. Marketability Risk
    D. Purchasing Power Risk

_____ 1. Also known as liquidity risk. The risk that a security cannot be sold quickly at a fair market price.

_____ 2. Also known as inflation risk. The risk of continually rising prices on investments.

___ 3. Also known as default risk The risk that principal may be lost due to issuer failure.

___ 4. Also known as systematic risk. The risk that principal may be lost due to price volatility.

True or False?

___ 5. Interest rate risk is generally associated with equity investments.

___ 6. Default risk is the risk of losing invested principal due to the issuer's financial failure.

___ 7. Reinvestment risk is most problematic when interest rates are rising.

___ 8. Liquidity risk is also known as systematic risk.

___ 9. Bonds backed by the federal government tend to have very low credit risk.

See page 332 for answers and rationale.

Summary

Congratulations! You have just completed Lesson 1, the longest of the four lessons that comprise your Series 6 exam material. Although this is the longest section, it is not the most heavily tested area; 23 questions on your Series 6 exam are about securities, the markets in which they trade and the risks associated with them. These questions can be selected from a broad spectrum of detail.

As you review, be sure you pay close attention to the risks associated with various investments and the objectives different securities satisfy. This area is quite heavily tested on the Series 6 exam. In addition, be sure to have a sound understanding of the differences between equity and debt and the marketplaces in which they trade.

The highlights of this lesson are presented on the following Hotsheet:

Equity Securities Hotsheet

Stock Classifications:
- Authorized—number of shares corporation is permitted to issue
- Issued—has been sold to the public
- Treasury—repurchased by corporation; no voting rights, receives no dividends
- Outstanding—Number of shares held by the public

- Treasury = Issued – Outstanding
- Outstanding = Issued – Treasury

Stock Valuations:
- Par—assigned accounting value
- Book—liquidation or net worth value
- Market—value determined by supply and demand

Preemptive Rights: Allow shareholders to maintain proportionate interest

Voting Rights: Directors, issuance of convertible bonds or preferred stock; *not* on dividend payment or amount

Stock Splits:
- Normal – More shares, less value per share, same total value before and after
- Reverse – Less shares, more value per share, same total value before and after

Preferred Stock:
- Par value = $100
- Stated (fixed) dividend rate
- Priority over common stock in liquidation and dividend payment
- Typically no voting rights

Current Yield: *Annual* dividends divided by current market price

Stock Points:

1 point = $1	$\frac{1}{8}$ = .125	$\frac{1}{4}$ = .25	$\frac{3}{8}$ = .375
$\frac{5}{8}$ = .625	$\frac{3}{4}$ = .75	$\frac{7}{8}$ = .875	$\frac{1}{2}$ = .5

Rights:
30–45 day duration

Strike price below market

Trade as a separate security

Available to existing shareholders only

One right per share outstanding

Warrants:
Long term

Strike price above market

Trade as separate security

Offered as "sweeteners"

ADRs:
- No preemptive rights
- Dividends in dollars
- Investors have voting rights

Investment Grade: Baa or BBB and above, based on default risk, ability to pay interest and principal when due

Call Features:
- Called by issuer when interest rates are falling; no interest after call
- Issuer cannot call during call protection period

Refunding: Refinancing at a lower rate, done when interest rates are declining

Bond Yields: Current yield = annual interest ÷ current market price

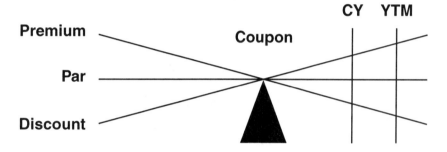

Corporate Bonds:
- Called funded debt
- Secured: Mortgage, collateral trust (backed by securities), equipment trust certificates
- Unsecured: backed by full faith and credit, debentures and subordinated debentures

Convertibles: Par ÷ conversion price = conversion ratio; new price/conversion ratio = parity price of common; conversion ratio × common stock price = parity price of bonds

Governments: Bills quoted at a discount, notes and bonds in 32nds; notes/bonds are callable, bills are not; Treasury STRIPS are backed in full by the U.S. government

Agencies: Ginnie Maes are backed in full by U.S. government

CMOs: Corporate instrument with tranches; taxable monthly interest

Money Markets:
- Commercial paper: most heavily traded; corporate issue; issued at a discount, 270-day max maturity
- Negotiable CD: minimum face of $100,000, issued by banks
- Bankers' Acceptances: Time draft, letter of credit for foreign trade; 270-day max maturity

Interest Rates: Fed funds rate most volatile, established by market; Discount rate set by FRB

Municipals:
- GOs backed by taxes, Revenues backed by user fees, IDRs may be taxable
- Interest is not taxable at the federal level

Underwriting:
- Firm commitment – underwriters act as principal, financial risk
- Best efforts – underwriters act as agent, no financial risk
- Corporate underwriters must be NASD members

Trading:
- Listed securities are exchange traded in auction market
- Unlisted securities trade OTC; price is negotiated
- Third market is listed securities trading OTC

Broker-Dealers:
- Agent = Broker = Commissions
- Dealer = Principals = Markups

Settlement Dates:
- Regular Way: Corps and Munis, T + 3; Governments, T + 1
- Cash settlement: same day
- Reg T settlement: T + 5

Frozen Accounts: If no extension granted from SRO, 90-day freeze, amounts of less than $1,000 can be ignored

Ex-dates:
- Two business days before record date (regular way)
- Business day after record date (cash settlement and mutual funds)
- *DERP*—order of dates is declaration, ex, record, payable
- *D, R and P* determined by Board of Directors, NASD determines ex-date
- Buy before the ex-date to get the dividend

Money Supply:
- Fiscal policy – set by government through taxes and spending
- Monetary policy – set by FRB through discount rate, FOMC (most used tool) and reserve requirement (most drastic)

Lesson 1 Practice Exam

1. If the German mark has depreciated relative to the U.S. dollar, then

   I. goods produced in Germany become less expensive in the United States
   II. goods produced in Germany become more expensive in the United States
   III. goods produced in the United States become less expensive in Germany
   IV. goods produced in the United States become more expensive in Germany

   A. I and III
   B. I and IV
   C. II and III
   D. II and IV

2. An investor owns 100 shares of common stock in ABC Corporation. ABC Corporation allows for statutory voting in Board of Directors elections. If there are five positions to be voted on for the Board, the investor has

   A. 500 votes for each of the positions
   B. a total of 500 votes which may be cast in any manner
   C. 100 votes for each of the five positions
   D. 20 votes for each of the five positions

3. All of the following types of securities trade in the secondary market EXCEPT

   A. debentures
   B. open-end investment company shares
   C. closed-end investment company shares
   D. municipal bonds

4. Which of the following corporate bonds would be considered the safest investment for an investor?

   A. A rated unsecured bond
   B. A rated secured bond
   C. AAA rated unsecured bond
   D. BBB rated secured bond

5. Which of the following types of preferred stock may pay a dividend that is greater than the dividend stated on the face of the certificate?

   I. Straight
   II. Cumulative
   III. Convertible
   IV. Participating

   A. I and II
   B. I, II and III
   C. II and III
   D. II and IV

6. Which of the following are characteristics of general obligation (GO) municipal bonds?

   I. They are backed by the revenue generated from the facility that was built with the proceeds of the bond issue.
   II. Interest paid is tax free at the federal level.
   III. They are issued by agencies of the federal government.
   IV. They are backed by the taxing power of the issuing municipality.

   A. I and III
   B. I, III and IV
   C. II and III
   D. II and IV

7. Which of the following are characteristics of a zero-coupon bond?

   I. The bond pays interest on a semiannual basis.
   II. The bond is purchased at a discount from its face value.
   III. The investor has locked in the rate of return.
   IV. The bond is taxed each year on an "as earned" basis.

   A. I and II
   B. I and III
   C. I, II and III
   D. II, III and IV

8. Which of the following statements are true with regard to Government National Mortgage Association (GNMA) Securities?

    A. Investors receive a monthly check representing both interest and a return of principal.
    B. The minimum purchase is $25,000.
    C. Investors own an undivided interest in a pool of mortgages.
    D. All of the above

9. Which of the following statements describing current yield is correct?

    A. The terms *current yield* and *total return* are identical.
    B. Current yield is calculated by dividing the current market price of an investment into its annual interest or dividend.
    C. Current yield compares an investment's current price to its price at the end of the previous year.
    D. Current yield can be used to express the income return on a bond but not on a stock or a mutual fund.

10. Which of the following statements about collateralized mortgage obligations are true?

    I.   CMOs are backed by the U.S. government.
    II. CMOs are broker-dealer sponsored pools of mortgages.
    III. CMOs are exempt from taxation at the federal level.
    IV. CMOs cannot include municipal issues.
    A. I and III
    B. I and IV
    C. II and III
    D. II and IV

11. The Federal Open Market Committee is concerned with rising inflation. To counteract this concern the FOMC should

    A. increase the reserve requirement
    B. sell U.S. Treasury securities in the open market
    C. increase the federal funds rate
    D. increase the discount rate

12. Which of the following provides the right to buy a corporation's stock for the longest period of time?

    A. Warrant
    B. Long Put
    C. Long Call
    D. Pre-emptive right

13. An investor owns a 9% convertible bond issued by the XYZ Corporation, which is a subsidiary of the ABC Corporation. The bond is convertible at $25. This investor may convert the bond into

    A. 4 shares of common stock of the ABC Corporation
    B. 4 shares of common stock of the XYZ Corporation
    C. 40 shares of common stock of the ABC Corporation
    D. 40 shares of common stock of the XYZ Corporation

14. Where are securities NOT listed on an exchange traded?

    A. Only through INSTINET
    B. On the over-the-counter market
    C. On a regional exchange in the same state where the security was issued
    D. All securities must be listed in order to trade publicly.

15. Regulation T addresses the extension of credit from

    A. broker-dealers to customers
    B. banks to broker-dealers
    C. banks to customers
    D. both banks and broker-dealers to customers

16. Which of the following would be considered money market instruments?

    I. A Treasury bond with 11 months to maturity
    II. 10 shares of preferred stock sold within 270 days
    III. An American Depository Receipt held for less than one year
    IV. A $200,000 negotiable certificate of deposit

    A. I, II and III
    B. I and IV
    C. II and III
    D. II, III and IV

17. A conservative customer is in the 28 percent federal income tax bracket. She notifies her representative that she has a high-grade corporate bond maturing in the near future and wishes to invest the proceeds in another bond as soon as possible to continue her income stream from the interest. After research, the representative discovers a municipal General Obligation bond rated Moody's Baa, with a coupon rate of 5 percent. The representative has also researched a corporate bond paying a 6.5 percent coupon and carrying a Standard & Poor's rating of BBB. Considering the client's situation, which bond should the representative recommend?

    A. The corporate bond because it pays a higher interest rate and the investor wants regular income
    B. The municipal bond because it carries a higher rating from Moody's even though the income is lower
    C. The corporate bond because it provides the same income but has a higher rating
    D. The municipal bond because the after-tax income is greater and its rating equals the corporate bond's

18. Which of the securities listed below is issued WITHOUT a stated rate of return?

    A. Treasury bond
    B. Treasury bill
    C. Preferred stock
    D. Treasury note

19. All of the following statements about preferred stock and bonds are true EXCEPT

    A. they are both debt instruments
    B. they both have a fixed rate of return
    C. they are both senior to common stock at the dissolution of a corporation
    D. the prices of both are directly influenced by interest rates

20. An investor purchased a corporate bond for 97⅜. If the bond is sold for 99⅜ the investor has a profit of

    A. $.20
    B. $2.00
    C. $20.00
    D. $200.00

21. Which of the following statements about bid and asked prices are correct?

    I. Market makers buy at the bid and sell at the asked.
    II. Market makers buy at the asked and sell at the bid.
    III. Customers buy at the bid and sell at the asked.
    IV. Customers buy at the asked and sell at the bid.

    A. I and III
    B. I and IV
    C. II and III
    D. II and IV

22. An issuer offers a large block of new stock to the public through an investment banker who is acting as principal. This is most likely which of the following types of underwritings?

    A. Firm commitment
    B. All-or-none
    C. Best Efforts
    D. Stand-by

23. Which of the following debt securities has the least amount of credit risk?

    A. Mortgage bonds
    B. Debentures
    C. Equipment trust certificates
    D. Collateral trust certificates

Answers and Rationale

1. **B.** If the German mark falls in value relative to the U.S. dollar, goods produced by the United States become more expensive in Germany. Goods produced in Germany become less expensive in the United States. (Page 19) [18421]

2. **C.** Statutory voting allows investors one vote for each share of stock they own. This investor has 100 votes for each of the five voting positions on the Board of Directors. (Page 7) [18428]

3. **B.** Open-end investment company shares (mutual funds) are available in the primary market only. There is no secondary trading of mutual fund shares. Shares are redeemed by the issuing fund. (Page 75) [18430]

4. **C.** AAA as the highest rating that a bond can receive from the rating services. Even though the AAA bond is unsecured, it is still considered the safest due to its AAA rating. (Page 35) [18432]

5. **D.** Cumulative preferred stockholders have the right to receive skipped dividends of the corporation and can receive a dividend in arrears plus the current year's dividend. Participating preferred stockholders have the right to receive a share of the excess profits of the corporation. (Page 14) [18437]

6. **D.** General Obligation bonds are backed by the full faith and credit (and taxing authority) of the issuing municipality. The interest that is paid on municipal bonds is exempt from taxation at the federal level. Municipal revenue bonds are backed by revenues generated from the use of the facility. Municipal bonds are issued by government levels other than the federal government. (Page 64) [18441]

7. **D.** Zero coupon bonds are bought at a discount from their face value. The investor has locked in a rate of return because the maturity value of the bond is known at the time of purchase. The bond pays no interest each year, but is taxed as if it did. (Page 47) [18449]

8. **D.** GNMA certificates provide for an undivided interest in a portfolio of mortgages, and pay monthly interest and principal. The minimum purchase of a GNMA is $25,000. (Page 59) [18450]

9. **B.** Current yield is calculated by dividing the annual income distribution from an investment (interest for bonds and dividends for stock or mutual funds) by the current market value (price) of the security. The current return calculation does not factor price movement over time, or reinvestment of distributions, and thus does not express an investment's total return. (Page 41) [18460]

10. **D.** Collateralized mortgage obligations (CMOs) are broker-dealer-sponsored mortgage pools. They are not backed by the U.S. government. Like other corporate instruments, they are subject to taxation at all levels. Regulations prohibit CMOs from including municipal issues. (Page 60) [18465]

11. **B.** The FOMC buys and sells U.S. Treasury securities to impact the money supply. To counteract inflation, the FOMC needs to put more dollars into the money supply. When the money supply is increased, interest rates fall. The FOMC does not set the reserve requirement or the discount rate; these are tools of the Federal Reserve Board (FRB). The Federal Funds rate is determined by market supply and demand of excess reserves between banks. (Page 90) [18466]

12. **A.** A warrant allows an investor a long-term right to buy an issuer's stock. The expiration period of a warrant is generally a minimum of five years, but may extend through the lifetime of the holder. Long calls are options that give the holder the right to buy stock, but typically expire within nine months. Pre-emptive rights are short-term rights to buy stock and usually expire within 30–45 days. Long puts are rights to sell. (Page 24) [18475]

13. **D.** To calculate the number of shares that a bond is convertible into, divide the bond's par value ($1,000) by the conversion price ($25).

Because the bond was issued by the XYZ Corporation, this bond is convertible into 40 shares of XYZ Corporation's common stock.   (Page 50) [18482]

14. **B.** Securities not listed on an exchange are traded on the over-the-counter market. INSTINET is used by institutional investors for fourth market trades. The location of the issue has no bearing on whether or not the issue is listed on a regional exchange.   (Page 75) [18490]

15. **A.** Regulation T deals with the extension of credit from broker-dealers. Regulation U covers the extension of credit from banks.
(Page 80) [18495]

16. **B.** Money market securities are high grade and liquid debt securities with less than one year to maturity. Preferred stock and ADRs are equity securities. The T-bond with less than one year to maturity and a negotiable CD are money market instruments.   (Page 66) [18504]

17. **D.** The municipal and corporate bonds have equal safety because Standard & Poor's BBB rating is equivalent to Moody's Baa. Both bonds are investment grade bonds. The municipal bond has a higher tax-equivalent yield than the corporate bond. This is determined with the following formula: Municipal yield $\div$ (1 – tax bracket) = .05 $\div$ .72 = 6.94 percent. A corporate bond, of equivalent quality, would have to pay 6.94 percent to be equivalent to the federally tax-free bond.
(Page 63) [18508]

18. **B.** Treasury bills are not issued with a stated coupon rate. Instead, they are sold through auctions at a discount to their par value of $10,000. They then mature to their face amount and the discount represents the interest earned. Treasury bonds and Treasury notes are issued with a stated rate of interest, and interest is paid semi-annually. Preferred stock has a stated rate of dividend, however, it is not guaranteed. The stated rate of dividend is only paid if declared by the Board of Directors.   (Page 55) [18518]

19. **A.** Preferred stock is an equity instrument because it represents an ownership interest in a corporation. However, because of its stated dividend rate, the price of preferred stock, like the price of bonds, is directly influenced by changes in interest rates. Debt securities and preferred stock are senior to common stock in corporate dissolutions.   (Page 12) [18520]

20. **C.** This investor has a profit of two points, or $20. Remember, bond points are worth $10 each. The actual dollar prices of the bonds are computed as follows: 97⅜ = 970 + 3.75 (⅜ of $10) = $973.75; 99 ⅜ = 990 + 3.75 = 993.75.   (Page 55) [18529]

21. **B.** Customers buy stock at the asked price, which means that market makers must sell at the asked price. Customers sell to market makers at the bid price, which is the price that a market maker will pay to buy the customer's stock. Simply remember that "Customers buy at the asked." You can then remember that market makers do the opposite and easily solve questions like this.
(Page 76) [18530]

22. **A.** An investment banker (or underwriter) acting as principal in an underwriting has taken on financial liability for the offering. Investment bankers act as principal in firm commitment underwritings.   (Page 73) [18531]

23. **A.** The lowest amount of credit risk (also called default risk) is found in mortgage bonds because they are backed by a mortgage on real property which is typically quite stable in value. Equipment trust certificates are backed by equipment, which depreciates as it is used, and collateral trust certificates are backed by securities, which may fluctuate in value regularly; these issues are considered to have greater credit risk that mortgage bonds. Debentures are unsecured corporate bonds; they have the highest amount of credit risk of the types of bonds listed.
(Page 101) [18534]

Investment Company Products

Investment company products offer a diversified portfolio of securities, professional management and reduced transaction costs. Because of these attractive features, they are very popular with investors today. Mutual funds, one form of investment company, currently manage trillions of dollars for investors.

This lesson is the most heavily tested lesson. The Series 6 exam will ask you 36 questions on these products and their features. Be sure to spend sufficient study time reviewing and practicing this information.

After completing this lesson you should be able to:

- List and describe the three types of investment companies defined by the Investment Company Act of 1940
- Compare and contrast open-and closed-end management companies
- List several situations that require a majority vote of the outstanding shares
- Identify and explain five significant roles in the operation of an investment company
- List and describe the unique features and benefits of mutual fund shares
- Compare and contrast three different methods for collecting fees for the sale of shares
- Discuss tax consequences of mutual fund distributions
- Compare and contrast contractual plans under the Investment Company Act of 1940 and the Investment Company Act of 1970
- Compare and contrast features of individual, joint and discretionary accounts
- List and describe at least five characteristics of UGMA accounts

Investment Company Offerings

An investment company is a corporation or trust that pools investors' money and then invests in securities on their behalf. By investing these pooled funds as a single large account jointly owned by every investor in a company, the investment company management attempts to invest and manage funds for people more efficiently than the individual investors could themselves.

Investment Company Purpose

Like corporate issuers, investment companies raise capital by selling shares to the public. Investment companies must abide by the same registration and prospectus requirements imposed by the Securities Act of 1933 on every other issuer. Investment companies are also subject to regulations regarding how their shares are sold to the public. The Investment Company Act of 1940 provides for SEC regulation of investment companies and their activities.

Customers often invest in investment companies because they believe a professional money manager should be able to outperform the average investor in the market.

Types of Investment Companies

The Investment Company Act of 1940 classifies investment companies into three broad types: face-amount certificate companies (FACs); unit investment trusts (UITs); and management investment companies

Face-Amount Certificate Companies

A face-amount certificate is a contract between an investor and an issuer in which the issuer guarantees payment of a stated ("face amount") sum to the investor at some set date in the future. In return for this future payment, the investor agrees to pay the issuer a set amount of money either as a lump sum or in periodic installments. If the investor pays for the certificate in a lump sum, the investment is known as a fully paid face-amount certificate. Issuers of these investments are called, naturally enough, face-amount certificate companies. Very few face-amount certificate companies operate today because tax law changes have eliminated their tax advantages.

 **Test Topic Alert!**

You will see no more than one or two questions involving face amount certificate companies. For the test you should remember that:

- Face amount certificates pay a fixed rate of return.
- Face amount certificates do not trade in the secondary market; they are redeemed by the issuer.
- Face amount certificate companies are classified as investment companies.

FIGURE 2.1   Classification of Investment Companies

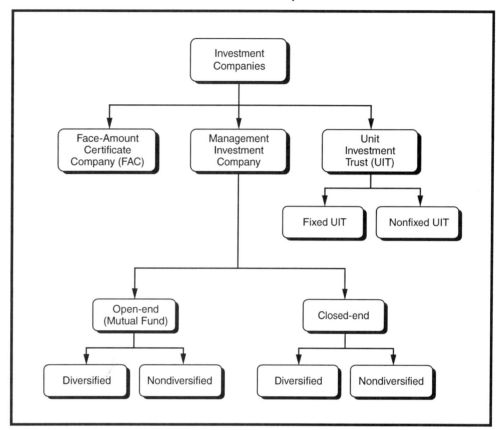

Unit Investment Trusts

A UIT is an investment company organized under a trust indenture. The primary characteristics follow:

- They do not have Boards of Directors.
- They do not employ investment advisers.
- They do not actively manage their own portfolios (trade securities).

A UIT functions as a holding company for its investors. UIT managers typically purchase other investment company shares or government and municipal bonds. They then sell redeemable shares, also known as *units* or *shares of beneficial interest*, in its portfolio of securities. Each share is an undivided interest in the entire underlying portfolio. Because UITs are not managed, when any securities in the portfolio are liquidated, the proceeds must be distributed.

A UIT may be fixed or nonfixed. A fixed UIT typically purchases a portfolio of bonds and terminates when the bonds in the portfolio mature. A nonfixed UIT purchases shares of an underlying mutual fund. Under the Investment Company Act of 1940, the trustees of both fixed and nonfixed UITs must maintain secondary markets in the units, thus guaranteeing liquidity to shareholders.

 Take Note: Let's get a clear picture of how a unit investment trust works. Think of it just like a mutual fund—up to a point. Both fixed UITs and mutual funds are comprised of a pool of securities in which investors own a proportionate share.

The big difference is that mutual funds *actively* trade their portfolios; a portfolio manager gets paid a fee to buy low and sell high as needed to meet the objectives of the fund. UIT portfolios usually are not traded; they are fixed trusts. The advantage to the investor is that they own a diversified interest but they do not have to pay a management fee—the biggest expense of mutual fund ownership. The downside is that the UIT portfolio is not traded in response to market conditions.

Test Topic Alert!

Expect to see several questions related to UITs. You should know the following features:

- UITs are not actively managed; there is no Board of Directors (BOD) or investment adviser.
- UIT shares (units) are not traded in the secondary market; they must be redeemed by the trust.
- UITs are investment companies as defined under the Investment Company Act of 1940.

Management Investment Companies

The most familiar type of investment company is the management investment company, which actively manages a securities portfolio to achieve a stated investment objective. A management investment company is either closed-end or open-end. Initially, both closed- and open-end companies sell shares to the public; the difference between them lies in the type of securities they market and where investors buy and sell their shares in the primary or secondary market.

Closed-End Investment Companies

When a closed-end investment company wants to raise capital for its portfolio, it conducts a common stock offering. For the initial offering, the company registers a fixed number of shares with the SEC and offers them to the public, with a prospectus, for a limited time through underwriters. The fund's capitalization is fixed unless an additional public offering is made at some future time. Closed-end investment companies can issue bonds and preferred stock as well.

Closed-end investment companies are often called *publicly traded funds*. After the stock is sold in the initial offering, anyone can buy or sell shares in the secondary market, either on an exchange or over the counter (OTC). Supply and demand determine the bid price (price at which an investor can sell) and the ask price (price at which an investor can buy). Closed-end fund shares may trade at a premium or discount to the shares' net asset value (NAV).

Open-End Investment Companies

An open-end investment company, or **mutual fund**, does not specify the exact number of shares it intends to issue. It registers an open offering with the SEC. With this registration type, the open-end investment company can raise an unlimited amount of investment capital by continuously issuing new shares. Conversely, when investors liquidate holdings in a mutual fund, the fund's capital shrinks because the fund redeems shares. The offering never "closes" because the number of shares the company can offer is unlimited. Any person who wants to invest in the company buys shares directly from the company or its underwriters at the public offering price (POP). A mutual fund's POP is the net asset value (NAV) per share plus a sales charge. A mutual fund's NAV is calculated by deducting the fund's liabilities from its total assets. NAV per share is calculated by dividing the fund's NAV by the number of shares outstanding. Calculating NAV will be covered in detail later in this lesson.

The shares an open-end investment company sells are *redeemable securities*. When an investor sells shares, the company redeems them at their NAV. For each share an investor redeems, the company sends the investor money for the proportionate share of the company's net assets. Therefore, a mutual fund's capital shrinks when investors redeem shares, although the NAV per share does not fall.

 Take Note: An easy way to remember the features of a closed-end company is to think about what would be true for any corporate security. For example:

- Where do shares of closed-end companies trade? Like corporates, in the secondary market
- What types of securities can closed-ends issue? Like corporations, common, preferred and bonds
- Can fractional shares be purchased? Like corporates, only full shares can be purchased
- When must a prospectus be used? Like corporates, only in the IPO
- No prospectus is given when the shares are purchased in a secondary market transaction.

You are likely to see three to four questions that require your understanding of these features. Try this method to simplify the process!

TABLE 2.1   Comparison of Open-End and Closed-End Investment Companies

Characteristic	Open-End	Closed-End
Capitalization	Unlimited; continuous offering of shares.	Fixed; single offering of shares.
Issues	Common stock only; no debt securities; permitted to borrow.	May issue common, preferred and debt securities.
Shares	Full or fractional.	Full only.
Offerings and Trading	Sold and redeemed by the fund only. Continuous primary offering. Must redeem shares.	Initial primary offering. Secondary trading OTC or on an exchange. Does not redeem shares.
Pricing	NAV plus sales charge. Selling price is determined by a formula found in the prospectus.	CMV plus commission. Price is determined by supply and demand.
Shareholder Rights	Dividends (when declared), voting.	Dividends (when declared), voting, preemptive.
Ex-date	Set by board of directors.	Set by the exchange or the NASD.

Quick Quiz 2.1 Determine whether each statement describes an open-end or a closed-end company. Write "O" for open-end and "C" for closed-end.

____ 1. Trades in the secondary market

____ 2. Investors may purchase fractional shares

____ 3. Can issue common stock, preferred stock and bonds

____ 4. Are sold with prospectus during IPO only

____ 5. Issues a fixed number of shares

____ 6. Ex-date is set by the Board of Directors

___ 7. Do not trade in the secondary market; shares must be redeemed.

___ 8. Price is set by supply and demand.

___ 9. Usually called "mutual funds"

___ 10. Selling price usually includes a sales charge

See page page 333 for answers.

Diversified and Nondiversified

Diversification provides risk management that makes mutual funds popular with many investors. However, not all investment companies feature diversified portfolios.

Diversified. Under the Investment Company Act of 1940, an investment company qualifies as a diversified investment company if it meets the following **75-5-10** test:

- *75 percent* of total assets must be invested in securities issued by companies other than the investment company itself or its affiliates. Cash on hand and cash equivalent investments (short-term government and money-market securities) are counted as part of the 75 percent required investment in outside companies.
- No more than *5 percent* of total assets can be invested in any one corporation's securities.
- The investment company can own no more than *10 percent* of an outside corporation's outstanding voting class securities (common stock).

Nondiversified. A nondiversified investment company fails to meet the 75-5-10 test.

An investment company that specializes in one industry is not necessarily a nondiversified company. Some investment companies choose to concentrate their assets in an industry or a geographic area, such as health care, technology stocks or northeast coast company stocks. These are known as *specialized funds* or *sector funds*. An investment company that invests in a single industry can still be considered diversified as long as it meets the 75-5-10 test.

✓ *Take Note:* Be sure to remember that both open- and closed-end companies can be diversified or nondiversified.

Quick Quiz 2.2   1. Which of the following are covered under the Investment Company Act of 1940?

    I. Unit investment trusts
    II. Face-amount companies
    III. Open-end management companies
    IV. Closed-end management companies

    A. I and II only
    B. I, III and IV only
    C. III and IV only
    D. I, II, III and IV

2. What kind of investment company has NO provision for redemption of outstanding shares?

    A. Open-end company
    B. Closed-end company
    C. Unit investment trust
    D. Mutual fund

3. Diversified management companies must be invested so that

    I. they own no more than 5 percent of the voting stock of a single company
    II. no more than 5 percent of their assets are invested in any one company
    III. they own no more than 10 percent of the voting stock of any one company
    IV. if they own more than 25 percent of a target company, they do not vote the stock

    A. I and II
    B. I, II and IV
    C. II and III
    D. II, III and IV

4. According to the Investment Company Act of 1940, an investment company with a fixed portfolio, redeemable shares and no management fee is classified as a

    A. face-amount certificate company
    B. management company
    C. unit investment trust
    D. closed-end investment company

5. Open-end investment companies, but not closed-end investment companies

   I. can make continuous offerings of shares provided the original registration statement and prospectus are periodically updated
   II. can be listed on registered national exchanges
   III. always redeem their shares
   IV. can issue only common stock

   A. I, II and III
   B. I and III
   C. I, III and IV
   D. II and IV

See page 333 for answers and rationale

Investment Company Registration

A company must register with the SEC as an investment company if:

- the company is in the business of investing in, reinvesting in, owning, holding or trading securities; or
- 40 percent or more of the company's assets are invested in securities. (Government securities and securities of majority-owned subsidiaries are not used in calculating the 40 percent limitation.)

A company must meet certain minimum requirements before it may register as an investment company with the SEC. An investment company cannot issue securities to the public unless it has:

- private capitalization (seed money) of at least $100,000 of net assets;
- 100 investors; and
- clearly defined investment objectives.

If the investment company does not have 100 shareholders and $100,000 in net assets, it can still register a public offering with the SEC if it can meet these requirements within 90 days of registration.

The company must clearly define an investment objective under which it plans to operate. Once defined, the objective may be changed only by a majority vote of the company's outstanding shares.

Open-End Companies. In addition, the act of 1940 requires open-end companies to have:

- no more than one class of security and
- a minimum asset-to-debt ratio of 300 percent.

Because open-end investment companies may issue only one class of security (common stock), they are permitted to borrow from banks as long as a company's asset-to-debt ratio is not less than 3-to-1—that is, debt coverage by assets of at least 300 percent, or no more than one-third of assets from borrowed money.

 **Take Note:** Mutual funds may borrow money from banks but not from investors. Borrowing money from investors is like issuing bonds, and only closed-end companies may issue bonds. Keep in mind that when borrowing money from the bank, the fund must have at least $3 of total assets for every $1 borrowed.

Test Topic Alert!

Be cautious of questions that ask about the asset-to-debt ratio described above. If the question specifically asks about the *asset-to-debt ratio*, the answer to the question is 3:1, or 300 percent. But, if it asks about the *debt-to-asset ratio*, the correct answer is 1:3, or 33 percent. READ carefully to avoid careless mistakes!

SEC Registration and Public Offering Requirements

Investment companies must file registration statements with the SEC, provide full disclosure and generally follow the same public offering procedures required of other corporations when issuing securities. In filing for registration, an investment company must identify:

- the type of investment company it intends to be (i.e., open-end or closed-end);
- plans the company has to raise money by borrowing;
- the company's intention, if any, to concentrate its investments in a single industry;
- plans for investing in real estate or commodities;
- conditions under which investment policies may be changed by a vote of the shares;
- the full name and address of each affiliated person; and
- a description of the business experience of each officer and director during the preceding five years.

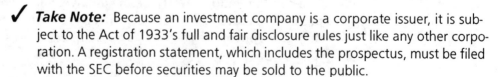 **Take Note:** Because an investment company is a corporate issuer, it is subject to the Act of 1933's full and fair disclosure rules just like any other corporation. A registration statement, which includes the prospectus, must be filed with the SEC before securities may be sold to the public.

In filing for registration, an investment company must identify the overall investment intentions of the fund and background information on affiliated persons, officers and directors.

Continuous Public Offering Securities

The SEC treats the sale of open-end investment company shares as a continuous public offering of shares, which means all sales must be accompanied by a prospectus. The financial information (statements) in the prospectus must be dated not more than 16 months prior to the sale. With closed-end funds, only the initial public offering of stock is sold with a prospectus.

 **Test Topic Alert!**

Here are three important test points regarding investment company prospectuses that you are likely to see in test questions:

1. Mutual funds must always be sold with a prospectus because they are continuous *primary* offerings. New securities must always be sold with a prospectus.
2. Closed-end funds must be sold with a prospectus in their IPO only. When they are trading in the secondary market, closed-end funds need not be sold with a prospectus.
3. Information provided to the public in a prospectus can be no more than 16 months old. The Act of 1933 requires that information disclosed to an investor is *current* and complete.

Purchasing Mutual Fund Shares on Margin. Because a mutual fund is considered a continuous primary offering, Regulation T of the Federal Reserve Board prohibits the purchase of mutual fund shares on margin. Margin is the use of money borrowed from a brokerage firm to purchase securities. Mutual fund shares may be used as collateral in a margin account, however, if they have been held fully paid for more than 30 days.

 Take Note: In margin accounts, investors borrow money from broker-dealers to purchase securities. Broker-dealers acquire funds to loan by pledging customer securities to the bank as collateral. Mutual funds may be used in this way. However, they cannot be purchased using borrowed funds. Mutual funds are considered new issues and rules prohibit the purchase of new issues on the margin.

Registration of Investment Company Securities

After filing as an investment company under the act of 1940, the investment company must register with the SEC any securities it intends to sell. The registration of shares takes place under the Securities Act of 1933.

Registration Statement and Prospectus

The registration statement an investment company must file consists of two parts. Part 1 is the prospectus that must be furnished to every person to whom the company offers the securities. Part 1 is also called an **N1-A prospectus** or a **summary prospectus**. Part 2 is the document containing information that need not be furnished to every purchaser, but must be made available for public inspection. Part 2 is called the Statement of Additional Information (SAI). The prospectus must contain any disclosure that the SEC requires. The fact that all publicly issued securities must be registered with the SEC does not mean that the SEC in any way approves the securities. For that reason, every prospectus must contain a disclaimer similar to the following on its front cover:

> These securities have not been approved or disapproved by the Securities and Exchange Commission nor has the Commission passed on the accuracy or adequacy of this prospectus. No state has approved or disapproved this offering. Any representation to the contrary is a criminal offense.

✓ **Take Note:** Investors who purchase mutual funds must receive a prospectus no later than the time of solicitation. They do not automatically receive the statement of additional information; this supplementary information is available upon request from the mutual fund.

Also, as with any other security, the SEC does not approve mutual funds for sale; they are released for sale with sufficient disclosure for an investor to make an informed investment decision.

Restrictions on Operations

The SEC prohibits a mutual fund from engaging in the following activities unless the fund meets stringent disclosure and financial requirements:

- purchasing securities on margin;
- selling securities short;
- participating in joint investment or trading accounts; and
- acting as distributor of its own securities, except through an underwriter.

The fund must specifically disclose these activities, and the extent to which it plans to engage in these activities, in its prospectus.

✓ **Take Note:** Short selling is a securities industry practice that involves selling shares that are not owned. To do this, investors borrow shares from the broker-dealer by putting up collateral in a margin account. The borrowed shares are then sold with the hopes that their market price will fall. If the market price does fall, the short seller can buy back the borrowed shares at a lower price to repay the broker-dealer. The difference in the price at which the shares are sold and the lower price at which they are bought to repay the broker-dealer is the profit to the investor. However, if the price goes up instead, the potential for loss is unlimited.

Note that in general investors *buy low* and *sell high* to make a profit; a short sale involves the same steps only in a different order. In a short sale investors *sell high,* then *buy low.*

 Test Topic Alert!

The test may ask which mutual fund trading activities *may* be prohibited by the SEC. The right answer choices include margin account trading, short selling and naked (uncovered) options trading strategies. *Covered* option transactions are permissible, but *naked* strategies are generally considered too risky.

Shareholders' Right to Vote

Before any change can be made to a fund's published bylaws or objectives, shareholder approval is mandatory. In voting matters, it is the majority of shares voted for or against a proposition that counts, not the majority of people voting. Thus, one shareholder holding 51 percent of all the shares outstanding can determine a vote's outcome.

Among the changes that require a majority vote of the shares outstanding are:

- issuing or underwriting other securities;
- purchasing or underwriting real estate;
- making loans;
- changing subclassification (for example, from open-end to closed-end or from diversified to nondiversified);
- changing sales load policy (for example, from a no-load fund to a load fund);
- changing the nature of the business (for example, ceasing business as an investment company); and
- changing investment policy (for example, from income to growth or from bonds to small capitalization stocks)

In addition to the right to vote on these items, shareholders retain all rights that stockholders normally possess.

 Test Topic Alert!

Be careful when answering questions to discern correctly between *shares* voting and *shareholders* voting in mutual fund matters. Remember, a majority vote of the outstanding shares is what is required to approve such things as sales load or investment company objectives changes.

Quick Quiz 2.3 True or False?

_____ 1. Mutual funds are generally prohibited from using covered options strategies.

_____ 2. A majority vote of the outstanding shareholders is required to change the investment objectives of a mutual fund.

_____ 3. Mutual fund shares may be purchased on margin, but cannot be used as collateral in margin accounts.

_____ 4. Open-end companies must have 100 shareholders and $100,000 of assets before they can operate as an investment company.

_____ 5. Mutual funds are required to file registration statements with the SEC before shares are sold to the public.

_____ 6. Mutual funds are considered continuous secondary offerings of securities.

_____ 7. An open-end investment company must maintain a debt-to-asset ratio of 3 to 1.

_____ 8. Closed-end companies are generally considered mutual funds.

See page 333 for answers and rational

Management of Investment Companies

Five parties work together to help an investment company operate: a Board of Directors, investment adviser, custodian, transfer agent and underwriter. Figure 2.2 shows the organizational structure of a fund.

Board of Directors

Like publicly owned corporations in general, a management investment company has a CEO, a team of officers and a Board of Directors (BOD), to serve the interests of its investors. The officers and directors concern themselves with policy and administrative matters. They do not manage the investment portfolio. As with other types of corporations, the shareholders

FIGURE 2.2 Organization Structure of Fund

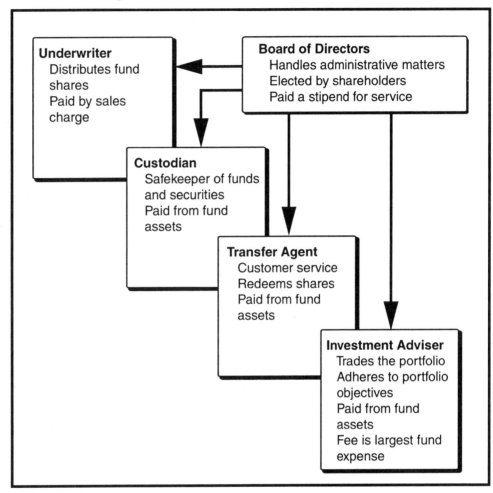

of an investment company elect the Board of Directors to make decisions and oversee operations.

A management investment company's Board of Directors pulls together the different parts of a mutual fund:

- It defines the type of fund(s) to offer, such as growth, income, combination or sector.
- It defines the fund's objective.
- It approves and hires the transfer agent, custodian and investment adviser.

The Act of 1940 restricts who may sit on an investment company's Board of Directors. The act requires at least 40 percent of the directors to be independent or noninterested persons. A noninterested person is only connected with the investment company in her capacity as a director. A noninterested person is not connected with the investment company's investment adviser, transfer agent or custodian bank. This means that no more than 60 percent of the board members may be interested persons, including attorneys on retainer, accountants and any persons employed in similar capacities with the company.

Also, no individual who has been convicted of a felony of any type or a misdemeanor involving the securities industry may serve on aBoard of Directors, nor may any person who has been either temporarily or permanently barred from acting as an underwriter, a broker, a dealer or an investment company by any court.

 **Test Topic Alert!**   Be cautious of questions that ask about members of a mutual fund's Board of Directors. If the question specifically asks how many directors can be *interested* persons, the answer is 60 percent. But, if it asks about how many must be *non-interested*, the correct answer is a minimum 40 percent.

Investment Adviser

An investment company's board of directors contracts with an outside investment adviser or portfolio manager to invest the cash and securities in the fund's portfolio, implement investment strategy, identify the tax status of distributions made to shareholders and manage the portfolio's day-to-day trading. Naturally, the adviser must adhere to the objective stated in the fund's prospectus. The adviser cannot transfer the responsibility of portfolio management to anyone else.

The investment adviser earns a management fee, typically a set annual percentage of the portfolio asset value, which is paid from the fund's net assets. In addition, if the investment adviser consistently outperforms a specified market performance benchmark, he or she usually earns an incentive bonus.

An investment company cannot contract with an investment adviser who has been convicted of a securities-related felony unless the SEC has granted an exemption. In addition, an investment company cannot lend money to its investment adviser.

 **Test Topic Alert!**   Listed below are some testable points about a mutual fund's investment adviser:

1. The adviser trades the portfolio to meet the investment objectives, but cannot change them.
2. The adviser is given a two-year contract by the Board of Directors, but the contract is subject to annual approval by the Board or a majority vote of the outstanding shares.

3. The adviser's fee is the largest single management expense associated with fund ownership, and is a percentage of the assets that are managed.
4. The adviser must inform shareholders of the tax status of fund distributions.
5. The responsibilities of the investment adviser cannot be transferred to a third party.
6. The adviser must be registered with the SEC according to the Investment Advisers Act of 1940.

Custodian

To protect investors' assets, the act of 1940 requires each investment company to place its securities in the custody of a bank or a stock exchange member broker-dealer. The bank or broker-dealer performs an important safekeeping role as custodian of the company's securities and cash, and it receives a fee for its services. Often, the custodian handles most of the investment company's clerical functions. The custodian may, with the consent of the investment company, deposit the securities it is entrusted to hold in one of the systems for the central handling of securities established by the NASD or the NYSE. These systems make it easier to transfer or pledge securities. Once securities are placed in the system, most such transfers can be accomplished with a simple bookkeeping entry rather than physical delivery of the securities.

Once an investment company designates a custodian and transfers its assets into the custodian's safekeeping, the custodian must:

- keep the investment company's assets physically segregated at all times;
- allow withdrawal of assets only under SEC rules; and
- restrict access to the account to certain officers and employees of the investment company

 **Test Topic Alert!**

For the exam you should know the following information about the custodian:

1. The custodian is generally a commercial bank.
2. The custodian is the safekeeper of the assets of the fund.
3. The custodian periodically audits the fund's assets to assure that they are properly accounted for.
4. The custodian is paid a fee from the assets of the fund.

Transfer Agent (Customer Services Agent)

The transfer agent's functions include issuing, redeeming and canceling fund shares, handling name changes for the fund, sending customer confirmations and fund distributions and recording outstanding shares so distributions are properly made.

The transfer agent can be the fund custodian or a separate service company. The fund pays the transfer agent a fee for its services.

 **Test Topic Alert!**   Two important points about the transfer agent are:

> 1. The transfer agent issues and redeems shares and handles other customer service work.
> 2. The transfer agent is paid a fee from the assets of the fund.

Underwriter

A mutual fund's underwriter, often called the sponsor or distributor, is appointed by the Board of Directors and receives a fee for selling and marketing the fund shares to the public. The open-end investment company sells its shares to the underwriter at the current NAV, but only as the underwriter needs the shares to fill customer orders. The underwriter is prohibited from maintaining an inventory of open-end company shares. The underwriter is compensated by adding a sales charge to the share's NAV when it makes sales to the public.

In general, a mutual fund may not act as its own distributor or underwriter. An exception exists for no-load and 12b-1 funds.

 **Test Topic Alert!**   Below are critical test points about a fund's underwriter:

> 1. The underwriter is also called the sponsor or distributor.
> 2. Funds can generally not act as their own underwriter. However, a fund *is* allowed to act as its own underwriter under *Section 12b*-1 of the Act of 1940. Many funds today follow this section, and *12b-1 distribution fees* are very common.
> 3. Fund underwriters must be NASD member firms.
> 4. Underwriters cannot inventory mutual fund shares.
> 5. Underwriters are compensated from the sales charge, *not* the assets of the fund.

✓ *Take Note:* It's important to note that all parties that work together in the operation of a mutual fund are paid from the net assets of the fund *except* the underwriter. The underwriter's compensation comes from sales charges.

Information Distributed to Investors

Investors must be provided with specific information when purchasing and tracking mutual funds.

Prospectus The prospectus must be distributed to an investor before or during any solicitation for sale. The prospectus contains information on the fund's objective, investment policies, sales charges and management expenses, and services offered. It also discloses 1-, 5- and 10-year performance histories.

The statement of additional information typically contains the fund's consolidated financial statements, including:

- the balance sheet;
- statement of operations;
- income statement; and
- portfolio list at the time the statement was compiled.

Financial Reports The act of 1940 requires that shareholders receive financial reports at least semiannually (twice per year). One of these must be an audited annual report. The reports must contain:

- the investment company's balance sheet;
- a valuation of all securities in the investment company's portfolio as of the date of the balance sheet (a portfolio list);
- the investment company's income statement;
- a complete statement of all compensation paid to the Board of Directors and to the advisory board; and
- a statement of the total dollar amount of securities purchased and sold during the period.

In addition, the company must send a copy of its balance sheet to any shareholder who requests one in writing between semiannual reports.

Additional Disclosures The SEC also requires the fund to include in its prospectus or annual reports the following:

- a discussion of those factors and strategies that materially affected its performance during its most recently completed fiscal year;
- a line graph comparing its performance to that of an appropriate broad-based securities market index; and
- the name(s) and title(s) of the person(s) primarily responsible for the fund portfolio's day-to-day management.

✓ *Take Note:* On the test, don't confuse financial reports of the fund with shareholder account statements. The fund must distribute financial reports to shareholders semiannually. The annual report must be audited; the semiannual reports can be unaudited.

Account statements are typically sent monthly to shareholders with active accounts, or quarterly to inactive accounts.

Quick Quiz 2.4

1. The custodian of a mutual fund usually does which of the following?

   A. Approves changes in investment policy
   B. Holds the cash and securities of the fund and performs clerical functions
   C. Manages the fund
   D. Does cleaning and related duties on the fund's properties

2. Investment company financial statements are sent to shareholders

   A. monthly
   B. quarterly
   C. semiannually
   D. annually

3. The role of a mutual fund's underwriter is to

   A. hold the fund's assets and perform clerical responsibilities
   B. determine when dividends should be distributed
   C. market shares
   D. provide investment advisory services

4. When a bank is serving as the custodian of a mutual fund, it always

   A. manages the portfolio
   B. signs all margin agreements
   C. holds the cash and securities and performs other clerical functions
   D. serves as the distributor of the fund and manages interactions with other underwriters

5. Typically, the largest single expense of a mutual fund is the

   A. custodian fee
   B. registration fee
   C. management fee
   D. brokerage fee

See page 334 for answers and rationale.

Characteristics of Mutual Funds

A mutual fund is a pool of investors' money invested in various securities as determined by the fund's objective. Mutual funds have several unique characteristics.

The Mutual Fund Concept

A mutual fund must redeem shares at the net asset value. Unlike other securities, mutual funds offer guaranteed marketability: there is always a willing buyer for the shares.

Each investor in the mutual fund's portfolio owns an undivided interest in the portfolio. All investors in an open-end fund are mutual participants. No one investor has a preferred status over any other investor because mutual funds issue only one class of common stock. Each investor shares mutually with other investors in gains and distributions derived from the investment company portfolio.

Each investor's share in the fund's performance is based on the number of shares owned. Mutual fund shares may be purchased in either full or fractional units, unlike corporate stock, which may be purchased in full units only. Because mutual fund shares can be fractional, the investor can think in terms of dollars rather than number of shares owned.

An investment company portfolio is elastic. Money is constantly being invested or paid out when shares are redeemed. The mutual fund portfolio's value and holdings fluctuate as money is invested or redeemed and as the value of the securities held by the portfolio rises and falls. The investor's account value fluctuates proportionately with the mutual fund portfolio's value.

Other mutual fund characteristics include the following:

- A professional investment adviser manages the portfolio for investors.
- Mutual funds provide diversification by investing in many different companies.
- A custodian holds a mutual fund's shares to ensure safekeeping.
- Most funds allow a minimum investment, often $500 or less, to open an account, and they allow additional investment for as little as $25.
- An investment company may allow investments at reduced sales charges by offering breakpoints, for instance, through larger deposits, a letter of intent or rights of accumulation.
- An investor retains voting rights similar to those extended to common stockholders, such as the right to vote for changes in the Board of Directors, approval of the investment adviser, changes in the fund's investment objective, changes in sales charges and liquidation of the fund.
- Many funds offer automatic reinvestment of capital gains and dividend distributions without a sales charge.
- An investor can liquidate a portion of his or her holdings without disturbing the portfolio's balance or diversification.
- Tax liabilities for an investor are simplified because each year the fund distributes a 1099 form explaining taxability of distributions.

- A fund may offer various withdrawal plans that allow different payment methods at redemption.
- Funds may offer reinstatements provisions that allow investors that withdraw funds to reinvest up to the amount withdrawn within 30 days with no new sales charge. This provision must be in the prospectus and is available one time only.

TABLE 2.2   Comparison of Common Stock and Mutual Fund Shares

Common Stock	Mutual Fund Shares
Dividends from corporate profits	Dividends from net investment income
Price of stock determined by supply and demand	Price of share determined by forward pricing - the next price calculated as determined by the fund's pricing policy
Traded on an exchange or the OTC market	Purchased from and redeemed by the investment company; no secondary trading
Sold in full shares only	Can purchase full or fractional shares
First security issued by a public corporation	Only security issued by a mutual fund
Carries voting rights	Carries voting rights
May carry preemptive rights	Does not carry preemptive rights
Ex-dividend: 2 business days prior to record date	Ex-dividend: typically the day after record date as set by the board of directors

✎ **Quick Quiz 2.5** True or False?

____ 1. Mutual fund shareholders own a divided interest in the fund's portfolio.

____ 2. A mutual fund shareholder's account value fluctuates proportionately with the mutual fund's portfolio value.

___ 3. The mutual fund's investment adviser is offered a two-year contract that is subject to annual approval.

___ 4. The transfer agent holds the mutual fund's securities to ensure safekeeping.

___ 5. Mutual funds issue only one class of common stock.

___ 6. The reinstatement provision allows reinvestment of withdrawn funds within 60 days at no load.

___ 7. To open an account, most funds require a minimum investment of at least $2,500.

___ 8. Mutual fund shareholders are allowed to vote on the frequency of dividend distributions.

See page 334 for answers and rationale.

Investment Objectives

Once a mutual fund defines its objective, the portfolio is invested to match it. The objective must be clearly stated in the mutual fund's prospectus and can be changed only by a majority vote of the fund's outstanding shares.

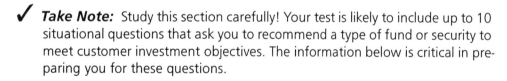 ***Take Note:*** Study this section carefully! Your test is likely to include up to 10 situational questions that ask you to recommend a type of fund or security to meet customer investment objectives. The information below is critical in preparing you for these questions.

Stock Funds

Common stock is normally found in the portfolio of any mutual fund that has growth as a primary or secondary objective. Bonds, preferred stock and blue chip stocks are typically used to provide income to mutual funds with income objectives.

Growth Funds. Growth funds invest in stocks of companies whose businesses are growing rapidly. Growth companies tend to reinvest all or most of their profits for research and development rather than pay dividends. Therefore, growth funds are focused on generating capital gains rather than income.

Blue chip or *conservative* growth funds invest in established and more recognized companies to achieve growth with less risk. Generally these companies have fairly large capitalization. These funds are sometimes called *large-cap* funds (capitalization of more than $10 billion).

Aggressive growth funds are sometimes called *performance funds* or *go-go funds*. These funds are willing to take greater risk to maximize capital appreciation. Some of these funds invest in newer companies with relatively small capitalization, (less than $5 billion capitalization) and are referred to as *small-cap* funds. Mid-cap funds are somewhat less aggressive and have capitalization of between $5 and $10 billion.

Income Funds. An income fund stresses current income over growth. The fund's objective may be accomplished by investing in the stocks of companies with long histories of dividend payments, such as utility company stocks, blue chip stocks and preferred stocks.

Option income funds invest in securities on which options can be written and earn premium income from writing options. They may also earn capital gains from trading options at a profit. These funds seek to increase total return by adding income generated by the options to appreciation on the securities held in the portfolio.

Growth and Income Funds. A growth and income fund, also called a combination fund, may attempt to combine the objectives of growth and current yield by diversifying its stock portfolio among companies showing long-term growth potential and companies paying high dividends.

Specialized (Sector) Funds. Many funds attempt to specialize in particular economic sectors or industries. Usually, the funds have a minimum of 25 percent of their assets invested in their specialties. Examples include gold funds (gold mining stock), technology funds and utility funds, among others.

Sector funds offer high appreciation potential, but may also pose higher risks to the investor.

Special Situation Funds. Special situation funds buy securities of companies that may benefit from a change within the companies or in the economy. Takeover candidates and turnaround situations are common investments.

Index Funds. Index funds invest in securities to mirror a market index, such as the S&P 500. An index fund buys and sells securities in a manner that mirrors the composition of the selected index. The fund's performance tracks the underlying index's performance.

Turnover of securities in an index fund's portfolio is minimal. As a result, an index fund generally has lower management costs than other types of funds.

Foreign Stock Funds. Foreign stock funds invest mostly in the securities of companies that have their principal business activities outside the United

States. Long-term capital appreciation is their primary objective, although some funds also seek current income.

International funds invest in the securities of foreign countries, while *global* funds invest in the securities of both the United States and foreign countries.

Balanced Funds

Balanced funds invest in stocks for appreciation and bonds for income. In a balanced fund, different types of securities are purchased according to a formula the manager may adjust to reflect market conditions. For example, a balanced fund's portfolio might contain 60 percent stocks and 40 percent bonds.

Asset Allocation Funds

Asset allocation funds split investments between stocks for growth, bonds for income and money-market instruments or cash for stability. Fund advisers switch the percentage of holdings in each asset category according to the performance, or expected performance, of that group.

A fund may have 60 percent of its investments in stock, 20 percent in bonds and the remaining 20 percent in cash. If the stock market is expected to do well, the adviser may switch from cash and bonds into stock. The result may be a portfolio of 80 percent in stock, 10 percent in bonds and 10 percent in cash. Conversely, if the stock market is expected to decline, the fund may invest heavily in cash and sell stocks.

Bond Funds

Bond funds have income as their main investment objective. Some funds invest solely in investment-grade corporate bonds. Others, seeking enhanced safety, invest in government issues only. Still others pursue capital appreciation by investing in lower rated for higher yields.

Corporate Bond Funds. Investors seeking high current income choose corporate bond funds. Because of their increased credit risk, these funds provide higher yields to investors than government and municipal bond funds.

Tax-Free (Tax-Exempt) Bond Funds. Tax-exempt funds invest in municipal bonds or notes that produce income exempt from federal income tax. Tax-free funds can invest in municipal bonds and tax-exempt money-market instruments.

U.S. Government and Agency Security Funds. U.S. government funds purchase securities issued by the U.S. Treasury or an agency of the U.S. government, such as Ginnie Mae. Investors in these funds seek current income and maximum safety.

Because Ginnie Mae funds are pools of home mortgages, they are susceptible to principal risk when interest rates fall and homeowners refinance their mortgages. Ginnie Mae funds yield slightly more than government securities funds.

Dual-Purpose Funds

Dual-purpose funds are **closed-end funds** that meet two objectives: Investors seeking income purchase income shares and receive all the interest and dividends the fund's portfolio earns. Investors interested in capital gains purchase the gains shares and receive all gains on portfolio holdings. The two types of shares in a dual fund are listed separately in the financial pages.

Money-Market Funds

Money-market funds are usually no-load, open-end mutual funds that serve as temporary holding tanks for investors who are most concerned with liquidity. "No-load" means investors pay no sales or liquidation fees. A fund manager invests the fund's capital in money-market instruments that pay interest and have short maturities. Interest rates on money-market funds are not fixed or guaranteed and change often. The interest these funds earn is computed daily and credited to customers' accounts monthly. Many funds offer check-writing privileges; however, checks normally must be written for amounts of $500 or more. The largest expense to investors is the management fee, which is usually around .5 percent.

The net asset value of money-market funds is set at $1 per share. Although this price is not guaranteed, a fund is managed in order not to "break the buck" regardless of market changes. Thus, the price of money-market shares does not fluctuate in response to changing market conditions.

Restrictions on Money-Market Funds. SEC rules limit the investments available to money-market funds and require certain disclosures to investors. Restrictions include the following:

- The front cover of every prospectus must prominently disclose that an investment in a money-market fund is neither insured nor guaranteed by the U.S. government and that an investor has no assurance the fund will be able to maintain a stable NAV. This statement must also appear in all literature used to market the fund.
- No more than 5 percent of a fund's assets may be invested in any one issuer's securities.
- Investments are limited to securities with remaining maturities of not more than 12 months, with the average portfolio maturity not exceeding 90 days.
- Investments are limited to eligible securities determined to have minimal risk. Eligible securities are defined as those rated by nationally recognized rating organizations (Standard & Poor's, Moody's, etc.) in one of the top two categories. (No more than 5 percent of the portfolio

may be in the second tier of ratings.) Comparable unrated securities must adhere to the definition of safety as provided by the rating organizations. (Tax-exempt money-market funds are exempt from certain parts of the requirement to invest only in rated securities.)

Hedge Funds

Hedge funds use aggressive strategies to generate income but hedge against market decline. These funds engage in short selling, in purchases and sales of options and margin account transactions. Hedge funds are *not* mutual funds, and are not investment companies as defined by the Investment Company Act of 1940. They are structured as limited partnerships.

✓ *Take Note:* When you see suitability questions on the test, the first step is to determine the customer's primary objective. In general, the following basic rules apply:

- Investors who are interested in *growth* should invest in stock funds.
- Investors who are interested in *income* should invest in bond funds.
- Investors who are concerned about *safety of principal* should invest in government bond funds.
- Investors who are concerned with *immediate liquidity* should invest in money market funds.

Of course, the secondary objective of the investor must also be taken into account. For example:

- Investors who are interested in *aggressive growth* should invest in technology stock funds or stock funds invested in new companies with cutting edge ideas. Aggressive funds or *small cap* funds are usually most suitable for younger investors who have high risk tolerance.
- Investors who are seeking *growth* but are more *conservative* should consider balanced growth funds, which are likely to be *large cap* funds. These funds are not as speculative as smaller cap and aggressive funds.
- Investors who are interested in *income* but want *safety of principal* should invest in a government bond fund.
- Investors seeking the *highest possible income with little concern for risk* should invest in a corporate bond fund.
- *High tax bracket* investors seeking *income* should invest in a municipal bond fund.
- Investors that are interested in *income-producing stock* should select a "blue chip" stock fund (a blue chip stock is a large company stock that has a consistently strong performance history and regularly pays dividends), a preferred stock fund or a utility stock fund (utility stocks historically pay high, consistent dividends).
- Investors seeking *safety of principal with high liquidity* should consider a money market fund

- Investors who wish to invest in a *portfolio that mirrors the performance of the stock market* should consider an index fund.
- *Asset allocation* funds provide a combination of stocks and bonds and allow the portfolio manager the flexibility to change the portfolio mix to react to market conditions.
- *Hedge funds* are for the speculative investor. They are not true mutual funds, but do provide investors with an undivided interest in a portfolio. They are considered suitable for investors with high risk tolerance.

Review these points carefully, as this information is heavily tested!

Quick Quiz 2.6

Match the investment objective with the most suitable fund recommendation

A. Balanced fund
B. Aggressive growth fund
C. Specialized fund
D. Blue chip stock fund

____ 1. Desires capital growth with minimal risk

____ 2. Wishes to maximize capital gains quickly with high risk tolerance

____ 3. Wishes to diversify securities and is conservative

____ 4. Wishes to invest in medical technology and is not risk averse

Match the objective with the type of fund

A. Conservative growth fund
B. Money market fund
C. Small cap fund
D. Balanced fund

____ 5. Capital gains/income/lower risk

____ 6. Capital gains/low risk

____ 7. Liquidity/low risk

____ 8. Capital gains/higher risk

Match the objective with the type of fund.

    A. Government bond fund
    B. Large cap fund
    C. Asset allocation fund
    D. Hedge fund

___ 9. Capital gains/income/lower risk

___ 10. Growth/high risk

___ 11. Growth/low risk

___ 12. Income/low risk

Match the description with the type of fund

    A. Ginnie Mae fund
    B. Special situation fund
    C. Asset allocation fund
    D. Index fund

___ 13. Purchase a large variety of assets to achieve capital gains, income and diversification

___ 14. Mimic stock market indices to achieve performance comparable to the market overall

___ 15. Achieve safety of principal with yields slightly higher than government bond fund

___ 16. Seek investments in companies with unusual opportunities

See page 335 for answers.

Comparing Mutual Funds

When comparing mutual funds, an investor should select funds that match his or her personal objectives. The investor will find many such investment companies.

When comparing funds with similar objectives, the investor should review information regarding the funds':

- performance;

- costs;
- taxation;
- portfolio turnover; and
- services offered.

Performance   Securities law requires that each fund disclose the average annual total returns for 1, 5 and 10 years or since inception. Performance must reflect full sales loads with no discounts. The manager's track record in keeping with the fund's objectives as stated in the prospectus is important as well.

 **Test Topic Alert!**

The test will require you to know that fund quotations of average annual return must be for 1-, 5- and 10-year periods or as long as the fund has operated.

Costs   Sales loads, management fees and operating expenses reduce an investor's returns because they diminish the amount of money invested in a fund.

Sales Loads

Historically, mutual funds have charged front-end loads of up to 8.5 percent of the money invested. This percentage compensates a sales force. Many low-load funds charge between 2 percent and 5 percent. Other funds may charge a back-end load when funds are withdrawn. Some funds charge ongoing fees under Section 12b-1 of the Investment Company Act of 1940. These funds deduct annual fees to pay for marketing and distribution costs. Sales loads are covered in detail later in this lesson.

Expense Ratio

A fund's expense ratio relates the management fees and operating expenses to the fund's net assets. All mutual funds, load and no-load, have expense ratios. The expense ratio is calculated by dividing a fund's expenses by its average net assets. An expense ratio of 1 percent means that the fund charges $1 per year for every $100 invested. Typically, aggressive funds and international funds have higher expense ratios.

Stock funds generally have expense ratios between 1 percent and 1.5 percent of a fund's average net assets. For bond funds, the ratio is typically between .5 percent and 1 percent.

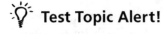 **Test Topic Alert!**

You may see a question on the exam that asks about the factors that are included in calculating a mutual fund's expense ratio. The Board of Directors stipend, the investment adviser's fee, the custodian fee and the transfer agent fee are all included. The sales load is not. The formula for the computation is:

$$\frac{\text{Fund expenses}}{\text{Average net assets}}$$

The fund's expense ratio is found in the prospectus and measures the efficiency of its management. The largest part of the expense ratio is the investment advisory fee.

Taxation Mutual fund investors pay taxes on capital gains the fund receives. These taxes are based on how long the fund owned the security it sold. Because tax rates for long-term gains are typically lower than for short-term gains, it is better for an investor in a high tax bracket to receive a long-term gain than a short-term gain.

Portfolio Turnover The costs of buying and selling securities, including commissions or markups and markdowns, are reflected in the portfolio turnover ratio. It is not uncommon for an aggressive growth fund to reflect an annual turnover rate of 100 percent or more. A 100 percent turnover rate means the fund replaces its portfolio annually. If the fund achieves superior returns, the strategy is working; if not, the strategy is subjecting investors to undue costs.

The portfolio turnover rate reflects a fund's holding period. If a fund has a turnover rate of 100 percent, it holds its securities, on average, for less than one year. Therefore, all gains are likely to be short term and subject to the maximum tax rate. On the other hand, a portfolio with a turnover rate of 25 percent has an average holding period of four years, and gains are likely taxed at the long-term rate.

Services Offered The services mutual funds offer include retirement account custodianship, investment plans, check-writing privileges, telephone transfers, conversion privileges, combination investment privileges, withdrawal plans and others. However, an investor should always weigh the cost of services provided against the value of the services to the investor.

Mutual Fund Marketing and Pricing

Mutual fund shares may be marketed in several ways; however, mutual fund shares are priced according to a set formula.

Marketing Mutual Fund Shares

A fund can use any number of methods to market its shares to the public. A discussion of some of the marketing methods various firms use follows.

Fund to Underwriter to Dealer to Investor

An investor gives an order for fund shares to a dealer. The dealer then places the order with the underwriter. To fill the order, the fund sells shares to the underwriter at the current NAV. The underwriter sells the shares to the dealer at the NAV plus the underwriter's concession (the public offering price less the dealer's reallowance or discount). The dealer sells the shares to the investor at the full public offering price (POP).

 **Test Topic Alert!**   Remember for test questions that fund underwriters (sponsors) must be NASD member firms. Only member firms can receive selling concessions.

Fund to Underwriter to Investor

The underwriter acts as dealer and uses its own sales force to sell shares to the public. An investor gives an order for fund shares to the underwriter. To fill the order, the fund sells shares to the underwriter at the current NAV. The underwriter then adds the sales charge and sells the shares to the investor at the POP. The sales charge is split among the various salespeople.

Fund to Investor

Some funds sell directly to the public without using an underwriter or a sales force and without assessing a sales charge. If an open-end investment company distributes shares to the public directly—that is, without the services of a distributor—and the fund offers its shares with no sales charge, the fund is called a no-load fund. The fund pays all sales expenses.

Fund to Underwriter to Plan Company to Investor

Organizations that sell contractual plans for the periodic purchase of mutual fund shares are called plan companies. Such a company purchases fund shares and holds them in trust for an individual purchasing the shares under a periodic payment plan.

Sales at the POP   Any sale of fund shares to a customer must be made at the public offering price. The NASD defines a customer as anyone who is not an NASD member. The route the sale takes is not important—the nonmember customer must be charged the POP. Only an NASD member acting as a dealer or an underwriter may purchase the fund shares at a discount from the issuer.

✓ **Take Note:** Remember—no discounts to the public or nonmember firms. Only member firms can receive a discount from the POP, and only if they have a written sales agreement.

Determining the Value of Mutual Fund Shares

Mutual funds must calculate the NAV of fund shares at least once per business day because purchase and redemption prices are based on the NAV. Most funds wait until after the NYSE closes (4:00 P.M. EST) before making their NAV calculations. The price of purchase or redemption orders for mutual fund shares is determined at the next NAV calculation after an order is entered. This is known as **forward pricing**.

✓ *Take Note:* If you were to call your broker-dealer right now to purchase or redeem mutual fund shares, you would not know the share price. The price you pay to buy shares, or receive if you redeem shares, is the price next calculated. The share price is typically calculated after the New York Stock Exchange closes for the day. Some funds, however, may choose to calculate more frequently. Read the prospectus to find out the specifics.

Net Asset Value per Share

When a customer buys mutual fund shares, he or she is charged the public offering price. The POP equals the NAV per share plus the sales charge. When a customer sells, the liquidation price always equals the current NAV.

To determine the fund's total NAV, the custodian totals the value of all assets and subtracts all liabilities.

Assets (Cash + Current value of securities) – Liabilities = Fund's NAV

The NAV per share is determined by dividing the total net assets by the number of shares outstanding.

$$\frac{\text{Fund's NAV}}{\text{Number of shares outstanding}} = \text{NAV per share}$$

In working with NAV calculations, a fund's total assets include everything of value the fund owns, not just the investment portfolio.

✓ *Take Note:* The NAV is like the bid price and the POP is like the ask price. Investors buy at the ask price and redeem at the NAV.

Changes in NAV

The NAV can change daily because of changes in the market value of a fund's portfolio. The events discussed below may change a fund's NAV per share:

- NAV per share increases when portfolio securities increase in value or when the portfolio receives investment income.
- NAV per share decreases when portfolio securities decrease in value or when portfolio income and gains are paid to shareholders.
- NAV per share does not change when shares are sold or redeemed or when portfolio securities are bought or sold. In these circumstances, the fund exchanges securities for cash so that the total net assets remain unchanged.

 **Test Topic Alert!**

Expect to see questions similar to the following:

1. Under which of the following circumstances does NAV per share decrease?

   I. Portfolio securities decrease in value.
   II. Dividends are distributed from the portfolio to shareholders.
   III. New shares are issued.
   IV. Shares are redeemed.

The correct choices are I and II. NAV per share decreases when the portfolio securities decline in value or when an income distribution is made from the portfolio to the shareholders. NAV does not change when shares are issued or redeemed. When shares are purchased, new money paid to the fund is off-set by a greater number of shares outstanding. Likewise, when shares a redeemed, the decrease in portfolio assets is offset by a decrease in shares outstanding.

Sales Charges

The NASD prohibits its members from assessing sales charges in excess of 8.5 percent of the POP on customers' mutual fund purchases. However, members selling mutual fund contractual plans may not assess sales charges in *excess of 9 percent* of the POP over the life of a fund. Mutual funds are free to charge lower rates *if they specify these rates in the prospectus.*

✓ **Take Note:** Be sure to note that a mutual fund's maximum sales charge is based on the POP *not* the NAV! The maximum load for mutual fund shares is 8.5 percent of the POP, unless sold through a contractual plan. The maximum sales charge for contractual plans is 9 percent of the POP over the life of the fund.

Most funds today charge somewhat lower sales loads. 5 percent to 6 percent is a typical maximum load for equity funds; 4 percent to 5 percent is a typical maximum load for bond funds.

Closed-End Funds

Closed-end funds do not have sales charges. An investor pays a brokerage commission in an agency transaction or pays a markup or markdown in a principal transaction. Closed-end funds may trade at a premium or discount to their net asset value.

Open-End Funds

All sales commissions and expenses are paid from the sales charges collected. Sales expenses include commissions for the managing underwriter, dealers, brokers and registered representatives, as well as all advertising and sales literature expenses.

Mutual fund distributors use three different methods to collect the fees for the sale of shares:

1. front-end loads (difference between POP and NAV)
2. back-end loads (contingent deferred sales loads)
3. 12b-1 sales charges (asset-based fees)

Front-End Loads

Front-end sales loads are the charges included in a fund's public offering price. The charges are added to the NAV at the time an investor buys shares. Front-end loads are the most common way of paying for the distribution services a fund's underwriter and broker-dealers provide.

 Take Note: Here's how a front-end load operates. Assume an investor deposits $10,000 with a mutual fund that has a 5% front-end load. The 5% load amounts to $500, which is deducted from the invested amount. In this example, $9,500 is invested in the fund's portfolio on the investor's behalf.

Back-End Loads

A back-end sales load, also called a contingent deferred load, is charged at the time an investor redeems mutual fund shares. The sales load, a declining percentage charge that is reduced annually (for instance, 6% the first year, 5% the second, 4% the third, etc.), is applied to the proceeds of any shares sold in that year. The back-end load is usually structured so that it drops to zero after an extended holding period. The sales load schedule is specified in a fund's prospectus.

 Take Note: With a back-end load, when an investor deposits $10,000 in a mutual fund, the full $10,000 is invested in the portfolio on the investor's behalf. The sales load is deducted only if the investor withdraws the money too soon. This type of sales charge is intended to discourage frequent trading in mutual fund accounts. Many back-end load funds also have 12b-1 fees.

12b-1 Asset-Based Fees

Mutual funds cannot act as distributors for their own fund shares except under Section 12b-1 of the Investment Company Act of 1940. 12b-1 permits a mutual fund to collect a fee for promoting, selling or related activity in connection with the distribution of its shares. Although the fee is determined *annually* as a flat dollar amount or as a percentage of the fund's average total NAV during the year, the Board of Directors must *review* the expenditures made under the plan at least quarterly. This "annual" fee is also deducted quarterly. The fee is disclosed in the fund's prospectus.

Requirements for 12b-1 fees include the following:

- The percentage of net assets charged must be reasonable. 12b-1 fees may range from ½ percent to ¾ percent of a fund's assets per year.
- The fee must reflect the anticipated level of distribution services.

The payments represent fees that would have been paid to an underwriter if sales charges had been negotiated for sales, advertising and marketing costs.

Approval. The 12b-1 plan must be approved initially and reapproved at least annually by a majority of the outstanding shares, the Board of Directors and those directors who are noninterested persons.

Termination. The 12b-1 plan may be terminated at any time by a majority vote of the noninterested directors and by a majority vote of outstanding shares.

Misuse of No-Load Terminology. A fund that has a deferred sales charge or an asset-based 12b-1 fee of more than .25 percent of average net assets may not be described as a no-load fund. To do so violates the NASD's Rules of Fair Practice; the violation is not alleviated by disclosures in the fund's prospectus.

 **Test Topic Alert!**

Expect at least three questions about 12b-1 fees on your Series 6 exam. You need to know the following points:

1. 12b-1 fees are annual charges that are reviewed quarterly.
2. Approval requires three votes: a majority of the outstanding shares, the full board and the uninterested members of the board.
3. Termination requires two votes: a majority of the outstanding shares and the uninterested members of the board.
4. Charges covered by 12b-1 fees included advertising, sales literature and prospectuses delivered to potential customers, *not* fund management expenses.
5. 12b-1 funds are not no-load funds.

Computing the Sales Charge Percentage

When the NAV and the POP are known, the sales charge percentage can be determined as shown below:

$$POP - NAV = \text{Sales charge (\$ amount)}$$

$$\frac{\text{Sales charge (\$ amount)}}{POP} = \text{Sales charge \%}$$

If the dollar amounts for the NAV and sales charges are specified, the formula for determining the POP of mutual fund shares is:

$$NAV + \text{Sales charge (\$)} = POP (\$)$$

A mutual fund prospectus must contain a formula that explains how the fund computes the NAV and how the sales charge is added. Note that the sales charge is always based on the POP, not on the NAV. To determine the POP, divide the NAV by 100 percent minus the sales charge percent. The formula is as follows:

$$\frac{NAV}{(100\% - \text{Sales Charge \%})} = POP$$

Because of the possible high front-end sales charge, mutual funds should be recommended for long-term investing.

✓ **Take Note:** Let's review the two calculations just covered.

Assuming a NAV of $10 and a POP of $10.50, what is the sales charge percentage?

The sales charge percentage is calculated by finding the sales charge amount ($10.50 – $10.00) and dividing by the POP. Remember, sales charge is a percentage of the *POP* not the NAV.

$$\$.50 \div \$10.50 = 4.7\% \text{ (when rounded)}$$

Assume a NAV of $10 and a sales charge of 5 percent. What is the POP?

The POP is found by dividing the NAV by 100 percent minus the sales charge percent.

In this example, $10 ÷ .95 = $10.53.

Remember that a little logic goes a long way on this exam. Your answer has to be more than the NAV, otherwise you goofed!

 **Test Topic Alert!**

Although we will review a number of mathematical computations in this lesson, please realize that the test is more concerned with your understanding of formulas than of actual calculations. Your entire exam will include no more than two to five mathematical computations. Continue to practice the calculations to assure your understanding.

Reductions in Sales Charges

The maximum permitted sales charge is reduced from 8½% to 6½% if an investment company does not offer certain features. To qualify for the maximum 8½% sales charge, the investment company must offer all of the following:

- breakpoints—a scale of declining sales charges based on the amount invested;
- automatic reinvestment of distributions at NAV; and
- rights of accumulation.

Breakpoints   The schedule of quantity purchase discounts that a mutual fund offers is called the fund's **breakpoints**. Breakpoints are available to any person. For a breakpoint qualification, "person" includes married couples, parents and their minor children, corporations and certain other entities. Investment clubs or associations formed for the purpose of investing do *not* qualify for breakpoints. The following table illustrates a breakpoint schedule:

Purchase	Sales Charge
$1 to $9,999	8½%
$10,000 to $24,999	7½%
$25,000 to $49,999	7%
$50,000 plus	6¼%

An investor can qualify for breakpoints in several ways. A large lump-sum investment is one method. Mutual funds offer additional incentives for an investor to continue to invest and qualify for breakpoints through a **letter of intent** (LOI) or **rights of accumulation**.

Test Topic Alert!   Be ready for the question that asks who is eligible for breakpoints. Married couples, parents with minor children and corporations are eligible for breakpoints. Parents with adult children and investment clubs are *not* eligible for breakpoints.

Breakpoint Sales. The NASD prohibits registered reps from making or seeking higher commissions by selling investment company shares in a dollar amount just below the point at which the sales charge is reduced. This violation is known as a *breakpoint sale*.

The NASD considers this practice contrary to just and equitable principles of trade. It is the responsibility of all parties concerned, particularly the principal, to prevent such practices.

✓ *Take Note:* Breakpoints offer a significant advantage to mutual fund purchasers; breakpoint sales, however, are a prohibited practice!

Letter of Intent

A person who plans to invest more money with the same mutual fund company may immediately decrease his overall sales charges by signing a **letter of intent**. In the LOI, the investor informs the investment company that he intends to invest the additional funds necessary to reach the breakpoint within 13 months.

The LOI is a one-sided contract binding on the fund only. However, the customer must complete the investment to qualify for the reduced sales charge. The fund holds the extra shares purchased from the reduced sales charge in escrow. If the customer deposits the money to complete the LOI, he receives the escrowed shares. Appreciation and reinvested dividends do not count toward the LOI.

Referring back to the sample breakpoint schedule, you see that a customer investing $9,000 is just short of the $10,000 breakpoint. In this situation, the customer might sign a letter of intent promising an amount that will qualify for the breakpoint within 13 months from the date of the letter. Investing an additional $1,000 within 13 months qualifies the customer for the reduced sales charge. Each investment is charged the appropriate sales charge at the time of purchase.

If the customer has not completed the investment within 13 months, he or she will be given the choice of sending a check for the difference in sales charges or cashing in escrowed shares to pay the difference.

Backdating the Letter. A fund often permits a customer to sign a letter of intent as late as the 90th day after an initial purchase. The LOI may be backdated by up to 90 days to include prior purchases, but may not cover more than 13 months in total. This means that if the customer signs the LOI 60 days after a purchase, he has 11 months to complete the letter.

✓ **Take Note:** Assume the following breakpoint schedule:

0–$9,999	5%
$10,000–$24,999	4%
$25,000–$49,000	3%
$50,000 +	2%

If an investor intends to deposit $50,000 in a mutual fund over a 13 month period and puts in $1,000 when the account is opened, the investor is charged a sales charge of 2 percent on the initial and every subsequent investment *if* a letter of intent has been signed. If the letter had not been signed, the sales charge on the initial amount of $1,000 would have been 5 percent based on this breakpoint schedule. The letter of intent allows for a discount on an installment plan purchase.

 **Test Topic Alert!**   Know the following information about letters of intent for possible test questions:

1. Letters of intent are good for a maximum of 13 months and may be backdated 90 days.
2. If the letter of intent is not completed, the sales charge amount that applies is based on the total amount that was actually invested.
3. Share appreciation and income paid by the fund do not count toward completion of the letter.

Rights of Accumulation

Rights of accumulation, like breakpoints, allow an investor to qualify for reduced sales charges. The major differences are that rights of accumulation:

- are available for subsequent investment and do not apply to initial transactions;
- allow the investor to use prior share appreciation to qualify for breakpoints; and
- do not impose time limits.

The customer may qualify for reduced charges when the total value of shares previously purchased and shares currently being purchased exceeds a certain dollar amount. For the purpose of qualifying customers for rights of accumulation, the mutual fund bases the quantity of securities owned on:

- the current value of the securities at either NAV or POP;
- total purchases of the securities at the actual offering price; or
- the higher of current NAV or the total of purchases made to date.

✔ **Take Note:** Assume the following breakpoint schedule:

0–$9,999	5%
$10,000–$24,999	4%
$25,000–$49,000	3%
$50,000 +	2%

An investor deposits $5,000 in a mutual fund but does not sign a letter of intent. The $5,000 grows to $10,000 over time, and the investor decides to invest another $15,000. If rights of accumulation exist, the new $15,000 is charged a sales charge of 3 percent, which is based on the new money plus the accumulated value in the account ($15,000 + $10,000 = $25,000). If rights of accumulation do not exist, the sales charge would have be 4 percent.

Combination Privilege

A mutual fund sponsor frequently offers more than one fund and refers to these multiple offerings as its **family of funds**. An investor seeking a reduced sales charge may be allowed to combine separate investments in two or more funds within the same family to reach a breakpoint.

Exchanges Within a Family of Funds

Many sponsors offer exchange or conversion privileges within their families of funds. Exchange privileges allow an investor to convert an investment in one fund for an equal investment in another fund in the same family, often without incurring an additional sales charge.

Mutual funds may be purchased at NAV under a no-load exchange privilege. Certain rules apply:

- Purchase may not exceed the proceeds generated by the redemption of the other fund.
- The redemption may not involve a refund of sales charges.
- The sales personnel and dealers must receive no compensation of any kind from the reinvestment.
- Any gain or loss from the redemption of shares must be reported for tax purposes.

Redemption of Fund Shares

A mutual fund must redeem shares within seven days of receiving a written request for redemption. If the customer holds the fund certificates, the mutual fund must redeem shares within seven days of the date the certificates and instructions to liquidate arrive at the custodian bank. The written request must be accompanied by a *signature guarantee*. The price at which shares are redeemed is the NAV; it must be calculated at least once per business day. The redemption requirement may be suspended when:

- the NYSE is closed other than for a customary weekend or holiday closing;
- trading on the NYSE has been restricted;
- an emergency exists that would make disposal of securities owned by the company not reasonably practical; or
- the SEC has ordered the suspension of redemptions for the protection of the company's securities holders.

Otherwise, the fund must redeem shares upon request.

Cancellation of Fund Shares

Because an open-end mutual fund is a continuous initial public offering, after a mutual fund share has been redeemed the share is destroyed. Unlike other corporate securities, mutual fund shares cannot be sold to other owners. An investor purchasing mutual fund shares receives new shares.

✔ **Take Note:** Here's a quick list of some sales charge test points for your review!

- The maximum sales charge allowed by the NASD is 8.5 percent of the POP.
- An investor buys and redeems shares at the price next calculated (forward pricing).
- Only NASD member firms can buy below the POP—*not* the public or nonmembers.
- The NAV does not change when new shares are issued or when shares are redeemed.
- 12b-1 fees are charged quarterly, but must be approved annually.
- Breakpoints are not allowed for investment clubs and a parent and child above the age of majority. They are allowed for corporations, husband and wife or a parent and minor child.
- A fund can only charge an 8 ½ percent sales load if it offers breakpoints, reinvestment at NAV and rights of accumulation.
- Mutual fund shares that have been redeemed are cancelled. They are never reissued.

 **Quick Quiz 2.7**

1. In order for a company to charge the maximum sales charge of 8½ percent, it must offer all of the following EXCEPT

   A. automatic reinvestment of dividends and capital gains at NAV
   B. breakpoints
   C. letter of intent
   D. rights of accumulation

2. A mutual fund is quoted at $16.56 NAV and $18.00 POP. The sales charge is

   A. 7½%
   B. 7¾%
   C. 8%
   D. 8½%

3. Redemption of a no-load fund may be made at the

   A. NAV minus the sales charge
   B. POP minus the sales charge
   C. NAV plus the sales charge
   D. NAV

4. Ms. Bruin purchased mutual fund shares with a net asset value of $7.82 and an 8 percent sales charge. She paid a sales charge of

   A. $.68
   B. $.74
   C. $.80
   D. $.87

5. Which of the following statements are true regarding a letter of intent and breakpoints?

   I. The letter of intent can be backdated a maximum of 30 days.
   II. The letter of intent is valid for 13 months.
   III. The investor is legally bound to meet the terms of the agreement.
   IV. The fund may hold shares in escrow.

   A. I and II
   B. II and III
   C. II and IV
   D. III and IV

6. Which of the following investors can take advantage of breakpoints?

   I. Individual
   II. Investment club
   III. Trust
   IV. Corporation

   A. I and II
   B. I, III and IV
   C. II, III and IV
   D. III and IV

See page 335 for answers and rationale.

Mutual Fund Distributions and Taxation

Distributions from mutual funds are derived from income received from portfolio securities or gains from the sale of portfolio securities. Whether taken in cash or reinvested, distributions are taxable.

Distributions from Mutual Funds

Mutual fund distributions are taxed according to the conduit theory, as described below.

The Conduit Theory Because an investment company is organized as a corporation or trust, you might assume its earnings are subject to tax. Consider, however, how an additional level of taxation shrinks a dividend distribution's value. Assume GEM Fund owns shares of Mountain Brewing Co. First, Mountain Brewing is taxed on its earnings before it pays a dividend. Then GEM Fund pays tax on the amount of the dividend it receives. Finally, the investor pays income tax on the distribution from the fund.

Triple taxation of investment income may be avoided if the mutual fund qualifies under Subchapter M of the Internal Revenue Code (IRC). If a mutual fund acts as a conduit, or pipeline, for the distribution of net investment income, the fund may qualify as a regulated investment company, subject to tax only on the amount of investment income the fund retains. The investment income distributed to shareholders escapes taxation at the mutual fund level.

Subchapter M requires a fund to distribute at least 90 percent of its net investment income to shareholders. The fund then pays taxes only on the undistributed 10 percent. If the fund distributes 89 percent, it pays taxes on 100 percent of net investment income.

 **Test Topic Alert!** A test question may ask you the tax consequences to a fund that distributes 98 percent of its net investment income. In this situation the fund does not pay taxes on the 98 percent that is distributed; it pays taxes only on the 2 percent of retained earnings.

Note that the Conduit theory may also be called the *Pipeline theory*.

Dividend Distributions A mutual fund may pay dividends to each shareholder in the same way corporations pay dividends to stockholders. Dividends are paid from the mutual fund's net investment income.

Net investment income includes gross investment income—dividend and interest income from securities held in the portfolio—minus operating expenses. Advertising and sales expenses are not included in a fund's operating expenses when calculating net investment income. Dividends from net investment income are taxed as ordinary income to shareholders.

✔ *Take Note:* An easy way to remember how net investment income is calculated is **D – I – E**.

Net investment income = Dividends + interest – expenses of the fund.

You may see a question on the test that asks for this calculation and gives you a list of items to exclude or include in the calculation. If you remember **D – I – E**, it will be easy for you to remember what items to include.

Net investment income is distributed to shareholders as dividends. Dividends paid to shareholders may be reinvested or taken in cash. The shareholder pays ordinary income taxes on the dividends in *either* case.

Capital Gains Distributions

The appreciation or depreciation of portfolio securities is unrealized capital gain or loss if the fund does not sell the securities. Therefore, shareholders experience no tax consequences. When the fund sells the securities, the gain or loss is **realized** and affects shareholder taxes.

Capital gains distributions are derived from realized gains. If the fund has held the securities for at least one year, the gain is a long-term capital gain, taxed at the long-term capital gains rate. The mutual fund may reinvest the gain or distribute it to shareholders. A long-term capital gains distribution may not be made more often than once per year.

Any gains distribution from a mutual fund is long term. A short-term gain is identified, distributed and taxed as an income distribution.

✓ *Take Note:* The terms *realized gains* and *unrealized gains* can be confusing. Think of an unrealized gain as a paper profit. If you had purchased a house for $150,000 and its value had appreciated to $200,000, you would experience an unrealized gain of $50,000. You would have no taxes to pay on these paper profits. However, if you had sold the house, the $50,000 would be taxable to you as a capital gain. The gain resulting from a sale is known as a *realized* gain. Unrealized profits are not taxable; realized profits are taxable as capital gains.

A mutual fund portfolio that has increased in value has unrealized profits. These are not taxable to investors. But, when the fund sells appreciated portfolio securities, it has realized profits. These profits are distributed as capital gains to shareholders. Shareholders can take these capital gain distributions in cash or reinvest them to purchase additional shares. In either case, these distributions are taxable as long-term capital gains to shareholders.

Capital gains distributions may be made no more than once per year.

Reinvestment of Distributions

Dividends and capital gains are distributed in cash. However, a shareholder may elect to reinvest distributions in additional mutual fund shares. The automatic reinvestment of distributions is similar to compounding interest. The reinvested distributions purchase additional shares, which may earn dividends or gains distributions.

✓ *Take Note:* Frequently, mutual funds allow reinvestment of dividend and capital gains distributions at the NAV. This means that investors are able to buy new shares without any sales load, a significant advantage that results in faster growth to the investor.

Typically, customers may systematically reinvest dividends and capital gains at less than the POP and can use them to purchase full and fractional shares as long as:

- shareholders who are not already participants in the reinvestment plan are given a separate opportunity to reinvest each dividend;
- the plan is described in the prospectus;
- the securities issuer bears no additional costs beyond those that it would have incurred in the normal payout of dividends; and
- shareholders are notified of the availability of the dividend reinvestment plan at least once every year.

A mutual fund may apply a reasonable charge against each dividend reinvestment.

If a company wishes to establish a plan through which investors can reinvest their capital gains distributions, as opposed to their dividends, at a discount to the POP, the following rules apply:

- The plan must be described in the prospectus.
- All participants must be given a separate opportunity to reinvest capital gains at each distribution.
- All participants must be notified at least once every year of the availability of the distribution reinvestment plan.

Taxation of Reinvested Distributions

Distributions are taxable to shareholders whether the distributions are received in cash or reinvested. The fund must disclose whether each distribution is from income or capital tax transactions. Form 1099, which is sent to shareholders after the close of the year, details tax information related to distributions for the year.

✓ **Take Note:** Just as with dividend distributions, whether capital gains are taken in cash or reinvested they are currently taxable to the shareholder. Dividends must be reported as ordinary income; capital gains distributions must be reported on the investor's capital gains schedule.

✎ **Quick Quiz 2.8** True or False?

____ 1. Unrealized gains of the portfolio are taxable to mutual fund shareholders.

____ 2. Capital gains distributions are typically paid quarterly.

____ 3. Mutual fund capital gains distributions are taxable to shareholders as short-term capital gains.

____ 4. Mutual funds pay dividends to shareholders from net investment income.

____ 5. IRC Subchapter M requires a fund to distribute a minimum of 90 percent of its net investment income.

____ 6. Funds that comply with IRC Subchapter M are considered registered investment companies

____ 7. Reinvested dividend distributions are not currently taxable to shareholders.

____ 8. Form 1099 classifies mutual fund distributions to shareholders.

See page 336 for answers and rationale.

Calculating Fund Yield

To calculate fund yield, divide the dividend paid from net investment income by the current offering price. Yield quotations must disclose the:

- general direction of the stock market for the period in question;
- fund's NAV at the beginning and the end of the period; and
- percentage change in the fund's price during the period.

Current yield calculations may be based only on income distributions for the preceding 12 months. Gains distributions may not be included in yield calculations. *Total return* is the return achieved if dividends and capital gains distributions were reinvested.

Most mutual funds with income objectives distribute dividends quarterly. A mutual fund must disclose the source of a dividend payment if it is from other than retained or current income.

 **Test Topic Alert!**   You are likely to see a test question similar to the following:

ABC mutual fund distributed dividends of $1.00 and capital gains of $1.00 in the past year. The current NAV of ABC shares is $19.50 and the POP is $20.00. What is the current yield of ABC shares?

The correct answer is 5 percent. Mutual fund yield is found exactly like the current yield on common stock:

$$\frac{\text{Annual dividends}}{\text{Current market price}}$$

The annual dividends of $1.00 divided by the POP price of $20.00 = current yield of 5 percent. Never include capital gains in the calculation of current yield.

The calculation of *total return* assumes the reinvestment of both dividends and capital gains.

Ex-Dividend Date

Unlike the ex-dividend date for other corporate securities, the ex-dividend date for mutual funds is set by the Board of Directors. Normally, the ex-dividend date for mutual funds is the day after the record date.

Selling Dividends

If an investor purchases fund shares just before the ex-dividend date, the fund shares' market value decreases by the distribution amount. The investor is also taxed on the distribution. A registered representative may not encourage investors to purchase fund shares before a distribution because of this tax liability. Doing so is **selling dividends**, a violation of NASD rules.

✓ *Take Note:* Selling dividends is a prohibited practice because the investor is immediately taxed on distributions received *and* the value of shares is reduced by the dividend distributed. So not only are investors subject to taxation, they have also experienced an immediate depreciation in the value of their shares.

Remember, the ex-date for mutual funds is determined by the BOD, but normally is the business day after the record date.

Fund Share Liquidations to the Investor   When an investor sells mutual fund shares, he must establish his cost base, or **basis**, in the shares to calculate the tax liability. A simple definition of cost base is the amount of money invested on which taxes have been paid. Upon liquidation, cost base represents a return of capital and is not taxed again.

Valuing Fund Shares

The cost base of mutual fund shares includes the shares' total cost, including sales charges, plus any reinvested income and capital gains. For tax purposes, the investor compares cost base to the amount of money received from selling the shares. If the amount received is greater than the cost base, the investor reports a taxable gain. If the amount received is less than the cost base, the investor reports a loss.

Calculate the gain or loss on mutual fund shares as illustrated below.

Total value of fund shares – Cost base = Taxable gain or loss

The investor does not receive a separate tax form from the mutual fund identifying the cost base of the shares sold. Recordkeeping for purchases and sales is the shareholder's responsibility.

 Take Note: To find the cost basis of mutual fund shares, add the price paid and all reinvested distributions. These distributions become part of the cost basis because they have already been taxed.

Assume that an investor bought shares for $10.00 and sold them for $15.00. The investor had reinvested dividend distributions of $1.00 per share and capital gains of $.50. What was the investor's cost basis and what was the investor's capital gain?

The cost basis in this example is found by adding the initial share cost and the reinvested distributions. ($10.00 + 1.00 + .50 = $11.50 cost basis). The capital gain is found by subtracting the cost basis from the sales proceeds. $15.00 – cost basis of $11.50 = capital gain of $3.50 per share.

If the shares had been sold for $11.00 instead, the investor would have experienced a capital loss of $.50 because the cost basis of $11.50 was $.50 greater than the sales proceeds of $11.00.

Calculating Net Gains and Losses

To calculate tax liability, taxpayers must first add all capital gains for the year. Then, they separately add all capital losses. Finally, they offset the totals to determine the net capital gain or loss for the year. Net capital losses are deductible against earned income up to a maximum of $3,000 per year. Any capital losses not deducted in a year may be carried forward indefinitely to be used in future years.

 Take Note: Assume an investor's capital gains schedule reports the following:

Capital Gains	Capital Losses
$20,000	$30,000

The investor experiences a net capital loss of $10,000 based on this information. Of this loss, $3,000 can be used to reduce the investor's ordinary income in the current tax year. The remaining $7,000 net capital loss may be carried forward indefinitely, and $3,000 per year can be used as a deduction until the full amount is used up.

Accounting Methods

If an investor decides to liquidate shares, he determines the cost base by electing one of three accounting methods: "first in, first out" (FIFO), share identification or average basis. If the investor fails to choose, the IRS assumes the investor liquidates shares on a FIFO basis.

First In, First Out

When FIFO shares are sold, the cost of the shares held the longest is used to calculate the gain or loss. In a rising market, this method normally creates adverse tax consequences.

Share Identification

When using the share identification accounting method, the investor keeps track of the cost of each share purchased and uses this information when deciding which shares to liquidate. He then liquidates the shares that provide the desired tax benefits.

Average Basis

The shareholder may elect to use an average cost basis when redeeming fund shares. The shareholder calculates average basis by dividing the total cost of all shares owned by the total number of shares. The shareholder may not change his decision to use the average basis method without IRS permission.

✓ **Take Note:** Assume an investor has purchased shares as follows:

1990: Cost basis $10.00

1995: Cost basis $20.00

If the investor wishes to redeem shares this year at the current NAV of $25.000, which shares would result in the least amount of capital gains taxation?

Redemption of the shares with the highest cost basis results in the least tax. Redemption of the 1995 shares would result in a gain of $5.00 per share ($25.00 – $20.00 = $5.00). However, if the investor redeems the 1990 shares the capital gain is $15.00 per share ($25.00 – $10.00 = $15.00).

Investors are entitled to choose which shares they wish to redeem first under the share identification method. If they do not choose, the IRS assumes FIFO. FIFO generally results in the largest taxation because the shares acquired earliest typically have the lowest basis. The IRS imposes the method that results in the biggest tax bill!

Other Mutual Fund Tax Considerations

Mutual fund investors must consider many tax factors when buying and selling mutual fund shares.

Withholding Tax

If an investor neglects or fails to include his or her tax ID number (Social Security number) when purchasing mutual fund shares, the fund must withhold 31 percent of the distributions to the investor as a withholding tax.

Cost Basis of Shares Inherited

The cost basis of inherited property is either stepped up or stepped down to its fair market value (FMV) at the date of the decedent's death.

Dividend Exclusions

Corporations that invest in other companies' stock may deduct 70 percent of the dividend received from taxable income. No similar exclusion exists for individual investors.

Taxation of Investment Returns

The taxation of investment returns can be summarized as follows:

- Income distributions: Taxed as ordinary income
- Capital gains distributions: Taxed at investor's capital gains tax rate
- Profit or loss on sale: Short- or long-term gain or loss depending on length of holding period and cost basis

Exchanges Within a Family of Funds

Even though an exchange within a fund family incurs no sales charge, the IRS considers a sale to have taken place, and if a gain occurs, the customer is taxed. This tax liability can be significant, and shareholders should be aware of this potential conversion cost.

Wash Sales

Capital losses may not be used to offset gains or income if the investor sells a security at a loss and purchases the same or a substantially identical security within 30 days before or after the trade date. The sale at a loss and the repurchase within this period is a **wash sale.**

 ***Take Note:*** Here are the test highlights about mutual fund distributions and taxation:

- Funds that comply with Subchapter M (the conduit theory) are known as Regulated Investment Companies.
- Mutual fund yield is calculated by dividing the annual dividend by the POP. Capital gains distributions are not included.

FIGURE 2.3   Wash Sale

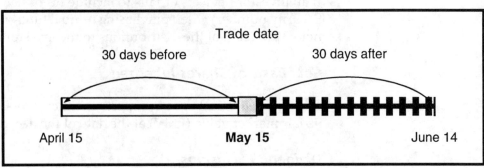

- When is the ex-date of a mutual fund? The best answer is as determined by the Board of Directors, but if that choice is not given, choose the business day after the record date.
- Dividends and capital gains are taxable whether reinvested or taken in cash.
- An investor's cost basis in mutual fund shares is what was paid to buy the share plus reinvested dividends and capital gains distributions.
- The IRS always assigns FIFO for share liquidation unless the investor chooses a different method.
- $3,000 of net capital loss may be used as a deduction against ordinary income each tax year. Any unused capital loss may be carried forward indefinitely.
- There is no tax exclusion available on dividends paid to individuals; corporation, however, may exclude 70 percent of dividends received from taxation.
- Although an exchange from one fund to another within the same family is not subject to a sales charge, it is a taxable event. Any gain or loss on the shares sold is reportable at the time of the exchange.
- When a shareholder dies, his or her shares are assigned a cost basis equal to the value of the shares on the date of death.

 Quick Quiz 2.9   1. Which of the following decides when a mutual fund goes ex-dividend?

    A. NASD
    B. NYSE
    C. SEC
    D. Board of Directors of the fund

2. The conduit theory

    A. is described in the Investment Company Act of 1940
    B. refers to a favorable tax treatment available to investment companies
    C. was developed by the NASD
    D. is stated in the SEC statement of policy

3. Your client owns shares in an open-end investment company. The shares are currently quoted in the newspaper at $10 bid and $10.80 ask. Within the past 12 months, the investment company has distributed capital gains of $l.20 per share and dividends of $.60 per share. What is the current yield on your client's shares?

    A. 1.8%
    B. 5.0%
    C. 5.6%
    D. 6.0%

See page 336 for answers and rationale

New Accounts

An account that is opened by a broker-dealer requires a completed new account form or new account card. An example of a typical new account form is shown in Figure 2.4.

A registered rep is required to fill out certain information on all new account forms:

- Full name of each customer who will have access to the account
- Address and telephone number (business and residence)
- Social Security number if individual, or tax identification number if other legal entity
- Occupation, employer and type of business
- Citizenship
- Whether the customer is of legal age (note that birth date is *not* required)
- Estimated income and net worth
- Investment objectives
- Bank and brokerage references
- Whether the customer is an employee of a member broker-dealer
- How the account was acquired
- Name and occupation of the person(s) with authority to make transactions in the account
- Signatures of the representative opening the account and a principal of the firm (note that the customer's signature is *not* required on the new account form

FIGURE 2.4   New Account Form

Greenback Securities, Inc.

Staking Your Financial Future
12654 Futurity Blvd.
Belmont, CA 99462

NEW ACCOUNT FORM

TAXPAYER ID NUMBER	☐ SSN ☐ TAX ID	AGE	BRANCH# RR#	ACCOUNT#	DATE

LEGAL NAME(S) AND MAILING ADDRESS	☐ HOME ☐ BUS

ACCOUNT TYPE ☐ CASH   ☐ OPTION
☐ MARGIN   ☐ COMMODITY

MARITAL STATUS ☐ MARRIED   ☐ SINGLE
☐ DIVORCED   ☐ WIDOWED

ACCOUNT REGIS. ☐ SINGLE   ☐ JTWROS
☐ JTIC   ☐ INV CLUB
☐ CORP   ☐ PARTNER
☐ RETIRE   ☐ OTHER

TELEPHONE NO. ☐ HOME ☐ BUS	TELEPHONE NO. ☐ HOME ☐ BUS	DIVIDENDS ☐ HOLD ☐ MAIL	U.S. CITIZEN? ☐ YES ☐ NO _____

IS THE CUSTOMER OR SPOUSE EMPLOYED BY, OR RELATED TO AN EMPLOYEE OF, ANY FINANCIAL INSTITUTION? ☐ YES ☐ NO   DUPLICATE ☐ YES   CONFIRMS? ☐ NO   **ATTACH SPECIAL INSTRUCTIONS**

EMPLOYMENT

EMPLOYER'S NAME   YEARS EMPLOYED

ADDRESS

TYPE OF BUSINESS   CLIENT'S OCCUPATION

DOCUMENTATION			OTHER (DESCRIBE)
MARGIN AGR	☐ PEND	☐ RCVD	_____
JOINT ACCT	☐ PEND	☐ RCVD	_____
TRADING AUTH	☐ PEND	☐ RCVD	_____
CORP/PART AGR	☐ PEND	☐ RCVD	_____
RETIRE ACCT	☐ PEND	☐ RCVD	_____
SIG CARD	☐ PEND	☐ RCVD	_____

REFERENCE

BANK NAME AND ADDRESS   ☐ CHECKING ☐ VERIFIED
☐ SAVINGS ☐ NOT VERIFIED

DOES CLIENT HAVE AN ACCOUNT WITH ANOTHER BROKERAGE FIRM? ☐ YES ☐ NO   IF YES, WITH WHAT FIRM?

SPOUSE

NAME   OCCUPATION   AGE

EMPLOYER   ADDRESS   ANNUAL INCOME

INVESTMENT EXPERIENCE	DOES CLIENT OR SPOUSE HAVE ANOTHER ACCOUNT WITH US? ☐ YES ☐ NO IF YES, LIST:	HOW WAS ACCOUNT ACQUIRED? ☐ WALK IN ☐ REFERRAL ☐ PHONE IN ☐ PROSPECT ☐ OTHER ☐ ACQUAINTANCE	OPTION TRADES ANTICIPATED ☐ BUY ONLY ☐ STRADDLES ☐ COV CALLS ☐ SPREADS ☐ COV PUTS ☐ COMBINS ☐ UNC OPTS ☐ OTHER

INVESTMENT OBJECTIVES
☐ GROWTH ☐ SPECULATION
☐ INCOME ☐ RETIREMENT
☐ GRO/INC ☐ TAX

IS CLIENT NOW OR HAS CLIENT EVER BEEN A CORPORATE OFFICER OR OWNER OF 10% OF ANY CORPORATION'S SECURITIES?
☐ YES ☐ NO
IF YES, NAME:
_____

INITIAL TRANSACTION
☐ BUY   DESCRIBE:
☐ SELL
☐ OTHER

INITIAL DEPOSIT

IS CLIENT FAMILIAR WITH OPTIONS?
☐ YES   ☐ NO
HAS CLIENT RECEIVED OCC PROSPECTUS?
☐ YES DATE
HAS CLIENT PREVIOUSLY TRADED OPTIONS?
☐ YES   ☐ NO
ARE OPTIONS SUITABLE?
☐ YES   ☐ NO

HOME ☐ OWN ☐ RENT
NO. OF DEPENDENTS _____
ANNUAL INC _____
NET WORTH _____

DISCRETIONARY AUTHORIZATION
☐ FULL ☐ LIMITED ☐ NONE

RR SIGNATURE	AGENT'S NAME AND ADDRESS
BRANCH MGR APPROVAL DATE	ROP SIGNATURE (OPTIONS APPROVAL)

✓ **Take Note:** Oddly enough, the birth date and the customer's signature are not required on the new account form! The rep is only required to know that the customer is above the age of majority. Minors cannot open accounts because they cannot make binding contracts.

The signatures required to open an account are the rep's and the principal's.

Accounts may be opened by any legally competent person above the age of majority. Legally incompetent individuals may not open accounts.

When opening an account, reps should know all essential facts about a customer's current financial situation, his or her present holdings, risk tolerance, needs and objectives. Such information should be updated periodically as situations change.

If a customer refuses to provide all information requested, the account may still be opened if the firm believes the customer has the financial resources necessary to support the account. The registered representative can only make recommendations if sufficient information has been given to determine suitability.

A partner or principal of the firm must approve every new account in writing on the new account form before or promptly after the completion of the first transaction in the account.

Account Ownership

Accounts can be opened with various types of ownership. The principal types of ownership are:

- Individual
- Joint
- Corporate
- Partnership

Trading Authorization

Accounts may be opened with someone other than the owner having the authority to buy and sell securities on behalf of the owner. This is known as *trading authorization* or *power of attorney*. The primary types of trading authorization are:

- **Discretionary**—a registered representative has been given written authorization from a customer to make trading decisions for the customer
- **Custodial**—an adult has been designated to act on behalf of a child, who is the beneficial owner of the account
- **Fiduciary**—a third party has been legally appointed to prudently manage the account on behalf of another person or entity

Payment Method

Customers may pay for securities with cash or on margin. In cash accounts, customers must pay the full purchase price of securities by the transaction settlement date. Margin accounts allow customers to borrow part of a security's purchase price from the broker-dealer.

Securities Traded   Customers must have special approval to make certain types of trades in their accounts, particularly options transactions. Normally, no special authorization is required to buy or sell stocks, bonds and mutual funds.

Opening New Accounts

Generally, any competent person of age may open an account. Any person declared legally incompetent may not. Fiduciary or custodial accounts may be opened for minors or legally incompetent individuals.

Approval and Acceptance of an Account   A partner or a principal of the firm must approve every new account in writing on the account form before or promptly after the completion of the first transaction in the account.

Documenting New Accounts

In addition to the new account form required for all accounts opened, other specific applications may be required including:

- Customer agreements
- Loan consent agreements
- IRA contracts
- Keogh forms
- Partnership agreements
- Corporate charters
- Simplified employee pension plan (SEP) applications
- Annuity contracts
- Trust documents
- Mutual fund applications
- Full or limited powers of attorney

Mailing Instructions

A customer gives specific mailing instructions when opening a new account. Statements and confirms may be sent to someone who holds power of attorney for the customer if the customer requests it in writing or if duplicate confirms are also sent to the customer. A member firm may hold a customer's mail for up to two months if the customer is traveling in the United States and for up to three months if the customer is abroad.

Retirement Accounts   Each type of personal and corporate retirement account has its own forms and applications. The most important are those that establish the firm's custodial relationship with the retirement account owner, necessary for Internal Revenue Service (IRS) reporting purposes.

Business Accounts   When a registered rep opens a business account of any type, he or she must establish three items:

1. the business's legal right to open an investment account;
2. an indication of any limitations that the owners, the stockholders, a court or any other entity has placed on the securities in which the business can invest; and
3. who will represent the business in transactions involving the account.

A copy of the legal documents that established the business usually contains this information and must be kept on file with the other account forms.

Trading Authorization/ Power of Attorney   A power of attorney or a discretionary power allows a party other than the account owner to make investment decisions for the account without consulting the account owner. When such authority has been established for an account, a signed copy of the document must be kept on file. If power of attorney or a discretionary power has been established for an account, the rep must keep a signed copy of the document on file.

Opening Accounts for Employees of Other Brokers

The National Association of Securities Dealers (NASD), the New York Stock Exchange (NYSE) and the Municipal Securities Rulemaking Board (MSRB) require broker-dealers to give permission or written notification to other broker-dealers regarding the establishment of accounts for certain individuals, including:

- employees of broker-dealers and
- spouses or minor children of broker-dealer employees.

NASD Requirements. NASD rules do not require an employee of one NASD member firm to get his employer's permission to open an account with another NASD member, but do require the firm opening the account to notify the customer's employer. The employee is responsible for disclosing that he or she is an associated person of an NASD member when opening the account. Duplicate confirmations and statements must be sent to the employer broker-dealer if the employer requests them.

 **Test Topic Alert!**   Be prepared for a question that asks about opening an account for an employee of another NASD firm. The following two steps must occur:

1. The individual's employer must receive notification that the account is being opened.
2. The employer may request duplicate confirmations.

Note that the duplicate confirmations are not *required* to be sent; they must be made available only upon request by the employing firm.

Quick Quiz 2.10

1. An employee of another NASD member broker-dealer would like to open an account with your firm. All of the following statements regarding the employee and the account are true EXCEPT the

   A. employer must receive duplicate copies of all transactions made in the account if requested
   B. employer must be notified of the opening of the account
   C. opening member must notify the employee in writing that the employer will be notified of the employee's intent to open the account
   D. broker-dealer holding the account must approve each transaction made by the person before entry of the order

2. All of the following customer information is required on a new account form EXCEPT

   A. name
   B. date of birth
   C. Social Security number
   D. occupation

3. A registered rep is permitted to open all of the following customer accounts EXCEPT

   A. individual account opened by the individual's spouse
   B. minor's account opened by a custodian
   C. corporate account opened by the designated officer
   D. partnership account opened by the designated partner

4. Which of the following must sign a new account form?

   I. Principal
   II. Registered representative
   III. Customer
   IV. Spouse of the customer

   A. I and II only
   B. I, II and III only
   C. II and III only
   D. I, II, III and IV

See page 336 for answers and rationale

Types of Accounts

When an account is opened, it is registered in the name(s) of one or more persons. They are the account owners and the only individuals who are allowed access to and control of the investments in the account.

Single Accounts   A single account has one beneficial owner. The account holder is the only person who can:

- control the investments within the account and
- request distributions of cash or securities from the account.

Joint Accounts   In a joint account, two or more adults are named on the account as co-owners, with each allowed some form of control over the account. In addition to the appropriate new account form, a joint account agreement must be signed, and the account must be designated as either joint tenants in common (TIC) or joint tenants with right of survivorship (JTWROS).

The account forms for joint accounts require the signatures of all owners. Both types of joint account agreements provide that any or all tenants may transact business in the account. Checks must be made payable to the names in which the account is registered and must be endorsed for deposit by all tenants, although mail need be sent to only a single address. To be in good delivery form, securities sold from a joint account must be signed by all tenants.

Joint Tenants in Common

JTIC ownership provides that a deceased tenant's fractional interest in the account is retained by that tenant's estate and is not passed to the surviving tenant(s).

Joint Tenants with Right of Survivorship

JTWROS ownership stipulates that a deceased tenant's interest in the account passes to the surviving tenant(s).

 **Test Topic Alert!**   The test might have questions pertaining to the following details about joint accounts:

- JTWROS—both parties must have equal interests
- JTIC—interest can be unequal

Parties in JTWROS and JTIC have an *undivided ownership interest.* In other words, they

- all own some of everything in the account;
- any party can make a trade; and
- checks or distributions must be made payable to all parties and endorsed by all parties.

Full Power of Attorney

A full power of attorney allows someone who is not the owner of an account to:

- deposit or withdraw cash or securities and
- make investment decisions for the account owner.

Custodians, trustees, guardians and other people filling similar legal duties are often given full power of attorney.

Limited Power of Attorney

A limited power of attorney allows an individual to have some, but not total, control over an account. The document specifies the level of access the person may exercise.

Discretionary Accounts

An account set up with preapproved authority for a registered rep to make transactions without having to ask for specific approval is a discretionary account. *Discretion* is defined as the authority to decide:

- what security;
- the number of shares or units; and
- whether to buy or sell.

Discretion does not apply to decisions regarding the timing of an investment or the price at which it is acquired. An order from a customer worded "Buy 100 shares of Microscam for my account whenever you think the price is right" is not a discretionary order.

Discretionary Authority. A customer can give discretionary power over his account(s) only by filing a trading authorization or a limited power of attorney with the broker-dealer. No transactions of a discretionary nature can take place without this document on file. Once authorization has been given, the customer is legally bound to accept the registered rep's decisions, although the customer may continue to enter orders on his own.

The customer may give discretion for the account only to a specific individual. If the registered rep leaves the firm or in any other way stops working with the account, the discretionary authority ends immediately.

Regulation of Discretionary Accounts. In addition to requiring the proper documentation, discretionary accounts are subject to the following rules:

- Each discretionary order must be identified as such at the time it is entered for execution.
- An officer or a partner of the brokerage house must approve each order promptly and in writing, not necessarily before order entry.
- A record must be kept of all transactions.
- No excessive trading may occur in the account, relative to the size of the account and the customer's investment objectives.
- To safeguard against the possibility of churning, a designated supervisor or manager must review all trading activity frequently and systematically.

✓ **Take Note:** If you are having any difficulty identifying a discretionary order, you might want to give the following method a try:

An order is discretionary if any one of the *three A's* are missing. The three A's are:

Activity
Amount
Asset

For example, if a customer asks a rep to sell 1,000 shares of XYZ stock, the order is not discretionary even though the customer did not specifically say when or at what price.

Activity = sell; *Amount* = 1,000 shares; *Asset* = XYZ stock. All three A's were defined.

However, if a customer asks a rep to buy 1,000 shares of the best computer company stock available, the order is discretionary. The *Asset* is missing, because the company was not defined.

How about this one! A customer wishes to buy 1,000 shares of XYZ whenever you think is price is best.

You're right if you said nondiscretionary. The A's were all defined. Omitting the time or the price does not make an order discretionary.

Uniform Gifts to Minors Act Accounts

Uniform Gifts to Minors Act (UGMA) and Uniform Transfers to Minors Act (UTMA) accounts require an adult or a trustee to act as custodian for a minor (the beneficial owner). Any kind of security—cash, life insurance, annuity contracts and other forms of property—may be given to the account without limitation.

Donating Securities

When a person makes a gift of securities to a minor under the UGMA laws, that person is the donor of the securities. A gift under UGMA conveys an indefeasible title; that is, the donor may not take back the gift, nor may the minor return the gift until she has reached the age of majority. Once the gift is donated, the donor gives up all rights to the property. When the minor reaches the specified age, the property in the account is transferred into her name.

Custodian

Any securities given to a minor through an UGMA account are managed by a custodian until the minor reaches the age of majority. The custodian has full control over the minor's account and can:

- buy or sell securities;
- exercise rights or warrants; and
- liquidate, trade or hold securities.

The custodian may also use the property in the account in any way he deems proper for the minor's support, education, maintenance, general use or benefit. However, the account is not normally used to pay basic expenses associated with raising a child, such as food and clothing.

Registered representatives must be aware of the following rules regarding UGMA custodial accounts:

- An account may have only one custodian and one minor or beneficial owner.
- A minor can be the beneficiary of more than one account and a person may serve as custodian for more than one UGMA as long as each account benefits only one minor.
- The donor of securities can act as custodian or can appoint someone else to do so.
- Unless acting as custodians, parents have no legal control over an UGMA account or the securities in it.

A registered representative is not responsible for determining whether an appointment is valid or whether a custodian's activities are appropriate.

Opening an UGMA Account

When opening an UGMA account, a rep must ensure that the account application contains the custodian's name, the minor's name and Social Security number, and the state in which the UGMA is registered.

Registration of UGMA Securities

Any securities in an UGMA account are registered in the custodian's name for the benefit of the minor; they cannot be registered in street name. Typically, the securities are registered to "Joan R. Smith as custodian for Brenda Lee Smith," for example, or a variation of this form. When the minor reaches the age of majority, all of the securities in the account will be registered in his or her name.

The gift of securities is considered complete when this registration has been completed.

Fiduciary Responsibility

An UGMA custodian is charged with fiduciary responsibilities in managing the minor's account. Certain restrictions have been placed on what is deemed to be proper handling of the investments in an UGMA. The most important limitations follow:

- UGMAs may be opened and managed as cash accounts only.
- A custodian may not purchase securities in an account on margin or pledge them as collateral for a loan.
- A custodian must reinvest all cash proceeds, dividends and interest within a reasonable period of time. Cash proceeds from sales or dividends may be held in a noninterest-bearing custodial account for a reasonable period, but should not remain idle for long.
- Investment decisions must take into account a minor's age and the custodial relationship; commodities futures, naked options and other high-risk securities are examples of inappropriate investments. Options may not be bought in a custodial account because no evidence of ownership is issued to an options buyer. Covered call writing is normally allowed.
- Stock subscription rights or warrants must be either exercised or sold.
- A custodian for an UGMA may not grant trading authority to a third party.
- A custodian may loan money to an account, but may not borrow from it.

A custodian may be reimbursed for any reasonable expenses he or she incurs in managing the account unless the custodian is also the donor.

Taxation

The minor's Social Security number appears on an UGMA account, and the minor must file an annual income tax return and pay taxes on any income exceeding $1,400 (1999) produced by the UGMA at the parent's top marginal tax rate, regardless of the source of the gift, until the minor reaches the age of 14. Exclusions are available, and they are indexed for inflation.

When the minor reaches age 14, the account will be taxed at the minor's tax rate.

Although the minor is the account's beneficiary and is responsible for any and all taxes on the account, in most states it is the custodian's responsibility to see that the taxes are paid.

Death of the Minor or Custodian If the beneficiary of an UGMA dies, the securities in the account pass to the minor's estate, not to the parents' or custodian's estate. In the event of the custodian's death or resignation, either a court of law or the donor must appoint a new custodian.

UTMAs Although almost identical to UGMA accounts, UTMA accounts have one distinguishing feature. The age of transfer can be postponed until the child reaches age 25.

Test Topic Alert! The test will most likely ask two–three questions about UGMA accounts. You should know the following information:

1. UGMA accounts must be one to one (one minor, one custodian).
2. Gifts under UGMA are irrevocable.
3. The gift can be of any size.
4. The donor (the giver of the gift) may be liable for gift tax on any gift of more than $10,000 in one year to one individual.
5. The child's Social Security number is on the account; the child is owner of the assets.
6. Speculative trading strategies are prohibited. No short selling, naked options or margin accounts.

Quick Quiz 2.11 1. Which of the following persons are considered fiduciaries?

  I. Executor of an estate
  II. Administrator of a trust
  III. Custodian of an UGMA/UTMA account
  IV. Conservator for a legally incompetent person

  A. I and II only
  B. I, II and III only
  C. III and IV only
  D. I, II, III and IV

2. A customer would like to open a custodial UGMA or UTMA account for his nephew, a minor. The uncle

   A. can open the account provided the proper trust arrangements are filed first
   B. can open the account and name himself custodian
   C. needs a legal document evidencing the nephew's parents' approval of the account
   D. can be custodian for the account only if he is also the minor's legal guardian

3. All of the following statements regarding customer accounts are true EXCEPT

   A. stock held in a custodial account may not be held in street name
   B. the customer who opens a numbered account must sign a statement attesting to ownership
   C. stock held under JTWROS goes to the survivor(s) in the event of the death of one of the tenants
   D. margin trading in a fiduciary account does not require any special consideration

4. An investor wishes to provide for his three nephews after his brother dies. Under the Uniform Gifts to Minors Act, which of the following actions may the investor take?

   A. Open one account for all three nephews
   B. Open three separate accounts and deposit cash and securities
   C. Open three separate accounts and deposit insurance policies
   D. Open three separate accounts and deposit fixed annuities

5. Securities owned by a donor and given to a minor under the Uniform Gifts to Minors Act become the property of the minor

   A. when the securities are paid for by the minor
   B. on the settlement date
   C. when the securities are registered in the custodian's name for the benefit of the minor
   D. when the donor decides to give the securities to the minor

See page 337 for answer and rationale

Mutual Fund Purchase and Withdrawal Plans

Mutual fund investors may select from among several methods by which to purchase mutual fund shares or withdraw money from the mutual fund account.

Types of Mutual Fund Accounts

When an investor opens an account with a mutual fund, she makes an initial deposit and specifies whether fund share distributions are to be made in cash or reinvested. If the customer elects to receive distributions in cash rather than reinvesting them, her proportionate interest in the fund is reduced each time a distribution is made. The customer may make additional investments in an open account at any time and in any dollar amount; that is, the law sets no minimum requirement, although each fund may set its own.

Accumulation Plans   Mutual funds have established several accumulation plans that allow investors to use the dollar cost averaging strategy.

Voluntary Accumulation Plan

A voluntary accumulation plan allows a customer to deposit regular periodic investments on a voluntary basis. The plan is designed to help the customer form regular investment habits while still offering some flexibility.

Voluntary accumulation plans may require a minimum initial purchase and minimum additional purchase amounts. Many funds offer automatic withdrawal from customer checking accounts to simplify contributions. If a customer misses a payment, the fund does not penalize him because the plan is voluntary. The customer may discontinue the plan at any time.

✓ **Take Note:** In a voluntary accumulation plan, once the account has been opened, investor can contribute nearly any sum with nearly any frequency they like.

Dollar Cost Averaging. One method of purchasing mutual fund shares is called dollar cost averaging, where a person invests identical amounts at regular intervals. This form of investing allows the individual to purchase more shares when prices are low and fewer shares when prices are high. In a fluctuating market and over a period of time the average cost per share is lower than the average price of the shares. However, dollar cost averaging does not guarantee profits in a declining market because prices may continue to decline for some time. In this case, the investor buys more shares of a sinking investment.

The following example illustrates how average price and average cost may vary with dollar cost averaging:

Month	Amount Invested	Price per Share	No. of Shares
January	$600	$20	30
February	$600	$24	25
March	$600	$30	20
April	$600	$40	15
Total	*$2,400*	*$114*	*90*

The average cost per share equals $2,400 (the total investment) divided by 90 (the total number of shares purchased), or $26.67 per share, while the average price per share is $28.50 ($114 ÷ 4). Average price per share is found by dividing total price paid per share by the number of investments made.

 **Test Topic Alert!**

It is possible that the test may ask you to calculate either the average cost or the average price per share. Review the calculation above as practice.

More importantly, understand the *concept* of dollar cost averaging. It involves investing a fixed amount of money every period, regardless of market price fluctuation. If the market price of shares is up, less shares are purchased; if the market price of shares is down more shares are purchased. Over time, if the market fluctuates, dollar cost averaging is likely to achieve a lower average cost per share than average price per share.

Recognize this phrase for the test: Dollar cost averaging is effective if the average cost per share is less than the average price per share. This method historically outperforms attempts to time the market, but can never be guaranteed.

Contractual Accumulation Plan

In a contractual plan, the investor signs an agreement to invest a specified dollar amount over a set period of time. Although called a contractual plan, the agreement is binding on the company only; the investor cannot be held to the contract. Contractual plans are discussed in more detail below.

Contractual Plans   A contractual plan, also called a periodic payment plan, enables a person to invest in a mutual fund on a periodic basis over a fixed period of time. The plan allows the individual to invest an amount that is typically less than the amount a mutual fund requires. An investor may begin a contractual plan for as little as $20 per month, with future payments of as little as $10 per month. The investor signs an agreement stating that he intends to invest a fixed number of dollars over a defined period of time. This agreement is not binding on the investor, but he may incur penalties if he terminates the plan before completion.

Characteristics of Contractual Plans

When a contractual plan is sold, two sales actually take place. First, the customer agrees to make periodic payments to a contractual plan company and is given a plan certificate issued by the company. Second, as the investor makes periodic payments, the plan company uses the money to buy shares in the mutual fund.

Contractual plan companies are organized as UITs. The customer's monthly payments buy units that are credited to the customer's plan account. The dollars represented by these units, in turn, are invested in shares the mutual fund issues.

Thus, a double sale occurs— the sale of units in the plan account and the sale of shares in the fund. Therefore, two prospectuses are required.

Plan companies also have their own plan custodians. The plan custodian has many of the same duties and functions as the investment company transfer agent.

Front-End Load and Spread Load

Whether a plan company operates under the Investment Company Act of 1940 or the Investment Company Act Amendments of 1970, the maximum sales charge allowable is 9 percent over the life of the plan.

TABLE 2.4   Comparison of Contractual Plans

Terms	1940 Act (Front-end Load)	1970 Act (Spread-load, or 27-H)
Max. sales charges (life)	9%	9%
Max. sales charges in any one year	50%	20%
Max. sales charges over four years	No limit set	16% average per year
45-day free-look letter	Refund of current NAV plus any sales charges	Refund of current NAV plus any sales charges
Termination within first 18 months	Refund of current NAV plus any sales charges in excess of 15% of total payments	Refund of NAV only

Front-End Load. The Investment Company Act of 1940 allows the plan company to collect sales charges of up to 50 percent of an investor's deposits in the first year. The act of 1940 plans are known as front-end-load plans.

Spread Load (27-H). The Investment Company Act Amendments of 1970, which amended paragraph 27h of the 1940 act, allow the plan company to charge up to 20 percent of an investor's deposit in any one year as long as the average charge over the first four years does not exceed 16 percent annually. This arrangement is known as a spread-load plan or 27-H plan.

✓ *Take Note:* Although contractual plans are not frequently sold today, the test may ask several questions about them.

"The Rule of 90" is an easy way to remember the important test points about contractual plans. Figure 2.5 shows how it works.

FIGURE 2.5   The Rule of 90

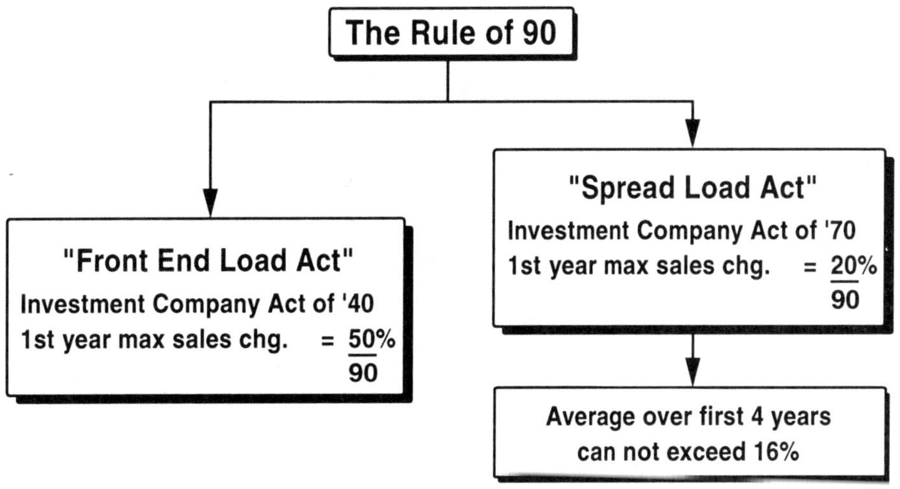

The Rule of 90 reminds you of the 9 percent sales load over the life of contractual plans. It also helps you remember the maximum sales charge in the first year under a contractual plan. Under the Act of 1940, 40 + what number = 90? The missing number is 50, and it represents the maximum sales charge in the first year. Following the same logic, the maximum first year sales charge under the Act of 1970 must be 20 percent.

Also, you are expected to know the names "Front end load Act" and "Spread load Act." An easy way to remember these acts is to think of "F's" for the Act of 40 (50 percent, front-end load) and "S's" for the Act of 1970 (Spread Load, 16 percent average).

Terminating a Plan

Under the provisions of the Investment Company Act of 1940, front-end load and spread-load plans must allow investors to change their purchase decisions.

Right of Withdrawal (45-day free look). A fund's custodian must provide each investor with a written notice detailing the total sales charges that will apply over the life of the plan. The notice must be sent within 60 calendar days of the date a contractual plan certificate is issued to the customer.

The customer may surrender the certificate and terminate the plan within 45 days from the mailing date of the custodian's written notice. If the customer surrenders the certificate within that time, she is entitled to:

- a 100 percent refund of all sales charges paid to date, plus
- the investment's current value (NAV).

The value of the fund shares liquidated at NAV may result in a profit or loss on the investment, depending on the NAV at the time of purchase.

After the 45-day free look period, the amount of refund depends on whether a plan company operates under the Act of 1940 or the Act of 1970.

Under the Act of 1940:

- termination after the 45-day free look but before the end of 18 months—investor receives the current NAV plus the amount of the sales charge in excess of 15 percent of the total amount of money invested
- termination after 18 months—investor receives NAV only

Under the Act of 1970:

- termination after the 45-free look—investor receives NAV only

✓ **Take Note:** The contractual plan administrator has 60 days to send out the 45-day free look letter! This letter offers a refund of 100 percent of sales charge plus the net asset value of the account within the 45-day period starting with the mailing date of the letter. This does not necessarily assure that an investor will get all of his money back. He may get more or less, depending on the NAV of the account.

After the 45-day free look period, refund provisions under the plan differ. The Act of 1970 is easy: after the 45-day free look period, the investor receives NAV only.

The Act of 1940 is a bit more complex. After the 45-day free look, but before the end of 18 months, the investor gets back NAV plus the amount of sales charge that exceeds 15 percent of the investment. After 18 months the investor is returned only the NAV.

If you were asked to calculate the refund under the Act of 1940 in the tenth month, look for an answer choice that is more than the NAV only, but less than the NAV plus the sales charge paid. Thinking logically will help eliminate unreasonable answers and save you a tedious math computation!

Quick Quiz 2.12 Match the following items to the appropriate descriptions below.

    A. Front-End Load Act
    B. 15
    C. 45
    D. 16

____ 1. Number of days in contractual plan free-look period

____ 2. Maximum average sales charge that can be withdrawn over the first four years of a Spread Load Act Plan

____ 3. The act that has allows a first year sales charge of 50 percent

____ 4. Sales charges in excess of this percentage of the investment amount must be returned after 45 days but before the end of 18 months under an Act of 1940 contractual plan

Match the following numbers to the best descriptions below.

    A. 9
    B. 60
    C. 18
    D. 20

____ 5. The plan company must send the free-look letter within this number of days.

____ 6. Maximum sales charge percent in the first year under an Act of 1970 plan

____ 7. After this number of months the refund under an Act of 1940 plan is NAV only.

_____ 8. Maximum sales charge over the life an Act of 1940 or Act of 1970 contractual plan

See page 337 for answers and rationale.

Withdrawal Plans

In addition to lump-sum withdrawals where customers sell all of their shares, mutual funds offer systematic withdrawal plans. Withdrawal plans are normally a free service. Not all mutual funds offer withdrawal plans, but those that do may offer plans that include the following.

Fixed Dollar

A customer may request the periodic withdrawal of a fixed dollar amount. Thus, the fund liquidates enough shares each period to send that sum. The amount of money liquidated can be more or less than the account earnings during the period.

Fixed Percentage or Fixed Share

Under a fixed-percentage or fixed-share withdrawal plan, either a fixed number of shares or a fixed percentage of the account is liquidated each period.

Fixed Time

Under a fixed-time withdrawal plan, customers liquidate their holdings over a fixed period of time.

Most mutual funds require a customer's account to be worth a minimum amount of money before a withdrawal plan may begin. Additionally, most funds discourage continued investment once withdrawals start.

Withdrawal Plan Disclosures

Withdrawal plans are not guaranteed. With fixed-dollar plans, only the dollar amount to be received each period is fixed. All other factors, including the number of shares liquidated and a plan's length, are variable. For a fixed-time plan, only the period of time is fixed; the amount of money the investor receives varies each period. Because withdrawal plans are not guaranteed, the registered rep must:

- never promise an investor a guaranteed rate of return;
- stress to the investor that it is *possible* to exhaust the account by over-withdrawing;
- state that during a down market it is possible that the account will be exhausted if the investor withdraws even a small amount; and
- never use charts or tables unless the SEC specifically clears their use.

✓ **Take Note:** Be sure to note that mutual fund withdrawal plans are *not guaranteed* in any way! Also, any charts and tables regarding withdrawal plans must be cleared by the SEC prior to use.

✎ **Quick Quiz 2.13** 1. Under which of the following circumstances will dollar cost averaging result in an average cost per share that is lower than the average price per share?

 I. The price of the stock fluctuates over a period of time.
 II. A fixed number of shares is purchased regularly.
 III. A fixed dollar amount is invested regularly.
 IV. A constant dollar plan is maintained.

 A. I and II
 B. I and III
 C. I, III and IV
 D. II and III

 2. All of the following statements regarding dollar cost averaging are true EXCEPT that

 A. dollar cost averaging results in a lower average cost per share
 B. dollar cost averaging is not available to large investors
 C. more shares are purchased when prices are lower
 D. in sales literature, dollar cost averaging cannot be referred to as *averaging the dollar*

 3. Which of the following is a risk of a withdrawal plan?

 A. The sales charge for the service is high.
 B. The cost basis of the shares is high.
 C. The plan is illegal in many states.
 D. The investor may outlive his or her income.

 4. An investor has requested a withdrawal plan from his mutual fund and currently receives $600 per month. This is an example of what type of plan?

 A. Contractual
 B. Fixed-share periodic withdrawal
 C. Fixed-dollar periodic withdrawal
 D. Fixed-percentage withdrawal

See page 337 for answers and rationale.

Tracking Investment Company Securities

Investment company prices, like those for individual securities, are quoted daily in the financial press. However, because various methods are used to calculate sales charges, as described below, the financial press provides several footnotes to explain the type of sales charge a mutual fund issuer uses. A registered representative must understand the presentation and meaning of the footnotes associated with investment company quotes so that he can accurately describe the quotes to the investing public.

Most newspapers carry daily quotes of the NAVs and offer prices for major mutual funds. A mutual fund's NAV is its bid price. The offer price, also called the *public offering price* or *POP*, is the ask price; it is the NAV plus the maximum sales charge, if any. The "NAV Chg." column reflects the change in NAV from the previous day's quote.

In Figure 2.6, look at the family of funds called ArGood Mutual Funds. ArGood Growth Fund is a part of this group; its net asset value, offering price and the change in its net asset value per share are listed. As stated previously, when a difference exists between the NAV and the offering price, the fund is a load fund. A no-load fund is usually identified by the letters "NL" in the "Offer Price" column. Look at the Best Mutual funds; they are a family of no-load funds.

FIGURE 2.6   Mutual Fund Quotations

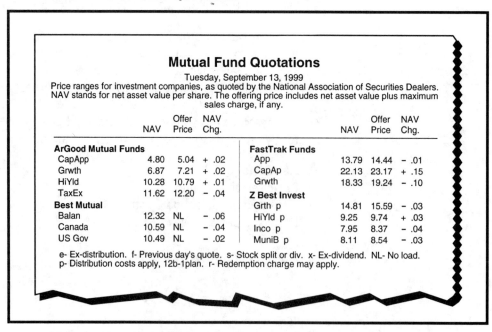

Mutual Fund Quotations

Tuesday, September 13, 1999

Price ranges for investment companies, as quoted by the National Association of Securities Dealers. NAV stands for net asset value per share. The offering price includes net asset value plus maximum sales charge, if any.

	NAV	Offer Price	NAV Chg.		NAV	Offer Price	NAV Chg.
ArGood Mutual Funds				**FastTrak Funds**			
CapApp	4.80	5.04	+ .02	App	13.79	14.44	− .01
Grwth	6.87	7.21	+ .02	CapAp	22.13	23.17	+ .15
HiYld	10.28	10.79	+ .01	Grwth	18.33	19.24	− .10
TaxEx	11.62	12.20	− .04	**Z Best Invest**			
Best Mutual				Grth p	14.81	15.59	− .03
Balan	12.32	NL	− .06	HiYld p	9.25	9.74	+ .03
Canada	10.59	NL	− .04	Inco p	7.95	8.37	− .04
US Gov	10.49	NL	− .02	MuniB p	8.11	8.54	− .03

e- Ex-distribution. f- Previous day's quote. s- Stock split or div. x- Ex-dividend. NL- No load. p- Distribution costs apply, 12b-1plan. r- Redemption charge may apply.

The final column shows the change in a share's net asset value since the last trading date. A plus (+) indicates an upward move, and a minus (–) indicates a downward turn.

From this information, you can calculate any mutual fund's sales charge. For example, find the FastTrak group of funds in Figure 2.6. The first entry is App.

Remember the formula for calculating the sales charge:

$$\text{Public offering price} - \text{NAV} = \text{Sales charge}$$

Therefore, in this case, the calculation is:

$$\$14.44 - \$13.79 = \$.65$$

To calculate the sales charge percentage, use the following formula:

$$\text{Sales charge} \div \text{Public offering price} = \text{Sales charge \%}$$

In this case, the calculation follows:

$$\$.65 \div \$14.44 = 4.5\%$$

You can also watch the movements of the fund's share value.

FIGURE 2.7   Standard & Poor's Mutual Fund Summary

Fund	Prin. Obj.	Type	Dec 31, 1998 Total Net Assets (MILS)	Cash & Equiv (MILS)	Net Assets per Share % Chg. from Prev. Dec. 31 At Dec. 31 1996	1997	1998	Min. Unit	Max. Sales Chg. %	$10,000 Invested 12-31-88 Now Worth	Price Record 1998 High	Low	NAV Per Sh as of 12-31-98 NAV per Shr.	Offer Price
Acorn	G	C	525.8	47.0	+ 3.9	+30.1	+15.4	$4,000	None	29,603	47.71	37.61	47.71	47.71
ALFA Securities	G	C	672.6	22.9	+33.5	+41.1	+21.6	$1,000	None	32,518	24.75	19.62	24.47	24.47
Alliance Fund	G	C	948.2	19.0	- 5.2	+29.5	+ 8.9	$250	5.5	24,661	9.67	6.96	9.45	10.00
Alliance Tech	G	C	200.8	10.0	- 16.4	+26.1	+12.0	$250	5.5	....	36.47	23.44	34.24	36.23
Amer Balanced	IS	B	202.0	24.0	+ 7.7	+27.1	+15.8	$500	8.5	27,889	12.61	10.92	12.32	13.46
Amer Cap Corp Bond	IS	BD	136.0	16.0	+ 9.2	+24.6	+10.8	$500	8.5	23,457	7.51	7.12	7.12	7.48
Amer Cap Mun Bond	I	TF	187.0	7.0	+10.0	+22.0	+15.9	$500	4.75	22,897	21.74	18.53	19.14	20.09
Analytic Opt Equity	GI	C	85.7	11.7	+ 6.6	+15.5	+10.2	$5,000	None	20,662	15.59	13.88	15.45	15.45
Axe-Houghton Bond	SIR	B	204.5	4.0	+ 5.8	+31.6	+21.5	$1,000	None	27,766	12.16	10.26	11.93	11.93
Axe-Houghton Stock	G	C	93.4	2.0	- 15.0	+31.1	+10.8	$1,000	None	28,394	11.46	8.25	11.13	11.13

Principal Objective: G-Growth; I-Income; R-Return on Capital; S-Stability; E-Objectives treated Equally; P-Preservation of Capital; Listed in order of importance. Type: B-Balanced; BD-Bond; C-Common; CV-Conv Bond and Prefd Stock; FL-Flexible; GB-Long-term Gov't; GL-Global; H-Hedge; L-Leverage; P-Preferred; PM-Precious Metals; O-Options; SP-Specialized; TF-Tax Free; ST-Short-term investments.

Stock guides such as Standard & Poor's include summaries of mutual funds for the year. Figure 2.7 shows a portion of a table taken from a Standard & Poor's Stock Guide; you can use it to evaluate mutual funds. To the right of the third fund listed on the table, Alliance Fund, the following information is listed:

- **Principal objective of the fund.** "G" means Alliance is a growth fund. Other objectives might be income, return on capital and stability; they are listed in the footnotes below the table.
- **Type of fund.** Alliance Fund is a "C" or common stock fund. Other types of funds are listed in the footnotes. They include the following:

B - balanced	**FL** - flexible
BD - bond	**H** - hedge
C - common	**L** - leverage
CN - Canadian	**P** - preferred
CT - common	**SP** - specialized
CV - convertible bond and preferred stock	**TF** - tax free

- **Total net assets.** This column lists total net assets at market value— that is, assets minus liabilities. Alliance Fund has total net assets of $948.2 million.
- **Cash and equivalents.** This column includes cash and receivables, short-term government securities and other money-market instruments less current liabilities. Cash and equivalents are part of the total net assets.
- **Percentage change in net assets per share.** These columns show a fund's performance over a specific period—in this case, from the previous December 31. For example, on December 31, 1997, Alliance Fund had a 29.5 percent increase in net asset value per share since December 31, 1996.
- **Minimum unit.** This is the minimum initial purchase of shares. For Alliance Fund, it is $250.
- **Maximum sales charge.** Alliance Fund charges 5.5 percent. If a fund is a no-load fund, it levies no sales charge.
- **Current worth of $10,000 invested December 31, 1988.** This column provides a gauge of a fund's performance over several years. In this case, $10,000 invested in Alliance Fund on December 31, 1988, would have more than doubled, growing to $24,661.
- **Price record.** From these columns, you can learn a share's percentage of appreciation from its low price of the year. To determine the percentage, subtract the low price from the latest NAV per share, then divide the difference by the low price. For example, during 1998 Alliance Fund sold at a low of 6.96. If on June 30, 1998 (the current date), its

NAV per share was 9.67, the appreciation would be computed as follows:

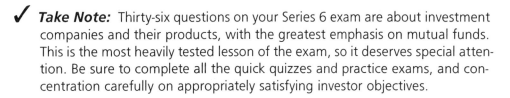

NAV	9.67
Low	− 6.96
	2.71

2.71 ÷ 6.96 = 38.93% Appreciation

- **NAV per share.** This column shows the current NAV per share, as well as the current POP.

✔ ***Take Note:*** Thirty-six questions on your Series 6 exam are about investment companies and their products, with the greatest emphasis on mutual funds. This is the most heavily tested lesson of the exam, so it deserves special attention. Be sure to complete all the quick quizzes and practice exams, and concentration carefully on appropriately satisfying investor objectives.

The highlights of this lesson are presented on the following Hotsheet.

Investment Company Products Hotsheet

Inv. Co. Act of 1940:
- Defines and regulates investment companies
- Three types: face amount certificate, unit investment trust, management company

Open-End Company:
- Mutual fund; continuous primary offering, redemption in seven calendar days, price by formula in prospectus, fractional shares

Closed-end Company:
- Trades in secondary market, issues debt and equity, fixed number of shares, sold with prospectus in IPO only

Diversified Status:
- *75 percent* invested in other companies; max of *5 percent* in any one company; can own no more than *10 percent* of a target company's voting stock
- Status applies to open- and closed-end companies

Registration Requirements:
- Minimum $100,000 capital, 100 investors, clearly defined investment objective
- Asset to debt ratio not less than 3 to 1 (300 percent)

Prohibited Investing:
- No purchases on margin, no short sales, no naked options sold

Shareholder Votes:
- Change investment objective, change sales load policy, change fund classification

Shareholder Reports:
- Annual audited report, semiannual unaudited report (two per year)

Sector Funds:
- Minimum of 25 percent of assets in area of specialty; more aggressive

Money-market Funds:
- No load, fixed NAV, check-writing privileges, daily interest

Performance History:
- 1, 5, 10 years (or fund's life if less than 10 years)

Sales Charge %:
- (POP – NAV) ÷ POP (NASD maximum of 8.5 percent of POP)

POP Calculation:
- NAV ÷ (100% – SC%)

12b-1 Charges:
- Distribution fee approved annually and charged quarterly; cannot be described as no-load fund if exceeds .25 percent.

8½% Sales Charge:
- Only if fund offers reinvestment at NAV, rights of accumulation, breakpoints

Letter of Intent:
- Must be in writing, maximum 13 months, can be backdated 90 days

Conduit Theory:
- IRC subchapter M. Fund is "regulated investment company" if it distributes a minimum of 90 percent of net investment income; fund taxed only on retained earnings.

Ex-dividend Date:
- Determined by BOD, typically business day after record date

Calculating Yield:
- Annual dividends/POP; capital gains distributions are not included.

Dollar Cost Averaging:
- Produces an average cost per share that is lower than average price per share; no guarantees allowed

Contractual Plans:
- Refunds:

  Front End Load Act
  - Before 45 days: NAV + 100% SC
  - After 45 days, before 18 months: NAV + SC exceeding 15% of investment
  - After 18 months: NAV only

  Spread Load Act
  - Before 45 days: NAV + 100% SC
  - After 45 days: NAV only

- Objectives:
- *Growth* = stock funds
- *Income* = bond funds
- *Safety of principal* = government bond funds
- *Immediate liquidity* = money market funds
- *Aggressive growth* = technology stock funds or stock funds invested in new companies, small caps
- *Conservative growth* = blue chip stock funds
- *Highest possible income with little concern for risk* = corporate bond fund
- *High tax bracket seeking income* = municipal bond fund
- *Income-producing stock* = blue chip stock fund, preferred stock fund, utility stock fund
- *Mirror performance of the stock market overall* = index fund

New Account Forms:
- Required for all accounts
- Birth date not required
- Customer signature not required for cash accounts; needed for margin accounts
- Signed by rep and approving principal

Account Approval:
- By principal, either prior to or promptly after the first transaction

Trading Authorization:	• Limited—third party can trade only • Full—third party can trade and withdraw cash and securities
Accounts for other Broker-Dealer Employees:	• NASD—prior written notification, duplicate confirms upon request only
Joint Accounts:	• All signatures required to open • Any party can trade • Distributions payable to all • Each owns undivided interest

JTWROS	JTIC
• equal ownership interest • Passes to survivor(s) at death; no probate	• unequal interests OK • Passes by will to heirs, probate

Discretionary:	• Authority from customer must be in writing • Account must be approved before the first trade • Principal must review discretionary accounts frequently for churning • Time and price not discretionary
UGMA:	• Cash accounts only • Minor is beneficial owner; minor's Social Security number on account • One minor, one custodian • No short sales, no options, no margins

Lesson 2 Practice Exam

1. From which of the following is the 12b-1 fee deducted?

   A. Public offering price of a share
   B. Difference in POP and NAV
   C. Investment advisory fee
   D. Asset value of the fund

2. A customer signs a contractual plan agreement and wants to know who the check should be made out to. You direct him to make the check payable to

   A. the mutual fund company
   B. the contractual plan company
   C. the broker-dealer firm
   D. his registered representative

3. Your customer, age 29, makes $42,000 annually and has $10,000 to invest. Although he has never invested before, he wants to invest in something "exciting." Which of the following should you suggest?

   A. An aggressive growth fund because the customer is young and has many investing years ahead
   B. A growth and income fund because the customer has never invested before
   C. A balanced fund because when the stock market is declining, the bond market will perform well
   D. Your customer should provide more information before you can make a suitable recommendation.

4. Which of the following statements regarding taxable investment company returns to investors is true?

   A. Dividend distributions are reported on IRS form 1099-DIV.
   B. Dividends are distributed quarterly and capital gains are distributed semiannually.
   C. Capital gains are generated from an investment company's net investment income.
   D. Capital gains are generated when portfolio assets are sold but not when investor shares are redeemed.

5. According to the Investment Company Act of 1940, which of the following are required to start an open-end Investment Company?

   I. $100,000 of net worth
   II. $1,000,000 of net worth
   III. 100 investors
   IV. A clearly defined investment objective

   A. I and III
   B. I, III and IV
   C. II and III
   D. II, III and IV

6. A retired individual seeking income has $200,000 to invest. Which of the following would be the LEAST suitable portfolio?

   A. Small-cap stock fund, municipal bond fund and money market fund
   B. Municipal bond fund, U.S. Treasury bond fund
   C. Small-cap stock fund, medium-cap stock fund
   D. Balanced fund, medium-cap stock fund

7. Your customer feels she is overburdened with taxes and would like relief. You discuss the Favorable Municipal Bond Fund with her and advise her of the tax treatment of the distributions. Which of the following would be correct advice?

   A. Dividends and capital gains are federally tax exempt and may even be state exempt if issues in the portfolio are issues in her state of residence.
   B. Dividends and capital gains are federally tax exempt but only the dividends may qualify for state exemption.
   C. Dividends are federally tax exempt and capital gains are subject to taxation.
   D. Both dividends and capital gains are taxable at favorable capital gains rates.

8. Which of the following statements regarding mutual fund redemption fees is correct?

   A. They are not charged by no-load funds.
   B. They are used to defray fund distribution costs.
   C. They are typically 2 percent or less of the redeemed value.
   D. They are also known as 12b-1 fees.

9. You are considering an investment in the Flying High Fund. Because you desire long-term capital appreciation, which section of the prospectus would you consult to determine if this fund is appropriate?

   A. Investment Policies and Restrictions
   B. How the Funds Are Managed
   C. Tax Treatment of Distributions
   D. The Investment Objectives

10. Who is required to sign the new account form?

   A. The customer only
   B. The registered representative only
   C. Both the principal and the registered representative
   D. The customer, the registered representative and the principal

11. Who sets a mutual fund's ex-dividend date?

   A. Its Board of Directors
   B. The shareholders
   C. The NASD
   D. The exchange on which the mutual fund trades

12. Which of the following is an advantage to a customer who invests in a contractual plan?

   A. The customer may invest with a low load.
   B. The customer may invest with small deposits.
   C. Because of plan completion insurance, a beneficiary will receive an immediate death benefit if the contract holder dies.
   D. Contractual plans are available in virtually all states.

13. A mutual fund has $3,000,000 in assets. What is the maximum amount it may borrow?

   A. $0
   B. $1,000,000
   C. $3,000,000
   D. $9,000,000

14. Amalgamated Investments is a nondiversified, closed-end investment company with assets of $20,000,000 whose shares are traded OTC. Amalgamated wishes to make an investment in Hoopla, Inc., a company worth $2,000,000. What is the maximum amount that Amalgamated can invest in Hoopla, Inc.?

   A. $100,000
   B. $200,000
   C. $1,000,000
   D. $2,000,000

15. A unit investment trust can best be described as

    I. a managed investment company
    II. a nonmanaged investment company
    III. a company that issues redeemable securities
    IV. a company that issues securities that are actively traded in the secondary marketplace

    A. I and III
    B. I and IV
    C. II and III
    D. II and IV

16. All of the following charges are included in the computation of a mutual fund's expense ratio EXCEPT

    A. fee paid to Board of Directors members
    B. sales load paid to the underwriters
    C. investment adviser fee
    D. transfer agent fee

17. A client invested in XYZ Bond mutual fund five years ago. The client took dividend distributions in cash and reinvested capital gains distributions into more shares of XYZ Bond mutual fund. Interest rates have declined over the past five years. Which of the following statements is true?

    A. The client's proportionate interest in the fund has not changed.
    B. The reinvested capital gains have accumulated tax deferred.
    C. NAV per share of XYZ Bond mutual fund increased.
    D. The dividend distributions were subject to capital gains taxation.

18. The Board of Directors of an open-ended investment company may vote to determine a change in all of the following EXCEPT

    I. the securities in the mutual fund portfolio
    II. the sponsoring underwriter
    III. the investment objective
    IV. the custodian

    A. I and III
    B. I and IV
    C. II and III
    D. II and IV

19. An XYZ open-ended bond fund advertising its returns must show all of the following EXCEPT

    A. share prices based on the highest possible sales charge
    B. current yield based on annual dividends and capital gains, divided by POP
    C. average annual total returns for 1-, 5-, and 10-year periods
    D. total returns quotations based on the most recent calendar quarter

20. How do closed-end investment companies differ from open-end investment companies?

    I. Closed-end companies register their shares with the SEC; open-end companies do not.
    II. Closed-end companies shares are sold with prospectus only in IPOs; open-end shares solicitations must always be accompanied by a prospectus.
    III. Closed-end companies issue a fixed number of shares; there is no limit on the number of shares issued by an open-end company.
    IV. Closed-end companies can only sell shares to institutional investors; open-end companies can sell to any investor.

    A. I and II only
    B. II and III only
    C. II and IV only
    D. I, II, III, and IV

21. Which of the following statements about mutual funds is NOT correct?

    A. Mutual funds are also referred to as open-end investment companies.
    B. When investors sell mutual fund shares, the shares are redeemed at their net asset value.
    C. Mutual funds can continually issue new shares.
    D. The POP of a mutual fund is the net asset value minus any sales charges.

22. Which of the following statements concerning UGMA accounts is correct?

    A. UGMAs must have only one custodian and one minor.
    B. UGMAs may have several custodians but only one minor.
    C. UGMAs may have only one custodian but several minors.
    D. UGMAs may have several custodians and several minors.

23. When a mutual fund does not assess a distribution charge, it is called a

    A. 12b-1 fund
    B. back-end load fund
    C. no-load fund
    D. level-load fund

24. What is the cost basis for mutual fund shares that are transferred at the death of the owner?

    A. The original price of purchase
    B. The current price of purchase if bought in the secondary market
    C. The net asset value of the shares at the time of transfer
    D. The net asset value of the shares at the end of tax year prior to the transfer

25. Discretionary authority is required for a registered representative to determine

    I. Which security to buy or sell
    II. The best time to enter the order
    III. The best price to execute the order
    IV. The number of shares

    A. I and IV only
    B. II and III only
    C. II and IV only
    D. I, II, III, and IV

26. Which of the following causes an increase in NAV?

    I. The fund purchases $10 million in portfolio securities.
    II. Investment income is received by the fund.
    III. The securities in the portfolio appreciate.
    IV. Capital gains are distributed by the fund.

    A. I and III only
    B. II and III only
    C. II and IV only
    D. I, II, III and IV

27. All of the following are correct regarding capital gains taxation EXCEPT

    A. A mutual fund sells a security at a profit and reinvests the capital gains. This is a realized capital gain and is a taxable event to the shareholder.
    B. A mutual fund holds a security after it has appreciated. Although it is not sold, the security's appreciation is a taxable event to the shareholder.
    C. If the fund has realized capital gains, they are typically distributed at year end and taxed as capital gains to the shareholder.
    D. Realized profits on securities held for more than 12 months are taxed as capital gains to the shareholder.

28. All of the following are true regarding joint account registration EXCEPT

    A. Customers one, two and three have a JTWROS. Each deposits funds into the account. One of the three tenants must be designated to make trades for the account.
    B. Two customers have a JTIC account. Customer one deposits $5,000 and customer two deposits $10,000 into the account. If one joint owner dies, her assets will go to her estate. Both parties can place a trade.
    C. If an account has a joint registration, distributions must be made payable to all.
    D. Two customers have a JTWROS. If one customer were to die, his shares would be assumed by the survivor.

29. Your customer is a retired widower aged 71. He is seeking a mutual fund to provide a moderate level of income in addition to his Social Security and pension. He is extremely conservative when investing and wishes to preserve capital. Which of the following funds is most suitable?

    A. Balanced fund
    B. U.S. Government Bond fund
    C. Sector fund
    D. Gold fund

30. Under NASD advertising rules, a money market mutual fund with a portfolio composed primarily of U.S. government short-term obligations and NAV that has never varied from $1.00 per share may state which of the following?

    A. The portfolio of the fund is principally invested in U.S. government short-term debt instruments and an NAV of $1.00 will be maintained.
    B. The fund has a portfolio invested primarily in short-term U.S. government debt instruments for stability of principal and regular interest. The fund's NAV has, since the inception of the fund, never varied from $1.00. The fund will make every effort to maintain the NAV at $1.00; however, past performance is not an indicator of future results.
    C. The portfolio of the fund is invested principally in U.S. government short-term debt instruments. Because these investments are guaranteed by the full faith and credit of the U.S. government, the fund provides guaranteed protection from default and loss of principal for its investors.
    D. Money market mutual funds invested primarily in U.S. Treasury bills will maintain a stability of NAV at $1.00 per share because T-Bills are guaranteed to mature at face amount and are backed by the full faith and credit of the U.S. government

31. The Acme Double-Whammy Combination fund has dual objectives of capital appreciation and current income. Last year the fund paid quarterly dividends of $.25 per share, and capital gains of $.10 per share. The annualized growth rate of the fund was 15 percent. The current net asset value (NAV) of the fund is $28.50 and the current public offering price (POP) is $30. Advertising and sales literature of the fund may report the current yield of the fund to be

   A. .83%
   B. 3.33%
   C. 3.85%
   D. 27.2%

32. Assuming that expense ratios for the funds listed are identical, rank the funds below in order, from lowest to highest yield.

   I. Municipal bond fund
   II. Government bond fund
   III. Corporate bond fund

   A. I, II, III
   B. I, III, II
   C. II, I, III
   D. III, II, I

33. Which of the following statements about dollar cost averaging is true?

   A. It is effective if smaller dollar purchases are made when the market prices rise.
   B. When the market fluctuates it will result in a lower average cost per share.
   C. It will protect investors from losses in a falling market.
   D. It is most effective when the market remains constant.

34. A shareholder has redeemed some mutual fund shares that were purchased over a period of 10 years. If the shareholder has not indicated on his tax return the specific dates of purchase and cost of the shares that were redeemed, the IRS will follow which of the following methods in determining the cost basis of shares redeemed?

   A. Average cost of purchase
   B. FIFO
   C. LIFO
   D. Step up in basis

35. The total return of a mutual fund is equal to

   A. the return attained by reinvestment of all dividend and capital gains distributions
   B. annualized fund dividends divided by the current POP
   C. all realized and unrealized capital appreciation
   D. the reinvestment of all unrealized dividend and capital gain income

36. Your 45 year-old client is interested in obtaining the highest current income possible from his investment. He is willing to accept fluctuations in investment principal. Which of the following would best suit this client's investment objective?

   A. High yield bond fund
   B. Aggressive growth fund
   C. Tax-free money-market fund
   D. Balanced fund

Answers and Rationale

1. **D.** A 12b-1 fee is charged against the asset value of the fund and is based on a percentage of the average annual assets. (Page 147) [18399]

2. **B.** When a customer makes payments into a contractual plan, checks are made payable to the contractual plan company. Customer checks should never be made payable to a registered representative. (Page 179) [18413]

3. **D.** It is necessary to get more information about this customer and his definitions of an "exciting" investment opportunity before making any recommendations. A thorough suitability and risk tolerance analysis should be performed before a recommendation is made. (Page 167) [18416]

4. **A.** Investment company distributions are reported to shareholders on IRS form 1099-DIV. Dividends are paid as declared by the Board of Directors; capital gains are paid annually. Dividends, not capital gains, are paid from the company's net investment income. Capital gains are generated when an investor redeems appreciated shares of the investment company. (Page 158) [18424]

5. **B.** To start an investment company the Investment Company Act of 1940 requires $100,000 of net assets, 100 investors and a clearly defined investment objective. (Page 121) [18429]

6. **C.** A retired individual who requires income should invest in bond or blue-chip stock funds, not growth. Remember this question asks for the least appropriate choice. (Page 136) [18434]

7. **C.** Dividends from municipal bond funds are tax-exempt because they represent tax-exempt interest paid to the portfolio. Capital gains distributions are taxable. (Page 137) [18435]

8. **C.** Redemption fees are charged by some mutual funds when investors sell back shares to the fund. They are usually 2 percent or less of the redemption value of all the fund shares. They may be charged by no-load funds, typically as a means of discouraging frequent switching of fund choices. 12b-1 fees are a separate charge against the net asset value for fund distribution costs. (Page 153) [18438]

9. **D.** Of the prospectus sections listed, the Investment Objectives section is the fund's goals for trading the portfolio. (Page 135) [18448]

10. **C.** Both the registered representative and the principal are required to sign the new account form (sometimes called the new account card). The representative signs to introduce the new account to the firm. The principal signs to accept the account on the firm's behalf. The customer is NOT required to sign the new account form. (Page 165) [18452]

11. **A.** A mutual fund's ex-dividend date is established by its board of directors. An NASD rule governs the ex-dividend date for stock and certain closed-end funds. Mutual funds do not trade on exchanges. Shareholders have no voice in matters regarding dividend distributions. (Page 160) [18454]

12. **B.** The opportunity to invest with small deposit amounts is an advantage of contractual plans. Contractual plans do not offer low loads; their average lifetime loads are higher than those of traditional mutual funds, with first-year loads as high as 50 percent under certain plans. Plan completion insurance operates to ensure that the plan is completed, and thus provides no immediate death benefit to a beneficiary. Because many state securities departments will not register contractual plans, they are not available in all states. (Page 179) [18456]

13. **B.** The Investment Company Act of 1940 mandates that a mutual fund must have $3 of assets for each $1 it borrows. (Page 122) [18461]

14. **D.** Amalgamated can purchase all of Hoopla, Inc. ($2,000,000). A nondiversified company is not subject to the 75/5/10 rule of diversification for management companies.
(Page 119) [18462]

15. **C.** A unit investment trust is a nonmanaged investment company that issues redeemable securities. There is no active investment manager, which means that once the securities for the trust have been selected they are held. UIT units do not trade in the secondary marketplace.
(Page 115) [18467]

16. **B.** The expense ratio of a mutual fund is calculated by dividing the expenses of the fund by the fund's average net assets. Fund expenses include the fee paid to Board of Directors members, the investment adviser's fee, the custodian's fee, the transfer agent's fee and 12b-1 distribution charges. The sales load paid to the underwriters is not an expense of the fund. (Page 142) [18468]

17. **C.** When interest rates decline, bond prices increase. The increased value of bonds in the portfolio causes an increase in the NAV. The client's ownership interest in the fund decreased as dividend distributions were received in cash. The dividend distributions were taxable each year as ordinary income. Reinvested capital gains or dividends are currently taxable. Earnings in mutual fund portfolios do not accumulate tax deferred.
(Page 158) [18473]

18. **A.** Changes in the mutual fund portfolio are determined by the investment adviser. A change in the fund's investment objective must be approved by a majority of outstanding shares. The Board of Directors may change the sponsoring underwriter and custodian. (Page 121) [18480]

19. **B.** Current yield is calculated by dividing annual dividends by the POP; capital gains are not included. Advertising must reflect the highest possible sales charge (no breakpoints) and average annual total returns for one-, five- and ten-year periods (or since inception if a new fund). It must base total return quotations on the most recent calendar quarter returns. (Page 159) [18484]

20. **B.** Closed-end companies issue a fixed number of shares, whereas open-end companies do not specify the number of shares to be issued. Both types of companies register issues with the SEC, and any investor can invest in both types of company shares. (Page 116) [18486]

21. **D.** Mutual funds, or open-end investment companies, can continually issue new shares. Mutual fund shares are sold or redeemed at the net asset value next calculated. Each share's price of purchase (POP) is based on the net asset value of each share PLUS sales charges. (Page 117)[18487]

22. **A.** An UGMA account may have only one custodian as a trustee for the account of one minor. Multiple custodians or minors are not permitted.
(Page 174) [18488]

23. **C.** No-load funds do not assess a fee for sales or distribution of fund shares. Front-end loads are deducted when shares are purchased; back-end loads are charged when shares are sold; an annual asset-based percentage is deducted if the fund operates with a level-load.
(Page 138) [18489]

24. **C.** The cost basis for shares transferred at death is the net asset value of the shares at the time of transfer, also called the fair market value.
(Page 163) [18491]

25. **A.** Discretionary authority allows the registered representative to choose which security, the number of shares, and whether to buy or sell. Deciding the best time and the best price are NOT discretionary actions. (Page 172) [18493]

26. **B.** Dividends and interest received by the fund and appreciation of the portfolio cause an increase in NAV. The purchase of securities with cash results in no change of NAV because the outlay of cash is offset by the increased value of portfolio securities. Any distributed by the fund would cause a decrease in NAV. (Page 145) [18496]

27. **B.** An unrealized capital gain results in an increase in NAV but is not taxable to the share-

holder until it is realized, or sold.
(Page 157) [18497]

28. **A.** A joint account registration allows all tenants to place trades, regardless of their contributions. In JTIC account, the interest of a deceased tenant passes to the estate; in a JTWROS account the interest of the deceased passes to the surviving tenant. (Page 171) [18501]

29. **B.** A U.S. government bond fund is the safest alternative and would preserve capital. Sector and gold funds are speculative. Balanced funds do not necessarily preserve capital because of stock within the portfolio. (Page 137) [18502]

30. **B.** Even when fully invested in U.S. government securities, money-market mutual funds are specifically prohibited from implying a government guarantee or insurance on their portfolios. The principal value of these instruments is continually subject to market value fluctuation. Mutual funds may state their past performance history with the caveat that past performance is not an indicator of future results. (Page 138) [18511]

31. **B.** According to NASD rules, current yield on a mutual fund is the annualized dividend divided by the POP. Gains and growth cannot be included when advertising current yield. The current yield of 3.33 percent is calculated as follows: ($.25 × 4) ÷ $30. = .3333 × 100 = 3.33%. (Page 159) [18512]

32. **C.** Corporate bonds have the greatest amount of credit risk and, therefore, the highest yield. Government bond funds yield more than municipal bond funds because interest paid on government bonds is taxable. (Page 137) [18547]

33. **B.** Dollar cost averaging is effective when the market price of securities is fluctuating and investors continue to invest a fixed amount of money every period. Under these circumstances, the average cost per share is lower than the average price that would have been paid for shares over the same period. Dollar cost averaging is not effective in a constant market and does not protect investors from loss in a falling market.
(Page 178) [18550]

34. **B.** If another method is not indicated on an investor's tax return, the IRS will assume the FIFO (first in, first out) method of accounting in determining the cost basis of the shares redeemed. Investors may choose to identify shares redeemed only if the cost of the shares and the date of purchase is recorded on the tax return. The average method is applied when all shares are redeemed.
(Page 162) [18565]

35. **A.** The calculation of a fund's total return assumes reinvestment of the all dividend distributions, capital gains distributions and appreciation.
(Page 159) [18587]

36. **A.** Because this investor's objective is income, a bond fund is suitable. Investors who are willing to accept risk and who are interested in high income should invest in corporate bond funds with some risk of principal. These bond funds are known as high yield corporate bond funds. (Page 135) [18602]

Variable Contracts and Retirement Plans

OVERVIEW

Variable annuities and variable life insurance have become popular tools in retirement and estate planning. Series 6 registered representatives frequently assist clients with various types of qualified and nonqualified plans to meet retirement goals. Variable products are popular products for meeting these needs, but may only be sold if representatives are also insurance licensed.

The Series 6 exam will ask 16 questions on these topics. After completion of this lesson, you should be able to:

- List the similarities between variable annuities and mutual funds
- Describe the phases of the annuity contract
- Determine fluctuations in monthly payouts based on comparison of the assumed interest rate (AIR) and separate account rate of return
- Describe the taxation of annuity withdrawals
- Differentiate the features of traditional whole life, variable life and universal variable life policies
- Describe the impact of the AIR on variable life death benefit and cash value accumulation
- Describe the 1035 Exchange provision
- Compare and contrast the features of qualified and nonqualified plans
- Identify eligibility and contribution rules for Individual Retirement Accounts, Keoghs and 403(b) plans
- List penalties that affect retirement plan investors
- Specify ERISA guidelines for the regulation of retirement plans

Annuity Plans

An annuity is a life insurance company product that was designed to provide supplemental retirement income. The term *annuity* specifically refers to a stream of income payments that is guaranteed for life. Because of the guarantee, this product is unique from other securities products that have been discussed.

Types of Annuity Contracts

Life insurance companies offer two basic annuity products: fixed annuities and variable annuities.

Both products require that the purchaser make deposits to the insurance company, either in a lump sum or over a period of time, and then at some point begin to withdraw the funds. Although designed to provide monthly income for the life of the annuitant, withdrawals are frequently taken in lump sums or random withdrawals.

Fixed Annuities In a fixed annuity, investors pay premiums to the insurance company that are invested in the company's general account. The insurance company is then obligated to pay a guaranteed amount of payout (typically monthly) to the annuitant based on how much was paid in. Note that the insurer guarantees a rate of return and, therefore, bears the investment risk. Because the insurer is at risk, this product is not a security. An insurance license, but not a securities registration, is required to sell fixed annuities.

A significant risk is associated with fixed annuities: purchasing power risk. The fixed payment that the annuitant receives loses buying power over time due to inflation.

 Take Note: To understand the risk of the fixed annuity, consider the following example:

An individual who purchased a fixed annuity in 1960 began to receive monthly income of $375 in 1980. Years later this amount, which seemed a sufficient monthly income at the time, is no longer enough income to live on.

Variable Annuities Insurance companies introduced the variable annuity as an opportunity to keep pace with inflation. For this potential advantage, the investor assumes the investment risk rather than the insurance company. Because the investor takes on this risk, the product is considered a security. It must be sold with a prospectus and by individuals who are both insurance licensed and registered representatives.

FIGURE 3.1   Fixed Annuity

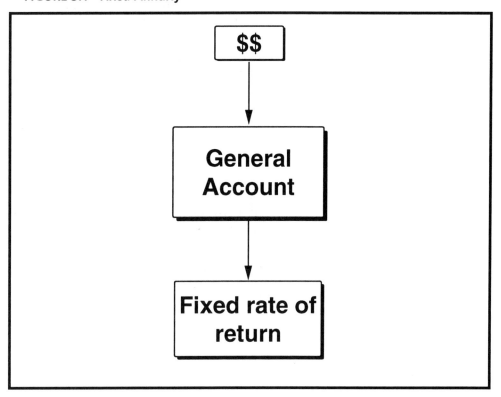

FIGURE 3.2   Variable Annuity

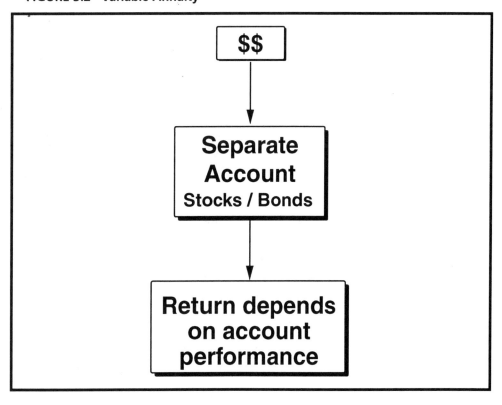

As with a fixed annuity, the purchaser makes payments to the insurer. However, the premium payments for variable annuities are invested in the *separate account* of the insurer. This account is separated from the general funds of the insurer because it is invested differently. Investments include common stock, bonds and mutual funds, with the objective of achieving growth that will match or exceed the rate of inflation. Although annuitants are guaranteed monthly income for life, the amount of monthly income received is dependent on the performance of the separate account. Monthly income either increases or decreases, as determined by the separate account's performance.

Investors may purchase a combination annuity to receive the advantages of both the fixed and variable annuities. In a combination annuity, the investor contributes to both the general and separate accounts, which provides for guaranteed payments as well as inflation protection.

FIGURE 3.3   Investing Variable Annuity Premium Dollars

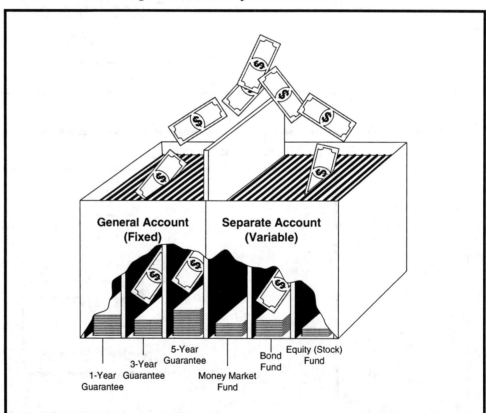

The key features of both products are summarized in Table 3.1.

Table 3.1 Key Features of Fixed Annuities and Variable Annuities

	Fixed Annuity	*Variable Annuity*
Payments made with:	after-tax dollars	after-tax dollars
Payments invested in:	the general account	the separate account
Portfolio of:	fixed income securities and real estate	equity, debt, or mutual funds
Who assumes the investment risk?	Insurer	Annuitant
Is it a security?	No	Yes
Rate of Return:	Guaranteed	Depends on performance of separate account
Administrative Expenses are:	Fixed	Fixed
Income Guaranteed:	for life	for life
Monthly Payments:	never fall below guaranteed minimum	may fluctuate up or down
Purchasing Power Risk Protection?	Yes	typically provides some protection
Regulation	Subject to insurance regulation	Subject to insurance & securities regulation

Comparison of Mutual Funds and Variable Annuities

As described previously, the separate account of the variable annuity consists of the purchasers' funds pooled together and is invested in a diversified portfolio of stocks, bonds and mutual funds. Investors own a proportionate share of these securities, and the value of their shares rises and falls based on the performance of the securities in the pool. This is precisely how mutual funds perform; the separate account of a variable annuity is operated and regulated just like a mutual fund. Consider the comparison in Table 3.2.

If the investment manager of an insurance company is responsible for selecting the securities to be held within the separate account, the separate account is *directly managed* and must be registered under the Investment Company Act of 1940 as an open-end management investment company. However, if the investment manager of the insurance company passes the portfolio management responsibility to another party, the separate account is *indirectly managed* and must be registered as a Unit Investment Trust under the Act of 1940.

TABLE 3.2   Mutual Funds vs. Variable Annuities

	Mutual Fund	Variable Annuity
Sales Load	8 1/2% max, 9% for contractual plans	8 1/2% max
Pricing	NAV calculated once per business days	Unit value calculated once per business day
Share Value	Depends on performance of fund	Depends on performance of separate account
Regulated by	Act of 1933 Act of 1934	Act of 1933 Act of 1934
	Investment Company Act of 1940	Investment Company Act of 1940
	Investment Advisor's Act of 1940	Investment Advisor's Act of 1940
	(portfolio manager receives fee)	(Separate account manager receives fee)

Although there are many similarities in mutual funds and variable annuities, there are *two* extremely significant features that differentiate the two products. *The earnings on dollars invested into a variable annuity accumulate tax deferred.* Mutual funds periodically distribute dividends and capital gains, and all of these distributions are typically taxable upon receipt. Such distributions are never paid directly to owners of annuities; instead, they increase the value of units in the separate account. Tax liability is postponed until withdrawals take place. This feature of tax-deferred growth has established the annuity as a popular product for retirement accumulation. As with other retirement products, if withdrawals are made prior to age 59½, a 10 percent penalty is applied to the earnings.

The second unique feature of a variable annuity is that it offers the advantage of guaranteed lifetime income. Mutual fund shareholders are offered no guarantees on income provided.

 Take Note: Remember the similarity of annuities and mutual funds when you take the Series 6 exam. In fact, if an annuity question stumps you, try substituting the term *mutual fund* for variable annuity before you give up! For practice, try these Quick Quiz questions.

Quick Quiz 3.1

1. Which of the following represent rights of an investor who has purchased a variable annuity?

    I.   Right to vote on proposed changes in investment policy
    II. Right to approve changes in the plan portfolio
    III. Right to vote for the investment adviser
    IV. Right to make additional purchases at no sales charge

    A. I and III
    B. I and IV
    C. II and III
    D. II and IV

2. Which of the following statements are true regarding both variable annuities and mutual funds?

    I.   They contain managed portfolios.
    II. An owner's account value typically passes to his estate at the time of his death.
    III. They are regulated by the Investment Company Act of 1940.
    IV. All investment income and realized capital gains are taxable to the owner in the year they are generated.

    A. I and III
    B. I and IV
    C. II and III
    D. II and IV

See page 338 for answers and rationale

✓ **Take Note:** It is also critical that you remember the unique tax feature of variable annuities: *Earnings accumulate tax-deferred.* Because of this feature, brokerage firms, banks and insurance companies sell a lot of annuities.

Quick Quiz 3.2

1. What has the greatest effect on the value of annuity units in a variable annuity?

    A. Changes in the Standard & Poor's index
    B. Cost-of-living index
    C. Fluctuations in the securities held in the separate account
    D. Changes in stock market prices

2. Variable annuity salespeople must register with the

    I.   SEC
    II. state banking commission
    III. NASD
    IV. state insurance department

    A. I, II and III
    B. I and III
    C. I, III and IV
    D. II and IV

3. A variable annuity contract guarantees a

    I.   rate of return
    II. fixed mortality expense
    III. fixed administrative expense

    A. I and II only
    B. I and III only
    C. II and III only
    D. I, II and III

4. Separate accounts are similar to mutual funds in that both

    I.   may have diversified portfolios of common stock
    II. are managed by full-time professionals
    III. give investors voting rights

    A. I and II only
    B. I and III only
    C. II and III only
    D. I, II and III

5. Which of the following information must be included in a prospectus describing variable annuities to clients?

    I.   Summary explanation in nontechnical terms of the contract's principal features
    II. Statement of the separate account's investment policy
    III. Statement of the separate account's net investment return for the past 10 years
    IV. Statement of the deductions and charges against the gross premium, including all commissions paid to agents for each policy year the commissions are to be paid

    A. I and II only
    B. I, II and III only
    C. III and IV only
    D. I, II, III and IV

See page 338 for answers and rationale.

Purchasing Annuities   An investor is offered a number of options when purchasing an annuity. Payments to the insurance company can either be made with a single lump-sum investment, or periodically on a monthly, quarterly or annual basis.

A *single premium deferred annuity* is purchased with a lump sum, but payment of benefits is delayed until a later date selected by the annuitant.

A *periodic payment deferred annuity* allows investments over time. Benefit payments for this type of annuity are always deferred until a later date selected by the annuitant.

An *immediate annuity* is purchased with a lump sum, and the payout of benefits usually commences within 60 days.

 **Test Topic Alert!**   Remember for a test question that there is no such thing as an *immediate deferred annuity*!

Accumulation Stage   The variable annuity has two distinct phases. The growth phase is its *accumulation phase*, while the payout phase is its *annuity phase*. A contract owner's interest in the separate account is known as either accumulation units or annuity units depending on the contract phase. Both accumulation units and annuity units vary in value based on the separate account's performance.

At some point, the annuitant may begin to take income from the account. This is known as the *annuitization* of the contract. Technically, the value of the accumulation units is converted into a fixed number of annuity units. These annuity units are then used to provide monthly income guaranteed for the life of the annuitant.

FIGURE 3.4   Annuitization

Annuitization

Accumulation Phase	Annuity Phase
Accumulation Units	Annuity Units

Receiving Distribution from Annuities

Annuity Payout Options   An annuity offers several payment options for money accumulated in the contract. The investor can withdraw the funds randomly, in a lump sum or annuitize the contract (receive monthly income).

If annuitization is chosen, the actuarial department of the insurance company determines the initial value for the annuity units and the amount of the first month's annuity payment. At this time, an *assumed interest rate* (AIR) is established. The AIR is a conservative projection of the performance of the separate account over the estimated life of the contract. It is only relevant in the annuity phase of the contract.

The value of each annuity unit and the annuitant's subsequent monthly income will vary, depending on separate account performance as compared to the AIR. To determine whether the monthly income will increase, decrease or stay the same as the previous month, the following rules are applied:

- If separate account performance is greater than the AIR, the monthly income is more than the previous month's payment
- If separate account performance is equal to the AIR, the monthly income stays the same as the previous month's payment
- If separate account performance is less than the AIR, the monthly income is less than the previous month's payment

✓ **Take Note:** Although the AIR formula sounds logical, sometimes it can be confusing when you look at the numbers. Let's try an example—remember to follow the rules you just learned!

Assume an AIR of 4 percent. Assume also that the actuaries have determined the first month's payment to be $1,000.

Month 2: Separate account performance is 8 percent. Does monthly income go up, go down or stay the same?

The monthly payment goes up! Remember, you must compare the 8 percent rate of the separate account to the AIR. Since 8 percent is greater than 4 percent, the payment increases. Don't worry about the amount of the increase—it is actuarially determined. For illustrative purposes, we'll pretend it goes up to $1,100.

Month 3: Separate account performance drops to 6 percent. Does monthly income go up, go down or stay the same?

Although you might be tempted to say "goes down," because the separate account performance fell, the payment still increases. The separate account return is greater than the 4 percent AIR. We'll pretend the monthly payment increases to $1,200.

Month 4: Separate account performance is 4 percent. What happens to monthly income?

According to the rules, when separate account performance equals the AIR, the monthly income does not change. The monthly income amount is $1,200.

Month 5: Separate account performance is 3 percent. What happens to monthly income?

You're correct if you're thinking that it falls. When the separate account return is less than the AIR the monthly income is lower than the previous month. We'll pretend it drops to $1,100.

Month 6: Separate account performance is 3 percent again. What happens to monthly income?

	Month 1	Month 2	Month 3	Month 4	Month 5	Month 6
AIR	4%	4%	4%	4%	4%	4%
Separate Account Return	0	8%	6%	4%	3%	3%
Monthly Payment	$1000	$1100	$1200	$1200	$1100	$1000

Don't be tempted to say that it stays the same as the previous month! Yes, the separate account performance did not change, but you must follow the AIR rule. Because the separate account return is less than the AIR, the monthly income decreases.

Do you think you've mastered the AIR concept? Complete the Quick Quiz to be sure.

Quick Quiz 3.3

1. A customer invests in a variable annuity. At age 65, she chooses to annuitize. Under these circumstances, which of the following statements are true?

   I. She will receive the annuity's entire value in a lump-sum payment.
   II. She may choose to receive monthly payments for the rest of her life.
   III. The accumulation unit's value is used to calculate the total number of annuity units.
   IV. The accumulation unit's value is used to calculate the annuity unit's value.

   A. I and III
   B. I and IV
   C. II and III
   D. II and IV

2. An investor is in the annuity period of a variable annuity purchased 15 years ago. During the present month, the annuitant receives a check for an amount that is less than the previous month's payment. Which of the following events caused the annuitant to receive the smaller check?

   A. The account's performance was less than the previous month's performance.
   B. The account's performance was greater than the previous month's performance.
   C. The account's performance was less than the assumed interest rate.
   D. The account's performance was greater than the assumed interest rate.

3. An insurance company offering a variable annuity makes payments to annuitants on the 15th of each month. The contract has an assumed interest rate of 3 percent. In July of this year, the contract earned 4 percent. In August the account earned 6 percent. If the contract earns 3 percent in September, the payments to annuitants will be

   A. greater than the payments in August
   B. less than the payments in August
   C. the same as the payments in August
   D. less than the payments in July

See page 338 for answers and rational.

Annuity Payout Options

At the time of annuitization, the annuitant is required to select an annuity payout option. The choices that are tested on Series 6 are:

- Life income
- Life with period certain
- Joint and last survivor

Life annuity/straight life. If an annuitant selects the life income option, the insurance company will pay the annuitant for life. When the annuitant dies, there are no continuing payments to a beneficiary.

✓ **Take Note:** This probably wouldn't have been a good choice if the annuitant died after receiving only one month's payment! With the life income option, all money accumulated that wasn't paid out at the time of the annuitant's death would belong to the insurer.

The following options are a little less risky because they allow for payments to a beneficiary.

Life annuity with period certain. To guarantee that a minimum number of payments are made even if the annuitant dies, the life with period certain option can be chosen. The contract will specifically allow the choice of a period of 10 or 20 years, for example. The length of the period certain is a choice that is made when a payout option is selected. The annuitant is guaranteed monthly income for life with this option, but if death occurs within the period certain, a named beneficiary receives payments for the remainder of the period.

✔ *Take Note:* To illustrate this option, assume a client selects a life annuity with a 10-year period certain. If the annuitant lives to be 150 years old, annuity payments are still made by the insurer. But, if the annuitant dies after receiving payments for two years, the beneficiary will receive payments for eight more years.

Joint life with last survivor annuity. The joint life with last survivor option guarantees payments over two lives. It is often used for husbands and wives. If the husband were to die first, his wife would continue to receive payments as long as she lives. If the wife were to die first, the husband would receive payments as long as he lives.

 **Test Topic Alert!** There is a risk-reward trade-off with these payout options. The test is likely to look at payout options in questions similar to the following:

Which of the following annuity options typically pays the largest monthly income?

A. Life only
B. Joint life with last survivor
C. Life with 10-year period certain
D. Contingent deferred option

A. Life only. Remember that there is no beneficiary with this option. Greater risk means greater reward

Are you puzzled about the Contingent deferred option in Choice D? Frequently the test will tempt you with distracters that really sound good. If you haven't seen the term before, don't choose the answer. The important terms will have been discussed in your lessons.

One more question:

Which of the following annuity options is likely to provide the smallest monthly income?

A. Life only
B. Joint life with last survivor
C. Life with 10-year period certain
D. Life with 20-year period certain

B. Joint life with last survivor. There is a cost in monthly income amount for the guarantee on two lives.

✎ **Quick Quiz 3.4** Match each of the following terms with the appropriate description.

A. Accumulation unit
B. Joint and last survivor annuity
C. Deferred annuity
D. Variable annuity

____ 1. Delays distributions until the owner elects to receive them

____ 2. Determines an annuitant's interest in the insurer's separate account during accumulation stage of an annuity

____ 3. Performance of a separate account determines value

____ 4. Annuity payments continue as long as one of the annuitants remains alive

Match each of the following terms with the appropriate description.

A. Assumed interest rate
B. Immediate annuity
C. Life income with period certain
D. Separate account

____ 5. Contract starts to pay the annuitant immediately following its purchase

____ 6. Forms the basis for projected annuity payments, but is not guaranteed

____ 7. Holds funds paid by variable annuity contract holders

____ 8. If the annuitant dies before a specified time expires, payments go to the annuitant's named beneficiary.

See page 339 for answers.

Taxation of Annuities

All contributions to annuities are made with after-tax dollars, unless the annuity is part of a qualified retirement plan. When contributions are made with after-tax dollars, these already taxed dollars are considered the investor's cost basis and are not taxed when withdrawn. The earnings in excess of the cost basis are taxed as ordinary income when withdrawn.

✔ **Take Note:** Always assume that the annuity is nonqualified unless the question specifically states otherwise. Let's take a look at an example.

Assume that an investor has contributed $100,000 to a variable annuity. The annuity is now worth $150,000. Two questions: What is the investor's cost basis, and what amount is taxable upon withdrawal?

Because this is a nonqualified annuity, contributions were made with after-tax dollars. The cost basis is equal to the contributions, so $100,000 is the answer to the first question. The taxable amount at withdrawal will be the earnings of $50,000.

Because annuities are designed to supplement retirement income and provide tax-deferred growth, withdrawals before age 59½ are subject to the 10 percent early withdrawal penalty and ordinary income tax like other retirement plans.

When an investor chooses to annuitize or selects a monthly income payout option, each month's payment is considered partly a return of cost basis and partly earnings. Only the earnings portion is taxable. The amount of each payment considered a return of cost basis is determined by dividing the annuity owner's cost basis by the annuitant's life expectancy.

 **Test Topic Alert!**   You will *not* be asked to calculate the amount of each annuity payment that is taxable or nontaxable. However, you may be asked a question similar to the following:

The amount of each month's annuity payment that is considered by the IRS as a return of cost basis is determined by which of the following calculations?

A. LIFO
B. FIFO
C. Cost basis divided by life expectancy
D. Income averaging

The correct answer is C. The calculation that is made to identify the portion of each month's income that is a return of the after-tax dollars invested (the investor's cost basis) is:

Annuity owner's cost basis ÷ Annuitant's life expectancy.

Many contract owners choose lump-sum or random withdrawals over the annuity option. If either of these choices is made, *last-in, first-out* (LIFO) taxation applies. The IRS requires that all earnings are withdrawn first, and are taxed at ordinary income rates. After earnings are completely withdrawn there is no additional taxation, because the cost basis has already been taxed.

✓ *Take Note:* Let's go back to our previous example:

> Assume: $100,000 after-tax contributions (cost basis)
> $50,000 earnings
> $150,000 total account value

If the investor makes a random withdrawal of $60,000, what are the tax consequences?

Remember that LIFO applies—the IRS wants tax revenue as early as possible! Those earnings that accumulated tax deferred are now fully taxable.

The investor must pay ordinary income taxes on the first $50,000 withdrawn, because that is the amount of earnings. And, if the investor is under age 59½, an extra 10 percent early withdrawal tax applies—ouch! The remaining $10,000 is a return of the cost basis and is not taxed.

By the way, any answer choice that mentions capital gains taxation on annuities or retirement plans is WRONG! There is only ordinary income tax on distributions from annuities and retirement plans.

🖉 **Quick Quiz 3.5**

1. Ms. Charolais purchases a nonqualified variable annuity at age 60. Before the contract is annuitized, she withdraws some of her funds. What are the consequences?

    A. 10 percent penalty plus payment of ordinary income on all funds withdrawn
    B. 10 percent penalty plus payment of ordinary income on all funds withdrawn in excess of basis
    C. Capital gains tax on earnings in excess of basis
    D. Ordinary income tax on earnings in excess of basis

2. Distributions from both an IRA and a variable annuity are subject to which of the following forms of taxation?

    A. Short-term capital gains
    B. Long-term capital gains
    C. Ordinary income
    D. No tax is due.

3. What is the capital gains tax rate that an individual pays on appreciation in the reserves held for his variable annuity in a separate account while the contract is in the accumulation period?

A. 0 percent
B. 10 percent
C. 25 percent
D. 50 percent

See page 339 for answers and rationale.

The Table 3.3 summarizes the tax treatment of annuity contracts.

TABLE 3.3   Effects of Investment Returns on Annuity Payouts

IF the realized rate of return:	THEN the value of the annuity unit:	AND the payout in relation to the previous payout:
Increases above AIR	Increases	Increases
Decreases below AIR	Decreases	Decreases
Stays the same as AIR	Stays the same	Stays the same

 **Test Topic Alert!**   The test may ask a question about taxation of early withdrawals or surrender of the contract before annuitization similar to the following:

An annuity contract owner, age 45, surrenders his annuity to buy a home. Which of the following statements best describes the tax consequences of this action?

A. Ordinary income taxes and a 10 percent early withdrawal penalty will apply to all money withdrawn
B. Capital gains tax will apply to the amount of the withdrawal that represents earnings; there will be no tax on the cost basis
C. Ordinary income taxes and a 10 percent early withdrawal penalty will apply to the amount of the withdrawal that represents earnings; there will be no tax on the cost basis
D. Ordinary income taxes apply to the amount of the withdrawal that represents earnings; the 10 percent early withdrawal penalty does not apply to surrenders.

    C. Interest earnings are always withdrawn first and are taxable as ordinary income. They are also subject to the 10 percent early withdrawal penalty when withdrawn prior to age 59½. Note that this tax treatment is no different than random or lump-sum withdrawal tax treatment.

Another potential tax question follows:

After the death of the annuitant, beneficiaries under a life and 15-year period certain option are subject to

    A. capital gains taxation on the total amount of payments received
    B. ordinary income taxation on the total amount of payments received, plus a 10 percent withdrawal penalty if the annuitant was under the age of 59½
    C. ordinary income taxation on the amount of the payment that exceeds the cost basis
    D. tax-free payout of all remaining annuity benefits

    C. Payments from the annuity to the beneficiary through a period certain option are taxed in the same way as all other annuity payments: benefits over the amount of the cost basis are taxable as ordinary income. However, no 10 percent penalty applies in this situation.

Life Insurance

A life insurance policy is a contract between an insurance company and an individual that is designed to provide financial compensation to the policy owner's beneficiaries in the event of the policy owner's death.

Many types of life insurance contracts are available; each type serves a different need. We will focus on those contracts that use separate accounts to fund the death benefits and that are considered "securities," as defined by the Securities Act of 1933.

Whole Life Insurance   Also known as permanent or cash value insurance, whole life insurance (WLI) provides protection for the "whole of life." Coverage begins on the date of issue and continues to the date of the insured's death, provided the premiums are paid. The benefit payable is the face amount of the policy, which remains constant throughout the policy's life. The premium is set at the time of the policy's issue and it, too, remains level for the policy's life.

Cash Values

Unlike term insurance, which provides only a death benefit, whole life insurance combines a death benefit with an accumulation, or a savings element. This accumulation, commonly referred to as the policy's cash value, increases each year the policy is kept in force. In traditional whole life insurance, the insurer invests reserves in conservative investments (for example, bonds, real estate, mortgage loans and so on). Because of the low risk of such investments, the insurer can guarantee the policy's cash value and the non-forfeiture options that are based on that cash value. Traditional life insurance reserves are held in the insurer's general accounts.

Universal Life Insurance

Universal life insurance (ULI) is a variation of whole life insurance, but it is considerably more flexible. Unlike whole life, ULI allows a policyowner to determine the amount and frequency of the premium payments and to adjust the policy face amount up or down to reflect changes in needs. As premiums are paid and cash values accumulate, interest is credited to the policy's cash value account. As long as the cash value account is sufficient to pay the monthly mortality and expense costs, the policy continues in force, whether or not the owner pays the premium. Of course, premium payments must be large enough and frequent enough to generate sufficient cash values. If the cash value account does not support the monthly deductions, the policy terminates.

Variable Life Policies

Variable life has many of the characteristics of whole life insurance. The main difference is the investment of policy reserves. In variable life policies, reserves are invested in the insurer's separate account, but the policyowner provides direction as to the investment choices. Policyowners may choose among common stock, bonds, money markets and other types of securities.

Cash value in the policy fluctuates with the performance of the separate account and is not guaranteed. Variable life policies provide policyowners with a minimum guaranteed death benefit. The benefit may increase above this minimum amount depending on investment results but can never fall below.

 Take Note: Note that because a variable life insurance policy has a *minimum death benefit*, the premiums necessary to fund this part of the death benefit are held in the insurer's general account. Any policy benefit that is *guaranteed* is invested in the insurer's *general* account.

Any premium above what is necessary to pay for the minimum death benefit is invested in the separate account. This portion of the premium is subject to investment risk. The death benefit can grow above the minimum guaranteed amount if the separate account performs well. The death benefit will never be less than the minimum guarantee, even if the separate account performs poorly.

TABLE 3.4   Comparison of Variable Life and Whole Life Policies

Variable Life	Whole Life
Premium is level and fixed.	Premium is level and fixed.
Premium is payable for life.	Premium is payable for life.
A minimum death benefit is guaranteed; benefit may fluctuate above minimum amount.	Death benefit is guaranteed and fixed; it remains level.
Cash value is not guaranteed; depends on performance of separate account.	Cash value is guaranteed.
Premiums are held in separate account(s).	Premiums are held in general account.
Reserves are maintained in separate accounts(s).	Reserves are maintained in general account.
Expenses are paid from investment income.	Expenses are paid from investment income.

Scheduled Premiums A scheduled-premium (or fixed-premium) VLI contract is—as stated earlier—issued with a minimum guaranteed death benefit. (The premiums for some variable life contracts are flexible. This is discussed later, under "Variable Universal Life.") A scheduled-premium VLI contract's death benefit is determined at issue, and evidence of insurability is required. The premium is calculated according to the policyowner's age and sex and the policy's face amount (guaranteed amount) at issue. Once the premium has been determined and the expenses have been deducted, the net premium is invested in a separate account the policyowner selects.

Charges and Expenses Charges and expenses are deducted either from the gross premium or from the separate account. The charges and expenses must be reasonable and as described in the VLI contract. When and how they are collected is important because it affects the amount of premium that may be invested in the separate account and the separate account's investment return.

Deductions from the Premium

Deductions from the gross premium normally reduce the amount of money credited to (invested in) the separate account. The greater the deductions, the less money available for the investment base in the separate account. Charges deducted from the gross premium include:

- administrative fee;
- sales load; and
- state premium taxes.

The administrative fee is normally a one-time charge to cover the cost of processing the application.

Deductions from the Separate Account

Deductions from the separate account normally reduce the investment return payable to the policyowner. Charges deducted from the separate account include:

- mortality risk fee (cost of insurance);
- expense risk fee; and
- investment management fee.

The mortality risk fee covers the risk that the policyowner may live for a period shorter than assumed. The expense risk fee covers the risk that the costs of administering and issuing the policy may be greater than assumed.

 Take Note: The test may ask you which charges are deducted from the gross premium and which are deducted from the separate account (the net premium).

Remember the acronym S-A-S to make it simple. The charges deducted from the *gross premium* are:

- **S**ales load
- **A**dministrative fee
- **S**tate premium taxes

Any other charges, like cost of insurance, expense risk fee and investment management fee are deducted from the net premium, which is invested in the separate account.

Assumed Interest Rate and Variable Death Benefit

The death benefit payable under a VLI policy equals the guaranteed death benefit plus the variable insurance amount. The variable insurance amount is based on a cumulative total of net investment return for the policy in all prior years, and it may be positive or negative. The death benefit must be calculated at least annually.

The effect that a change in earnings has on the contract's death benefit depends on a comparison of actual account performance and the performance assumed by the insurance company. If the separate account returns are greater than the AIR, additional funds are available to the policyowner. These extra earnings are reflected in an increase in death benefit and cash value. If the separate account returns equal the AIR, actual earnings meet estimated expenses, resulting in no change in benefit levels. Should the separate account returns be less than the AIR, the contract's death benefit may decrease; however, it may never fall below the amount guaranteed at issue.

An increase in account earnings, even if the account is earning more than the AIR, may not automatically increase the contract's death benefit. If the account returns have been less than the AIR for several months, the insurance company records these negative earnings. The death benefit will not increase until the account has earned a greater amount (earnings exceeding AIR) to offset the earlier negative performance.

Cash Value   The policyowner's cash values reflect the investments held in the separate account. The individual policy's cash value must be calculated at least monthly.

The cash value, like the death benefit, may increase or decrease depending on the separate account's performance. If performance has been negative, the cash value may decrease to zero, even if the contract has been in force for several years. The cash value cannot be negative, but the insurance company keeps track of negative performance. Therefore, like the death benefit, the cash value may not increase until prior negative performance has been offset.

 Take Note: The AIR has no affect on cash value accumulation in a variable life policy. The cash value will grow whenever the separate account has positive performance.

The AIR, however, does impact the death benefit. Just remember the rules you already learned for variable annuities. The rules for the death benefits are as follows:

- If the separate account performance is greater than the AIR, the death benefit will *increase*.
- If the separate account performance is equal to the AIR, the death benefit will *stay the same.*
- If the separate account performance is less than the AIR, the death benefit will *decrease.*

 **Test Topic Alert!**   You may see a question that asks about the frequency of certain calculations associated with variable life insurance policies. You should know the following:

- *Death benefits* are calculated annually.
- *Cash value* is calculated monthly.
- *Unit values* are calculated daily.

Loans   Like traditional whole life insurance (WLI), a VLI contract allows the insured to borrow against the cash value that has accumulated in the contract. However, certain restrictions exist. Usually, the insured may borrow only a percentage of the cash value. The minimum percentage that must be made available is 75 percent after the policy has been in force for three years. If the death benefit becomes payable during the period that a loan is outstanding, the loan amount is deducted from the proceeds payable.

If an extreme decline in account value occurs during the loan's term, the policyowner is liable for maintaining a positive net cash value in the account. If the loan amount exceeds the contract's net cash value, the policyowner must repay enough of the loan to restore the cash value to a positive amount. The insurance company notifies the policyowner when the account falls below the required amount. If a positive cash value is not restored within 31 days, the insurance company has the right to terminate the contract.

 **Test Topic Alert!**   Several testable facts about policy loans are as follows:

- 75 percent of the cash value must be available for policy loan after three years.
- The insurer is never required to loan 100 percent of the cash value. Full cash value is obtained by "surrendering" the policy to the insurer.
- If due to poor separate account performance the loan exceeds the policy cash value, the policyowner must make payment to the insurer within 31 days
- If the insured dies with a loan outstanding, the death benefit is reduced by the amount of the loan

Contract Exchange   During the early stage of ownership, a policyowner has the right to exchange a VLI contract for a traditional fixed-benefit WLI contract. The length of time this exchange privilege is in effect varies from company to company, but under no circumstances can the period be less than 24 months (federal law).

The exchange is allowed without evidence of insurability. If a contract is exchanged, the new WLI policy has the same contract date and death benefit as the minimum guaranteed in the VLI contract. The premiums equal the amounts guaranteed in the new WLI contract, as if it were the original contract.

Test Topic Alert!   Two testable facts about the contract exchange provision are as follows:

- The contract exchange provision must be available for a minimum of two years.
- No medical underwriting (evidence of insurability) is required for the exchange.

Sales Charges and Refunds

The separate accounts that fund VLI contracts are defined under the Investment Company Act of 1940 as periodic payment plans. They normally operate as either front-end load or spread-load plans.

Sales Charges

The sales charges on a fixed-premium VLI contract may not exceed 9 percent of the payments to be made over the life of the contract. The contract's "life" means the lesser of 20 years or the insured's life expectancy.

Refund Provisions

The refund provisions under VLI contracts differ from the refund provisions of the Investment Company Act of 1940. The insurer must extend a free look to the policyowner for 45 days from the execution of the application or for 10 days from the time the owner receives the policy, whichever is longer.

During the free-look period, the policyowner may terminate the policy and receive all payments made. Under other periodic payment plans, the sales charge and current net asset value are refunded, which may be more or less than the payments made.

The refund provisions extend for two years from issuance of the policy. If within the two-year period the policy owner terminates participation in the contract, the insurer must refund the contract's cash value (the value calculated after the insurer receives the redemption notice) plus all sales charges deducted in excess of 30 percent in the first year of the contract and 10 percent in the second year. After the two-year period has lapsed, only the cash value need be refunded; the insurer retains all sales charges.

 **Test Topic Alert!**

Several testable facts about sales charges and refunds are as follows:

Because variable life is considered a contractual plan, the maximum sales charge over the life of the contract is 9 percent. Variable annuities have a maximum sales charge of 8½ percent.

If a policy owner wants a refund within 45 days, he or she receives *all* money paid.

Refund provisions are for two years:

- For the first year, remember the refund is sales charges in excess of 30 percent of the premiums paid plus the cash value.
- For the second year, the refund is sales charges in excess of 10 percent of the premium paid plus. the cash value.

Thereafter, the policyowner has access to the cash value only.

Voting Rights   Contract holders receive one vote per $100 of cash value funded by the separate account. As with other investment company securities, changes in investment objectives and other important matters can be accomplished only by a majority vote of the separate account's outstanding shares or by order of the state insurance commissioner. Contract holders must be given the right to vote on matters concerning separate account personnel at the first meeting of contract holders within one year of beginning operations.

Test Topic Alert!   Don't confuse the voting rights of variable annuities and variable life. Variable annuities and mutual funds are the same: one vote per unit (share). Variable life is one vote per $100 of cash value.

 Quick Quiz 3.6 Match each of the following numbers with the best description below:

A. 75
B. 24
C. 9
D. 10

____ 1. Sales charge percent of premium kept if cancellation is in the second year

____ 2. Minimum amount of cash value that must be available for a policy loan after three years

____ 3. Number of months contract exchange provision must be in place

____ 4. Maximum sales charge allowed over life of variable life contract

See page page 339 for answers.

Variable Universal Life   Variable universal life (VUL) is a flexible-premium variable life product. Sometimes referred to as universal variable life, VUL combines certain characteristics of a variable life policy, such as a variable death benefit and variable cash value, and certain characteristics of universal life, principally that the policyowner may adjust the premium payments and death benefit according to changing needs. He also can choose from one or more separate accounts with differing investment objectives to fund the VUL policy.

The policyowner may choose the premium payment schedule and, if the policy's cash value is sufficient, he can adjust the premium payments. As long as the cash value is sufficient to pay the expenses deducted from the separate account, the policy will not lapse. The cash value and, indirectly, the death

TABLE 3.5   Comparison of Variable Life and Variable Universal Life Policies

Variable Life	Variable Universal Life
Premiums are fixed as to timing and amount.	Premiums are discretionary as to timing and amount.
Fees and charges are deducted from premium payments.	Fees and charges are deducted from cash value.
Policy lapses are due to failure to pay premium.	Policy lapses are due to insufficient cash value.
Initial minimum death benefit is guaranteed based on premiums; adjustments are not allowed.	Death benefit may equal policy's face amount or face amount plus cash value; face amount cannot be less than a predetermined percentage of cash value (100% to 250%).
Investment experience does not affect premiums due.	Investment experience affects duration of policy; that is, earnings must be enough to pay for face amount.
Premiums and minimum death benefits are fixed.	Policy owner may directly adjust death benefit with additional premium or less premium, subject to policy minimums and underwriting requirements (insurability).

benefit are linked to the separate account's investment performance. Like VLI policies, VUL policies are subject to state and federal regulation.

✓ **Take Note:** Note that only variable universal life has flexible premiums. The "universal" aspect of the policy gives the policyholder complete flexibility.

Quick Quiz 3.7 Choose "W" for Whole Life, "V" for Variable Life and "U" for Universal Variable Life. More than one may apply.

____ 1. Features a stated premium

____ 2. Always has some guaranteed death benefit

___ 3. Features a guaranteed cash value

___ 4. Cash value not guaranteed

___ 5. Policy loans available

See page 339 for answers.

Tax Treatment to the Policyholder

During the life of the policy, net investment income (from dividends and interest paid to the separate account) and capital gains (both realized and unrealized) are not taxable to the policyholder. There is also no tax liability when a loan is taken against the cash value.

If the policy is surrendered, policy proceeds equal to the amount of premiums paid are tax free. The premiums paid are considered the cost basis of the policy. Any earnings over the cost basis are treated as income to the policyholder.

A death benefit that is paid to the beneficiary of a life insurance policy is exempt from federal taxation as income. However, the full amount of the policy's death benefit is includable in the estate of the deceased policyowner for federal estate tax purposes.

1035 Exchange Provision. The IRS allows variable annuity and variable life policyholders to exchange their policies without tax liability. For example, if a variable life policyholder wanted to exchange his policy to that of another company, he could transfer all values from the old policy into the new policy without recognizing any tax consequences. This 1035 Exchange provision applies to transfers from fixed policies to variable policies and vice versa. It also applies to transfers of life insurance to annuities; however, it cannot be used for transfers from an annuity to a life insurance policy.

Quick Quiz 3.8 True or False?

___ 1. Death benefit are taxable as income to beneficiaries.

___ 2. Policy death benefits are excluded from the estate of the deceased policyowner.

___ 3. The cost basis of an insurance policy is equal to the premiums paid.

_____ 4. A 1035 Exchange from an insurance policy to an annuity is not permitted.

_____ 5. A 1035 Exchange can be made between fixed and variable policies.

_____ 6. When a policy is surrendered, any earnings in excess of the cost basis are subject to taxation as capital gains.

_____ 7. Proceeds from policy loans are not taxable to the policyholder.

See page 340 for answers.

Retirement Planning

An important goal for many investors is to provide themselves with retirement income. Many individuals accomplish this through corporate retirement plans, others set up their own plans, and some have both individual and corporate retirement plans.

Nonqualified Retirement Plans

Retirement plans are categorized as *qualified* or *nonqualified*. The primary difference between the two types is whether or not the contributions are tax deductible. Both plans allow tax-deferred growth on earnings attributable to plan contributions.

Table 3.6 summarizes the important features of qualified and nonqualified plans.

Types of Plans   Deferred compensation and payroll deduction programs are two types of nonqualified retirement plans. Both plans may be used to favor certain employees (typically executives) because nondiscrimination rules are not applicable to nonqualified plans.

✔ *Take Note:* When a plan is *nondiscriminatory*, it means that all persons that meet certain criteria must be eligible to participate. In a *discriminatory* plan, the employer can choose to provide benefits to certain employees but exclude others.

A nonqualified deferred compensation plan is a contractual agreement between a company and an employee, in which the employee agrees to defer receipt of current income in favor of payout at retirement. It is assumed that the employee will be in a lower tax bracket at retirement age. These plans are

TABLE 3.6 Qualified vs. Nonqualified Plans

Qualified Plans	Nonqualified Plans
Contributions currently tax deductible	Contributions are not currently tax deductible
Plan approved by the IRS	Plan does not need IRS approval
Plan cannot discriminate	Plan can discriminate
Tax on accumulation is deferred	Tax on accumulation is deferred
All withdrawals taxed	Excess over cost base taxed
Plan must be in writing	Plan must be in writing
Plan is a trust	Plan is not a trust
Strict IRS and Labor Dept. reporting and disclosure	Limited reporting and disclosure

not available to company board members, because they are not considered employees for retirement planning purposes.

Deferred compensation plans may be somewhat risky, because the employee covered by the plan has no right to plan benefits if the business fails. In this situation, the employee becomes a general creditor of the firm. Covered employees may also forfeit benefits if they leave the firm before retirement.

When the benefit is payable at the employee's retirement, it is taxable as ordinary income to the employee. The employer is entitled to the tax deduction at the time the benefit is paid out.

Payroll deduction plans allow employees to authorize their employer to deduct a specified amount for retirement savings from their paychecks. The money is deducted after taxes are paid, and may be invested in any number of retirement vehicles at the employee's option.

 **Test Topic Alert!**   For the NASD exams, 401(k) plans are considered salary reduction plans NOT payroll deduction plans. In any test question you see, assume payroll deduction plans are nonqualified.

Quick Quiz 3.9

1. Each of the following is an example of a qualified retirement plan EXCEPT a

   A. deferred compensation plan
   B. 401 (k) plan
   C. pension and profit-sharing plan
   D. defined benefit plan

2. A corporate profit-sharing plan must be in the form of a(n)

   A. trust
   B. conservatorship
   C. administratorship
   D. beneficial ownership

3. Which of the following statements is(are) true of deferred compensation plans?

   I.   They are available to a limited number of select employees.
   II. They must be nondiscriminatory.
   III. They cannot include corporate officers.
   IV. They cannot include members of the Board of Directors.

   A. I
   B. I and IV
   C. II
   D. III and IV

4. Adam Grizzly invests in a tax-qualified variable annuity. What is the tax treatment of the distributions he receives?

   A. Partially tax free; partially ordinary income
   B. Partially tax free; partially capital gains
   C. All ordinary income
   D. All capital gains

See page 340 for answers and rationale.

Individual Retirement Accounts

Individual retirement accounts (IRAs) were created to encourage people to save for retirement in addition to other retirement plans in which they participate. Anyone who has earned income is allowed to make an annual contribution of up to $2,000 or 100 percent of earned income, whichever is less. Earned income is defined as income from work, such as wages, salaries, bonuses, commissions, tips, etc., and alimony. Income from investments is not considered earned income. If the contribution limit is exceeded, a 6 percent excess contribution applies to the amount over the allowable portion (unless corrected shortly thereafter as defined by IRS rules).

Individuals with nonworking spouses are allowed to contribute up to a total of $4,000 split between two accounts. This benefit is known as the **spousal IRA contribution** and is only available to couples filing joint tax returns.

Contributions to IRAs must be made by April 15 of year following the tax year. Individuals may contribute until age 70½, provided they have earned income.

Distributions may begin without penalty after age 59½ and must begin by April 1 of the year after the individual turns 70½. Distributions before age 59½ are subject to a 10% penalty as well as regular income tax, except in the event of the following:

- death;
- disability;
- first time homebuyer for purchase of a principal residence;
- education expenses for the taxpayer, a spouse, child or grandchild;
- medical premiums for unemployed individuals;
- medical expenses in excess of defined AGI (adjusted gross income) limits; or
- substantially equal payments over life expectancy.

If distributions do not begin by April 1 of the year after the individual turns 70½ a 50 percent insufficient distribution penalty applies. It is applicable to the amount that should have been withdrawn based on IRS life expectancy tables. Ordinary income taxes also apply to the full amount.

Contributions to IRAs may or may not be tax deductible. Contributions are fully deductible, regardless of income, if the investor is ineligible to participate in any qualified plan. If eligible to participate in other qualified plans, contributions are deductible if the taxpayer's AGI falls within established income guidelines. Table 3.7 summarizes these deductibility rules.

✔ *Take Note:* Do not memorize the tax-deductible IRA contribution limits in the preceding table. Your test will not ask you about these specific limits because they are being phased in gradually.

In general, the test focuses on the ability to *contribute to* rather than *deduct* IRA contributions. With any qualified plan question that you see, assume that contributions have been made on a pre-tax basis unless otherwise specified.

Certain investments are not permitted for funding IRAs. Collectibles, such as antiques, gems, rare coins, works of art and stamps are not acceptable. Life insurance contracts cannot be purchased within an IRA. Municipal bonds are

TABLE 3.7   Phaseout Ranges

Year	Phaseout Range for Single Definition	Phaseout Range for Married Individuals Filing Jointly (Modified AGI)
Before 1998*	$25,000 to $35,000	$40,000 to $50,000
1998	$30,000 to $40,000	$50,000 to $60,000
1999	$31,000 to $41,000	$51,000 to $61,000
2000	$32,000 to $42,000	$52,000 to $62,000
2001	$33,000 to $43,000	$53,000 to $63,000
2002	$34,000 to $44,000	$54,000 to $64,000
2003	$40,000 to $50,000	$60,000 to $70,000
2004	$45,000 to $55,000	$65,000 to $75,000
2005	$50,000 to $60,000	$70,000 to $80,000
2006	$50,000 to $60,000	$75,000 to $85,000
2007 and after	$50,000 to $60,000	$80,000 to $100,000

*Before 1998, not only was the phaseout range less than what it was to become, but it was applied to both spouses even if only one was covered by an employer-sponsored plan. This is no longer true.

considered inappropriate because the benefit of their tax-free interest is lost within a retirement plan.

Certain investment practices are also considered inappropriate. No short sales of stock, speculative option strategies or margin account trading are permitted within IRAs or any other retirement plan. Covered call writing is, however, permissible because it does not increase risk.

Ineligible Investments	Ineligible Investment Practices
Collectibles	Short Sales of Stock
Life Insurance	Speculative Option Strategies
Municipal Bonds	Margin Account Trading

✓ *Take Note:* A quick tip for you: although life insurance is not allowed within IRAs, other life insurance company products, like annuities, are. Annuities are frequently used as funding vehicles for IRAs.

Also, in case you are wondering what investments are appropriate for IRAs, here is a partial list:

- Stocks
- Bonds
- Mutual funds (other than municipal bond funds)
- Unit Investment Trusts (UITs)
- Limited partnerships
- Government securities
- U.S. government-issued gold and silver coins
- Annuities

Individuals may move their investments from one IRA to another IRA or from a qualified plan to an IRA. These movements are known as either *rollovers* or *transfers.*

A rollover occurs when an IRA account owner takes temporary ownership of IRA account funds when moving the account to another custodian. Rollovers may take place once in a 12-month period and must be completed within 60 days. 100 percent of the funds withdrawn must be rolled into the new account or they will be subject to tax and the 10 percent early withdrawal penalty if applicable.

If a participant in an employer-sponsored qualified plan leaves his place of employment, he may move plan assets to a conduit IRA. If the employee takes possession of the funds, the 60-day rule of rollovers applies and 20 percent of the distribution must be withheld. The employee may then apply for a refund of the 20 percent withheld on his next income tax return. The 20 percent withholding is avoided if the distribution is made payable directly to another custodian instead of the employee.

IRA assets may be directly transferred from an IRA or qualified plan. A transfer occurs when the account assets are sent directly from one custodian to another, and the account owner never takes possession of the funds. There is no limit on the number of transfers that may be made during a 12-month period.

Roth IRAs Created in 1997, Roth IRAs allow after-tax (nondeductible) contributions of up to $2,000 per individual and $4,000 per couple, split between two accounts. Earnings accumulate tax deferred as in typical IRA accounts. The advantage of these IRAs is that distributions that satisfy holding period requirements are not taxable. Penalty-free withdrawals may begin after the money has been within a Roth IRA at least five years and the IRA owner is at least 59½ years of age. The 10 percent early distribution penalty is waived for death, disability and first-time homebuyers purchasing a principal residence. Withdrawals from Roth IRAs are not required to commence at age 70½.

Education IRAs   Education IRAs, like Roth IRAs were created in 1997. These IRAs allow after-tax contributions of up to $500 per student per year for children younger than 18. Contributions may be made by any adult, as long as the total contribution per child does not exceed $500 in one year. Distributions are tax free as long as the funds are used for higher education.

Test Topic Alert!   Assume questions are about traditional IRAs unless they specifically state *Roth* or *Education*.

Below are some key test points to remember about these newer forms of IRAs.

ROTH IRA

- Maximum contribution of $2,000 per year per individual
- Contributions are *not* tax deductible.
- Distributions are tax free *if* taken after age 59½ *and* money has been in the account for at least five years.
- Distributions are not required to begin at age 70½.
- No 10 percent early distribution penalty for death, disability and first-time home purchase

EDUCATION IRA

- Contribution limit is $500 per year per child under age 18.
- Contributions can be made by adults other than parents; total for one child is still $500.
- Contributions are *not* tax deductible.
- Distributions are tax free if taken prior to age 30 and used for post-secondary education expenses.

SEP-IRAs   A Simplified Employee Pension (SEP) plan is a qualified plan that offers ease of administration to small business owners. Employees open IRAs, and the employer makes contributions on their behalf. Employee contributions may be made into the same IRA accounts. An employer is allowed to contribute up to 15 percent of an employee's salary, up to a maximum of $30,000, each year. Any employee that is at least 21 years of age, has worked for the employer for three of the past five years, and has received at least $400 of compensation (as of 1998) in the current year is eligible to participate.

Quick Quiz 3.10

1. An individual who is less than age 70½ may contribute to an IRA

    A. if he has earned income
    B. provided he is not covered by a pension plan through an employer
    C. provided he does not own a Keogh plan
    D. provided his income is between $40,000 and $50,000 if married and $25,000 and $35,000 if single

2. An individual, who is 50 years of age, wants to withdraw funds from her IRA. The withdrawal will be taxed as

    A. ordinary income
    B. ordinary income plus a 10 percent penalty
    C. capital gains
    D. capital gains plus a 10 percent penalty

3. Premature distribution from an IRA is subject to a

    A. 5 percent penalty plus tax
    B. 6 percent penalty plus tax
    C. 10 percent penalty plus tax
    D. 50 percent penalty plus tax

4. Which of the following individuals will NOT incur a penalty on an IRA withdrawal?

    A. Man who has just become totally disabled
    B. Woman who turned 59 a month before the withdrawal
    C. Person, age 50, who decides on early retirement
    D. Man in his early 40s who uses the money to buy a second home

5. Which of the following statements regarding IRAs is NOT true?

    A. IRA rollovers must be completed within 60 days of receipt of the distribution.
    B. Cash-value life insurance is a permissible IRA investment, but term insurance is not.
    C. The investor must be under 70½ years of age to open and contribute to an IRA.
    D. Distributions may begin at age 59½ and must begin by the year after the year in which the investor turns 70½.

6. Which of the following statements about SEP-IRAs is true?

    A. They are used primarily by large corporations.
    B. They are used primarily by small businesses.
    C. They are set up by employees.
    D. They cannot be set up by self-employed persons.

7. Which of the following statements is true of both traditional IRAs and Roth IRAs?

    A. Contributions are deductible.
    B. Withdrawals at retirement are tax free.
    C. Earnings on investments are not taxed immediately.
    D. To avoid penalty, distributions must begin the year after the year the owner reaches age 70½.

8. What is the maximum amount that may be invested in an education IRA in one year?

    A. $500 per parent
    B. $500 per child
    C. $500 per couple
    D. $2,000 per couple

See page 340 for answers and rationale.

KEOGH (HR-10) Plans

Keogh plans, also known as *HR-10* plans, are qualified plans intended for self-employed persons and owner-employees of unincorporated businesses or professional practices filing Schedule C with the IRS.

With most Keogh plans, business owners or self-employed persons are allowed to contribute the lesser of 25 percent of after-contribution earnings or $30,000. Contributions for eligible employees must be at the same percentage rate.

✔ **Take Note:** Let's talk about the Keogh contribution limit. Although the rules state a maximum of 25 percent of after-contribution earnings, practically speaking, think 20 percent when answering questions involving the business owner. Here's why:

Assume a self-employed business owner has gross income of $100,000. What is his maximum Keogh contribution?

100,000 x 20% = $20,000. $20,000 is the contribution limit.

The employer's after contribution earnings are $80,000. As you can see, $20,000 is 25 percent of $80,000, just as the rule states. The reason the rule is stated this way is because the contribution percentage that is applied to eligible employees is the *after-contribution* percentage of the employer.

TABLE 3.8   Differences Between Keogh Plans and IRAs

Characteristic	Keogh Plans	IRAs
Source of contributions	Employer; employee may also make nondeductible contributions.	Employee.
Permissible investments	Most equity and debt securities, U.S. government-minted precious-metal coins, annuities and cash-value life insurance.	Most equity and debt securities, U.S. government-minted precious-metal coins and annuities.
Nonpermissible investments	Term insurance and collectibles.	Term insurance, collectibles and cash-value life insurance.
Change of employer	Lump-sum distribution can be rolled over into an IRA within 60 days.	Does not apply.
Penalty for excess contribution	10% penalty.	6% penalty.
Taxation of distributions	Taxed as ordinary income. 5 year forward averaging through 1999.	Taxed as ordinary income.
Penalty for early distribution.	10% if before age 59 1/2.	10% if before age 59 1/2.

This means the boss's contribution is less than that for an employee earning the same pay. The IRS considers this fair because the boss receives the advantage of tax deductions for contributions made. Now, if the employer had an employee making $40,000, the Keogh contribution would have to be how much? The answer is $10,000, because 25%, the employer's after-contribution percentage, is the factor that must be used.

Use 20% of *gross earnings* if the question pertains to the business owner or employer, and 25% if the question pertains to contributions for employees.

 **Test Topic Alert!**

To calculate the amount of annual contribution, pay careful attention to whether the question pertains to the employee or the employer. Multiply compensation by .25 for employees, and multiply by .20 for the employer.

If a business with a Keogh plan has one boss and one employee, and both earn $100,000 a year, what is the maximum allowable contribution for each?

Employer: $100,000 x .20 = $20,000

Employee: $100,000 x .25 = $25,000

Employees may be permitted to make nondeductible contributions to Keogh plans. In any case, the earnings accumulate tax free.

Eligible employees must be allowed to participate in Keogh plans. ERISA eligibility rules apply. Employees are eligible if they:

- have worked at least 1,000 hours in the year;
- have completed one or more years of continuous employment; and
- are at least 21 years of age.

A comparison of the Keogh plans and IRAs is shown in Table 3.8.

 Quick Quiz 3.11 1. Who among the following may participate in a Keogh plan?

 I. Self-employed doctor
 II. Analyst who makes money giving speeches outside regular working hours
 III. Individual with a full-time job who has income from freelancing
 IV. Corporate executive who receives $5,000 in stock options from his corporation

 A. I only
 B. I and II only
 C. I, II and III only
 D. I, II, III and IV

2. Which of the following are characteristics of a Keogh plan?

 I. Dividends, interest and capital gains are tax deferred.
 II. Distributions after age 70½ are tax free.
 III. Contributions are allowed for a nonworking spouse.
 IV. Lump-sum distributions are allowed.

 A. I and II
 B. I and III
 C. I and IV
 D. II and III

3. Which of the following disqualify a person from participation in a Keogh plan?

 A. Turning age 70 eight months ago
 B. Having a salaried position in addition to self-employment
 C. A spouse who has company-sponsored retirement benefits
 D. Owning an IRA

4. An individual earned $75,000 in royalties from his writings; $5,000 from interest and dividends; $2,000 from long-term capital gains in the stock market; and $3,000 from rents on two cottages. He can contribute to his Keogh plan

A. $12,570
B. $12,750
C. $15,000
D. $18,750

See page 341 for answers and rationale.

403(b) Plans

403(b) plans are a form of tax-sheltered annuity (TSA) available to employees of the following organizations:

- public educational institutions (403b institutions);
- tax exempt organizations (501(c)3 organizations); and
- religious organizations.

In general, the clergy and employees of charitable institutions, private hospitals, colleges and universities, elementary and secondary schools and zoos and museums are eligible to participate if they are at least 21 and have completed one year of service. 403(b) plans are sometimes referred to a tax-sheltered annuities (TSAs) or tax-qualified annuities.

403(b) plans are funded by elective employee deferrals. The employee may contribute up to $10,000 each year. The deferred amount is excluded from the employee's gross income and earnings accumulate tax free until distribution. A written salary reduction agreement must be executed between the employer and the employee.

Employer contributions may also be made, and are subject to the contribution limits of all defined contribution plans under ERISA: the lesser of 25 percent of participant's compensation or $30,000 per year. Historically, plan funds were invested in fixed or variable annuities; today, however, plan funds may be invested in mutual funds and CDs as well.

As with other qualified plans, a 10 percent penalty is applied to distributions before age 59½.

 **Test Topic Alert!**   You might see a question that asks if a student can be a participant in a 403(b). The answer is "no," because the plan is only available to employees.

Corporate Retirement Plans

Corporate pension plans fall into one of two categories: defined benefit or defined contribution. A defined benefit plan promises a specific benefit at retirement that is determined by a formula involving typical retirement age, years of service and compensation. The amount of the contribution must be determined by actuarial calculation because it involves complex assumptions about investment returns, future interest rates and other matters. This type of plan may be used by firms that wish to favor older key employees, because a much greater amount can be contributed for those with only a short time until retirement.

Defined contribution plans are much easier to administer. The current contribution amount is specified by the plan; however, the benefit that will be paid at retirement is unknown. A typical defined contribution formula might be 5 percent of salary. Employer contributions are limited to the lesser of 25 percent of the plan participants' compensation or $30,000.

Distributions from both defined benefit and defined contribution plans are eligible for five-year income averaging through 1999.

Profit-sharing plans are a popular form of defined contribution plan. These plans do not require a fixed contribution formula and allow contributions to be skipped in years of low profits. Their flexibility and ease of administration have made them a popular retirement plan option for employers.

 Take Note: All defined benefit and defined contribution plans, other than profit-sharing plans, require an annual contribution. Employers may skip contributions to profit-sharing plans in unprofitable years.

401(k) plans are the most popular form of retirement plan today. This type of defined contribution plan allows the employee to elect to contribute a percentage of salary to his or her retirement account. Contributions are excluded from the employee's gross income and accumulate tax deferred. Employers are permitted to make matching contributions up to a specified percentage of the employee's contributions. 401(k) plans permit certain hardship withdrawals.

 **Test Topic Alert!**   Below are important features of defined benefit and defined contributions. Be ready to identify these for test questions:

DEFINED BENEFIT	DEFINED CONTRIBUTION
• Benefit amount fixed	• Benefit amount varies
• Contribution determined by formula based on age, salary, years of service	• Contribution amount fixed
• Sponsor assumes investment risk	• Participant assumes investment risk
• Favors older key employees	• Plan favors younger employees with more time to accumulate funds for retirement

✎ **Quick Quiz 3.12**   Match each of the following terms with the appropriate description.

A. Defined benefit plan
B. Keogh plan
C. Spousal IRA contributions
D. Payroll deduction plan

___   1. Nonqualified plan in which an employee authorizes regular reductions from his or her check

___   2. Specifies the total amount an employee will receive at retirement

___   3. Qualified retirement plan for self-employed individuals and unincorporated businesses

___   4. IRA contributions made for a nonworking husband or wife

Match each of the following terms with the appropriate description.

A. Profit-sharing plan
B. Qualified plan
C. Deferred compensation plan
D. Rollover
E. Defined contribution plan

___   5. A qualified plan that specifies an employer's annual funding

___   6. Employees receive a portion of profits from a business

___   7. Movement of funds from one retirement plan to another, generally within a specified period of time

___   8. Nonqualified retirement plan in which an employee delays receipt of current compensation, generally until retirement

___   9. Plan meeting standards set by the Employee Retirement Income Security Act

See page 341 for answers.

ERISA

The Employee Retirement Income Security Act (ERISA) of 1974 was established to prevent abuse and misuse of pension funds. ERISA guidelines apply to private sector (corporate) retirement plans and certain union plans not public plans like those for government workers.

Test Topic Alert!   You may see a question that asks for the type of plans that ERISA regulates. Remember that ERISA applies to *private sector* plans (corporate) only. It does not apply to plans for federal or state government workers (*public sector* plans).

Significant ERISA provisions include:

- **Participation:** Identifies eligibility rules for employees. States that all employees must be covered if they are 21 years or older and have performed one year of full-time service, which ERISA defines as 1,000 hours.
- **Funding:** Requires that funds contributed to the plan be segregated from other corporate assets. Plan trustees have the responsibility to administer and invest the assets prudently and in the best interest of all participants. IRS contribution limits must be observed.
- **Vesting:** Employees are entitled to their entire retirement benefit within a certain number of years of service, even if they leave the company.
- **Communication:** The plan document must be in writing, and employees must be given annual statements of account and updates of plan benefits.
- **Nondiscrimination:** All eligible employees must be impartially treated through a uniformly applied formula.
- **Beneficiaries:** Beneficiaries must be named to receive an employee's benefits at his or her death.

Quick Quiz 3.13 1. Regulations regarding how contributions are made to tax-qualified plans relate to which of the following ERISA requirements?

    A. Vesting
    B. Funding
    C. Nondiscrimination
    D. Reporting and disclosure

2. Which of the following determines the amount paid into a defined contribution plan?

    A. ERISA-defined contribution requirements
    B. Trust agreement
    C. Employer's age
    D. Employee's retirement age

3. Your customer works as a nurse in a public school. He wants to know more about participating in the school's TSA plan. Which of the following statements is(are) correct?

    I. Contributions are made with before-tax dollars.
    II. He is not eligible to participate.
    III. Distributions before age 59½ are normally subject to penalty tax.
    IV. Mutual funds and CDs are available investment vehicles.

    A. I, II and III
    B. I and III
    C. I, III and IV
    D. II

4. Which of the following statements is true of a defined benefit plan?

    A. All employees receive the same benefits at retirement.
    B. All participating employees are immediately vested.
    C. High-income employees near retirement may receive much larger contributions than younger employees with the same salary.
    D. The same amount must be contributed for each eligible employee.

5. The requirements of the Employee Retirement Income Security Act apply to pension plans established by which of the following?

    A. U.S. government workers
    B. Only public entities, such as the City of New York
    C. Only private organizations, such as Exxon
    D. Both public and private organizations

See page 341 for answers and rationale.

✓ ***Take Note:*** Sixteen questions on your Series 6 exam are about variable contracts and retirement plans. Many of the questions describe concepts that differ from "real-world" applications of these products, but you must know these concepts the NASD way to be successful on the exam. Be sure to practice questions on this lesson thoroughly and, as always, read each question and all the answer choices VERY CAREFULLY!

Variable Annuities Hotsheet

Fixed Annuity:
- Guaranteed rate of return
- Insurance company has investment risk
- Subject to purchasing power risk
- Fixed income guaranteed for life
- Not a security

Variable Annuity:
- Rate of return dependent on separate account performance
- Investor has investment risk
- Sold with prospectus
- Can keep pace with inflation
- Variable income guaranteed for life; principal is not guaranteed

Accumulation Phase:
- Investor pays money to insurer
- Units vary in number and in value

Annuity Phase:
- Investor receives payments from insurer
- Fixed number of units, vary in value

Purchase Methods:
- Periodic deferred—paid in installments, payouts taken later
- Single premium immediate—lump-sum payment, payouts begin immediately, no accumulation period
- Single premium deferred—lump-sum payment, payouts taken later

Payout Methods:
- Lump sum or random withdrawals
- Annuitization (monthly income guaranteed for life)
- Life Income—no beneficiary, largest monthly payment
- Life with Period Certain—minimum guaranteed period
- Joint Life with Last Survivor—annuity on two lives; smallest monthly payment

AIR:
- Used to determine monthly income
- Income goes up from previous month if separate account performance is greater than AIR
- Income stays the same as previous month if separate account performance is equal to AIR

- Income falls from the previous month if separate account performance is less than the AIR

Taxation:
- Monthly income: part return of cost basis, part taxable; proportion determined by exclusion ratio
- Lump sum/random withdrawals: LIFO applies; earnings withdrawn first, taxable as ordinary income; no tax on remainder because it is a return of cost basis

Regulated By:
- Act of 1933; Act of 1934; Investment Company Act of 1940; Investment Advisers Act of 1940
- State Insurance Departments; Federal insurance law

Variable Life Insurance Hotsheet

	WHOLE LIFE	VARIABLE LIFE
Premium	Fixed	Fixed
Cash Value	Guaranteed	No guarantee
Death Benefit	Guaranteed and fixed	Minimum guaranteed, variable
Loan Privilege	100 percent of cash value allowed	Usually up to 90 percent of cash value allowed
Investment of Premiums	General account	Separate account
Investment Risk	Insurer	Policyowner
Regulation	State insurance regulations; not a security	State insurance and security regulations; NASD, SEC

Contract Exchange:
- 24 months to exchange variable to fixed

Policy Refunds:
- Full refund within free-look period (45 days)
- First year: Cash value plus 30 percent
- Second year: Cash value plus 10 percent

Calculations:
- Death benefit—annually; cash value—monthly

AIR:
- Death benefit fluctuates based on comparison of separate account performance to AIR
- Cash value is not affected by AIR

Voting Rights:
- 1 vote per $100 of cash value

Loan Provision:

- Minimum of 75 percent available after three years; up to maximum of 90 percent

Retirement Plans Hotsheet

Nonqualified plans:

- Nondeductible contributions, can be discriminatory
- Examples are payroll deduction, deferred compensation
- Risk of deferred compensation is employer failure

IRAs:

- Maximum contribution is $2,000, or 100 percent of earned income
- Spousal IRA allows $4,000 between two spouse filing joint returns, split between two accounts
- No life insurance or collectibles as contributions
- 10 percent penalty, plus applicable ordinary income tax, on withdrawals before age 59½
- 6 percent excess contribution penalty
- 50 percent insufficient distribution penalty (insufficient if after 70½)
- One rollover allowed each 12 months to be completed within 60 days
- Unlimited trustee to trustee transfers

SEPs:

- Qualified plan that allows employers to contribute money to employee IRAs
- Contribution max = 15 percent of employee salary up to $30,000
- Contributions immediately vested

Roth IRAs:

- New IRA that allows after-tax contributions, possible tax-free distributions
- Maximum contribution of $2,000 per individual, $4,000 per couple
- Does not require distributions to begin at age 70½

Education IRAs:

- New IRA that allows after-tax contributions for children under age 18
- Maximum contribution is $500 per year per child
- Tax-free distributions if funds are used for higher education

Keoghs (HR-10):

- Available to self-employed persons, owners of unincorporated businesses and professional practices
- Contribution max is lesser of 20 percent of gross for employer (25 percent for employee) or $30,000
- All employees must participate if age 21 or older, employed more than one year, work more than 1,000 hours per year
- Life insurance may be held within the plan
- Distributions in lump sums are eligible for five-year income averaging through 1999

TSAs (403(b) plans):	• Available to employees of non-profit organizations • Typically funded by elective employee salary reductions, usually no cost basis
Pension Plans:	• Require annual contribution
Defined Benefit:	• Based on formula factoring age, salary years of service, calculated by actuary; favor older key employees
Defined Contribution:	• Simpler to administer, contribution is typically a percent of salary • Five-year income averaging available on distributions through 1999
Profit-Sharing Plans:	• Annual contribution not required, great investment and contribution flexibility
Withholding Rule:	• 20 percent withholding applied to distributions from qualified plans made payable to participant
ERISA:	• Protects participants in corporate (private) plans, not public plans • Rules for funding, vesting, nondiscrimination, participation, communication

Lesson 3 Practice Exam

1. An annuity may be purchased under which of the following methods?

   I. Single payment deferred annuity
   II. Single payment immediate annuity
   III. Periodic payment deferred annuity
   IV. Periodic payment immediate annuity

   A. I and II only
   B. I, II and III only
   C. III and IV only
   D. I, II, III and IV

2. All the statements below regarding the exchange of a cash value life insurance policy for an annuity under Internal Revenue Code Section 1035 are correct EXCEPT

   A. An annuity acquired under a Section 1035 exchange can be designed to provide income over one or more lifetimes.
   B. Permanent life insurance can be exchanged for an annuity contract without generating the adverse tax consequences generally associated with surrendering a life insurance policy.
   C. The exchange of a life insurance policy for an annuity may appeal to taxpayers who feel they have too much life insurance and too little retirement income.
   D. Under Section 1035, a tax free exchange may only occur if the original contract is exchanged for a contract issued by the same insurance company.

3. The owner of a variable life contract has a death benefit that is subject to fluctuation. However, a specified death benefit is provided regardless of market performance. This policy feature is called the

   A. guaranteed face amount
   B. contractual death benefit
   C. policy guaranteed death benefit
   D. minimum guaranteed death benefit

4. A customer interested in tax shelter is considering the purchase of either a variable annuity or variable life insurance. In discussing the merits of the respective contracts, a registered representative can state that all of the following characteristics are common to both contracts EXCEPT

   I. all gains are tax-deferred
   II. the AIR is a factor in determining certain values
   III. fixed contributions are required
   IV. contract owners have the right to vote

   A. I and II
   B. I, II and III
   C. III
   D. III and IV

5. Tax-free distributions from a Roth IRA can be taken

   A. when the money has been in an account for five taxable years, and the owner is at least 59½
   B. when the owner buys rental property after holding the money in an account for five taxable years
   C. when an immediate family member becomes disabled
   D. only for medical emergencies

6. A 60-year-old male customer is interested in investing in a variable life annuity. Which of the following would you consider to be the least important in the investment decision?

   A. The customer's investment objective
   B. The customer's gender
   C. The performance history of the variable annuity
   D. The investment choices available in the variable annuity

7. Which of the following IRAs are funded only with after-tax contributions and provide tax-free distributions?

   I. Traditional IRAs
   II. Roth IRAs
   III. Education IRAs
   IV. SEP-IRAs

   A. I and III
   B. I and IV
   C. II and III
   D. I, II, III, and IV

8. An investor owns a variable life insurance policy on his wife. The policy names their daughter as the beneficiary. Presuming his wife dies, which statement below correctly describes the tax consequence associated with this policy?

   A. The death benefit will be taxable to the wife's estate upon distribution.
   B. The death benefit will not be taxable to the daughter upon distribution.
   C. The policyowner can deduct premiums paid into the policy in the year they are paid.
   D. There will be no federal income tax on any distribution if the variable life insurance separate account includes only municipal bonds.

9. The AIR (assumed interest rate) for your customer's variable annuity contract is 5 percent. In February, the separate account earned 7 percent. In March, the separate account earns 5 percent. The April annuity payment will be

   A. higher than the March payment
   B. lower than the March payment
   C. equal to the March payment
   D. equal to the original payment amount at the time of annuitization

10. Your customer, a self-employed, incorporated small businessperson wishes to establish a Keogh plan for herself and her two employees. According to IRS rules, which of the following is correct?

   A. She may contribute a maximum of 25 percent of after-contribution earnings for herself and must contribute the same percentage for her eligible employees.
   B. Her Keogh plan must be established as a defined benefit plan.
   C. Her Keogh plan is not subject to IRS approval.
   D. She and her employees are not eligible for a Keogh plan.

11. Under the Employee Retirement Income Security Act of 1974 (ERISA), all of the following guidelines for the regulation of retirement plans are true EXCEPT

   A. all qualified plans require a written plan document
   B. a corporation in business for three years is required to establish a retirement plan for employees
   C. funds contributed to a retirement plan are required to be segregated from corporate assets
   D. fully vested employees are entitled to the accumulated retirement accounts if they leave the employer

12. A customer has a variable life policy and has made two annual premium payments. From the first year's premium, $600 was deducted in sales charges. From the second year's premium, $400 was deducted. If the customer terminates the policy before the end of the second year, which of the following statements is true?

   A. The customer is not entitled to a policy refund but may exchange the policy into a traditional whole life policy.
   B. The customer is refunded all premiums paid.
   C. The customer is refunded a portion of premiums paid.
   D. The customer receives the policy cash value only.

13. A registered representative presenting a variable life insurance (VLI) policy proposal to a prospect must disclose which of the following about the insured's rights of exchange of the VLI policy?

    A. The insurance company will allow the insured to exchange the VLI policy for a traditional whole-life policy within 45 days from the date of the application or 10 days from policy delivery, whichever is longer.

    B. Federal law requires the insurance company to allow the insured to exchange the VLI policy for a traditional whole-life policy issued by the same company for two years with no additional evidence of insurability.

    C. Within the first 18 months the insured may exchange the VLI policy for either a whole-life or universal variable policy issued by the same company with no additional evidence of insurability.

    D. The insured may request that the insurance company exchange the VLI policy for a traditional whole life policy issued by the same company within two years. The insurance company retains the right to have medical examinations for underwriting purposes.

14. An annuitant received payments until his death from a nonqualified variable annuity. At his death, his wife received a lump sum payment from the annuity. This example illustrates a

    A. straight life annuity
    B. cash balance annuity
    C. joint and last survivor annuity
    D. unit refund annuity

15. Guaranteed cash value is a standard feature found in which of the policies listed below?

    A. Whole life
    B. Term life
    C. Variable life
    D. Whole life and variable life

Answers and Rationale

1. **B.** A periodic payment immediate annuity would be rather difficult to provide. As the annuitant is contributing, he or she would also be receiving.   (Page 211) [14901]

2. **D.** Under Internal Revenue Code Section 1035, to accomplish a tax-free exchange of a life insurance contract for an annuity (or for another life insurance contract), no requirement exists that both contracts are issued by the same insurance company. The intent of Section 1035 is to permit tax-free exchange of a (cash value) life insurance policy for an annuity or a life insurance policy for another life insurance policy. A policyholder approaching retirement may have a reduced insurance need but a greater need for retirement income, and may choose to exchange the policy for an annuity designed to provide monthly income for one, or more, lifetimes. An annuity may also be exchanged for another company's annuity under Section 1035.   (Page 229) [18111]

3. **D.** While a VLI contract's death benefit can increase if the separate account performs well, it can also decrease. However, it can never fall below the minimum guaranteed death benefit.
               (Page 221) [18423]

4. **C.** The AIR affects the death benefit in variable life insurance and the payout in a variable annuity. All gains are deferred until withdrawn. Only variable life requires a fixed contribution (scheduled premiums). Both contracts have voting privileges.   (Page 222) [18425]

5. **A.** Tax-free distributions from a Roth IRA can begin after the money has been in an account for five taxable years and the owner reaches age 59½, dies, becomes disabled or purchases a home for the first time.   (Page 235) [18431]

6. **B.** Because payouts for males and females are actuarially equal, gender is not a significant consideration in the purchase of a variable annuity. The customer's investment objective, past performance of the variable annuity and available fund choices are critical considerations.
               (Page 204) [18439]

7. **C.** Roth IRAs and Education IRAs are funded entirely with after-tax contributions, and distributions are tax free. SEP-IRAs are funded with pretax dollars and have taxable distributions. Traditional IRAs are funded with pretax or after-tax dollars (depending on the income level) and distributions that exceed after-tax contributions are taxable.   (Page 235) [18443]

8. **B.** Death benefits under variable (and other) life insurance policies are generally not taxable to a beneficiary. Premiums are not deductible to the owner of the policy (payor). Presuming the insured is not the owner of the policy, the policy's death benefit is not included in the estate at death. Because of the tax-free build up of life insurance cash values, variable life insurance products do not offer lower-yielding municipal bond subaccounts among their separate account choices.
               (Page 229) [18453]

9. **C.** When the separate account return is equal to the AIR, the monthly payment amount does not change. The April payment will be equal to the March payment. The payment increases if the separate account is greater than the AIR and decreases if the separate account performance is less than the AIR.   (Page 212) [18458]

10. **D.** Keogh plans are only available to self-employed, non-incorporated businesses. This customer and her employees cannot participate in a Keogh plan because the business is incorporated.
               (Page 238) [18472]

11. **B.** Corporations are never required to sponsor retirement plans for employees, but if a corporation has a retirement plan for its employees, it must follow ERISA guidelines. (Page 244) [18481]

12. **C.** The variable life refund provision allows for a return of a portion of the premiums paid within the first two policy years. There is a 24-

month contract exchange provision that allows variable policyowners to convert to traditional whole life policies without evidence of insurability. (Page 226) [18505]

13. **B.** Federal law requires that issuers of variable life insurance policies allow exchange of these policies for traditional whole-life policies issued by the same company for a period of no less than two years. The exchange must be made without additional evidence of insurability.
(Page 225) [18510]

14. **D.** When the unit refund option is chosen, the insurer pays the annuitant a minimum number of payments and at death, the survivor receives the balance of the account in a lump-sum payment. In a joint and last survivor annuity, payments continue as long as either spouse is alive. A straight life annuity pays only to the annuitant; at death the account balance reverts to the insurer. There is no such thing as a cash balance annuity.
(Page 215) [18567]

15. **A.** Traditional whole life policies offer guaranteed cash values and death benefits. The insurer maintains the investment risk by promising a fixed rate of policy return, regardless of investment performance. Term insurance is pure insurance protection and builds no cash value. Variable life cash value is not guaranteed; cash value may be available depending on the performance of investments in the separate account. (Page 221) [18571]

4

Securities Industry Regulations

OVERVIEW

The Securities Industry Regulations lesson, the final lesson of your Series 6 course, is a critical one for your future in the industry. It addresses the regulatory framework of the industry: the laws you must understand and follow in order to practice as a Series 6 registered representative. Firms and reps are not only required to comply with SEC rules, but must also comply with the rules of the self regulatory organizations (SROs)—the NASD, New York Stock Exchange (NYSE) and others—as well as house rules developed by your firm internally. The intent of these rules is to protect the public, and your career depends on your ability to follow the rules and regulations of the industry.

Your Series 6 exam includes 25 questions on Securities Industry Regulation. Be sure to proceed carefully through this lesson and the exercises provided to master the details of each regulation.

After completing this lesson you should be able to

- Describe the scope and boundaries of the following major securities legislation
    - Securities Act of 1933
    - Securities Exchange Act of 1934
    - Maloney Act of 1938
    - Investment Advisers Act of 1940
    - Securities Investor Protection Act of 1970
    - Insider Trading Act of 1988
    - Telephone Consumer Protection Act of 1991
    - Blue-Sky Laws
- Define the role of the SEC in the securities industry
- Define the role of the NASD in the securities industry
- Explain the relationship between the SEC and SROs
- Describe the role and responsibilities of a firm's principal

- Define advertising and sales literature and describe applicable disclosure and filing rules
- List and describe at least 10 sales practices prohibited of Series 6 registered representatives
- Compare and contrast the Code of Procedure and the Code of Arbitration

The Regulation of New Issues

After the devastating market crash of 1929, Congress examined the cause and passed laws to prevent its recurrence. The Securities Act of 1933 was the first of the regulations enacted in response to the crash.

The Securities Act of 1933. Investigation of the conditions that led to the 1929 market crash determined that investors had little protection from fraud in the sale of new issues of securities. Rumors, exaggerations and unsubstantiated claims led to excessive speculation in newly issued stock. Congress passed the Securities Act of 1933 to require issuers of new securities to file registrations statements with the SEC in order to provide investors with complete and accurate information. New securities that are subject to the Act's requirements are called *nonexempt* issues. *Exempt* securities are not subject to these requirements.

✓ **Take Note:** Make sure you have a clear understanding of these terms!

NONEXEMPT means "must register with the SEC under the Act of 1933." Think of corporate issues as *nonexempt.*

EXEMPT means "not required to register with the SEC." Think of government securities and municipals as *exempt.*

Listed below are the most important provisions of the Act of 1933.

- Issuers of nonexempt securities must file registration statements with the SEC.
- Prospectuses must be provided to all purchasers of new, nonexempt issues for full and fair disclosure.
- Fraudulent activity in connection with underwriting and issuing of all securities is prohibited.
- Criminal penalties are assessed for fraud in the underwriting and sale of new issues.

✓ **Take Note:** If a question on your exam discusses the "new issue market" or "primary market," or any activity associated with the sale of new issues, the regulation involved is the Act of 1933. Remembering a few key words will help you make this association. Think:

Act of 1933 =	• New issues
	• Underwriting
	• Registration Statement
	• Prospectus
	• Primary Market

Registration of Securities

The Securities Act of 1933 requires new issues of corporate securities to be registered with the SEC. The corporate issuer does so by filing a registration statement. Most of the registration statement becomes the prospectus.

✔ **Take Note:** To simplify, think of the Act of 1933 as the *Paper Act* because of the registration statement and prospectus. Although you will not see this term on the exam, it reminds you of the paperwork requirements for full and fair disclosure.

State Registration. State securities laws, also called *blue-sky laws*, require state registration of securities, broker-dealers and registered reps. An issuer or investment banker may blue-sky an issue by one of the following three methods:

1. **Qualification.** The issuer files with the state independent of federal registration, and must meet all state requirements.
2. **Coordination.** The issuer registers simultaneously with the state and the SEC. Both registrations become effective on the same date.
3. **Filing (Notification).** Certain states allow some issues to blue-sky by having the issuer notify the state of SEC registration. In this case, the state requires no registration statement, although certain other information must be filed and specific financial criteria must be met.

Exempt Securities. The Act of 1933 provides specific exemptions from its registration provisions. Among the exemptions are the following *issuers:*

- The U.S. government
- U.S. municipalities and territories
- Non-profit religious, educational and charitable organizations
- Common carriers whose activities are regulated by the Interstate Commerce Commission

Certain *securities* are also exempt. They include:

- Bankers' acceptances
- Commercial paper

These securities are exempt from the Act's registration requirements only if their maturities are 270 days or less.

 **Test Topic Alert!**   You may see a question on your exam similar to the following:

The Securities Act of 1933 regulates all of the following activities EXCEPT

A. delivery of prospectuses for full and fair disclosure
B. registration of securities at the state level
C. underwriting of new issues
D. securities fraud in the primary market

The correct answer is **B**. The Securities Act of 1933 regulates *federal* registration of new issues with the SEC. The Uniform Securities Act regulates the registration of securities at the *state* level. Registering at the state level is called *blue-skying* the issue.

The Prospectus   After an issuer files a registration statement with the SEC, a 20-day cooling-off period begins. During the cooling-off period, the SEC reviews the security's registration statement and can issue a stop order if the statement does not contain all of the required information.

FIGURE 4.1   The Three Phases of an Underwriting

Issuer files registration statement with the SEC   Cooling-off period   Effective date— offering period may begin

Prior to the filing of the registration statement, no sales can be solicited and no prospectus can circulate.

No one can solicit sales during the cooling-off period, but indications of interest can be solicited with a red herring.

Sales can now be solicited, but the firm must use a final prospectus.

Red Herring. A registered representative may discuss the issue with prospects during the cooling-off period and provide them with preliminary information through the **red herring** (preliminary prospectus). The red herring is used to gauge investor reactions and gather **indications of interest**. It must carry a legend, printed in red, that declares that a registration statement has been filed with the SEC but is not yet effective. The final offering price and underwriting spread are not included in the red herring.

SEC rules prohibit the sale of public offering securities without a prospectus, which means that no sales are allowed until the final prospectus is available.

Tombstone Ads. During the cooling-off period, sales of the security and related activities are prohibited. Nonbinding indications of interest may be gathered with the preliminary prospectus. Although the use of advertising and sales literature are generally prohibited, an exception is made for **tombstone ads**. These announcements, typically published in financial periodicals, offer information to investors; they do not offer the securities for sale. Issuers are not required to publish tombstones, but may do so to announce an upcoming issue of securities.

FIGURE 4.2   Federal Farm Credit Bank Bonds Tombstone

New Issue   September 26, 1999

Federal Farm Credit Banks Consolidated Systemwide Bonds

8.30% $1,366,000,000
CUSIP NO. 313311 NG3   DUE APRIL 1, 2000
Interest on the above issue payable at maturity

Dated October 1, 1999   **Price 100%**

The Bonds are the joint and several obligations of
the Thirty-seven Federal Farm Credit Banks and are issued under the
authority of the Farm Credit Act of 1971. The Bonds are not Government
obligations and are not guaranteed by the Government.

Bonds are Available in Book-Entry Form Only.

Federal Farm Credit Banks Funding Corporation

90 William Street, New York, N.Y. 10038   The Farm Credit System

Maxwell J. Leveridge
President

This announcement appears as a matter of record only.   SM

The following list of Dos and Don'ts clarifies allowable activity during the cooling-off period.

DO	DON'T
Gather indications of interest	Offer securities for sale
Distribute red herrings	Distribute final prospectuses
Publish tombstone ads	Disseminate advertising material
	Disseminate sales literature
	Take orders
	Accept postdated checks

Quick Quiz 4.1   Answer "Y" if the activity is permitted during the cooling-off period and "N" if it is not.

____ 1. Indications of interest are gathered

____ 2. Tombstone ads are published

____ 3. Sales literature is sent to future clients

____ 4. Postdated checks are accepted

____ 5. Red herrings are provided to potential customers

____ 6. Orders are taken

____ 7. An offer to sell the new stock when available is published in a newspaper

See page 342 for answers.

The Final Prospectus (Summary Prospectus). When the registration statement becomes effective, the issuer amends the preliminary prospectus and adds information, including the final offering price and the underwriting spread for the final prospectus. Registered representatives may then take orders from those customers who indicated interest in buying during the cooling-off period.

A copy of the final prospectus must precede or accompany all sales confirmations. The prospectus should include all of the following information:

- description of the offering;
- offering price;
- selling discounts;
- offering date;
- use of the proceeds;
- description of the underwriting, but not the actual contract;
- statement of the possibility that the issue's price may be stabilized;
- history of the business;
- risks to the purchasers;
- description of management;
- material financial information;
- legal opinion concerning the formation of the corporation;
- SEC disclaimer; and
- SEC review.

SEC Disclaimer

The SEC reviews the prospectus to ensure that it contains the necessary material facts, but it does not guarantee the disclosures' accuracy. Furthermore, the SEC does not approve the issue, but simply clears it for distribution. Implying that the SEC has approved the issue violates federal law. Finally, the SEC does not pass judgment on the issue's investment merit. The front of every prospectus must contain a clearly printed SEC disclaimer specifying the limits of the SEC's review procedures. A typical SEC disclaimer clause reads as follows:

> *These securities have not been approved or disapproved by the Securities and Exchange Commission or by any State Securities Commission nor has the Securities and Exchange Commission or any State Securities Commission passed upon the accuracy or adequacy of this prospectus. Any representation to the contrary is a criminal offense.*

The information supplied to the SEC becomes public once a registration statement is filed

 Take Note: Any answer choice that says the SEC *approves* or *disapproves* an issue of securities is a wrong answer! The SEC does not approve or disapprove—it *clears* or *releases* issues of securities for sale. When the SEC has completed their review, the registration becomes effective.

 **Quick Quiz 4.2**

1. This Can't Be Sushi (TCBS) will be offering $8,000,000 of its common stock in its home state and in three other states. For the offering to be cleared for sale by the SEC, TCBS must file a(n)

   A. offering circular
   B. standard registration statement
   C. letter of notification
   D. nothing

2. Which of the following pieces of information is NOT required in a preliminary prospectus?

   A. Written statement in red that the prospectus may be subject to change and amendment and that a final prospectus will be issued
   B. Purpose for which the funds being raised will be used
   C. Final offering price
   D. Financial status and history of the company

3. Which of the following statements about a red herring is FALSE?

   A. A red herring is used to obtain indications of interest from investors.
   B. The final offering price does not appear in a red herring.
   C. Additional information may be added to a red herring at a later date.
   D. A registered rep may send a copy of the company's research report with it.

4. As a registered representative, you can use a preliminary prospectus to

   A. obtain indications of interest from investors
   B. solicit orders from investors for the purchase of a new issue
   C. solicit an approval of the offering from SEC
   D. obtain the NASD's authorization to sell the issue

5. If the SEC has cleared an issue, which of the following statements is true?

   A. The SEC has guaranteed the issue.
   B. The underwriter has filed a standard registration statement.
   C. The SEC has endorsed the issue.
   D. The SEC has guaranteed the accuracy of the information in the prospectus.

See page 342 for answers and rationale

Civil Liabilities Under the Act of 1933   The seller of any security being sold by prospectus is liable to purchasers if the registration statement or prospectus contains false statements, misstatements or omissions of material facts. Any person acquiring the security may sue any or all of the following:

- those who signed the registration statement;
- directors and partners of the issuer;
- anyone named in the registration statement as being or about to become a director or partner of the company;
- accountants, appraisers and other professionals who contributed to the registration statement; and
- the underwriters.

Freeriding and Withholding: Hot Issues

Hot issues are new issues of public offering securities that are so popular that they trade immediately above their offering price in the secondary market. Member firms are not allowed to hold back any part of these issues from the public. They are prohibited from buying hot issue securities for their own trading accounts. The following list of persons are also prohibited from purchasing hot issues:

- the underwriters;
- the firm's employees;
- immediate family members of employees that are financially supported (immediate family includes parents, children, brothers, sisters, spouses and in-laws); and
- anyone else who is financially dependent on persons associated with the broker-dealer.

A member's failure to make a bona fide offering at the POP is considered **freeriding and withholding**, and a violation of the NASD's Conduct Rules.

Exceptions

Under certain circumstances, limited amounts of a hot issue may be sold to the following people.

Nonsecurities Persons Associated with the Underwriting. This category includes any person who acts in a business or professional capacity in connection with a public offering, such as a finder, an accountant, an attorney, a financial consultant or another person performing a fiduciary service for the managing underwriter, and any person who is supported financially by a person in this category. A person in this category should not be allowed to purchase a hot issue unless it can be proved that she regularly and routinely buys similar public offering securities. In other words, it is the person's normal investment practice.

Officers and Certain Employees of Financial Institutions. This category includes senior officers of banks, savings and loans, insurance companies, investment companies, investment advisers and other types of institutional investors, as well as any person who is supported financially by a person in this category.

Immediate Family Members. A family member who is *not* materially supported by any securities industry personnel may buy a hot issue if he purchases the issue from a broker-dealer that does not employ the restricted person and if the:

- family member has a history of purchasing similar securities;
- purchase size is consistent with his normal investment practice;
- sale is of an insubstantial amount compared to the total amount available; and
- total of all sales of the security to all classified accounts is not disproportionate to the amount the dealer has available for sale.

 *Take Note:* Anytime you see the terms *freeriding and withholding* on the Series 6 exam, immediately think of hot issues. Remember, hot issues occur when the demand for a new issue exceeds its supply, which causes the price to immediately increase in the secondary market. Hot issues are off limits to all registered reps and brokerage firms!

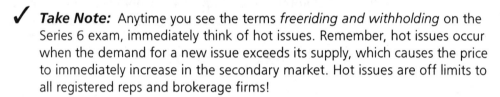 **Test Topic Alert!**   Be ready for a question on *freeriding and withholding* similar to the following:

NASD rules prohibit all of the following from purchasing hot issues of securities EXCEPT

A.   a janitor employed by a broker-dealer
B.   the son of a registered representative who lives in a neighboring city
C.   a cousin of a registered representative who lives in the rep's home
D.   the underwriter of the hot issue

The correct answer is B. Immediate family members that are not financially supported by an employee of a member firm may buy hot issues *if* this is their normal investment pattern and the amount they are buying is insubstantial. All employees of broker-dealers, all persons financially supported by employees of broker-dealers and underwriters of the issue are prohibited from purchasing under all circumstances.

The Regulation of Trading

As the Securities Act of 1933 regulates primary issues of securities, the Securities Exchange Act of 1934 regulates secondary trading.

✓ *Take Note:* As with the Act of 1933, a few key words help identify the Act of 1934 in your test questions. If you see any of the following, think:

Act of 1934 = Secondary market
Outstanding Securities
Trading Activities

As a further "shortcut," think of the Act of 1934 as the People Act. It regulates all the persons involved in trading securities on behalf of customers.

One other tip: Remember, although certain securities are exempt from the registration requirements of the Act of 1933, no security is exempt from the antifraud provisions of the Act of 1934. This statement just means that certain securities are exempt from registration and prospectus requirements, but you can't use fraud in the trading of any security, exempt or nonexempt.

✓ *Take Note:* In October 1996, Congress passed a bill titled the National Securities Markets Improvement Act of 1996 (NSMIA). The law extensively amended many provisions of the Securities Act of 1933, The Securities Exchange Act of 1934, the Trust Indenture Act of 1939, the Investment Company Act of 1940, and the Investment Advisers Act of 1040. It created and defined the *covered security*, referred to under state security laws as F*ederal covered security*. As many provisions of the act preempt sections of state securities laws, especially registration laws, the act effectively moved power to the Fed and away from the state.

The way the act affects Series 6-registered persons is that it affects securities that are registered under the Investment Act of 1940 (that is, securities issued by open and closed-end mutual funds, UITs, and FACs).

The Securities Exchange Act of 1934

The 1934 act, known as the **Exchange Act**, formed the SEC and gave it the authority to regulate the securities exchanges and the OTC markets to maintain a fair and orderly market for the investing public.

The Securities Exchange Act of 1934 addresses the:

- creation of the SEC
- regulation of exchanges

- regulation of credit by the Federal Reserve Board (FRB)
- registration of broker-dealers
- regulation of insider transactions, short sales and proxies
- regulation of trading activities
- regulation of client accounts
- customer protection rule
- regulation of the OTC market
- net capital rule and financial responsibility for broker-dealers

The Securities Exchange Act of 1934 requires exchange members, broker-dealers that trade securities OTC and on exchanges, and individuals who make securities trades for the public to be registered with the SEC.

🖉 **Quick Quiz 4.3** Determine whether each phrase below describes the Act of 1933 or the Act of 1934:

____ 1. Prohibits fraud in the primary markets

____ 2. Requires registration of broker-dealers

____ 3. Created the SEC

____ 4. Requires nonexempt issuers to file registration statements

____ 5. Prohibits fraudulent trading practices

____ 6. The "Paper Act"

____ 7. Regulates underwriting activity

____ 8. Regulates extension of credit by brokerage firms

____ 9. Regulates client accounts

____ 10. The "People Act"

See page 343 for answers.

The Securities and Exchange Commission   Composed of five commissioners appointed by the President of the United States and approved by the Senate, the SEC enforces the 1934 act by regulating the securities markets and behavior of market participants.

Registration of Exchanges and Firms   The 1934 act requires national securities exchanges to file registration statements with the SEC. By registering, exchanges agree to comply with and help enforce the rules of this act. Each exchange gives the SEC copies of its bylaws, constitution and articles of incorporation. An exchange must disclose to the SEC any amendment to exchange rules as soon as it is adopted.

The act of 1934 also requires companies that list their securities on the exchanges and certain firms traded OTC to register with the SEC. An SEC-registered company must file quarterly and annual reports (Form 10Q and 10K, respectively) informing the SEC of its financial status and providing other information.

Regulation of Broker-Dealers

Broker-dealers must comply with SEC rules and regulations when conducting business. A broker-dealer that does not comply is subject to:

- censure;
- limits on activities, functions or operations;
- suspension of its registration (or one of its associated person's license to do business);
- revocation of registration;
- fine; or
- civil monetary penalties.

Although a broker-dealer must register with the SEC, the broker-dealer may not claim that this registration in any way implies that the Commission has passed upon or approved the broker-dealer's financial standing, business or conduct. Any such claim or statement is a misrepresentation.

The Maloney Act

An amendment to the Act of 1934, the Maloney Act of 1938, permitted the establishment of a national securities association of broker-dealers transacting business in the OTC market. The Maloney Act permitted the NASD to act as the self-regulatory organization (SRO) of the OTC. SROs, such as the NASD, the NYSE, the MSRB (Municipal Securities Rulemaking Board) and others, must be registered with the SEC. Although they are permitted to make rules for their member firms, the SROs are all subject to regulation by the SEC.

✓ **Take Note:** The *Maloney Act* chartered the NASD as the SRO of the OTC! If you understand the meaning of all of these acronyms, you are doing well with securities vocabulary! Count on a question that asks what act chartered the NASD as a self-regulatory organization. Because the Series 6 is an NASD exam, the NASD wants you to know that it was brought into existence by the Maloney Act.

Financial Statements Sent to Customers

Every broker-dealer must provide its customers with copies of its financial statements. A customer is any person for whom the broker-dealer holds funds or securities or anyone who has made a securities transaction at any time up to one month before the date of a financial statement. Other broker-dealers, partners or officers of broker-dealers, and subordinated lenders are not considered customers.

Fingerprinting

Registered broker-dealers must have fingerprint records made for all of their employees, directors, officers and partners and must submit those fingerprint cards to the U.S. attorney general for identification and processing. Broker-dealer employees (typically clerical) are exempt from the fingerprinting requirement if they:

- are not involved in securities sales;
- do not handle or have access to cash or securities or to the books and records of original entry relating to money and securities; and
- do not supervise other employees engaged in these activities.

An additional exemption applies to broker-dealers and their employees involved exclusively in the sales of mutual fund shares, unit investment trusts and variable contracts, if certificates for these securities are not ordinarily issued.

Regulation of Credit

The Act of 1934 authorized the Federal Reserve Board (FRB) to regulate margin accounts, the credit extended for the purchase of securities. Within FRB jurisdiction are:

- **Regulation T** — regulates the extension of credit by broker-dealers
- **Regulation U** — deals with the extension of credit by banks and other financial institutions

The 1934 Act prohibits the extension of credit based on new issue securities as collateral for 30 days. Mutual funds, even though continuously offered as new securities, may be used as collateral as long as they have been held for 30 days. Although mutual fund shares can be used as collateral in a margin account, they can never be purchased on margin.

✓ **Take Note:** For an easy way to remember **Reg U**, think of the term *U-banks*. It should help remind you that *Reg U* regulates the extension of credit from *banks* to their customers. *Reg T* regulates the extension of credit from broker-dealers to their customers.

The Investment Advisers Act of 1940

The purpose of the Investment Advisers Act of 1940 is to require individuals in the business of giving investment advice for compensation to register as investment advisers with the SEC. Anyone who provides advice for a flat fee or a percentage of assets managed is subject to registration under this act.

✔ **Take Note:** Persons who must register under this act include financial planners, pension consultants, investment counselors and investment advisory services. Anyone who receives a *fee* for investment advising must register.

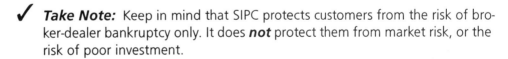

Securities Investor Protection Corporation

After numerous brokerage firm defaults in the 1960s, the Securities Investor Protection Act was passed in 1970 to protect customers from broker-dealer failure or insolvency. This act intensified broker-dealer financial requirements and also created the Securities Investor Protection Corporation (SIPC).

SIPC is an independent government-sponsored corporation that collects annual assessments from broker-dealers. These assessments create a general insurance fund for customer claims from broker-dealer failure. All broker-dealers that are registered with the SEC must be SIPC members except for:

- broker-dealers handling only mutual funds or unit trusts;
- broker-dealers handling only variable annuities or insurance; and
- investment advisers are also exempt from SIPC membership.

Firms that fail to pay their SIPC assessments cannot engage in the brokerage business.

✔ **Take Note:** Keep in mind that SIPC protects customers from the risk of broker-dealer bankruptcy only. It does **not** protect them from market risk, or the risk of poor investment.

Protection of Customers   If a firm is suspected by the SEC or any SRO of a violation of its minimum net capital requirements, a notification is made to SIPC. If SIPC believes that a violation has occurred or that the firm is insolvent, it will petition a court to appoint a liquidating trustee, and the firm ceases doing business. When a liquidation proceeding takes place, the order of events is as follows:

- Securities held in customer name are delivered to the registered owners.
- Cash and street name securities are distributed on a pro-rata basis.

- SIPC funds are distributed to meet remaining claims up to the maximum allowed per customer.
- Customers with excess claims become general creditors of the broker-dealer.
- The valuation date for customer securities claims is generally the day that the court appoints a trustee to oversee the liquidation.

Customer Account Coverage

Under SIPC, customer accounts are covered to a maximum of $500,000, with cash claims not to exceed $100,000 of that total. Each separate customer may enter a claim up to the $500,000 limit for all accounts in the customer's name. Table 4.1 provides examples of customer coverage limits.

TABLE 4.1   SIPC Coverage Limits

Examples of Customer Coverage Limits	
John Doe — Cash account John Doe — Margin account	1 customer = $500,000 coverage
John and Mary Doe — Joint account	1 customer = $500,000 coverage
John Doe as Custodian for Jane Doe	1 customer = $500,000 coverage

Commodities or futures contracts are not covered by SIPC because they are not considered securities.

 Take Note: Be sure to recognize that SIPC coverage is per customer, not per account. Use the "C" in SIPC to help you remember that each customer is entitled to $500,000 of coverage on all of the customer's accounts combined. Cash and margin accounts are combined for SIPC coverage purposes.

Advertising SIPC Membership

Broker-dealers are required to include their SIPC membership on all advertising, but may not imply that SIPC coverage is more than it actually is, or that its benefits are unique to only that firm. The term "SIPC" may not appear larger than the firm's own name. Also, all member firms must post a sign that indicates SIPC membership.

Fidelity bonds

Firms that are required to join SIPC must also purchase a blanket fidelity bond. The purpose of this bond is to protect against employee loss or theft of customer securities. The minimum coverage amount is $25,000, although firms may require additional coverage based on their scope of operations. A firm must review the sufficiency of its fidelity bond coverage once per year.

Test Topic Alert!   Expect at least one question on your exam that is very similar to the following:

SIPC provides coverage up to $500,000

A. with no more than $50,000 in cash
B. with no more than $100,000 in cash
C. with no more than $150,000 in cash
D. in cash or securities

The correct answer is B. SIPC coverage is $500,000 per separate customer account, with coverage of cash and cash equivalents not to exceed $100,000.

Insider Trading and Securities Fraud Enforcement Act of 1988

Although the Securities Act of 1934 prohibited the use of insider information in making trades, the Act of 1988 specifies penalties for insider trading and securities fraud. An **insider** is any person who has access to nonpublic information about a company. Inside information is any information that has not been disseminated to, or is not readily available to, the general public.

The act prohibits insiders trading on or communicating nonpublic information. Both "tippers" (the person who gives the tip) and "tippees" (the person who receives the tip) are liable, as is anyone who trades on information that he or she knows or should know is not public, or has control over the misuse of this information. No trade need be made for a violation to occur; even a personal benefit of a nonfinancial nature could lead to liability under the rules.

The key elements of tipper and tippee liability under insider trading rules are as follows:

- Does the tipper owe a fiduciary duty to a company/its stockholders? Has he or she breached it?
- Does the tipper meet the personal benefits test (even something as simple as enhancing a friendship or reputation)?
- Does the tippee know or should the tippee have known that the information was inside or confidential?
- Is the information material and nonpublic?

 Take Note: Even a slip of the tongue by a corporate insider could create liability under these rules! The SEC has a greatly broadened scope of authority for investigating and prosecuting the abuse of inside information under this act.

Written Supervisory Procedures. All broker-dealers must establish written supervisory procedures specifically prohibiting the misuse of inside information. Additionally, they must establish policies that restrict the passing of potentially material nonpublic information between a firm's departments. This barrier against the free flow of sensitive information is known as a *Chinese wall* or *fire wall*.

Penalties   The SEC can investigate any person suspected of violating any of the provisions of the Insider Trading Act. If the SEC determines that a violation has occurred, civil penalties of up to the greater of $1 million or 300 percent of profits made or losses avoided may be levied. Violators may also face criminal penalties of up to 10 years in jail.

Quick Quiz 4.4

1. Which of the following statements is true of a client not covered by SIPC in a broker-dealer bankruptcy?

    A. He becomes a secured creditor.
    B. He becomes a general creditor.
    C. He becomes a preferred creditor.
    D. He loses his investment.

2. A client has a special cash account with stock valued at $460,000 and $40,000 in cash. The same client also has a joint account with a spouse that has a market value of $320,000 and $180,000 in cash. SIPC coverage is how much?

    A. $460,000 for the special cash account and $320,000 for the joint account
    B. $500,000 for the special cash account and $420,000 for the joint account
    C. $500,000 for the special cash account and $500,000 for the joint account
    D. Total of $1 million for both accounts

3. SIPC uses which of the following to determine the value of customer claims when a broker-dealer becomes insolvent?

    A. Market value on the date the broker-dealer becomes insolvent
    B. Market value on the date a federal court is petitioned to appoint a trustee
    C. Market value on the date the trustee pays the customers their balances
    D. Average market value from the time a trustee is appointed to the payment date

4. Which of the following statements is NOT true regarding the civil penalties that may be imposed for insider trading violations under the Securities Exchange Act of 1934?

   A. A civil penalty may be imposed only on a person who is registered under a securities act.
   B. The violation for which the penalty may be imposed is defined as "buying or selling securities while in possession of material, nonpublic information."
   C. The SEC may ask a court to impose a penalty of up to three times the loss avoided or profit gained on an illegal transaction.
   D. Improper supervision may cause a broker-dealer firm to be liable to pay a penalty if one of its representatives commits an insider trading violation.

5. Under the Securities Exchange Act of 1934, insiders include which of the following?

   I. Attorney who writes an offering circular for a company
   II. Bookkeeper in a company's accounting department
   III. Wife of a company's president
   IV. Brother of a company's president

   A. I only
   B. II only
   C. II, III and IV only
   D. I, II, III and IV

See page 343 for answers and rationale

The National Association of Securities Dealers

The National Association of Securities Dealers (NASD) is the OTC industry's SRO. It was formed to help regulate the securities industry, specifically the over-the-counter marketplace, under the supervision of the SEC. The NASD is a membership corporation—that is, the NASD does not issue capital stock. The NASD's purposes and objectives are to:

- promote the investment banking and securities business, to standardize principles and practices, to promote high standards of commercial honor and to encourage the observance of federal and state securities laws;
- provide a medium for communication among its members, and between its members, the government and other agencies;

- adopt, administer and enforce the NASD's Conduct Rules (formerly known as Rules of Fair Practice) and rules designed to prevent fraudulent and manipulative practices, as well as to promote just and equitable principles of trade; and
- promote self-discipline among members and to investigate and adjust grievances between the public and members as well as between members.

Districts. The NASD divides the United States into 13 districts to facilitate its operation. Each district elects a district committee to administer NASD rules. A committee has a maximum of 12 members who serve for three years.

Within each district, the **Department of Enforcement** handles trade practice complaints. The NASD executive committee, made up of members of the Board of Governors, manages NASD national affairs.

NASD Dues, Assessments and Other Charges

The NASD is funded by assessments of member firms' registered reps and applicants and by annual fees. The annual fee each member pays includes a(n):

- basic membership fee;
- assessment based on gross income;
- fee for each principal and registered representative; and
- charge for each branch office.

Failure to pay dues can result in suspension or revocation of membership.

Use of the NASD's Corporate Name

NASD members cannot use the NASD name in any manner that would suggest that the NASD has endorsed a member firm. The members may use the phrase "member of the NASD" as long as the firm places no undue emphasis on it.

✓ **Take Note:** Neither the NASD nor the SEC approve the way a representative or firm conducts business. To suggest otherwise is prohibited. Consider the following situation:

A registered representative gives you the following business card:

> *James P. Mellon*
> *(555) 234-5678*
>
> **NASD Registered**
> **Representative**
>
> ABC Associates

Is there anything wrong with this business card?

Yes! Note that the large and bold print used to identify the NASD affiliation could mislead the recipient of this business card into thinking that James Mellon is actually associated with the NASD. The NASD cannot be more prominent than the name of the rep's firm. Someone might mistakenly be led to believe that the NASD *approves* of or endorses this rep.

NASD Manual NASD policies are specified in the NASD Manual. The manual describes four sets of rules and codes by which the OTC market is regulated:

1. **Conduct Rules (formerly the Rules of Fair Practice).** The Conduct Rules set out fair and ethical trade practices that member firms and their registered representatives must follow when dealing with the public.
2. **Uniform Practice Code.** This code established the Uniform Trade Practices, including settlement, good delivery, ex-dates, confirmations, don't know (DK) procedures and other guidelines for broker-dealers to follow when they do business with other member broker-dealer firms.
3. **Code of Procedure.** This code describes how the NASD hears and handles member violations of the Conduct Rules.
4. **Code of Arbitration Procedure.** This code governs the resolution of disagreements and claims between members, registered representatives and the public; it addresses monetary claims, not violations of the Conduct Rules.

NASD Membership and Registration

The NASD's Board of Governors establishes rules, regulations and membership eligibility standards. At present, the following membership standards and registration requirements are in place.

Broker-Dealer Registration

Any broker-dealer registered with the SEC is eligible and may apply for membership in the NASD. Any person who effects transactions in securities as a broker, a dealer or an investment banker also may register with the NASD, as may municipal bond firms. Application for NASD membership carries the applying firm's specific agreement to:

- comply with the association's rules and regulations;
- comply with federal securities laws; and
- pay dues, assessments and other charges in the manner and amounts fixed by the association.

A membership application is made to the NASD district office in the district in which the applying firm has its home office. If a district committee passes on the firm's qualifications, the firm can be accepted into NASD membership.

Associated Person Registration

Any person associated with an NASD member firm who intends to engage in the investment banking or securities business must be registered with the NASD as an associated person. Anyone applying for registration with the NASD as an associated person must be sponsored by a member firm.

Qualifications Investigated. Before submitting an application to enroll any person with the NASD as a registered representative, a member firm must check the person's business reputation, character, education, qualifications and experience. As part of the application process, the member firm must certify that it has made an investigation and that the candidate's credentials are in order.

Failure to Register Personnel. A member firm's failure to register an employee who performs any of the functions of a registered rep may lead to disciplinary action by the NASD.

Postregistration Rules and Regulations

Registered Persons Changing Firms. NASD registration is nontransferable. If a registered person leaves one member firm to join another firm, he must terminate registration at the first firm on a U-5 form and reapply for registration with the new employing member firm on a U-4 form. If a person terminates his registration with one firm, he must register with another firm within two years or he will be required to requalify for his license.

✓ *Take Note:* An individual cannot transact business as a registered representative unless he is associated with a broker-dealer. A representative's license is no longer effective when he leaves a firm.

Continuing Commissions. An individual must be registered to sell securities. A registered rep who leaves a member firm—upon retirement, for instance—may continue to receive commissions on business placed while employed. However, the rep must have a contract to this effect before leaving the firm. A deceased representative's heirs also may receive continuing commissions on business the representative placed if a contract exists.

Notification of Disciplinary Action. A member firm must notify the NASD if any associated person in the firm's employment is subjected to disciplinary action by one of the following:

- national securities exchange or association;
- clearing corporation;
- commodity futures market regulatory agency; or
- federal or state regulatory commission.

The notification must include the individual's name and the nature of the action.

A member firm also must notify the NASD of disciplinary action the firm itself has taken against an associated person and the nature of the action.

Terminations. If an associated person voluntarily ends his employment with a member, his NASD registration ceases 30 calendar days from the date the NASD receives written notice from the employing member firm. Whenever any registered person's employment is terminated, the member firm must notify the NASD and the NYSE in writing within 30 calendar days. If a firm terminates its membership, it is subject to complaints filed against it under the Code of Procedure for a period of two years.

Terminating Reps Under Investigation. If a registered representative or another associated person is under investigation for federal securities law violations or has disciplinary action pending against him from the NASD or any other SRO, a member firm may not terminate its business relationship with the person until the investigation or disciplinary action has been resolved. However, the NASD will backdate the effective date of the person's termination as a registered representative.

Exemptions from Registration

Certain people are *not* required to register with the NASD as associated persons.

Foreign Associates. Non-U.S. citizens employed by NASD member firms, usually in Canadian or overseas branch offices, are not subject to registration and licensing with the association. This does not include U.S. citizens living and working in overseas or Canadian branch offices, however. Each exempted foreign associate must agree not to engage in securities business in any country or territory under U.S. jurisdiction and not to do business with any U.S. citizen or national or resident alien.

Clerical Personnel and Corporate Officers. A member firm's clerical employees need not register with the NASD. Corporate officers who are not involved with the member's investment banking business also are exempt from registration.

Employees in Other Specific Functions. Employees registered with an exchange as floor members who work or trade only on the floor or who transact business only in exempted securities or commodities are exempt from registration.

State Registration

In addition to registering with the NASD, registered reps and broker-dealers must register with the state securities administrator in each state in which they intend to do business.

Quick Quiz 4.5 True or False?

_____ 1. The wife of a deceased rep may continue to receive commissions based on a verbal agreement with the former employer.

_____ 2. A foreign representative of a foreign broker-dealer is not required to register with the NASD if it engages in business with a U.S citizen.

_____ 3. A member firm is required to investigate the background and character of any person it may hire.

_____ 4. A representative terminates its registration with a firm by filing a U-5 form.

_____ 5. If a representative is registered with the NASD, state registration is not necessary.

_____ 6. A member firm's clerical staff must register with the NASD.

_____ 7. Broker-dealers may not use the phrase *member of the NASD* on any sales literature they prepare.

See page 343 for answers and rationale

Qualification Examinations

To become a registered representative or principal, an individual must pass the appropriate licensing examination(s).

Registered Representatives
All associated persons engaged in the investment banking and securities business are considered registered representatives, including any:

- assistant officer who does not function as a principal;
- individual who supervises, solicits or conducts business in securities; and
- individual who trains people to supervise, solicit or conduct business in securities.

Limited Securities Representative License (Series 6)

The Series 6 Investment Company/Variable Contract Products Limited Representative license allows a representative to sell open-end investment companies, new issues of closed-end investment companies and variable products. The Series 6 can serve as a prerequisite for the Series 26 principal exam.

General Securities Representative License (Series 7)

A Series 7 general securities license allows a registered representative to sell almost all types of securities products. A general securities rep cannot sell commodities futures unless he or she has a Series 3 license.

 **Test Topic Alert!**

You may see at least one question on the exam that asks you what a Series 6 registered representative can or cannot sell. Try the following:

A Series 6 registered representative is permitted to sell all of the following except:

A. face amount certificates
B. aggressive growth mutual fund shares
C. closed-end company shares in the secondary market
D. unit investment trusts

The correct answer is C. Although a Series 6 registered representative is permitted to sell closed-end company shares in their primary offering stage (with prospectus), once they begin trading in the secondary market, they must be sold by a Series 7 registered representative. A Series 7 registration is required to transact business in the secondary market.

Sometimes questions on the exam introduce terms as "distracters" that you may not recognize. Remember that a Series 6 representative *cannot* transact business in REITs (real estate investment trust units), limited partnerships or DPPs (direct participation programs). Don't worry about the features of these investments; just realize that a Series 6 rep can't sell them!

Registered Principals

Anyone who manages or supervises any part of a member's investment banking or securities business must be registered as a principal with the NASD. This includes people involved solely in training associated persons. Principals are required to review every customer order, all customer correspondence and the handling of all customer complaints. Unless the member firm is a sole proprietorship, it must employ at least two registered principals, one of whom must be registered as a general securities principal.

General Securities Principal License (Series 24)

Any person actively engaged in managing a member's securities or investment banking business, including supervising, soliciting and conducting business, or in training persons associated with the member must qualify by examination and register with the NASD as a general securities principal. The Series 7 is a prerequisite for the Series 24 principal examination.

Investment Company Principal License (Series 26)

The Series 26 Investment Company/Variable Contract Products Limited Principal license entitles a principal to supervise the solicitation, purchase or sale of mutual funds and variable annuities. The Series 6 is a prerequisite for the Series 26 principal examination.

 Take Note: A general rule to remember for your exam is that anyone who manages, trains or supervises reps must register as a principal. Each firm must have a minimum of *two* registered principals. Also, note that officers, directors and partners must register as principals.

Ineligibility and Disqualifications

A person may not act as a registered representative or principal unless he or she meets the NASD's eligibility standards regarding training, experience and competence.

Statutory Disqualification. Disciplinary sanctions by the SEC, another SRO, a foreign financial regulator or a foreign equivalent of an SRO can be cause for statutory disqualification of NASD membership. An individual applying for registration as an associated person will be rejected if that person:

- has been or is expelled or suspended from membership or participation in any other SRO or from the foreign equivalent of an SRO;
- is under an SEC order or an order of a foreign financial regulator denying, suspending or revoking his registration or barring him from association with a broker-dealer; or

- has been found to be the cause of another broker-dealer or associated person being expelled or suspended by another SRO, the SEC or a foreign equivalent of an SRO.

Any of the following also can automatically disqualify an applicant for registration:

- misstatements willfully made in an application for membership or registration as an associated person;
- a felony conviction, either domestic or foreign, or a misdemeanor conviction involving securities or money within the past 10 years; and
- court injunctions prohibiting the individual from acting as an investment adviser, an underwriter or a broker-dealer or in other capacities aligned with the securities and financial services industry.

Quick Quiz 4.6 The following matching exercise will review your grasp of some significant numbers associated with NASD rules:

A. 30
B. 24
C. 10
D. 2

___ 1. The minimum number of principals a firm must have

___ 2. All securities firms must have one of these to manage and supervise

___ 3. The number of days a broker-dealer has to notify the NASD of a rep's termination

___ 4. A felony conviction within this number of years can disqualify an individual from registration

See page 344 for answers.

NASD Definitions

The terms below have specific meanings to the NASD.

Associated Person (AP) of a Member. Any employee, manager, director, officer or partner of a member broker-dealer or another entity (issuer, bank, etc.) or any person controlling, controlled by or in common control with that member.

Broker. (1) An individual or a firm that charges a fee or commission for executing buy and sell orders submitted by another individual or firm. (2) The role of a brokerage firm when it acts as an agent for a customer and charges the customer a commission for its services. (3) Any person engaged in the business of effecting transactions in securities for the accounts of others who is not a bank.

Completion of the Transaction. Completion of the transaction occurs when a customer pays any part of the purchase price to the broker-dealer for a security he has purchased, or delivers a security he has sold. If the customer makes payment to the broker-dealer before the payment is due, completion of the transaction occurs when the broker-dealer delivers the security.

Customer. Any individual, person, partnership, corporation or other legal entity who is not a broker, dealer or municipal securities dealer—that is, the public.

Dealer. (1) The role of a brokerage firm when it acts as a principal in a particular trade. A firm acts as a dealer when it buys or sells a security for its own account and at its own risk, then charges the customer a markup or markdown. (2) Any person engaged in the business of buying and selling securities for his or her own account, either directly or through a broker, who is not a bank.

Member. A member of the NYSE can be defined as one of the 1,366 individuals owning a seat on the New York Stock Exchange. A member of the NASD is any individual, partnership, corporation or other legal entity admitted to membership in the NASD.

Security. Under the Act of 1934, any note, stock, bond, investment contract, variable annuity, profit-sharing or partnership agreement, certificate of deposit, option on a security or other instrument of investment commonly known as a security.

Quick Quiz 4.7 The following matching exercise will test your knowledge of important NASD definitions:

    A. dealer
    B. associated person
    C. member
    D. broker

___ 1. The NASD permits only firms to become one of these

___ 2. Compensated by a commission in securities transactions

___ 3. Compensated by a markup/markdown in securities transactions

___ 4. Someone controlling or controlled by a member firm

See page 344 for answers.

Continuing Education

All registered representatives are subject to NASD continuing education requirements and must periodically complete a *regulatory element* and a *firm element.*

Regulatory Element. The regulatory element of the Continuing Education requirement is completed at a Sylvan Learning Center on the second anniversary of registration and every three years thereafter. It requires participation in an exercise involving industry regulation and ethics in dealing with customers.

If registered representatives fail to complete the required regulatory element, their registrations become inactive and they cannot conduct business activities. Registrations that remain inactive for two years are terminated.

Firm Element. Any registered representative who has direct contact with customers in the sale of securities is subject to the firm element requirement on an annual basis. A member firm must design a written training program that covers the following topics:

- regulatory requirements that apply to business performed by the representative;
- suitability and ethical sales practices; and
- overall investment features and related risk factors.

Communications with the Public

Although the general public often uses the terms interchangeably, the NASD and the NYSE expect principals and representatives to recognize the difference between "advertising" and "sales literature."

Advertising and Sales Literature

The major difference between advertising and sales literature is how the NASD member selects the audience. If the member *cannot* select the audience, it is advertising; if the member *can* select the audience, it is sales literature.

Advertising. Advertising includes copy, support graphics and other support materials intended for:

- publication in newspapers, magazines or other periodicals;
- radio or television broadcast;
- prerecorded telephone marketing messages and tape recordings;
- videotape displays;
- signs or billboards;
- motion pictures and filmstrips;
- electronic (computer) communication devices;
- telephone directories; and
- any other use of the public media.

Sales Literature. Sales literature is any written communication distributed to customers or the public in general or available to people upon request that does not meet the definition of "advertising." Standardized sales pitches, telephone scripts and seminar tapes are all considered sales literature and, therefore, are subject to the same rules and regulations that apply to sales literature. Sales literature also includes materials such as:

- circulars;
- research reports;
- market letters;
- form letters;
- option worksheets;
- performance reports and summaries;
- text prepared and used for educational seminars;
- telemarketing scripts; and
- reprints and excerpts from any advertisement, sales literature or published news item or article.

Sales literature can be distributed in written, oral or electronic form.

✓ *Take Note:* One final point on definitions of advertising and sales literature:

Internet communications are a common occurrence within the securities industry and are subject to NASD rules on public communications. If you have any questions on such communications it may be helpful to know the following information:

- A Website is considered advertising.
- An e-mail sent to a group of persons is considered sales literature.
- An e-mail sent to one person only is considered correspondence.

Form Letters. According to the NASD, a form letter is a sales letter that contains sections or statements identical in essence to statements made or contained in other sales letters. As with all other forms of sales literature, these must be approved in advance by the principal and maintained in a file for a period of three years from the date of their first use.

✓ *Take Note:* Be careful of questions that ask you to differentiate between advertising and sales literature according to the NASD definition.

Think of advertising as *nontargeted*. There is no control over who will read, see or hear it.

Think of sales literature as *targeted* material. It is given or mailed to a specific recipient.

Whether a communication is classified as advertising or sales literature, it must still be approved by a principal **before** use. It must also be kept on file for **three years** from the date of first use.

Quick Quiz 4.8   Test yourself on your mastery of these definitions by choosing "A" (advertising) or "SL" (sales literature) for each of the following public communications:

___ 1. Billboard

___ 2. Seminar

___ 3. Radio broadcast

___ 4. Form letter

___ 5. Research report

___ 6. Recruitment ad

___ 7. Circular

___ 8. Telemarketing script

___ 9. Telephone directory

___ 10. Copies of a published mutual funds article distributed to prospective clients

See page 344 for answers.

Test Topic Alert!   Test your mastery of advertising and sales literature identification with the following question:

NASD rules on advertising specifically apply to which of the following?

A. Yellow page telephone listing
B. Market research reports
C. Telemarketing scripts
D. All of the above

The correct answer is A. The question asks about *advertising,* not sales literature. Of the choices offered, only a Yellow page listing is defined by the NASD as advertising.

Generic Advertising (Rule 135a). Generic advertising promotes securities as an investment medium, but does not refer to any specific security. Generic advertising often includes information about:

- the securities investments that companies offer;
- the nature of investment companies;
- services offered in connection with the described securities;
- explanations of the various types of investment companies;
- descriptions of exchange and reinvestment privileges; and
- where the public can write or call for further information.

All generic advertisements must contain the name and address of the registered sponsor of the advertisement. A generic advertisement can be placed only by a firm that offers the type of security or service described.

✔ *Take Note:* To clarify the rule on generic advertising, think of the following: a brokerage firm is not permitted to *advertise* no-load mutual funds if it does not *sell* them. The firm must have available for sale the type of security or service it advertises.

Tombstones (Rule 134 Advertisements). An underwriter is limited in what it can publicly state about a security in registration. Under Rule 134, advertising copy and other sales materials need not be filed with the SEC as part of the registration statement if the body copy is limited to:

- the name of the issuer of the securities being offered;
- a brief description of the business in the offering;
- the date, time and place of the meeting at which stockholders will vote on or consent to the proposed transaction;
- a brief description of the planned transaction; or
- any legend or disclaimer statement required by state or federal law.

Advertisements that meet these restrictions are more commonly known as tombstones or Rule 134 advertisements. They are not required to be accompanied by a prospectus, but must state where a prospectus can be obtained. Any advertising copy in a tombstone must also contain the following disclaimers:

- the communication does not represent an offer to sell the securities described—securities are sold by prospectus only;
- the name and address of the person or firm to contact for a prospectus; and
- a response to this advertisement does not obligate the prospect to a buying commitment of any kind.

Mutual Fund Tombstone Ads. Investment company tombstone ads are permitted to contain additional information under SEC Rule 134. Tombstone ads may include:

- the investment company's classification and subclassification;
- the type of fund (common stock fund, bond fund, balanced fund, etc.); and
- whether the fund emphasizes income or growth.

Funds may also describe investment policies and objectives, services, principal officers, year of incorporation and aggregate net asset value if the advertisement includes the following legend:

> *For more complete information about (fund's name) including charges expenses send for a prospectus from (name and address). Read it carefully before you invest or send money.*

 Take Note: Although tombstone advertisements and generic advertising are both *general* in nature, the differences between the two are as follows:

- Generic ads may name only the principal underwriter, but tombstone ads may name the specific investment company *and* the principal underwriter.
- Generic ads do not refer to a specific security, but tombstones identify the specific securities being advertised.

Approval and Filing Requirements

Approval

A registered principal of the member firm must approve each advertisement and piece of sales literature before use and, if applicable, before filing with the NASD. For advertisements or sales literature specific to options, the material must be approved by a registered options principal (ROP) or compliance ROP. A supervisory analyst must approve research reports.

Filing Requirements

All advertisements and sales literature must be on file with the member for a period of three years; for the first two years, the file must be kept in an easily accessible place. This file must include the name(s) of the person(s) who prepared the material and approved its use.

If the NASD determines that a member's advertising departs from the standards of fair dealing and good faith, it may require the member to file all advertising and sales literature with the Association's advertising department 10 days before use. The District Business Conduct Committee (DBCC) notifies the member in writing of the types of material to be filed and the length of time the filing requirement is in effect.

Filing with the NASD. A new member firm (one that has been in business for less than one year) is required to file any advertising or sales literature with the NASD advertising department *10 days before use*. Beyond one year there is no filing requirement, but the firm is still subject to NASD spot checks.

Investment Company. All member firms must file advertising and sales literature relating to investment company securities with the NASD's advertising department no later than 10 days after first use or publication. This requirement applies to communications regarding mutual funds, variable contracts and unit investment trust. Both old and new firms are subject to this filing rule.

✓ *Take Note:* Whether a communication is classified as advertising or sales literature, it must still be approved by a principal **before** use. It must also be kept on file for **three years** from the date of first use.

The NASD advertising department does not *approve* advertising. It just provides comments back to the broker-dealer on problems in the ad.

Also, note that investment company advertising and sales literature must *always* be filed with the NASD advertising department within 10 days of first use regardless of the age of the firm. The 10-day *pre-filing* requirement applies to *new* firms only and covers advertising for all types of securities products. After the first year, firms are only subject to filing requirements on investment company products.

Spot Checks

Members' advertising and sales literature are subject to spot checks by the NASD. Upon written notice, a member must submit all material the NASD advertising department requests.

Exceptions to Filing Requirements

The following types of advertisements or sales literature are excluded from filing and spot check procedures:

- those relating solely to changes in a member's name, personnel, location, ownership, business structure, officers or partners, telephone, facsimile or teletype numbers; and
- those for internal distribution only and not distributed to the public.

Excluded from the filing requirements are prospectuses, preliminary prospectuses, offering circulars and similar documents used in connection with the offering of securities that have been filed with the SEC or any state. If the security is exempt from registration requirements, any sales literature or advertising need not be filed.

🖉 **Quick Quiz 4.9** True or False?

___ 1. A member firm's investment company advertising material must be submitted to the NASD advertising department for approval before it is used.

___ 2. A principal of the firm must approve all sales literature within 10 days of first use.

___ 3. New firms are required to file all securities advertising material and sales literature with the NASD advertising department 10 days prior to use.

___ 4. Member firm investment company advertising and sales literature is not subject to NASD spot checks.

___ 5. Memos stamped "for internal use only" must be approved by a principal prior to distribution.

See page 344 for answers and rationale.

NASD Rules Concerning Public Communications

Securities rules and regulations protect the general public from unscrupulous investment professionals.

The two main problems the NASD's code of professionalism addresses in advertising and sales literature are omissions and distortions of material facts. In general, all communications from a member to the public must be based on principles of fair dealing and good faith. A communication should provide sound basis for evaluating the facts in regard to the product, service or industry promoted. Exaggerated, unwarranted or misleading statements are strictly prohibited.

Identification of Source. In general, sales literature—including market letters and research reports—must identify the member firm's name; the person or firm that prepared the material if copy was prepared outside the member firm; and the date the material was first used.

If the literature contains information that is not current, that fact should be stated in the material.

Customer Recommendations

A member should have reasonable grounds for believing that a security is a suitable investment for a customer before recommending its purchase. Investment recommendations must be consistent with customer needs, financial capability and objectives. Investment recommendations should be in a customer's best interest, not the registered representative's. Each investment should be explained fully, especially its risks. At no time should customers own investments that could put them at risk beyond their financial capacity.

Disclosure Requirements. Proposals and written presentations that include specific recommendations must have reasonable basis to support the recommendations. The member must offer to provide, upon request, investment information that supports the recommendation. The price of the security at the time the recommendation is made must be disclosed.

A recommendation may be supported by performance of past recommendations if it includes:

- price or price range of the recommended security at the date and time that the recommendation is made;
- market's general direction;
- availability of information supporting the recommendation;
- any recommendations made of similar securities within the past 12 months, including the nature of the recommendations—buy, sell or hold;
- whether the firm intends to buy or sell any of the recommended security for its own account;
- whether the firm is a market maker in the recommended security;
- whether the firm or its officers or partners own options, rights or warrants to buy the recommended security;
- whether the firm managed or co-managed a public offering of the recommended security or any other of the same issuer's securities during the past three years; and
- all recommendations (gainers and losers) the firm made over the period of time in question.

The time span covered in the list of recommendations must run through consecutive periods, without skipping periods in an attempt to hide particular recommendations or negative price performance data.

A knowledgeable investor uses this type of information to determine whether a recommendation is appropriate for his or her situation. In addition to meeting these information requirements, the firm making the recommendation must not:

- imply that any guarantees accompany the recommendation;
- compare the recommended security to dissimilar products;
- make fraudulent or misleading statements about the recommended security; or
- make any predictions about the recommended security's future performance or potential.

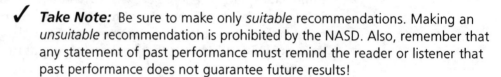 **Take Note:** Be sure to make only *suitable* recommendations. Making an *unsuitable* recommendation is prohibited by the NASD. Also, remember that any statement of past performance must remind the reader or listener that past performance does not guarantee future results!

Other Communication Prohibitions

Claims and Opinions Couched as Facts and Conclusions

It violates regulations to pass off opinions, projections and forecasts as guarantees of performance.

Testimonials. Testimonials and endorsements by celebrities and public opinion influencers related to specific recommendations or investment results must not mislead or suggest that past performance indicates future performance. If a member firm pays a fee or other compensation to a person for a testimonial or an endorsement, it must disclose this fact.

If a broker-dealer assembles a sales piece about a particular investment company that includes testimonials by one or more customers, the sales piece must state that:

- past performance does not indicate future performance;
- the company compensated the person who made the testimonial, if this is true; and
- the person making the testimonial has the qualifications to do so (these qualifications must be listed), if the testimonial implies that the statement is based on the customer's special experience or knowledge.

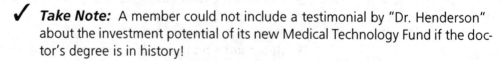 **Take Note:** A member could not include a testimonial by "Dr. Henderson" about the investment potential of its new Medical Technology Fund if the doctor's degree is in history!

Offers of Free Service. It is unprofessional to use offers of free service if, in fact, the respondent must assume obligations of one sort or another. Reports, analyses or other services offered to the public must be furnished entirely free and without condition or obligation.

Other Rules. The following are some additional rules regarding unprofessional practices:

- A communication must not state or imply that research facilities are more extensive than they actually are.
- Hedge clauses, caveats and disclaimers must not be used if they are misleading or inconsistent with the material's content.
- Ambiguous references to the NASD or other SROs must not be made with the aim of leading people to believe that a broker-dealer acts with the endorsement and approval of the Association or one of the other SROs. If the NASD's name or logo is used in a member's sales literature, it must not appear in a typeface larger or more prominent than the one used for the member's own name.

✓ **Take Note:** Remember this business card?

> *James P. Mellon*
> *(555) 234-5678*
>
> ## NASD Registered Representative
>
> ABC Associates

The name of the NASD should never appear larger than the name of the member. The size of the type and the bold print may mislead the public into thinking Mr. Mellon is in some way *endorsed* by the NASD, which would be a violation.

Use of Members' Names

General Standards. No material fact is to be omitted if the omission causes the advertisement or literature to be misleading. As a result, all advertising and sales literature must:

- clearly and prominently disclose the NASD member's name;
- clearly describe the relationship between the NASD member and the named entities and products when multiple entities and products are being offered;
- clearly disclose the relationship of an individual and an NASD member when an individual is named in the communication;
- not use or refer to nonexistent degrees or designations; and
- not use degrees or designations in a misleading manner.

Fictional Names. A fictional name or DBA (doing business as) designation is permitted if the name is filed with the NASD and the SEC.

Other Designations. A member may designate a portion of its business using a phrase such as "division of," "service of" or "securities offered through" only if a bona fide division exists. The member name must be clearly designated and the division be clearly identified as a division of the member.

Recruitment Advertising   Companies that advertise to attract new registered reps are regulated by the same Conduct Rules that cover companies advertising investment products. The advertisements must be truthful, informative and fair in representing the opportunities in the industry and must not contain exaggerated or unwarranted claims.

The advertisements may not emphasize the salaries of top-paid salespeople without revealing that they are not representative, and the ads may not contain any other statements that may be misleading or fraudulent.

Broker-dealers are permitted, in this one instance, to run blind advertisements—that is, advertisements that do not list a company's name.

✓ **Take Note:** Recruitment ads are the only form of advertising not required to disclose the identity of the member firm. Such an ad is allowed to request someone to "Send a resume to P.O. Box 54321" without stating the name of the firm.

Interviews

Once a company starts interviewing potential employees, it is the principal's responsibility to see that both the industry and the job opportunity are represented honestly. Any discussions of the business must present both the upside and the downside of the position and should not misrepresent the average employee's compensation.

Quick Quiz 4.10   True or False?

____ 1. It is permissible to omit facts in advertising an sales literature.

____ 2. Testimonials in investment company advertising are prohibited.

____ 3. Firms are not allowed to offer "free services."

____ 4. The price of the recommended security must always be disclosed at the time the recommendation is made.

____ 5. A recommendation showing past performance must include all recommendations made of similar securities within the past six months.

See page 344 for answers and rationale.

Specific Rules for Investment Company Sales Literature

SEC Rule 156 establishes additional guidelines for mutual fund sales literature. Any investment company sales literature that omits material facts, contains untrue statements or is misleading is illegal. Sales literature may be considered misleading because of:

- inaccurate reports of investment performance;
- predictions made of future income or capital gains based on past performance;
- unsubstantiated claims about the skills of the investment company's management;
- exaggeration of the backgrounds of officers and directors;
- omissions of the shortcomings of investment performance;
- information reported out of context;
- distorted or incomplete performance comparisons to other investments or indices;
- presenting potential benefits without providing equal prominence to possible risks; and
- omission of information about general economic and financial conditions.

These restrictions apply to any form of communication where an offer to sell is made. Even spoken words are considered part of the company's sales literature. Registered representatives must tell the complete truth in presentations and not imply investment performance or guarantees that do not exist.

✓ *Take Note:* In sales presentations, the downside of an investment opportunity must be as highly emphasized as its upside.

If in a sales presentation a representative draws additional charts or graphs to depict performance, the representative is in violation of Rule 156. All charts and graphs must be approved prior to use.

✓ *Take Note:* Reps are prohibited from marking or highlighting information on prospectuses distributed to prospective buyers by this rule!

Advertising Performance Data   Investment companies frequently choose to advertise measures of performance, such as return on investment or total return. When mutual funds, variable annuities and unit investment trusts advertise such performance data, additional requirements apply under SEC Rule 482. Funds are not required to include performance data in advertising.

Funds are limited to quoting the following performance information:

- average annual total return;
- current yield;
- tax equivalent yield; and

- a historical measure of performance reflecting all of these elements of return.

Total Return. Total return is calculated by assuming the reinvestment of dividends and capital gains distributions. The computation of total return must be made in accordance with standardized procedures. If the average annual total return is included, the quotations must for 1-, 5- and 10-year periods, or since inception if the fund is new. The periods over which the computation has been made must be identified.

Advertising Yield. If the fund chooses to disclose yield, current yield must be calculated according to standardized procedures. The base period of the calculation must be identified, and the computation must reflect a 30-day period.

An advertisement containing performance data must clearly state that what is shown is *past* performance, and that investment returns and principal values fluctuate. The ad must further state that an investor who redeems shares may receive more or less than the original cost. Money market funds are not required to state the risks of principal fluctuation.

Rule 482 also requires that the maximum amount of any sales load or nonrecurring fee is disclosed in the advertisement. Funds may alternatively choose *not* to disclose such fees, but if they do, a disclosure statement must identify that the deduction of such fees is not reflected and that performance would be reduced if fees were deducted.

Performance data must be *current*. The rule assumes that data from the most recent calendar quarter is current.

Recommending Funds

When recommending mutual funds to clients as investments and when using advertisements or sales literature developed for those investments, a broker-dealer should:

- use charts or graphs showing a fund's performance over a period of time long enough to reflect variations in value under different market conditions, generally a period of at least 10 years;
- reveal the source of the graphics;
- separate dividends from capital gains when making statements about a fund's cash returns;
- not state that a mutual fund is similar to or safer than any other type of security;
- reveal a fund's highest sales charge, even if the client appears to qualify for a breakpoint; and
- not make any fraudulent or misleading statements or omissions of facts.

Periodic Payment Plans. Mutual fund plans that make periodic payments (frequently sold in this manner so investors receive the benefits of dollar cost averaging) cannot be described in advertisements or sales literature without the disclosure that:

- a profit is not assured;
- they do not provide protection from losses in a declining market;
- the plans involve continuous investments regardless of market fluctuations; and
- an investor should consider her financial ability to continue purchases during periods of declining prices.

Review of NASD Regulations

The following summarizes the NASD regulations regarding advertising and sales literature:

- A principal must approve all advertising and sales literature before use and before filing with the NASD.
- All advertising and sales literature must be kept in a separate file for a minimum of three years.
- All advertising and sales literature concerning registered investment companies must be filed within 10 business days of first use by any member acting as a principal underwriter for the securities. With each filing, the member must provide the actual or anticipated date of first use.
- New members must file with the NASD all advertising they produce or distribute during their first year at least 10 days before first use and must provide the actual or anticipated date of first use with each filing.
- The NASD may require any member to resume filing all of its advertising and sales literature before use.

 **Test Topic Alert!**   The three questions below represent typical testable material about mutual fund advertising.

1. Which of the following activities is permissible in mutual fund sales presentation?

    A. Highlighting charts or graphs in the fund prospectus
    B. Comparing capital gains distributions between a stock fund and a U.S. government bond fund
    C. Creating a new chart on a separate sheet of paper to clarify a question raised by the customer
    D. Informing the customer of the tax status of dividend distributions

    D. It is appropriate for a representative to identify the tax status of dividend distributions in a mutual fund sales presentation. It is prohibited to make unfair comparisons, mark on the prospectus or create new charts or graphs and use them without approval.

2. All of the following must be disclosed in a mutual fund advertisement containing performance data EXCEPT

    A. investment returns fluctuate
    B. the SEC disclaimer stating that the securities have not been approved or disapproved by the SEC
    C. investors who redeem shares may receive more or less than the original cost
    D. data represents past performance

    B. The SEC disclaimer is not required in advertising material. The "no approval" clause must be included in the prospectus.

3. Which of the following statements about advertising mutual fund performance is true?

    A. A comparison must be provided to a market index most similar to the portfolio securities.
    B. The fund's total return must be included for a minimum period of one year.
    C. The advertisement must disclose the maximum amount of load or fee.
    D. All funds, including money markets, must make a disclosure about fluctuation of principal.

    C. In performance advertisements, the maximum sales load or other non-recurring fee must be disclosed. Comparisons to market indices are not required. Disclosure about fluctuation of principal is required for all funds except money market funds. The minimum period for total return is 10 years, or since the funds inception, whichever is shorter.

Legal Recourse of
Customers

The Securities Exchange Act of 1934 and the Acts of 1933 and 1940 all contain sections prohibiting the use of any fraudulent or manipulative device in the selling of securities to the public.

The rules make it unlawful for any person to use the mails or any facilities of interstate commerce to "employ, in connection with the purchase or sale of any security, any manipulative or deceptive device in contravention of such rules and regulations as the Commission may prescribe as necessary." In essence, this passage states simply that an act is unlawful if the SEC says it is, and the enforcement of the intent of the act is not to be limited by the letter of the law.

Statute of Limitations. Any client may sue for damages if he or she believes that a broker-dealer used any form of manipulative or deceptive practices in the sale of securities. The client must bring the lawsuit within three years of the manipulative act and within one year of discovery of the manipulation or deception.

Telephone Communications with the Public

The Telephone Consumer Protection Act of 1991 (TCPA), administered by the Federal Communications Commission (FCC), was enacted to protect consumers from unwanted telephone solicitations. A telephone solicitation is defined as a telephone call initiated for the purpose of encouraging the purchase of or investment in property, goods or services. The act governs commercial calls, recorded solicitations from autodialers and solicitations and advertisements to facsimile machines and modems. The act requires an organization that performs telemarketing—cold calling in particular—to:

- maintain a "do-not-call list" of customers who do not want to be called and keep a customer's name on the list for 10 years from the time the request is made;
- institute a written policy on maintenance procedures for the do-not-call list;
- train reps on using the list;
- ensure that reps acknowledge and immediately record the names and telephone numbers of customers who ask not to be called again;
- ensure that anyone making cold calls for the firm informs customers of the firm's name and telephone number or address;
- ensure that telemarketers do not call a customer within 10 years of a do-not-call request; and
- ensure that a telephone solicitation occurs only between the hours of 8:00 A.M. and 9:00 P.M. of the time zone in which the customer is located.

The act exempts calls:

- made to parties with whom the caller has an established business relationship or where the caller has prior express permission or invitation;
- made on behalf of a tax-exempt nonprofit organization;
- not made for a commercial purpose; and
- made for legitimate debt collection purposes.

✓ **Take Note:** Fax communications *are* subject to the Telephone Consumer Protection Act. Internet communications and e-mail, however, *are not.*

Quick Quiz 4.11

1. Which of the following parties is covered under the Telephone Consumer Protection Act of 1991?

   A. University survey group
   B. Nonprofit organization
   C. Church group
   D. Registered representative

2. Which of the following must a rep do when making cold calls?

   I. Immediately record the names and telephone numbers of customers who ask not to be called again
   II. Inform customers of the firm's name and telephone number or address
   III. Limit calls to between the hours of 8:00 A.M. and 9:00 P.M. of the time zone in which customers are located
   IV. Not call customers who make a do-not-call request

   A. I and II only
   B. I and IV only
   C. II and III only
   D. I, II, III and IV

See page 345 for answers and rationale.

Ethics in the Securities Industry

Ethical Business Practices   The securities industry is governed by a very strict code of ethics. Unacceptable behavior is subject to sanctions ranging from fines and reprimands to expulsion from the industry or jail. Business behavior and practices are measured against clear standards for fairness and equity.

Securities industry regulators work to prevent and detect unethical behavior. Investigators regularly examine activity at all levels -- from large firms to investment advisers to registered reps to individual investors. Even the most junior of broker-dealer employees is expected to adhere to high standards of business ethics and commercial honor in dealing with the public, customers, broker-dealer firms and the industry.

 Take Note: NASD rules and other industry regulations basically remind reps not to lie, cheat or steal when dealing with customers! If you are uncertain about a question on prohibited practices or ethics, you are likely to be headed in the right direction if you choose the most conservative response.

Prohibited Practices

The following practices in customer dealings are prohibited at all times.

Manipulative and Fraudulent Devices

NASD member firms are strictly prohibited from using manipulative, deceptive or other fraudulent tactics or methods to induce a security's sale or purchase. The statute of limitations under the Act of 1934 is three years from the alleged manipulation and within one year of discovering it. No dollar limit is placed on damages in lawsuits based on allegations of manipulation.

Private Securities Transactions

The NASD's Conduct Rules define a **private securities transaction** as any sale of securities outside an associated person's regular business and his employing member. Private securities transactions are also known as **selling away**.

Notification. If an associated person wishes to enter into a private securities transaction, that person must:

- provide prior written notice to his or her employer;
- describe in detail the proposed transaction;
- describe in detail his or her proposed role in the transaction; and
- disclose whether he or she has or may receive compensation for the transaction.

If the associated person wishes to enter into the transaction or business activity for compensation, the employing member may approve or disapprove the associated person's participation. If the member approves the participation, it must treat the transaction as if it is being done on its own behalf by entering the transaction on its own books and supervising the associated person during the transaction. If the member disapproves the transaction, the associated person may not participate in it.

If the associated person has not received or will not receive compensation for the private securities transaction, the employing member must acknowledge that it has received written notification and may require the associated person to adhere to specified conditions during his participation.

Transactions that the associated person enters into on behalf of immediate family members and for which the associated person receives no compensation are excluded from the definition of private securities transactions. Also excluded are personal transactions in investment company and variable annuity securities.

Outside Employment

An associated person cannot work for any business other than his member firm without providing written notice to his broker-dealer.

A passive investment, such as the purchase of a limited partnership unit, is not considered an outside employment or business activity, even if the purchaser receives money as a result of the investment. An associated person may make a passive investment for his own account without providing written notice to or receiving written approval from the employing broker-dealer.

Fair Dealing

The NASD's Conduct Rules and the laws of most states require broker-dealers, registered reps and investment advisers to inquire into a customer's financial situation before making any recommendation to buy, sell or exchange securities. This includes determining the client's other security holdings, income, expenses and financial goals and objectives.

The following activities violate the fair dealing rules:

- recommending any investment that isn't suitable for the customer's financial situation and risk tolerance;
- short-term trading of mutual funds;
- setting up fictitious accounts to transact business that otherwise would be prohibited;
- making unauthorized transactions or use of funds;
- recommending purchases that are inconsistent with the customer's ability to pay; and
- committing fraudulent acts, such as forgery and the omission or misstatement of material facts.

Excessive Trading

Excessive trading in a customer's account to generate commissions, rather than to help achieve the customer's stated investment objectives, is an abuse of fiduciary responsibility known as *churning*. Churning occurs due to either excessive frequency or excessive size of transactions.

To prevent such abuses, self-regulatory organizations require that a principal of the member firm review all accounts, especially those in which a registered rep or an investment adviser has discretionary authority.

Influencing Employees of Other Firms

Broker-dealers cannot distribute business-related compensation, either cash or noncash gifts or gratuities, to the employees of other member firms. However, a broker-dealer may give other firms' employees some form of compensation without violating the rules if:

- the compensation is not conditional on sales or promises of sales;
- it has the employing member's prior approval; and
- the compensation's total value does not exceed the annual limit set by the NASD Board of Governors (currently $100 per year) or the MSRB (currently $100 per year).

The limit on gifts from mutual fund underwriters is more restrictive. Underwriters may not make gifts to representatives in connection with the distribution of investment company shares in excess of $50.

Employment Contracts. This rule does not apply to legitimate employment contracts in which an employee of one firm supplies or performs services for another firm. The leasing of another firm's employee is acceptable provided a written employment agreement specifies the employment duties and compensation and the person's employer, the temporary employer and the employee give their written consent.

 Take Note: For questions on the gift limit rule, remember to differentiate between broker-dealers and underwriters. The gift limit for broker-dealers is **$100**, but the limit for mutual fund underwriters is **$50**.

Selling Dividends

It is improper to recommend that an investor buy mutual fund or stock shares just before a dividend distribution. The fund shares' market value will decrease by the distribution amount, and the customer will incur a tax liability on the distribution. A registered rep is forbidden to encourage an investor to purchase shares before a distribution because of this tax liability, and doing so is a violation known as **selling dividends**.

Breakpoint Sales

In a breakpoint sale, a customer unknowingly buys investment company shares in an amount just below an amount that would qualify the investment for a reduction in sales charges. As a result, the customer pays a higher dollar amount in sales charges, which reduces the number of shares purchased and increases the cost basis per share.

Encouraging a customer to purchase in such a manner, or remaining silent when a customer unknowingly requests such a transaction, is unethical and violates the NASD Conduct Rules.

✓ **Take Note:** Remember, a *breakpoint* is a good thing. It allows the investor a volume discount when buying mutual fund shares. A *breakpoint sale*, however, is a prohibited practice.

Borrowing and Lending

Registered reps and investment advisers must not borrow money or securities from a customer unless the customer is a bank, a broker-dealer or another financial institution in the business of lending money.

Registered reps and investment advisers may not lend money or securities to a customer. This prohibition does not include broker-dealers making margin loans or investment advisers lending money as part of their normal business practices.

✓ **Take Note:** Note that money can be borrowed from customers if the customer is a bank or other financial institution in the business of lending money.

Misrepresentations

Registered reps and investment advisers may not misrepresent themselves or their services to clients or potential clients. Included in this prohibition are misrepresentations covering:

- qualifications, experience and education;
- nature of services offered; and
- fees to be charged.

It is a misrepresentation to inaccurately state or fail to state a material fact regarding any of the above.

Research Reports

An investment adviser or a broker-dealer is prohibited from presenting to a client research reports, analyses or recommendations prepared by other persons or firms without disclosing the fact that the adviser did not prepare them. An adviser or a broker-dealer may base a recommendation on reports or analyses prepared by others, as long as these reports are not represented as the adviser's or broker-dealer's own.

Conflicts of Interest

An investment adviser must disclose in writing to a client any areas in which the adviser's interests conflict or could potentially conflict with those of the client. Examples of such conflicts include:

- affiliation(s) between an adviser and any product suppliers;
- compensation arrangements for advisory services to clients in addition to compensation from such clients for such services; and
- charging a client a fee for providing investment advice when the adviser or the adviser's employer will receive a commission for executing securities transactions based on that advice.

Guarantees and Sharing in Customer Accounts

Broker-dealers, investment advisers and registered reps cannot guarantee any customer against a loss or guarantee a gain. Members, advisers and representatives are also prohibited from sharing in any profits or losses in a customer's account. An exception is made if a joint account has received the member firm's prior written approval and the registered representative shares in the profits and losses only to the extent of his proportionate contribution to the joint account.

If the member firm authorizes such a **shared account**, any such sharing must be directly proportionate to the financial contributions each party makes. If a member or an associated person shares an account with a member of that person's immediate family, directly proportionate sharing of profits and losses is not mandatory.

Immediate family members include parents, mother-in-law or father-in-law, husband or wife, children and any relative to whom the officer or employee in question contributes financial support.

 Take Note: It is permissible for an agent to share in an account with a customer *if* the agent has written consent from both the customer and the employing firm and shares in profits and losses proportionate to his contribution. In this situation, it is permissible to commingle agent and customer funds. Please note that a firm and a customer can *never* have a joint account.

Misuse of Nonpublic Information

Every investment adviser must establish, maintain and enforce written policies and procedures to prevent the use of nonpublic inside information.

Fiduciary Information

During the normal course of business, employees of member firms will have access to proprietary information regarding individual customers and securities issuers. Such information is to be treated with strict confidentiality.

Confidentiality of Customer Information. Broker-dealer and investment adviser employees may not divulge any personal information about customers without a customer's express permission. This includes security positions, personal and financial details and trading intentions.

Numbered Accounts. For privacy reasons, a customer may have a designated account identified with a number or a letter rather than a name if the member has a signed statement from the customer claiming ownership of that account.

Confidentiality of Issuer Information. When a member broker-dealer serves an issuer as a paying agent, a transfer agent or an underwriter or in another similar capacity, the member has established a fiduciary relationship with that issuer. In this role, the member may obtain confidential information.

The member cannot use the information it obtains through its fiduciary role unless the securities issuer specifically asks and authorizes the member to do so.

Quick Quiz 4.12

Match the following terms with the appropriate description below.

A. Selling away
B. Breakpoint sale
C. Selling dividends
D. Material facts
E. Excessive trading

____ 1. Encouraging a purchase below the amount that would qualify for a reduction in sales load

____ 2. Omitting these in a recommendation violates NASD rules

____ 3. Encouraging a customer purchase just prior to a distribution

____ 4. Also called churning

____ 5. A prohibited practice without the broker-dealer's knowledge and consent

See page 345 for answers.

Artificial Transactions. Transactions intended to portray an artificial market for a stock are strictly prohibited. These transactions are sometimes called "matching" or "matched buy/sell orders."

Summary of Ethical Practices

Ethical behavior in the securities industry can be summarized as follows:

- Do not cheat or steal.
- Do not fabricate information or lie.
- Disclose any conflicts of interest.
- Know what investments are suitable for your customers' needs.

Criminal Penalties

A person who is convicted of willfully violating federal securities regulations, or of knowingly making false or misleading statements in a registration document, can be fined up to $1 million, sentenced to prison for not more than 10 years, or both. The maximum fine is $2.5 million for other than a natural person (broker-dealers or other businesses).

Assistance to Foreign Authorities   The SEC is pledged to help foreign regulatory authorities investigate any person who has violated, is violating or is about to violate any laws or rules relating to securities matters.

✐ Quick Quiz 4.13

Test your knowledge of prohibited business practices with the following exercises. Use "U" for unlawful and "L" for lawful.

____ 1. An agent explains to a mutual fund client that because the fund is invested in government securities, the client will not lose principal.

____ 2. A customer calls his representative and informs him to immediately buy 1,000 shares of a top Internet company. The representative enters an order for 1,000 shares of XYZ, which has been a market leader all week.

____ 3. An agent receives a call from the wife of his client, advising him to sell his XYZ stock. The agent refuses the order.

____ 4. A client writes a scathing letter to his agent regarding stocks that the agent had recommended that had subsequently performed very poorly. The agent calls the client and disposes of the letter after the client is calmed.

____ 5. A representative borrows $10,000 from his client, First Federal Bank of Oconomowoc, Wisconsin.

____ 6. An agent explains that because he is so convinced of the value of ABC Company stock, he will buy it back from the client if it is not up 10 percent in three months.

____ 7. An agent contacts her client and suggests that he buy a total of 1,000 shares of ABC stock, but that he buy 100 shares on 10 different days to try and time the market.

See page 345 for answers and rationale

Code of Procedure and Code of Arbitration Procedure

Code of Procedure

The NASD's Code of Procedure is a guide to settle complaints that arise between and among members and associated persons.

It is the task of the NASD Department of Enforcement to determine whether a charge or complaint is valid and, if so, to take appropriate disciplinary action against the offending member firm or associated person.

Regular Complaint Procedure

Sources of Complaints. Most complaints are filed by NASD examiners who regularly audit each member firm's books, bringing any evidence of wrongdoing to the attention of the Department of Enforcement. When a customer, another member firm or one of the NASD's committees lodges a complaint, one of the first steps in the proceedings is to have an NASD examiner inspect the accused member's books in an effort to substantiate or discredit the complaint.

Complaint Resolution Process. The first official action occurs when the Department of Enforcement notifies the accused member (or associated person) of the specifics of the complaint, identifying who has filed the complaint and requesting a response from the accused member within 25 calendar days of the service of the complaint.

Request for Hearing. When the regular complaint proceeding is chosen, typically the member firm either denies the charge or makes an offer of settlement. The complainant (the party complained against) can accept the offer or demand a formal hearing.

Venue. Once a complaint has been filed, it is usually scheduled to be heard before a committee in the district in which the member has its home office or in the district in which the branch office is located.

Hearing Panels. A hearing panel is convened that consists of Department of Enforcement members, all of whom are associated persons with member firms. Hearing panels, at times, also may consist of members of the NASD's Market Regulation Committee.

Decision of the Committee. The Department of Enforcement either upholds a rule violation or dismisses the complaint. Either way, the department issues a written decision and announces the sanctions imposed on the member firm as disciplinary action. The Department of Enforcement's decision becomes final after 45 calendar days.

Penalties. If the Department of Enforcement finds that a rule violation has occurred, it may impose one or more of the following disciplinary actions:

- censure;
- fine (unlimited);
- suspension of NASD registration;
- expulsion of a member firm; or
- barring of the associated person from association with all members.

Appeal and Review. If the Department of Enforcement finds in favor of the complainant, the member firm (or associated person) has 25 calendar days from notification to appeal the decision to the NASD **National Adjudicatory Council (NAC)**. The board may opt to review and may or may not overturn the department's decision. The call for review by the NAC must be made within 45 days of the department's hearing.

Settlement Procedure. The member may offer to make a settlement at any time during the proceedings, but such offer might not be accepted.

Payment of Fines and Costs. All fines levied as penalties for rule violations against a member firm must be paid promptly after the date of the Department of Enforcement's decision or, if that decision was appealed, after the final date of the National Adjudicatory Council's decision.

Appeal to SEC. The complainant or the respondent can appeal to the SEC for a review of the judgment if it wishes, and finally from the SEC to the Federal Courts (the Supreme Court if necessary).

Acceptance, Waiver and Consent

The *Acceptance, Waiver and Consent* procedure applies to minor rule violations. If the Department of Enforcement has reason to believe a violation has occurred and the member firm or associated person does not dispute the violation, a minor rule violation letter may be offered.

If the letter is accepted, the respondent waives the right to a hearing and any appeal. The maximum penalty that can be imposed under acceptance, waiver and consent is $2,500 per respondent, plus possible public censure. If the letter is rejected, a regular complaint proceeding is initiated.

✓ *Take Note:* To remember the purpose of the Code of Procedure, think of it as "the COP" and remember that the COP handles complaints.

Also, note that the NASD has the authority to impose virtually any disciplinary action, other than a jail sentence, against a rep or firm that has violated the Conduct Rules.

 **Test Topic Alert!**   Be sure to remember that the maximum penalty under Acceptance, Waiver and Consent is $2,500. This is a very typical test question!

Code of Arbitration Procedure

The Code of Arbitration Procedure offers participants a relatively easy method of settling disputes at a cost that is usually significantly lower than that of more formal procedures. Arbitration should not be confused with disciplinary proceedings under the Code of Procedure.

Matters Eligible for Submission. Any dispute or controversy may be submitted to the NASD's National Arbitration Committee for resolution and settlement. A claimant begins the proceedings by filing a statement of claim, a signed submission agreement and any supporting documents with the Director of Arbitration. A dispute or controversy eligible for arbitration must be submitted within six years of its occurrence.

Required Submissions. Internal disputes between member firms and between associated persons must be submitted for resolution and settlement in arbitration.

Arbitration Involving Customers. Customers are under no obligation to submit any dispute to the NASD's National Arbitration Committee. For them, arbitration is strictly optional; although a customer can take a member firm or an associated person before an arbitration panel on demand, neither a member firm nor an associated person can demand that a customer submit to arbitration. The customer must consent to arbitration in writing.

 **Test Topic Alert!**   Be ready for an arbitration question that asks about customer arbitrations. Customers *can* initiate arbitration against firms, but firms *cannot* initiate arbitration against customers unless the customer has given written consent.

No Redress Through the Courts. All parties to an NASD arbitration proceeding forfeit any civil court proceedings while the arbitration is in progress. Findings under the Code of Arbitration are binding on all parties involved in the dispute.

NASD National Arbitration Committee. The NASD maintains a pool of arbitrators consisting of industry people and public representatives. Arbitration panels are convened as needed to hear cases.

Simplified Industry Arbitration. Disputes not involving customers can be submitted for resolution under simplified industry arbitration procedures provided a claim's dollar amount does not exceed $25,000. Claims of $25,000 or less are heard by panels of one, two or three arbitrators. The arbitrators review evidence and written pleadings from both sides of the dispute and render a decision.

Simplified Customer Arbitration. As with simplified industry arbitration, the dollar amount in a simplified customer arbitration proceeding must not exceed $25,000. A single arbitrator hears such claims.

Arbitration Awards. The arbitration panel attempts to render decision within 30 business days.

Failure to Act Under Arbitration Procedures. Failure to participate in good faith in a matter under arbitration or failure to honor an award an arbitration panel issues violates the Conduct Rules.

Amendments to the Code of Arbitration Procedure

The NASD has implemented amendments that make the Code of Arbitration Procedure uniform with other SROs' procedures. The major changes include the following:

- Disputes subject to arbitration now include the business of members as well as securities-related disputes.
- All parties have the right to challenge arbitrators, and arbitrators have the obligation to disclose potential conflicts of interest.
- When the amount in dispute exceeds $50,000, the number of arbitrators is no fewer than three nor more than five.
- Parties may agree to arrange private settlements or to withdraw from arbitration without panel approval.

✓ *Take Note:* Here's a tip to help you distinguish between Code of Procedure and Code of Arbitration Procedure in a test question:

If the question asks which section of the NASD rule manual addresses ethics complaints, choose the Code of Procedure (COP). Also, associate *disciplinary action* with the COP.

If the question asks which section applies to settling money disputes *between members*, or any problem between parties associated with the securities industry, choose the Code of Arbitration Procedure.

Arbitration is the industry choice over civil court because is it cheaper. There are no appeals, and decisions are binding on all parties.

TABLE 4.2   Summary of the Codes of Arbitration and Procedure

	Code of Procedure (Disciplinary Action)	Code of Arbitration (Dispute Settlement)
Description	Used in conjunction with formal complaints that a member firm or an associated person violated specific NASD rules and regulations.	Used to resolve disputes, claims and controversies that arise in the course of business, none of which are violations of NASD rules and regulations.
Monetary Redress	Used to fine and punish a member firm or an associated person for NASD rule violations as charged in the complaint if the charges are upheld.	Used to recover monetary damages allegedly suffered by the claimant as the result of disputed acts, practices or omissions by a member firm or an associated person.
Primary Complainant or Claimant	DBCC (or Board of Governors) lodging a complaint against a member firm or an associated person based on findings of misconduct, or on reasonable grounds for same, as determined by NASD auditors/examiners.	Customer in dispute with a member firm or an associated person; associated person in dispute with a member firm or another associated person; member firm in dispute with another member firm or an associated person.
Outcome of Proceedings	Respondent has 25 days to appeal a decision.	If panel of arbitrators rules in favor of the complainant, awards for monetary damage will be made.

✎ Quick Quiz 4.14   Match the following numbers with the appropriate description below. Answers may be used more than once.

A. 25
B. 30
C. 45

___ 1. Number of days to begin an appeal of a Department of Enforcement decision to the National Adjudicatory Council

___ 2. Number of calendar days to respond to a Department of Enforcement complaint notice

___ 3. Number of days after which a Department of Enforcement decision becomes final

___ 4. Number of days from the Department of Enforcement's decision the NAC has to call for decision review

___ 5. Number of business days for an arbitration panel to render a decision.

See page 345 for answers.

✔ **Take Note:** Twenty-five questions on your Series 6 exam are about securities industry regulation. This is the second-most heavily tested topic on the exam. Many of the questions describe practices that are obviously wrong, but the answer choices are tricky! Be sure to practice questions on this lesson thoroughly and, as always, read each question and all the answer choices VERY CAREFULLY!

Securities Industry Regulations Hotsheet

Act of 1933:
- The Paper Act
- Nonexempt issuers must file registration statements with the SEC
- Requires use of prospectus when selling new issues
- Requires full and fair disclosure of new issues
- Regulates primary market activity (issuing and underwriting)

Act of 1934:
- The People Act
- Regulates secondary market activity
- Created the SEC
- Requires registration of all reps and firms that trade securities for the public
- Oversees exchanges and OTC market
- No security is exempt from antifraud provisions (even if exempt from 1933 registration)

Maloney Act:
- Chartered the NASD as the SRO of the OTC
- Investment Advisers Act of 1940
- Requires registration of persons who receive flat fees or percentages for giving investment advice

Insider Trading Act of 1988:
- Tippers and tippees are guilty
- Penalties are up to the greater of $1,000,000 or three times profits made/losses avoided
- Broker-dealers must have written supervisory procedures

Telephone Consumer Protection Act:
- Must call noncustomers at home between 8 A.M. and 9 P.M.
- Firms must maintain "do-not-call list" and written procedures
- Not applicable to nonprofit organizations

Principals:
- Minimum of two per firm; manage, train and supervise
- Approve all accounts and client transactions

Felony Conviction:
- May be disqualified for 10 years (also for cash/securities misdemeanor)

Private Transactions:
- Not allowed without broker-dealer's knowledge and consent. Prior written notice and disclosure of compensation required. Passive investments not subject to this requirement.

Gift Limit:
- No more than $100 cash per year to employees of other member firms from broker-dealer
- No more than $50 cash per year from mutual fund underwriter

Selling Dividends:
- Prohibited practice due to tax liability

Breakpoint Sales:
- Encouraging customer to purchase below the opportunity for a discount;
- Prohibited practice

Research Reports:
- Must disclose if prepared by someone outside firm

Shared Accounts:
- Allowable only if firm grants prior written approval; sharing only in proportion to contribution

Continuing Commissions:
- Allowed to rep or heirs with bona fide contract

Financial Disclosure:
- Customers entitled to most recent balance sheet upon written request

NASD Communications:
- Advertising = nontargeted communications
- Sales literature = targeted communications
- Both must be approved by principal before use, filed for three years, two years easily accessible
- Investment company material must be filed with NASD within 10 days of use
- First year firms must file with NASD 10 days before first use
- Generic advertising is OK if product or service offered is available
- Name of member required except on recruitment ads
- Testimonials OK with disclosure of compensation

Recommendations:
- Must be suitable; disclose current price; potential conflicts of interest
- "Past performance does not guarantee future results"

Investment Company Recommendations:
- Advertising/sales literature must disclose 10-year period unless new fund
- Advertise based on highest charge; no breakpoint

COP:
- Respond to Department of Enforcement notice within 25 days
- DOE can administer any penalty other than jail
- Appeal from DOE to National Adjudicatory Council within 25 days
- Decision final after 45 days

Summary Complaint:
- Maximum fine $2,500 and/or censure

Code of Arbitration:
- Between members, with public only with written consent
- Decisions are final and binding on all parties
- Awards after 30 days
- Simplified is $25,000 for public and industry

Lesson 4 Practice Exam

1. A customer sends a letter of complaint to a registered representative's home. What should the representative do with the letter?

   A. Call the customer and attempt to remedy the situation.
   B. Take the letter to the representative's principal.
   C. File the letter in the customer file the representative maintains.
   D. Do nothing unless the customer contacts the representative again.

2. Which of the following changes on a U-4 form need to be communicated to the registered representative's broker-dealer and the NASD?

   A. Marital status
   B. Bankruptcy
   C. Birth of a child
   D. Purchase of property

3. Which of the following is(are) true regarding the Cold Calling Rule?

   I. The rule imposes a time limit on calls to customers.
   II. Cold calls cannot be made before 8 A.M. and after 9 P.M. in the contact's time zone.
   III. Upon request, contact names must be placed on a "don't call" list and the request must be honored.
   IV. Faxes can be sent at any time of the day.

   A. I, II and III only
   B. II and III only
   C. II, III and IV only
   D. I, II, III and IV

4. Your client has given you discretionary authority to trade her account. Market conditions have been volatile for the past six months and one of her investment objectives is long-term growth. Which of the following series of transactions would most likely describe churning?

   A. A total of 37 trades in the last three months in mid-cap stocks
   B. A total of 22 trades in the last month in mid-cap stocks
   C. A total of nine trades in the last month when the normal transactions activity has been three per month
   D. Total dollar value of the trades in the last month was $4,500 when the average each month was about $3,900

5. Under which of the following circumstances would a registered representative most likely be accused of a prohibited practice?

   A. Encouraging a customer to switch her mutual fund when her investment objective changes
   B. Encouraging a customer to switch her mutual fund when her tax status changes significantly
   C. Encouraging a customer to switch her mutual fund when the fund's ranking changed in the latest magazine ranking
   D. Encouraging a customer to switch her mutual fund because of significant retirement planning changes

6. A customer is displeased because her representative is not following instructions when placing orders. Which of the NASD codes addresses the filing of a complaint against the representative?

   A. Code of Conduct
   B. Uniform Practice Code
   C. Code of Procedure
   D. Code of Arbitration Procedure

7. A registered representative must register as an investment adviser if he or she is

    A. teaching a college course in economics
    B. making a stock recommendation
    C. giving a seminar on investing strategies
    D. providing investment advice and charging a fee for the advice

8. What should be done when a registered representative is aware of a client trading on inside information?

    A. The registered representative should confront the client directly.
    B. The principal should be informed immediately.
    C. The NASD Department of Market Regulation should receive written notification.
    D. The issuer of the security should be contacted.

9. Which of the following statement(s) regarding dividend distributions are correct?

    I.   Purchasing stock immediately before its ex-dividend date is in the customer's interest because the dividend will be received.
    II. Purchasing stock immediately before its ex-dividend date is NOT in the customer's best interest because the dividend is typically taxable to the customer.
    III. Selling dividends is permissible with mutual funds but not with common stock.
    IV. Selling dividends is a violation of NASD rules.

    A. I and II
    B. I and III
    C. II and IV
    D. I, III, and IV

10. Which of the following parties may buy a hot issue?

    A. A broker-dealer for its investment account
    B. The secretary of the registered principal of the broker-dealer
    C. The registered representative who deals only in mutual funds
    D. A cousin of a registered representative who lives in another city

11. An investor is considering a purchase of a new issue of Magna Containers Commercial Paper. This purchase is exempt from the

    I.   Antifraud provisions of the Securities Act of 1933
    II. Antifraud provisions of the Securities Act of 1934
    III. Prospectus requirements of the Securities Act of 1933 because Magna Containers is an exempt issuer
    IV. Prospectus requirements of the Securities Act of 1933 because Magna is an exempt security

    A. I and III
    B. II and III
    C. II and IV
    D. III and IV

12. Texas Powerful Light Company intends to issue 1,000,000 shares of common stock. A tombstone ad for Texas Powerful Light Company's stock

    A. is considered advertising and must be filed with the NASD
    B. can be published during the cooling-off period
    C. is considered an offer to sell securities by the SEC
    D. may be used instead of a prospectus to provide disclosure to potential investors

13. While cold-calling, a registered representative encounters an individual interested in buying open-ended investment company shares. The representative and the client meet to discuss alternative investment choices. The individual then writes a check for purchase of open-ended investment company shares without receiving a prospectus. The registered representative is in violation of

A. 1933 Act
B. 1934 Act
C. 1940 Act
D. All of the above

14. Under NASD filing requirements and review procedures, which of the following are true?

I. A new member firm must file investment company advertising 10 days prior to first use for one year.
II. A member firm in business over one year is subject to routine spot checks.
III. For advertisements that depart from NASD standards, established firms may be subject to pre-filing for one year.
IV. An established member firm must submit registered investment company advertisements within 10 days of first use.

A. I and II only
B. I and IV only
C. I, III, and IV only
D. I, II, III and IV

15. When a member firm terminates a registered representative, the representative must

A. destroy the original U-4 form
B. submit a U-5 form
C. notify the SEC immediately
D. All of the above

16. Under the NASD's Conduct Rules, which of the following are violations of the rules regarding fair and ethical treatment of customers?

I. Encouraging customers to purchase mutual fund shares just prior to the ex-date to assure that the customer receives the upcoming dividend
II. Recommending that a customer regularly move his assets among several fund families with similar investment objectives to ensure diversification and top performance
III. Recommending that a customer set up a scheduled investment program, depositing the same amount each period regardless of market value
IV. Assuring a customer that because dollar cost averaging is one of the most effective means of investing for the long term, his account is unlikely to suffer any losses

A. I and II
B. I, II and III
C. I, II and IV
D. I and III

17. According to NASD rules, which of the following brokerage firm employees is NOT required to be fingerprinted?

A. Registered principal
B. Firm receptionist
C. Administrative assistant who handles customer funds
D. Registered representative

18. A registered principal must approve all of the following before use EXCEPT

A. advertising
B. sales literature
C. form letter
D. prospectus

19. A prospectus must accompany or precede which of the following?

    A. A sales presentation held in person at the representative's office
    B. A mutual fund seminar invitation mailed to the home of a prospective customer
    C. A general information brochure given to a customer to explain the basic features of mutual fund ownership
    D. A television advertisement explaining the benefits of investing in mutual funds to accumulate retirement savings

20. A tombstone advertisement may include all of the following EXCEPT

    A. the fund's investment adviser
    B. performance data
    C. the classification or subclassification of the investment company
    D. information on the fund's investment policies

21. An individual who holds a Series 6 license may sell all of the following EXCEPT

    A. unit investment trusts
    B. REITs
    C. open-end company shares
    D. face amount certificates

22. If a registered representative wishes to take on part-time employment as a photographer, he is

    A. required to provide written notification to his principal
    B. required to obtain written approval from his principal because the job is not related to the securities industry
    C. required to give prior notice to the NASD
    D. prohibited from doing so, as part-time employment outside the industry is a violation of NASD rules

23. All of the following actions are violations of the NASD Conduct Rules EXCEPT

    A. delivering a prospectus 48 hours after the sale of a mutual fund takes place
    B. opening a cash account for a customer without the customer's signature
    C. offering to trade mutual fund shares for a customer
    D. offering mutual fund shares to a customer at a discount from the POP

24. All of the following communications require the review of a registered principal EXCEPT

    A. internal memos
    B. customer complaints
    C. form letters mailed to all customers
    D. a market letter

25. The NASD will deny a person's registration in all of the following situations EXCEPT

    A. the applicant is not qualified due to lack of experience
    B. the applicant was suspended by another SRO
    C. the applicant was convicted of a securities misdemeanor within the past ten years
    D. the applicant provided false information when filing the U-4 form

Answers and Rationale

1. **B.** Complaint letters must be given to the representative's principal. They must be filed in accordance with the NASD's conduct rules.
(Page 282) [18412]

2. **B.** The broker-dealer and the NASD must be notified if a registered representative files for bankruptcy. The other occurrences listed do not require NASD notification. (Page 278) [18414]

3. **B.** The Cold Calling Rule restricts cold callers to these rules but does not restrict the length of conversation. Faxes cannot be sent to the homes of noncustomers unless requested.
(Page 301) [18417]

4. **C.** Churning involves increases from the normal pattern, i.e., increased transactions or dollar volume that is primarily for the benefit of the registered representative. The only answer choice that shows a significant deviation from previous activity is C. Although choices A and B identify substantial activity, it cannot be determined that this is abnormal for the customer.
(Page 304) [18426]

5. **C.** Significant changes in an investor's investment objective, tax status or retirement planning may be justification for switching from one fund to another. "Chasing the leader" can result in continual tax exposures and possibly new sales loads. When a switch between funds occurs, the shareholder must recognize any capital gain or loss. (Page 304) [18427]

6. **C.** The Code of Procedure identifies the steps in the NASD complaint procedure. The Code of Conduct discusses ethical treatment of customers; the Uniform Practice Code standardizes procedures between member firms; the Code of Arbitration Procedure deals with settling monetary disputes within the brokerage industry.
(Page 310) [18433]

7. **D.** An individual who gives advice and charges a fee is required to register as an investment adviser. (Page 271) [18440]

8. **B.** When inside information is suspected in any trade, registered representatives must immediately contact their principal. All broker-dealers are required to have written supervisory procedures in place to address this situation.
(Page 274) [18445]

9. **C.** Encouraging a customer to buy a stock or a mutual fund immediately before the ex-dividend date is NOT in the customer's best interest because the dividend received is usually taxable. Because the share price will drop by approximately the amount of the dividend, the customer who waits until after the ex-dividend date buys the shares cheaper and avoids a taxable distribution. "Selling dividends" violates NASD conduct rules.
(Page 305) [18451]

10. **D.** Because the cousin of the registered representative is neither a supported nor an "immediate" family member of the broker-dealer employee, he or she may buy the hot issue with no restriction. Broker-dealers, as well as any of their employees are considered prohibited/restricted persons under the NASD's freeriding and withholding rules and may not buy hot issues.
(Page 265) [18459]

11. **C.** Magna Containers Commercial Paper is an exempt security and is not subject to the prospectus requirements of the Securities Act of 1933. No new security is exempt from the antifraud provisions of the Act of 1933. Magna Containers however, is not an exempt issuer because corporate issues are subject to Act of 1933 filing requirements. Issues of Magna stock or bonds are subject to filing requirements under the Act of 1933. This purchase is not subject to the antifraud provisions of the Act of 1934 until it begins trading in the secondary marketplace. (Page 267) [18464]

12. **B.** A tombstone ad may be published by an issuer of common stock during the cooling-off period. A tombstone for an equity issue is not considered advertising by the SEC and is not subject to

NASD filing requirements. A tombstone offers information by telling investors where they can acquire a prospectus about the issue; it does not replace a prospectus and does not offer to sell securities. (Page 261) [18471]

13. **A.** A registered representative must sell primary offerings of nonexempt issues with prospectus under the 1933 act. The 1934 Act regulates secondary market trading (mutual fund shares do not trade on the secondary market). Under the 1940 Act, the mutual fund issuer must register as an investment company. (Page 258) [18477]

14. **D.** All of the statements are true. (Page 290) [18483]

15. **B.** Whenever a registered representative leaves a member firm, a U-5 form must be submitted to the NASD. There is no requirement that the U-4 form on file with the NASD be destroyed or that the SEC be notified. (Page 278) [18485]

16. **C.** Answer I is the prohibited practice of "selling dividends," which subjects investors to adverse tax consequences. Answer II is the prohibited practice of switching funds, which may cause additional sales charges. Answer IV is prohibited because, although dollar cost averaging is a conservative method of investing, the representative can never "guarantee" a customer's account against loss. Answer III defines the practice of dollar cost averaging. (Page 304) [18516]

17. **B.** All registered persons and firm employees who handle customer funds and securities must be fingerprinted. (Page 270) [18582]

18. **D.** The NASD requires that all advertising and sales literature be approved by a registered principal before use. Because form letters are considered sales literature, they fall under this rule. Prospectuses are not considered advertising material and are not subject to approval under advertising rules. The SEC strictly defines prospectus content and disclosure. (Page 287) [18584]

19. **A.** Any offer or advertisement of mutual fund shares must be accompanied by a prospectus.

However, generic advertisements or purely informational material are exempt from this requirement. A prospectus must be given to all seminar attendees when they arrive, not when the invitations are mailed. The face-to-face meeting between the representative and the prospect is considered an offer and must be accompanied by prospectus. (Page 258) [18585]

20. **B.** Tombstones or tombstone-style advertising may include information about the fund's investment advisers, investment policies, objectives and services and the fund's classification or subclassification. Tombstones are not permitted to include performance information. (Page 289) [18589]

21. **B.** Individuals who hold Series 6 licenses are permitted to sell investment company products, which include: Unit investment trusts, face amount certificates, open-end company shares and primary offerings of closed-end company shares. Units in REITs (Real Estate Investment Trusts) can only be sold by Series 7-licensed individuals. (Page 281) [18590]

22. **A.** NASD rules require that prior written notice must be given to the principal if a representative becomes employed on a part-time basis. Note that written permission from the principal is not necessary. Prior NASD notice is not required. (Page 304) [18591]

23. **B.** Cash accounts may be opened for customers without obtaining their signatures; margin accounts, however, require customer signature for account opening. A prospectus must be delivered to a mutual fund customer no later than the time of purchase. Mutual fund shares do not trade in the secondary market. They must be redeemed. Discounts from the POP are available to member firms only. (Page 303) [18594]

24. **A.** Memos prepared for "internal use only" do not require review or approval of a registered principal prior to use. Registered principals must review and oversee the handling of customer complaints. They must also review and approve all forms of advertising and sales literature prior to

use. Form letters and market letters are examples of sales literature and are subject to prior approval.
(Page 291) [18595]

25. **A.** The NASD will prohibit registration of individuals who have lied on their application forms, who have been suspended or expelled by another self-regulatory organization or who were convicted of a felony or securities misdemeanor within the past 10 years. Lack of experience is not reason for denial of registration by the NASD.
(Page 282) [18597]

Quick Quiz Answers and Rationale

Quick Quiz 1.1 1. **B.**   2. **D.**   3. **C.**   4. **A.**

Quick Quiz 1.2 1. **C.** Owning either common or preferred stocks represents ownership (or equity) in a corporation. The other two choices represent debt instruments. Clients purchasing corporate or mortgage bonds are considered lenders, not owners.

2. **C.** Treasury stock is stock a corporation has issued but subsequently repurchased from investors in the secondary market. The corporation can either reissue the stock at a later date or retire it. Stock that has been repurchased by the corporation has no voting rights and is not entitled to any declared dividends.

3. **B.** Preemptive rights enable stockholders to maintain their proportionate ownership when the corporation wants to issue more stock. If a stockholder owns 5 percent of the outstanding stock and the corporation wants to issue more stock, the stockholder has the right to purchase enough of the new shares to maintain a 5 percent ownership position in the company.

4. **B.** With cumulative voting rights, this investor may cast 500 votes for the five directors in any way the investor chooses.

5. **D.** The cumulative method of voting gives an investor one vote per share owned, times the number of directorships to be elected. For example, if an investor owns 100 stock shares, and there are five directorships to be elected, the investor will have a total of 500 votes. The stockholder may cast all of his votes for one candidate, thereby giving the small investor more voting power.

6. **B.** Shareholder approval is required to change the stated value of stock, which occurs with a stock split. Decisions regarding payment of dividends or repurchase of stock are made by the board of directors (management only) since these are considered operational decisions.

7. **D.** The basic formula of the balance sheet is Assets = Liabilities + Net Worth.

Quick Quiz 1.3   1. **D.**   2. **A.**   3. **B.**   4. **C.**

Quick Quiz 1.4   1. **D.** ADRs are tradable securities issued by banks, with the receipt's value based on the underlying foreign securities held by the bank.

2. **C.** An ADR represents ownership of a foreign corporation. The ADR holder receives a share of the dividends and capital appreciation (or capital loss) offered by the foreign stock.

Quick Quiz 1.5   1. **B.** Warrants are issued with long-term maturities. They may be used as sweeteners in an offering of the issuer's stock or bonds. Warrants are not offered only to current shareholders. The exercise price of a warrant is typically above the market value of the stock at the time of issue.

2. **B.** Preferred stockholders have no right to maintain a percentage of ownership when new shares are issued (no preemptive rights). However, they do receive preference in dividend payment and company liquidation.

Quick Quiz 1.6   1. **D.**   2. **A.**   3. **C.**   4. **B.**

Quick Quiz 1.7   1. **B.**   2. **A.**   3. **B.**   4. **C.**   5. **B.**   6. **A.**

7. **C.**   8. **E.**   9. **A.**   10. **D.**   11. **C.**   12. **B.**

Quick Quiz 1.8   1. **A.** Call protection is most valuable to a purchaser when interest rates are falling because the attractive coupon will increase the market price of the bond. In the meantime, the holder is assured the higher return even though interest rates generally fall below the bond interest rate.

2. **B.** Annual interest / Current market price = Current yield

3. **B.** The customer purchased the 5 percent bond when it was yielding 6 percent, therefore at a discount. The customer sold the bond when other

bonds of like kind, quality and maturity were yielding 4 percent. The bond is now at a premium because the 5 percent coupon is attractive to other investors. The customer, therefore, made a capital gain on the investment.

4. **B.** With the same nominal yield, the discount bonds will generate higher yields. In addition to the interest payments received on an ongoing basis, the investor receives the amount of the discount at maturity.

5. **B.** Long-term bonds are not as liquid as short-term obligations.

6. **B.** Long-term debt prices will fluctuate more than short-term debt prices as interest rates rise and fall. Common stock prices are not directly affected by interest rates.

Quick Quiz 1.9   1. **D.**   2. **C.**   3. **B.**   4. **A.**

5. **C.**   6. **D.**   7. **A.**   8. **B.**

Quick Quiz 1.10   1. **A.** The order in a liquidation is as follows: the IRS (and other government agencies), secured debt holders, unsecured debt holders, general creditors (in most cases, unsecured debt holders are given a slight priority over all but the largest creditors), holders of subordinated debt, preferred stockholders, common stockholders.

2. **D.** Ogden 5s means 5 percent bonds. Five percent of $1,000 par equals $50 interest per bond annually. For 50 bonds, the annual interest is $2,500.

3. **A.** Coupon rates are not higher; they are lower because of the value of the conversion feature. The bondholders are creditors, and if the stock price falls, the conversion feature will not influence the bond's price.

4. **B.** The calculations are: $1,000 ÷ $20 = 50 shares for one bond. $800 bond price ÷ 50 shares = $16 parity price.

5. **B.** $1,000 par ÷ $125 conversion price = 8 shares per bond.

Quick Quiz 1.11   1. **D.**   2. **A.**   3. **B.**   4. **C.**

5. **A.** Collateralized mortgage obligations are collateralized by mortgages on real estate. They do not own the underlying real estate, so they are not considered to be backed by it.

6. **B.** Collateralized mortgage obligations are a type of mortgage-backed security. A CMO issue is divided into several tranches, which set priorities for payments of principal and interest.

Quick Quiz 1.12

1. **F.** Municipal securities are issued by state and local governments

2. **T.**

3. **F.** Revenue bonds are self-supporting and are backed by income from the use of the facility. GOs are backed by taxes.

4. **T.**

5. **T.**

6. **T.**

Quick Quiz 1.13

1. **D.** Newly issued Treasury bonds have a minimum maturity of 10 years. Money-market instruments have a maximum maturity of one year.

2. **C.** Commercial paper is normally issued for a maximum period of 270 days.

3. **B.** Negotiable certificates of deposit are issued primarily by banks and are backed by (guaranteed by) the issuing bank.

4. **C.** Commercial paper is a short-term promissory note issued by a corporation.

5. **B.** Bankers' acceptances are used in international trade to finance imports and exports. Eurodollars and ADRs are not money-market instruments.

6. **B.** The federal funds rate reflects the rate charged by member banks lending funds to member banks that need to borrow funds overnight to meet reserve requirements.

7. **B.** The federal funds rate is the interest rate that banks with excess reserves charge other banks that are associated with the Federal Reserve System and that need overnight loans to meet reserve requirements. Because the federal funds rate changes daily, it is the most sensitive indicator of interest rate direction.

Quick Quiz 1.14   1. **B.**   2. **A.**   3. **E.**   4. **D.**   5. **C.**

Quick Quiz 1.15   1. **B.**   2. **A.**   3. **D.**   4. **C.**

Quick Quiz 1.16   1. **D.**   2. **A.**   3. **C.**   4. **B.**

5. **F.** A shareholder must own the stock on the record date to receive the dividend.

6. **F.** The ex-date is two business days before the record date.

7. **F.** The buyer gets the dividend only if the stock is purchased before the ex-date. The seller gets the dividend if the transaction is on or after the ex-date.

8. **F.** The payable date is usually three to four weeks after the record date.

9. **T.**

Quick Quiz 1.17   1. **B.** When the Federal Open Market Committee purchases T bills in the open market, it pays for the transaction by increasing the reserve accounts of member banks, the net effect of which increases the total money supply and signals a period of relatively easier credit conditions. Easier credit means interest rates will decline and the price for existing bonds will rise.

2. **D.** Increased foreign investment in the United States (choice I) would raise the U.S. dollar's relative value. A decrease in U.S. interest rates (choice IV) would chase money out of the United States and increase the foreign currency's relative value.

3. **A.** Disintermediation is the flow of deposits out of banks and savings and loans into alternative, higher paying investments. It occurs when money is tight and interest rates are high because these alternative investments may then offer higher yields than S&Ls and banks. However, when interest rates are low, investors may prefer to keep their money in banks and S&Ls.

4. **D.** To curb inflation, the Fed can sell securities in the open market, thus changing the amount of U.S. government debt institutions hold. It can also raise the reserve requirements, discount rate or margin requirements. The Fed has no control over taxes, which are changed by Congress.

Quick Quiz 1.18

1. **A.** "Growth" refers to an increase in the value of an investment over time. This growth can come from increases in the value of the security, the reinvestment of distributions or both.

2. **D.** Direct participation programs or limited partnerships are illiquid investments because there is no immediate market for them.

3. **C.** Of the answers offered, in order to generate the greatest return a fixed-income security (a bond) is most suitable. Common stock is definitely not suitable; convertibles (either bonds or preferred) generally pay out a lower income rate than nonconvertibles because the investors receive benefit from the conversion feature; income bonds pay interest only if the corporation meets targeted earnings levels.

4. **D.** The GNMA mutual fund is the most suitable investment for an investor seeking monthly income. The other securities offer higher long-term growth potential, but they are not designed to provide monthly income.

Quick Quiz 1.19

1. **C.**   2. **D.**   3. **B.**   4. **A.**

5. **F.** Bonds are most affected by interest rate risk

6. **T.**

7. **F.** When interest rates are falling it is difficult to reinvest income distributions at comparable rates.

8. **F.** Market risk and systematic risk are synonymous terms that describe the risk of investors losing money due to market price volatility in the overall market.

9. **T.**

Quick Quiz 2.1   1. **C**   2. **O**   3. **C**   4. **C**   5. **C**

                          6. **O**   7. **O**   8. **C**   9. **O**   10. **O**

Quick Quiz 2.2   1. **D.**   All are covered under the act of 1940. Unit investment trusts, face-amount and management companies are all mentioned in this act. Remember, both open-end and closed-end management companies are subclassifications of management investment companies.

                          2. **B.**   The closed-end company does not redeem the shares that it issues. The closed-end company has a fixed capitalization and, like regular corporations, outstanding shares trade on the open market.

                          3. **C.**   A diversified investment company

                          - must have at least 75 percent of its assets invested in cash, securities or both;
                          - may have no more than 5 percent of its total assets invested in one company; and
                          - may own no more than 10 percent of the voting stock of a company.

                          4. **C.**   Unlike unit investment trusts, which issue redeemable securities, face-amount certificate companies issue installment certificates with guaranteed principal and interest. A unit investment trust has a diversified portfolio that, once established, does not change. Therefore, it cannot be called a "management company." A closed-end investment company is a type of management company.

                          5. **C.**   Open-end investment companies, but not closed-end investment companies, can make continuous offerings of shares, can redeem their shares and can issue only common stock.

Quick Quiz 2.3   1. **F.**   Mutual funds may use covered option strategies but typically not naked or uncovered options.

                          2. **F.**   A change in the investment objectives of the fund requires a majority vote of the outstanding *shares*.

                          3. **F.**   Mutual funds may be used as collateral in margin accounts, but may not be purchased on margin.

                          4. **T.**

5. **T.**

6. **F.** Mutual funds are continuous primary or "new" offerings of securities and must be sold with prospectus.

7. **F.** The debt-to-asset ratio of a mutual funds cannot exceed 1 to 3, or 33 percent.

8. **F.** Open-end companies are considered mutual funds.

Quick Quiz 2.4

1. **B.** The main functions of the custodian, usually a commercial bank, are to hold the fund's cash and assets for safekeeping and to perform related clerical duties.

2. **C.** Investment company financial statements must be sent to shareholders at least semiannually.

3. **C.** The underwriter markets the fund's shares. Answer A is the responsibility of the custodian, answer B is the responsibility of the Board of Directors and answer D is the responsibility of the manager.

4. **C.** The primary function of a mutual fund's custodian bank is to safeguard the physical assets of the fund, hold the cash and securities and perform other purely clerical functions. It does not manage the portfolio or serve in a selling capacity for the fund.

5. **C.** Typically, the largest single expense for a mutual fund is the management fee—the fee paid to the management company for buying and selling securities and managing the portfolio. A typical annual fee is ½ of 1 percent of the portfolio's asset value.

Quick Quiz 2.5

1. **F.** Mutual fund shareholders own an undivided interest in the fund's portfolio.

2. **T.**

3. **T.**

4. **F.** The custodian holds the fund's securities for safekeeping.

5. **T.**

6. **F.** The reinstatement provision allows for reinvestment of funds withdrawn within 30 days at no load.

7. **F.** The minimum investment required for most mutual funds is frequently $500 or less.

8. **F.** Like common shareholders, mutual fund shareholders do not vote on matters involving dividends.

Quick Quiz 2.6

1. **D.**	2. **B.**	3. **A.**	4. **C.**	5. **D.**	6. **A**
7. **B.**	8. **C.**	9. **C.**	10. **D.**	11. **B.**	12. **A**
13. **C.**	14. **D.**	15. **A.**	16. **B**		

Quick Quiz 2.7

1. **C.** The maximum sales load is 8½ percent *only* if the company offers rights of accumulation, breakpoints and automatic reinvestment at NAV, not at POP. LOI is not required.

2. **C.** The formula is sales cost divided by public offering price. The sales cost is the difference between NAV and POP, or $1.44 per share. $1.44 ÷ $18 = 8%.

3. **D.** No-load funds are redeemed at net asset value. Mutual funds may also charge a redemption fee, which is subtracted from the NAV.

4. **A.** To find the dollar amount of the sales charge when the NAV and the sales charge percentage are provided, calculate the complement of the sales charge by subtracting the sales charge from 100%. (100% – 8% = 92%.) Then divide the NAV by the complement of the sales charge to find the offering price ($7.82 / .92 = $8.50, the offering price). The dollar amount of the sales charge is the offering price minus the NAV. $8.50 – $7.82 = $.68, the sales charge.

5. **C.** Only choices II and IV are true. Choice I is false because the letter of intent can be backdated 90 days. Choice III is false because the investor is not required by law to satisfy the letter of intent although, in the case of default, he or she will pay a higher sales charge.

6. **B.** Breakpoint advantages are available only to *persons*. An investment club is not considered a person, however, trusts and corporations are.

Quick Quiz 2.8   1. **F.**   Unrealized gains, or paper profits, are not taxable to investors.

2. **F.**   Capital gains distributions may be made not more than annually.

3. **F.**   Mutual fund gains distributions are all long-term. Mutual fund short-term gains are distributed as income.

4. **T.**

5. **T.**

6. **F.**   Funds that comply with IRC subchapter M are considered regulated investment companies.

7. **F.**   Dividend distributions, whether taken in cash or reinvested, are taxable as ordinary income to shareholders.

8. **T.**

Quick Quiz 2.9   1. **D.**   The ex-date for a mutual fund is set by its Board of Directors.

2. **B.**   Regulated companies under Subchapter M of the IRS code are allowed to *pass through* income to beneficial owners without a tax at the fund level on the distributed income. This is known as *conduit* or *flow-through* of income and taxation.

3. **C.**   In open-end investment companies, current yield is calculated as follows: Annual dividends divided by asked price equals yield. Your client would find the yield of his open-end investment company as follows: $.60 ÷ $10.80 = 0.0555 = 5.55% (5.6% rounded).

Quick Quiz 2.10   1. **D.**   The broker-dealer has no obligation to approve every transaction prior to entry.

2. **B.**   The registered rep must ascertain that the customer is of legal age in that state, but is under no obligation to determine an exact birth date.

3. **A.**   A rep is not permitted to open an individual account in the name of another individual, even in the name of a spouse.

4. **A.**   To open a cash account, only the signatures of the registered rep introducing the account and the principal accepting the account are required.

For margin accounts, the signature of the customer is required on the margin agreement.

Quick Quiz 2.11

1. **D.** All of the persons listed have fiduciary responsibilities because they are entrusted with the authority to manage the money or property of others.

2. **B.** The donor may name himself the custodian of an UGMA or UTMA account. No documentation of custodial status is required to open an UGMA account. The custodian is not required to be the minor's legal guardian.

3. **D.** Trading on margin is prohibited to fiduciary accounts except under special circumstances and with the appropriate prior permission and documentation.

4. **B.** UGMA rules require that any UGMA account have only one beneficial owner and only one custodian. Cash and securities may be donated into the account, but insurance contracts and fixed annuities may not be donated.

5. **C.** Transfer of securities into the custodial account completes the gift. At that time the minor becomes the owner of the securities.

Quick Quiz 2.12

1. **C.**   2. **D.**   3. **A.**   4. **B.**

5. **B.**   6. **D.**   7. **C.**   8. **A.**

Quick Quiz 2.13

1. **B.** Dollar cost averaging benefits the investor if the same amount is invested on a regular basis over a substantial period of time, during which the price of the stock fluctuates. A constant dollar plan (choice IV) is one in which the investor maintains a constant dollar value of securities in the investment portfolio.

2. **B.** Dollar cost averaging is available to both small and large investors.

3. **D.** Mutual fund withdrawal plans are not guaranteed. Because principal values fluctuate, investors may not have sufficient income for their entire lives.

4. **C.** If the investor receives $600 a month, the dollar amount of the withdrawal is fixed; therefore, this must be a fixed-dollar plan.

Quick Quiz 3.1

1. **A.** Owners of variable annuities, like owners of mutual fund shares, have the right to vote on changes in investment policy and the right to vote for an investment adviser.

2 **A.** The act of 1940 regulates both mutual funds and variable annuities. Mutual funds owned in a single name typically pass to the owner's estate at death. Variable annuity proceeds, however, usually pass directly to the owner's designated beneficiary at death, like a typical insurance policy. Investment income and capital gains realized generate current income to the owner of mutual funds, but in variable annuities income is deferred until withdrawal begins.

Quick Quiz 3.2

1. **C.** Annuity unit price changes are based on changes of value of securities held in the separate account. This price change is a risk that is passed on to the investor in a variable annuity.

2. **C.** Variable annuity salespeople must be registered with the NASD and the state insurance commission. Registration with the NASD is *de facto* registration with the SEC. No registration is required by the state banking commission.

3. **C.** A variable annuity does not guarantee an earnings rate; however, it does guarantee payments for life (mortality) and normally guarantees that expenses will not increase above a specified level.

4. **D.** Separate accounts as well as mutual funds may contain diversified portfolios of securities and be managed by professional investment advisers. Voting rights for policy and management elections are available.

5. **D.** All of the information listed here must be presented in the prospectus distributed to clients.

Quick Quiz 3.3

1. **C.** When a variable contract is annuitized, the number of accumulation units is multiplied by the unit value to arrive at the total annuitization value. An annuity factor has been actuarially determined considering the investor's sex, age, mortality and payout option selected, for example. This factor

is used to establish the dollar amount of the first annuity payment. Future annuity payments will vary according to the separate account's value.

2. **C.** In the annuity period of a variable annuity, the amount received depends on the account performance compared to the assumed interest rate. If actual performance is less than the AIR, the payout's value declines.

3. **C.** The contract earned 3 percent in September. The assumed interest rate for the contract is 3 percent. Payment size will not change from the payment made the previous month.

Quick Quiz 3.4   1. **C.**   2. **A.**   3. **D.**   4. **B.**

5. **B.**   6. **A.**   7. **D.**   8. **C.**

Quick Quiz 3.5   1. **D.** Contributions to a nonqualified variable annuity are made with after-tax dollars. Distributions from a nonqualified plan represent both a return of the original investment made in the plan with after-tax dollars (a nontaxable return of capital) and the income from that investment. Because the income was deferred from tax over the plan's life, it is taxable as ordinary income once it is distributed.

2. **C.** All retirement account distributions exceeding cost basis are taxed at the owner's then current ordinary tax rate. The advantage of most retirement accounts is that withdrawals usually begin after an account owner is in a lower tax bracket (i.e., upon retirement).

3. **A.** Gains in a separate account are tax deferred. The annuitant pays ordinary income tax on the distribution upon receipt.

Quick Quiz 3.6   1. **D.**   2. **A.**   3. **B.**   4. **C.**

Quick Quiz 3.7   1. **W, V**   2. **W, V**   3. **W**   4. **V, U**   5. **W, V, U**

Quick Quiz 3.8   1. **F**   2. **F**   3. **T.**   4. **F**   5. **T**

6. **F**   7. **T**

Quick Quiz 3.9   1. **A.** A deferred compensation plan is considered a nonqualified plan because no IRS approval is required to initiate such a plan for employees. All qualified retirement plans need IRS approval.

2. **A.** All corporate pension and profit-sharing plans must be set up under a trust agreement. A plan's trustee has fiduciary responsibility for the plan.

3. **B.** Deferred compensation plans can be offered to select employees; however, board members are not considered employees.

4. **C.** Because the annuitant has no basis, all payments are considered ordinary income. In a nonqualified annuity, contributions are made with after-tax dollars, which establish the annuitant's basis. Annuity payments from a nonqualified annuity are treated as ordinary income to the extent that they exceed the basis.

Quick Quiz 3.10   1. **A.** Any individual with earned income who is under the age of 70½ may contribute up to $2,000 to an IRA. The deductibility of those contributions will be determined by that person's coverage under other qualified plans and by level of income.

2. **B.** All withdrawals from IRAs are taxed at the individual's ordinary income tax rate at the time of withdrawal. Distributions taken before age 59½ will incur an additional 10 percent penalty.

3. **C.** The penalty for premature withdrawals from an IRA or a Keogh account is 10 percent plus normal income tax. Excess contribution penalty is 6 percent, while the 50 percent penalty applies after age 70½.

4. **A.** Early withdrawals, without penalty, are permitted only in certain situations, such as death or qualifying disability.

5. **B.** Cash-value life insurance, term insurance and collectibles are not permissible investments in an IRA.

6. **B.** Small businesses and self-employed persons typically establish SEP-IRAs because they are much easier and less expensive than other plans for an employer to set up and administer.

7. **C.** The common factor for both traditional and Roth IRAs is that investment earnings are not taxed when earned. Traditional IRAs offer tax-deductible contributions, but withdrawals are generally taxed. Roth IRAs do not offer tax-deductible contributions, but qualified withdrawals are tax free. Traditional IRAs require distributions to begin in the year after the year an owner reaches age 70½, but this is not true for Roth IRAs.

8. **B.** Only $500 may be invested in each child's education IRA every year. If a couple has three children, they may contribute $1,500 in total, or $500 for each child.

Quick Quiz 3.11

1. **C.** A person with self-employment income may deduct contributions to a Keogh plan. Keogh plans are not available to corporations or their employees.

2. **C.** All interest, dividends and capital gains accumulated in a Keogh are tax deferred until their withdrawal (which must begin between age 59½ and the year after the year in which the account owner turns 70½). The account owner may choose to take distributions in the form of regular income payments or as a single lump sum.

3. **A.** Keogh contributions can only be made *prior* to the date on which an individual turns 70½.

4. **C.** Only the royalties count as self-employment- income; therefore, 20 percent of $75,000 equals $15,000.

Quick Quiz 3.12

1. **D.**	2. **A.**	3. **B.**	4. **C.**	
5. **E.**	6. **A.**	7. **D.**	8. **C.**	9. **B.**

Quick Quiz 3.13

1. **B.** "Funding" covers how an employer contributes to or funds a plan. "Vesting" describes how quickly rights to a retirement account turn over to the employee. "Nondiscrimination" refers to broad employee coverage by a plan. All retirement plans must meet ERISA's fiduciary responsibility reporting and disclosure requirements.

2. **B.** The retirement plan's trust agreement contains a section explaining the formula(s) used to determine the contributions to a defined contribution plan.

3. **C.** Because he is employed by a public school system, your customer is eligible to participate in the tax-sheltered annuity plan. Employee contributions to a TSA plan are excluded from gross income in the year in which they are made. As in other retirement plans, a penalty tax is assessed on distributions received before age 59½. Mutual funds, CDs and annuity contracts are among the investment choices available for TSA plans.

4. **C.** The rules regarding the maximum amount of contributions differ for defined contribution plans and defined benefit plans. Defined benefit plans set the amount of retirement benefits that a retiree receives as a percentage of the previous several years' salaries. For the highly paid individual nearing retirement, the defined benefit plan allows a larger contribution in a shorter period of time. Choice D describes a defined contribution plan rather than a defined benefit plan.

5. **C.** ERISA was established to protect the retirement funds of employees working in the private sector only. It does not apply to self-employed persons or public organizations.

Quick Quiz 4.1   1. **Y**   2. **Y**   3. **N**   4. **N**

5. **Y**   6. **N**   7. **N**

Quick Quiz 4.2   1. **B.** Because TCBS's is a corporate issue that will be sold in different states, the issuer must file a standard registration statement with the SEC.

2. **C.** A preliminary prospectus is issued before the price is established, and it does not include the eventual offering date or the spread.

3. **D.** A registered rep is prohibited from sending a research report with either a preliminary or a final prospectus.

4. **A.** A preliminary prospectus is used to obtain indications of interest from investors.

5. **B.** The SEC does not approve, endorse or guarantee the accuracy of a registration

Quick Quiz 4.3   1. **1933**   2. **1934**   3. **1934**   4. **1933**   5. **1934**   6. **1933**

7. **1933**   8. **1934**   9. **1934**   10. **1934**

Quick Quiz 4.4

1. **B.** Any customer claims that SIPC does not cover result in the customer becoming a general (unsecured) creditor of the company.

2. **B.** SIPC coverage is $500,000 per separate customer account, with cash not to exceed $100,000. Thus, in the single-name account, SIPC provides full coverage, while in the joint account, SIPC covers the full value of the securities, but only $100,000 of the $180,000 in cash. The remaining $80,000 becomes a general debt of the bankrupt broker-dealer.

3. **B.** Under SIPC rules, customer claims are valued on the day customer protection proceedings commence; this is the day a federal court is petitioned to appoint a trustee.

4. **A.** The penalty may be imposed on anyone who trades on inside information, not just persons registered under the act. The other statements are correct: choice B defines "insider trading"; the penalty is up to three times the profit gained or loss avoided (choice C); and an advisory firm may face a penalty for the actions of its representatives (choice D).

5. **D.** While the Act of 1934 defines an insider as an officer, a director or a 10 percent stockholder of a company, the courts have broadened the definition to include anyone who has inside information.

Quick Quiz 4.5

1. **F.** An agreement for continuing commissions must be a bona fide, written contract.

2. **F.** Foreign representatives are required to register if they attempt to transact business with U.S. citizens

3. **T.**

4. **T.**

5. **F.** Reps and firms must be registered with the NASD and all states in which they conduct business

6. **F.** Clerical staff is exempt from NASD registration.

7. **F.** The phrase *member of the NASD* is permissible providing there is no undue emphasis on it.

Quick Quiz 4.6   1. **D.**   2. **B.**   3. **A.**   4. **C.**

Quick Quiz 4.7   1. **C.**   2. **D.**   3. **A.**   4. **B.**

Quick Quiz 4.8   1. **A**   2. **SL**   3. **A**   4. **SL**   5. **SL**

6. **A**   7. **SL**   8. **SL**   9. **A**   10. **SL**

Quick Quiz 4.9

1. **F.** The NASD advertising department does not *approve* advertising. Investment company advertising must be filed within 10 days of first use.

2. **F.** Sales literature must be approved by a principal *prior to use*.

3. **T.**

4. **F.** All advertising and sales literature prepared by a member is subject to NASD spot checks.

5. **F.** Documents for internal use only are exempt from filing and approval requirements.

Quick Quiz 4.10

1. **T.** Only material facts must be disclosed.

2. **F.** Testimonials are permitted with proper disclosure.

3. **F.** Free services are allowed providing there are "no strings attached."

4. **T.** Any recommendation must include the price at the time of the recommendation.

5. **F.** The similar recommendations within the past 12 months must be included.

Quick Quiz 4.11   1. **D.** The Telephone Consumer Protection Act of 1991 covers all registered reps. Each firm must have a do-not-call list that every registered rep is required to check before soliciting any person. The act applies to commercial solicitation and does not include a university survey group or non-profit organization.

2. **D.** All of the choices are requirements of the Telephone Consumer Protection Act of 1991.

Quick Quiz 4.12   1. **B.**   2. **D.**   3. **C.**   4. **E.**   5. **A.**

Quick Quiz 4.13   1. **U.** It is unlawful to guarantee performance of any security. Even government bonds may lose principal value.

2. **U.** It is unlawful to enter a discretionary order without written authorization. This order is discretionary because the agent selected the company.

3. **L.** An agent must refuse to enter an order from someone other than the customer without proper written authorization.

4. **U.** All written customer complaints must be forwarded to the principal.

5. **L.** Agents may borrow money from customers that are recognized financial institutions only.

6. **U.** This agent is guaranteeing protection against loss, and this activity is prohibited.

7. **U.** The agent is churning the account by making excessive transactions for the purpose of generating extra commission.

Quick Quiz 4.14   1. **A.**   2. **A.**   3. **C.**   4. **C.**   5. **B.**

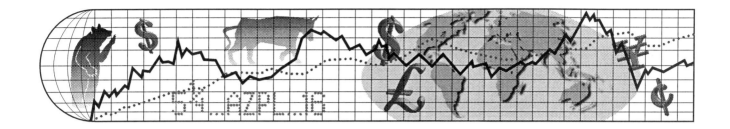

Glossary

A

account executive (AE) *See* registered representative.

accredited investor As defined in Rule 502 of Regulation D, any institution or individual meeting minimum net worth requirements for the purchase of securities qualifying under the Regulation D registration exemption.

An accredited investor is generally accepted to be one who:

- has a net worth of $1 million or more; or
- has had an annual income of $200,000 or more in each of the two most recent years (or $300,000 jointly with a spouse) and who has a reasonable expectation of reaching the same income level in the current year.

accrued interest The interest that has accumulated since the last interest payment up to, but not including, the settlement date and that is added to a bond transaction's contract price.

There are two methods for calculating accrued interest: the 30-day-month (360-day-year) method for corporate and municipal bonds and the actual-calendar-days (365-day-year) method for government bonds. Income bonds, bonds in default and zero-coupon bonds trade without accrued interest (flat). *See also* flat.

accumulation stage The period during which contributions are made to an annuity account. *See also* accumulation unit; distribution stage.

accumulation unit An accounting measure used to determine an annuitant's proportionate interest in the insurer's separate account during an annuity's accumulation (deposit) stage. *See also* accumulation stage; annuity unit; separate account.

act of 1933 *See* Securities Act of 1933.

act of 1934 *See* Securities Exchange Act of 1934.

adjusted gross income (AGI) Earned income plus net passive income, portfolio income and capital gains. *See also* tax liability.

administrator (1) A person authorized by a court of law to liquidate an intestate decedent's estate. (2) An official or agency that administers a state's securities laws.

ADR *See* American depositary receipt.

ADS *See* American depositary receipt.

advertisement Any promotional material designed for use by newspapers, magazines, billboards, radio, television, telephone recording or other public media where the firm has little control over the type of individuals exposed to the material. *See also* sales literature.

AE *See* registered representative.

agency basis *See* agency transaction.

agency issue A debt security issued by an authorized agency of the federal government. Such an issue is backed by the issuing agency itself, not by the full faith and credit of the U.S. government (except GNMA and Federal Import Export Bank issues). *See also* government security.

agency transaction A transaction in which a broker-dealer acts for the accounts of others by buying or selling securities on behalf of customers. *Syn.* agency basis. *See also* agent; broker; principal transaction.

agent (1) An individual or a firm that effects securities transactions for the accounts of others. (2) A person licensed by a state as a life insurance agent. (3) A securities salesperson who represents a broker-dealer or an issuer when selling or trying to sell securities to the investing public; this individual is considered an agent whether he actually receives or simply solicits orders. *See also* broker; broker-dealer; dealer; principal.

aggressive investment strategy A method of portfolio allocation and management aimed at achieving maximum return. Aggressive investors place a high percentage of their investable assets in equity securities and a far lower percentage in safer debt securities and cash equivalents, and they pursue aggressive policies including margin trading, arbitrage and option trading. *See also* balanced investment strategy; defensive investment strategy.

AGI *See* adjusted gross income.

AIR *See* assumed interest rate.

American depositary receipt (ADR) A negotiable certificate representing a given number of shares of stock in a foreign corporation. It is bought and sold in the American securities markets, just as stock is traded. *Syn.* American depositary share.

American Stock Exchange (AMEX) A private, not-for-profit corporation located in New York City that handles approximately one-fifth of all securities trades within the United States.

AMEX *See* American Stock Exchange.

annual compliance review The annual meeting that all registered representatives must attend, the purpose of which is to review compliance issues.

annual ROI The annual return on a bond investment, which equals the annual interest either plus the prorated discount or minus the prorated premium.

annuitant A person who receives an annuity contract's distribution.

annuitize To change an annuity contract from the accumulation (pay-in) stage to the distribution (payout) stage.

annuity A contract between an insurance company and an individual, generally guaranteeing lifetime income to the individual on whose life the contract is based in return for either a lump sum or a periodic payment to the insurance company. The contract holder's objective is usually retirement income. *See also* deferred annuity; fixed annuity; immediate annuity; variable annuity.

annuity unit An accounting measure used to determine the amount of each payment during an annuity's distribution stage. The calculation takes into account the value of each accumulation unit and such other factors as assumed interest rate and mortality risk. *See also* accumulation unit; annuity; distribution stage.

appreciation The increase in an asset's value.

approved plan *See* qualified retirement plan.

arbitration The arrangement whereby the NYSE's Board of Arbitration or a designated arbitration association hears and settles disagreements between members, allied members, member organizations and their employees. Nonmembers in dispute with members or employees may submit voluntarily to arbitration. *See also* simplified arbitration.

ask An indication by a trader or a dealer of a willingness to sell a security or a commodity; the price at which an investor can buy from a broker-dealer. *Syn.* offer. *See also* bid; public offering price; quotation.

asset (1) Anything that an individual or a corporation owns. (2) A balance sheet item expressing what a corporation owns.

asset allocation fund A mutual fund that splits its investment assets among stocks, bonds and other vehicles in an attempt to provide a consistent return for the investor. *See also* mutual fund.

assignment (1) A document accompanying or part of a stock certificate that is signed by the person named on the certificate for the purpose of transferring the certificate's title to another person's name. (2) The act of identifying and notifying an account holder that the option owner has exercised an option held short in that account. *See also* stock power.

associated person of a member (AP) Any employee, manager, director, officer or partner of a member broker-dealer or another entity (issuer, bank, etc.), or any person controlling, controlled by or in common control with that member. *See also* registered representative.

assumed interest rate (AIR) The net rate of investment return that must be credited to a variable life insurance policy to ensure that at all times the variable death benefit equals the amount of the death benefit. The AIR forms the basis for projecting payments, but it is not guaranteed.

auction market A market in which buyers enter competitive bids and sellers enter competitive offers simultaneously. The NYSE is an auction market. *Syn.* double auction market.

authorized stock The number of shares of stock that a corporation can issue. This number of shares is stipulated in the corporation's state-approved charter and may be changed by a vote of the corporation's stockholders.

average A price at a midpoint among a number of prices. Technical analysts frequently use averages as market indicators. *See also* index.

average price A step in determining a bond's yield to maturity. A bond's average price is calculated by adding its face value to the price paid for it and dividing the result by two.

B

back away The failure of an over-the-counter market maker to honor a firm bid and asked price. This violates the NASD Rules of Fair Practice.

back-end load A commission or sales fee that is charged when mutual fund shares or variable annuity contracts are redeemed. It declines annually, decreasing to zero over an extended holding period—up to eight years—as described in the prospectus. *Syn.* contingent-deferred sales load. *See also* front-end load.

balanced fund A mutual fund whose stated investment policy is to have at all times some portion of its investment assets in bonds and preferred stock as well as in common stock in an attempt to provide both growth and income. *See also* mutual fund.

balanced investment strategy A method of portfolio allocation and management aimed at balancing risk and return. A balanced portfolio may combine stocks, bonds, packaged products and cash equivalents.

balance sheet A report of a corporation's financial condition at a specific time.

balance sheet equation A formula stating that a corporation's assets equal the sum of its liabilities plus shareholders' equity.

banking act *See* Glass-Steagall Act of 1933.

basis point A measure of a bond's yield, equal to ¹⁄₁₀₀ of 1 percent of yield. A bond whose yield increases from 5.0 percent to 5.5 percent is said to increase by 50 basis points. *See also* point.

BD *See* broker-dealer.

bear An investor who acts on the belief that a security or the market is falling or will fall. *See also* bull.

bearer bond *See* coupon bond.

bear market A market in which prices of a certain group of securities are falling or are expected to fall. *See also* bull market.

beta coefficient A means of measuring the volatility of a security or a portfolio of securities in comparison with the market as a whole. A beta of 1 indicates that the security's price will move with the market. A beta greater than 1 indicates that the security's price will be more volatile than the market. A beta less than 1 means that it will be less volatile than the market.

bid An indication by an investor, a trader or a dealer of a willingness to buy a security; the price at which an investor can sell to a broker-dealer. *See also* offer; public offering price; quotation.

blue chip stock The equity issues of financially stable, well-established companies that have demonstrated their ability to pay dividends in both good and bad times.

blue-sky To register a securities offering in a particular state. *See also* blue-sky laws; registration by coordination; registration by filing; registration by qualification.

blue-sky laws The nickname for state regulations governing the securities industry. The term was coined in the early 1900s by a Kansas Supreme Court justice who wanted regulation to protect against "speculative schemes that have no more basis than so many feet of blue sky." *See also* Series 63; Series 65; Uniform Securities Act.

board of directors (1) Individuals elected by stockholders to establish corporate management policies. A board of directors decides, among other issues, if and when dividends will be paid to stockholders. (2) The body that governs the NYSE. It is composed of 20 members elected for a term of two years by the NYSE general membership.

Board of Governors The body that governs the NASD. It is composed of 27 members elected by both the NASD general membership and the Board itself.

bona fide quote An offer from a broker-dealer to buy or sell securities. It indicates a willingness to execute a trade under the terms and conditions accompanying the quote. *See also* firm quote; nominal quote.

bond An issuing company's or government's legal obligation to repay the principal of a loan to bond investors at a specified future date. Bonds are usually issued with par or face values of $1,000, representing the amount of money borrowed. The issuer promises to pay a percentage of the par value as interest on the bor-rowed funds. The interest payment is stated on the face of the bond at issue.

bond fund A mutual fund whose investment objective is to provide stable income with minimal capital risk. It invests in income-producing instruments, which may include corporate, government or municipal bonds. *See also* mutual fund.

bond quote One of a number of quotations listed in the financial press and most daily newspapers that provide representative bid prices from the previous day's bond market. Quotes for corporate and government bonds are percentages of the bonds' face values (usually $1,000). Corporate bonds are quoted in increments of ⅛, where a quote of 99⅛ represents 99.125 percent of par ($1,000), or $991.25. Government bonds are quoted in ⅟₃₂nds. Municipal bonds may be quoted on a dollar basis or on a yield-to-maturity basis. *See also* quotation; stock quote.

bond rating An evaluation of the possibility of a bond issuer's default, based on an analysis of the issuer's financial condition and profit potential. Standard & Poor's, Moody's Investors Service and Fitch Investors Service, among others, provide bond rating services.

bond swap The sale of a bond and the simultaneous purchase of a different bond in a like amount. The technique is used to control tax liability, extend maturity or update investment objectives. *Syn.* tax swap. *See also* wash sale.

bond yield The annual rate of return on a bond investment. Types of yield include nominal yield, current yield, yield to maturity and yield to call. Their relationships vary according to whether the bond in question is at a discount, at a premium or at par. *See also* current yield; nominal yield.

book-entry security A security sold without delivery of a certificate. Evidence of ownership is maintained on records kept by a central agency; for example, the Treasury keeps records of Treasury bill purchasers. Transfer of ownership is recorded by entering the change on the books or electronic files. *See also* coupon bond; registered; registered as to principal only.

book value per share A measure of the net worth of each share of common stock. It is calculated by subtracting intangible assets and preferred stock from total net worth, then dividing the result by the number of shares of common outstanding. *Syn.* net tangible assets per share.

branch office Any location identified by any means to the public as a place where a registered broker-dealer conducts business.

breakeven point The point at which gains equal losses.

breakpoint The schedule of sales charge discounts a mutual fund offers for lump-sum or cumulative investments.

breakpoint sale The sale of mutual fund shares in an amount just below the level at which the purchaser would qualify for reduced sales charges. This violates the NASD Rules of Fair Practice.

broad-based index An index designed to reflect the movement of the market as a whole. Examples include the S&P 100, the S&P 500, the AMEX Major Market Index and the *Value Line* Composite Index. *See also* index.

broker (1) An individual or a firm that charges a fee or commission for executing buy and sell orders submitted by another individual or firm. (2) The role of a firm when it acts as an agent for a customer and charges the customer a commission for its services. *See also* agent; broker-dealer; dealer.

broker-dealer (BD) A person or firm in the business of buying and selling securities. A firm may act as both broker (agent) and dealer (principal), but not in the same transaction. Broker-dealers normally must register with the SEC, the appropriate SROs and any state in which they do business. *See also* agent; broker; dealer; principal.

bull An investor who acts on the belief that a security or the market is rising or will rise. *See also* bear.

bull market A market in which prices of a certain group of securities are rising or will rise. *See also* bear market.

business cycle A predictable long-term pattern of alternating periods of economic growth and decline. The cycle passes through four stages: expansion, peak, contraction and trough.

business day A day on which financial markets are open for trading. Saturdays, Sundays and legal holidays are not considered business days.

C

call (1) An option contract giving the owner the right to buy a specified amount of an underlying security at a specified price within a specified time. (2) The act of exercising a call option. *See also* put.

callable bond A type of bond issued with a provision allowing the issuer to redeem the bond before maturity at a predetermined price. *See also* call price.

callable preferred stock A type of preferred stock issued with a provision allowing the corporation to call in the stock at a certain price and retire it. *See also* call price; preferred stock.

call buyer An investor who pays a premium for an option contract and receives, for a specified time, the right to buy the underlying security at a specified price. *See also* call writer; put buyer; put writer.

call date The date, specified in the prospectus of every callable security, after which the security's issuer has the option to redeem the issue at par or at par plus a premium.

call feature *See* call provision.

call price The price, usually a premium over the issue's par value, at which preferred stocks or bonds can be redeemed before an issue's maturity.

call protection A provision in a bond indenture stating that the issue is noncallable for a certain period of time (5 years, 10 years, etc.) after the original issue date. *See also* call provision.

call provision The written agreement between an issuing corporation and its bondholders or preferred stockholders giving the corporation the option to redeem its senior securities at a specified price before maturity and under certain conditions. *Syn.* call feature.

call risk The potential for a bond to be called before maturity, leaving the investor without the bond's current income. As this is more likely to occur during times

352

of falling interest rates, the investor may not be able to reinvest his principal at a comparable rate of return.

call writer An investor who receives a premium and takes on, for a specified time, the obligation to sell the underlying security at a specified price at the call buyer's discretion. *See also* call buyer; put buyer; put writer.

capital Accumulated money or goods available for use in producing more money or goods.

capital appreciation A rise in an asset's market price.

capital asset All tangible property, including securities, real estate and other property, held for the long term.

capital gain The profit realized when a capital asset is sold for a higher price than the purchase price. *See also* capital loss; long-term gain.

capitalization The sum of a corporation's long-term debt, stock and surpluses. *Syn.* invested capital. *See also* capital structure.

capital loss The loss incurred when a capital asset is sold for a lower price than the purchase price. *See also* capital gain; long-term loss.

capital market The segment of the securities market that deals in instruments with more than one year to maturity—that is, long-term debt and equity securities.

capital risk The potential for an investor to lose all money invested owing to circumstances unrelated to an issuer's financial strength. For example, derivative instruments such as options carry risk independent of the underlying securities' changing value. *See also* derivative.

capital stock All of a corporation's outstanding preferred stock and common stock, listed at par value.

capital structure The composition of long-term funds (equity and debt) a corporation has as a source for financing. *See also* capitalization.

capital surplus The money a corporation receives in excess of the stated value of stock at the time of first sale. *Syn.* paid-in capital; paid-in surplus. *See also* par.

cash account An account in which the customer is required by the SEC's Regulation T to pay in full for securities purchased not later than two days after the standard payment period set by the NASD's Uniform Practice Code. *Syn.* special cash account.

cash dividend Money paid to a corporation's stockholders out of the corporation's current earnings or accumulated profits. The board of directors must declare all dividends.

cash equivalent A security that can be readily converted into cash. Examples include Treasury bills, certificates of deposit and money-market instruments and funds.

cashiering department The department within a brokerage firm that delivers securities and money to and receives securities and money from other firms and clients of the brokerage firm. *Syn.* security cage.

cash transaction A settlement contract that calls for delivery and payment on the same day the trade is executed. Payment is due by 2:30 p.m. EST or within 30 minutes of the trade if it occurs after 2:00 p.m. EST. *Syn.* cash trade. *See also* regular way; settlement date.

catastrophe call The redemption of a bond by an issuer owing to disaster (for example, a power plant that has been built with proceeds from an issue burns to the ground).

CD *See* negotiable certificate of deposit.

certificate of deposit (CD) *See* negotiable certificate of deposit.

change (1) For an index or average, the difference between the current value and the previous day's market close. (2) For a stock or bond quote, the difference between the current price and the last trade of the previous day.

churning Excessive trading in a customer's account by a registered representative who ignores the customer's interests and seeks only to increase commissions. This violates the NASD Rules of Fair Practice. *Syn.* overtrading.

close The price of the last transaction for a particular security on a particular day.

closed-end management company An investment company that issues a fixed number of shares in an actively managed portfolio of securities. The shares may be of several classes; they are traded in the secondary marketplace, either on an exchange or over the counter. The shares' market price is determined by supply and demand, not by net asset value. *Syn.* publicly traded fund. *See also* dual-purpose fund.

CMV *See* current market value.

Code of Arbitration Procedure The NASD's formal method of handling securities-related disputes or clearing controversies between members, public customers, clearing corporations or clearing banks. Such disputes involve violations of the Uniform Practice Code rather than the Rules of Fair Practice. Any claim, dispute or controversy between member firms or associated persons must be submitted to arbitration.

Code of Procedure (COP) The NASD's formal procedure for handling trade practice complaints involving violations of the Rules of Fair Practice. The NASD District Business Conduct Committee (DBCC) is the first body to hear and judge complaints. The NASD Board of Governors handles appeals and review of DBCC decisions.

coincident indicator A measurable economic factor that varies directly and simultaneously with the business cycle, thus indicating the current state of the economy. Examples include nonagricultural employment, personal income and industrial production. *See also* lagging indicator; leading indicator.

collateralized mortgage obligation (CMO) A mortgage-backed corporate security. Unlike pass-through obligations issued by FNMA and GNMA, its yield is not guaranteed and it does not have the federal government's backing. These issues attempt to return interest and principal at a predetermined rate.

combination fund An equity mutual fund that attempts to combine the objectives of growth and current yield by dividing its portfolio between companies that show long-term growth potential and companies that pay high dividends. *See also* mutual fund.

combination preferred stock A type of preferred stock that combines two or more of the following preferred stock features: participating, cumulative, convertible, callable. *See also* preferred stock.

combination privilege A benefit offered by a mutual fund whereby the investor may qualify for a sales charge breakpoint by combining separate investments in two or more mutual funds under the same management.

commercial paper An unsecured, short-term promissory note issued by a corporation for financing accounts receivable and inventories. It is usually issued at a discount reflecting prevailing market interest rates. Maturities range up to 270 days.

commission A service charge an agent assesses in return for arranging a security's purchase or sale. A commission must be fair and reasonable, considering all the relevant factors of the transaction. *Syn.* sales charge. *See also* markup.

commissioner The state official with jurisdiction over insurance transactions.

Committee on Uniform Securities Identification Procedures (CUSIP) A committee that assigns identification numbers and codes to all securities, to be used when recording all buy and sell orders.

common stock A security that represents ownership in a corporation. Holders of common stock exercise control by electing a board of directors and voting on corporate policy. *See also* equity; preferred stock.

completion of the transaction As defined by the NASD, the point at which a customer pays any part of the purchase price to the broker-dealer for a security he has purchased or delivers a security he has sold. If the customer pays the broker-dealer before payment is due, the transaction's completion occurs when the broker-dealer delivers the security.

compliance department The department within a brokerage firm that oversees the firm's trading and market-making activities. It ensures that the firm's employees and officers abide by the rules and regulations of the SEC, exchanges and SROs.

concession The profit per bond or share that an underwriter allows the seller of new issue securities. The selling group broker-dealer purchases the securities from the syndicate member at the public offering price minus the concession. *Syn.* reallowance.

conduit theory A means for an investment company to avoid taxation on net investment income distributed to shareholders. If a mutual fund acts as a conduit for the distribution of net investment income, it may qualify as a regulated investment company and be taxed only on the income the fund retains. *Syn.* pipeline theory.

confirmation A printed document that states the trade date, settlement date and money due from or owed to a customer. It is sent or given to the customer on or before the settlement date. *See also* duplicate confirmation.

Consolidated Tape (CT) A New York Stock Exchange service that delivers real-time reports of securities transactions to subscribers as they occur on the various exchanges.
The Tape distributes reports to subscribers over two different networks that the subscribers can tap into through either the high-speed electronic lines or the low-speed ticker lines. Network A reports transactions in NYSE–listed securities. Network B reports AMEX–listed securities transactions, as well as reports of transactions in regional exchange issues that substantially meet AMEX listing requirements. *Syn.* Consolidated Ticker Tape; Tape; Ticker Tape.

Consolidated Ticker Tape *See* Consolidated Tape.

constant dollar plan A defensive investment strategy in which the total sum of money invested is kept constant, regardless of any price fluctuation in the portfolio. As a result, the investor sells when the market is high and buys when it is low.

constant ratio plan An investment strategy in which the investor maintains an appropriate ratio of debt to equity securities by making purchases and sales to maintain the desired balance.

constructive receipt The date on which the Internal Revenue Service considers that a taxpayer receives dividends or other income.

Consumer Price Index (CPI) A measure of price changes in consumer goods and services used to identify periods of inflation or deflation.

contingent-deferred sales load *See* back-end load.

contraction A period of general economic decline, one of the business cycle's four stages. *See also* business cycle.

contractionary policy A monetary policy that decreases the money supply, usually with the intention of raising interest rates and combating inflation.

contractual plan A type of accumulation plan in which an individual agrees to invest a specific amount of money in the mutual fund during a specific time period. *Syn.* penalty plan; prepaid charge plan. *See also* front-end load; mutual fund; spread load; voluntary accumulation plan.

control (controlling, controlled by, under common control with) The power to direct or affect the direction of a company's management and policies, whether through the ownership of voting securities, by contract or otherwise. Control is presumed to exist if a person, directly or indirectly, owns, controls, holds with the power to vote or holds proxies representing more than 10 percent of a company's voting securities.

control of securities A term used to indicate a broker-dealer's responsibilities with regard to securities in its possession. Under the SEC's customer protection rule, broker-dealers must maintain control procedures over customer funds and securities. Securities are considered to be under the control of or in the possession of a broker-dealer if they are in the broker-dealer's physical possession, are in an alternative location acceptable to the SEC or are in transit for a period of time that does not exceed SEC standards. *Syn.* possession of securities.

control person (1) A director, an officer or another affiliate of an issuer. (2) A stockholder who owns at least 10 percent of any class of a corporation's outstanding securities. *See also* affiliate; insider.

control security Any security owned by a director, an officer or another affiliate of the issuer or by a stockholder who owns at least 10 percent of any class of a corporation's outstanding securities. Who owns a security, not the security itself, determines whether it is a control security.

conversion parity Two securities, one of which can be converted into the other, of equal dollar value. A convertible security holder can calculate parity to help decide whether converting would lead to gain or loss.

conversion price The dollar amount of a convertible security's par value that is exchangeable for one share of common stock.

conversion privilege A feature the issuer adds to a security that allows the holder to change the security into shares of common stock. This makes the security attractive to investors and, therefore, more marketable. *See also* convertible bond; convertible preferred stock.

conversion rate *See* conversion ratio.

conversion ratio The number of shares of common stock per par value amount that the holder would receive for converting a convertible bond or preferred share. *Syn.* conversion rate.

conversion value The total market value of common stock into which a senior security is convertible.

convertible bond A debt security, usually in the form of a debenture, that can be exchanged for equity securities of the issuing corporation at specified prices or rates. *See also* debenture.

convertible preferred stock An equity security that can be exchanged for common stock at specified prices or rates. Dividends may be cumulative or noncumulative. *See also* cumulative preferred stock; noncumulative preferred stock; preferred stock.

cooling-off period The period (a minimum of 20 days) between a registration statement's filing date and the registration's effective date. In practice, the period varies in length.

coordination *See* registration by coordination.

corporate account An account held in a corporation's name. The corporate agreement, signed when the account is opened, specifies which officers are authorized to trade in the account. In addition to standard margin account documents, a corporation must provide a copy of its charter and bylaws authorizing a margin account.

corporate bond A debt security issued by a corporation. A corporate bond typically has a par value of $1,000, is taxable, has a term maturity and is traded on a major exchange.

corporation The most common form of business organization, in which the organization's total worth is divided into shares of stock, each share representing a unit of ownership. A corporation is characterized by a continuous life span and its owners' limited liability.

cost basis The price paid for an asset, including any commissions or fees, used to calculate capital gains or losses when the asset is sold.

coupon bond A debt obligation with attached coupons representing semiannual interest payments. The holder submits the coupons to the trustee to receive the interest payments. The issuer keeps no record of the purchaser, and the purchaser's name is not printed on the certificate. *Syn.* bearer bond. *See also* book-entry security; registered; registered as to principal only.

coupon yield *See* nominal yield.

CPI *See* Consumer Price Index.

credit risk The degree of probability that a bond's issuer will default in the payment of either principal or interest. *Syn.* default risk; financial risk.

cumulative preferred stock An equity security that offers the holder any unpaid dividends in arrears. These dividends accumulate and must be paid to the cumulative preferred stockholder before any dividends can be paid to the common stockholders. *See also* convertible preferred stock; noncumulative preferred stock; preferred stock.

cumulative voting A voting procedure that permits stockholders either to cast all of their votes for any one candidate or to cast their total number of votes in any proportion they choose. This results in greater representation for minority stockholders. *See also* statutory voting.

current assets Cash and other assets that are expected to be converted into cash within the next 12 months. Examples include such liquid items as cash and equivalents, accounts receivable, inventory and prepaid expenses.

current liabilities A corporation's debt obligations due for payment within the next 12 months. Examples include accounts payable, accrued wages payable and current long-term debt.

current market value (CMV) The worth of the securities in an account. The market value of listed securities is based on the closing prices on the previous business day. *Syn.* long market value. *See also* market value.

current price *See* public offering price.

current yield The annual rate of return on a security, calculated by dividing the interest or dividends paid by the security's current market price. *See also* bond yield.

CUSIP *See* Committee on Uniform Securities Identification Procedures.

custodial account An account in which a custodian enters trades on behalf of the beneficial owner, often a minor. *See also* custodian.

custodian An institution or a person responsible for making all investment, management and distribution decisions in an account maintained in the best interests of another. Mutual funds have custodians responsible for safeguarding certificates and performing clerical duties. *See also* mutual fund custodian.

customer Any person who opens a trading account with a broker-dealer. A customer may be classified in terms of account ownership, trading authorization, payment method or types of securities traded.

customer statement A document showing a customer's trading activity, positions and account balance. The SEC requires that customer statements be sent quarterly, but customers generally receive them monthly.

cyclical industry A fundamental analysis term for an industry that is sensitive to the business cycle and price changes. Most cyclical industries produce durable goods such as raw materials and heavy equipment.

D

DBCC *See* NASD District Business Conduct Committee.

dealer (1) An individual or a firm engaged in the business of buying and selling securities for its own account, either directly or through a broker. (2) The role of a firm when it acts as a principal and charges the cus-

tomer a markup or markdown. *Syn.* principal. *See also* broker; broker-dealer.

debenture A debt obligation backed by the issuing corporation's general credit. *Syn.* unsecured bond.

debt financing Raising money for working capital or for capital expenditures by selling bonds, bills or notes to individual or institutional investors. In return for the money lent, the investors become creditors and receive the issuer's promise to repay principal and interest on the debt. *See also* equity financing.

debt security A security representing an investor's loan to an issuer such as a corporation, a municipality, the federal government or a federal agency. In return for the loan, the issuer promises to repay the debt on a specified date and to pay interest. *See also* equity security.

declaration date The date on which a corporation announces an upcoming dividend's amount, payment date and record date.

deduction An item or expenditure subtracted from adjusted gross income to reduce the amount of income subject to tax.

default The failure to pay interest or principal promptly when due.

default risk *See* credit risk.

defensive industry A fundamental analysis term for an industry that is relatively unaffected by the business cycle. Most defensive industries produce nondurable goods for which demand remains steady throughout the business cycle; examples include the food industry and utilities.

defensive investment strategy A method of portfolio allocation and management aimed at minimizing the risk of losing principal. Defensive investors place a high percentage of their investable assets in bonds, cash equivalents and stocks that are less volatile than average.

deferred annuity An annuity contract that delays payment of income, installments or a lump sum until the investor elects to receive it. *See also* annuity.

deferred compensation plan A nonqualified retirement plan whereby the employee defers receiving current compensation in favor of a larger payout at retirement (or in the case of disability or death).

defined benefit plan A qualified retirement plan that specifies the total amount of money that the employee will receive at retirement.

defined contribution plan A qualified retirement plan that specifies the amount of money that the employer will contribute annually to the plan.

deflation A persistent and measurable fall in the general level of prices. *See also* inflation.

delivery The change in ownership or in control of a security in exchange for cash. Delivery takes place on the settlement date.

demand deposit A sum of money left with a bank (or borrowed from a bank and left on deposit) that the depositing customer has the right to withdraw immediately. *See also* time deposit.

depression A prolonged period of general economic decline.

derivative An investment vehicle, the value of which is based on another security's value. Futures contracts, forward contracts and options are among the most common types of derivatives. Institutional investors generally use derivatives to increase overall portfolio return or to hedge portfolio risk.

devaluation A substantial fall in a currency's value as compared to the value of gold or to the value of another country's currency.

dilution A reduction in earnings per share of common stock. Dilution occurs through the issuance of additional shares of common stock and the conversion of convertible securities.

discount The difference between the lower price paid for a security and the security's face amount at issue.

discount bond A bond that sells at a lower price than its face value. *See also* par.

discount rate The interest rate charged by the 12 Federal Reserve Banks for short-term loans made to member banks.

discretion The authority given to someone other than an account's beneficial owner to make investment decisions for the account concerning the security, the number of shares or units and whether to buy or sell. The authority to decide only timing or price does not constitute discretion. *See also* limited power of attorney.

discretionary account An account in which the customer has given the registered representative authority to enter transactions at the rep's discretion.

disintermediation The flow of money from low-yielding accounts in traditional savings institutions to higher yielding investments. Typically, this occurs when the Fed tightens the money supply and interest rates rise.

disposable income (DI) The sum that people divide between spending and personal savings. *See also* personal income.

distribution Any cash or other property distributed to shareholders or general partners that arises from their interests in the business, investment company or partnership.

distribution stage The period during which an individual receives distributions from an annuity account. *Syn.* payout stage. *See also* accumulation stage; accumulation unit.

District Business Conduct Committee *See* NASD District Business Conduct Committee.

diversification A risk management technique that mixes a wide variety of investments within a portfolio, thus minimizing the impact of any one security on overall portfolio performance.

diversified common stock fund A mutual fund that invests its assets in a wide range of common stocks. The fund's objectives may be growth, income or a combination of both. *See also* growth fund; mutual fund.

diversified management company As defined by the Investment Company Act of 1940, a management company that meets certain standards for percentage of assets invested. These companies use diversification to manage risk. *See also* management company; nondiversified management company; 75-5-10 test.

dividend A distribution of a corporation's earnings. Dividends may be in the form of cash, stock or property. The board of directors must declare all dividends. *Syn.* stock dividend. *See also* cash dividend; dividend yield; property dividend.

dividend payout ratio A measure of a corporation's policy of paying cash dividends, calculated by dividing the dividends paid on common stock by the net income available for common stockholders. The ratio is the complement of the retained earnings ratio.

dividends per share The dollar amount of cash dividends paid on each common share during one year.

dividend yield The annual rate of return on a common or preferred stock investment. The yield is calculated by dividing the annual dividend by the stock's purchase price. *See also* current yield; dividend.

DJIA *See* Dow Jones Industrial Average.

doctrine of mutual reciprocity The agreement that established the federal tax exemption for municipal bond interest. States and municipalities do not tax federal securities or properties, and the federal government reciprocates by exempting local government securities and properties from federal taxation. *Syn.* mutual exclusion doctrine; reciprocal immunity.

dollar cost averaging A system of buying mutual fund shares in fixed dollar amounts at regular fixed intervals, regardless of the share's price. The investor purchases more shares when prices are low and fewer shares when prices are high, thus lowering the average cost per share over time.

donor A person who makes a gift of money or securities to another. Once the gift is donated, the donor gives up all rights to it. Gifts of securities to minors under the Uniform Gifts to Minors Act provide tax advantages to the donor. *See also* Uniform Gifts to Minors Act.

Dow Jones averages The most widely quoted and oldest measures of change in stock prices. Each of the four averages is based on the prices of a limited number of stocks in a particular category. *See also* average; Dow Jones Industrial Average.

Dow Jones Industrial Average (DJIA) The most widely used market indicator, composed of 30 large, actively traded issues of industrial stocks. *See also* average.

dual-purpose fund A closed-end investment company that offers two classes of stock: income shares and capital shares. Income shares entitle the holder to share in the net dividends and interest paid to the fund. Capital shares entitle the holder to profit from the capital appreciation of all securities the fund holds. *See also* closed-end management company.

duplicate confirmation A copy of a customer's confirmation that a brokerage firm sends to an agent or an attorney if the customer requests it in writing. In addition, if the customer is an employee of another broker-dealer, SRO regulations may require a duplicate confirmation to be sent to the employing broker-dealer. *See also* confirmation.

E

earned income Income derived from active participation in a trade or business, including wages, salary, tips, commissions and bonuses. *See also* portfolio income; unearned income.

earnings per share (EPS) A corporation's net income available for common stock divided by its number of shares of common stock outstanding. *Syn.* primary earnings per share.

economic risk The potential for international developments and domestic events to trigger losses in securities investments.

EE savings bond *See* Series EE bond.

effective date The date the registration of an issue of securities becomes effective, allowing the underwriters to sell the newly issued securities to the public and confirm sales to investors who have given indications of interest.

elasticity The responsiveness of consumers and producers to a change in prices. A large change in demand or production resulting from a small change in price for a good is considered an indication of elasticity.

Employee Retirement Income Security Act of 1974 (ERISA) The law that governs the operation of most corporate pension and benefit plans. The law eased pension eligibility rules, set up the Pension Benefit Guaranty Corporation and established guidelines for the management of pension funds. Corporate retirement plans established under ERISA qualify for favorable tax treatment for employers and participants. *Syn.* Pension Reform Act. *See also* Title 1; Title 2; Title 3; Title 4.

endorsement The signature on the back of a stock or bond certificate by the person named on the certificate as the owner. An owner must endorse certificates when transferring them to another person. *See also* assignment.

EPS *See* earnings per share.

equity (EQ) Common and preferred stockholders' ownership interests in a corporation. *See also* common stock; preferred stock.

equity financing Raising money for working capital or for capital expenditures by selling common or preferred stock to individual or institutional investors. In return for the money paid, the investors receive ownership interests in the corporation. *See also* debt financing.

equity option A security representing the right to buy or sell common stock at a specified price within a specified time. *See also* option

equity security A security representing ownership in a corporation or another enterprise. Examples of equity securities include:
- common and preferred stock;
- interests in a limited partnership or joint venture;
- securities that carry the right to be traded for equity securities, such as convertible bonds, rights and warrants; and
- put and call options on equity securities.
See also debt security.

ERISA *See* Employee Retirement Income Security Act of 1974.

exchange Any organization, association or group of persons that maintains or provides a marketplace in which securities can be bought and sold. An exchange need not be a physical place, and several strictly electronic exchanges do business around the world.

Exchange Act *See* Securities Exchange Act of 1934.

exchange-listed security A security that has met certain requirements and has been admitted to full trading privileges on an exchange. The NYSE, the AMEX and regional exchanges set listing requirements for volume of shares outstanding, corporate earnings and other characteristics. Exchange-listed securities can also be traded in the third market, the market for institutional investors.

exchange market All of the exchanges on which listed securities are traded.

exchange privilege A feature offered by a mutual fund allowing an individual to transfer an investment in one fund to another fund under the same sponsor without incurring an additional sales charge.

ex-date The first date on which a security is traded that the buyer is not entitled to receive distributions previously declared. *Syn.* ex-dividend date.

ex-dividend date *See* ex-date.

executor A person given fiduciary authorization to manage the affairs of a decedent's estate. An executor's authority is established by the decedent's last will.

exempt security A security exempt from the registration requirements (although not from the antifraud requirements) of the Securities Act of 1933. Examples include U.S. government securities and municipal securities.

exempt transaction A transaction that does not trigger a state's registration and advertising requirements under the Uniform Securities Act. Examples of exempt transactions include:
- nonissuer transactions in outstanding securities (normal market trading);
- transactions with financial institutions;
- unsolicited transactions; and
- private placement transactions.

No transaction is exempt from the Uniform Securities Act's antifraud provisions.

exercise To effect the transaction offered by an option, a right or a warrant. For example, an equity call holder exercises a call by buying 100 shares of the underlying stock at the agreed-upon price within the agreed-upon time period.

exercise price The cost per share at which an option or a warrant holder may buy or sell the underlying security. *Syn.* strike price.

expansion A period of increased business activity throughout an economy; one of the four stages of the business cycle. *Syn.* recovery. *See also* business cycle.

expansionary policy A monetary policy that increases the money supply, usually with the intention of lowering interest rates and combatting deflation.

expense ratio A ratio for comparing a mutual fund's efficiency by dividing the fund's expenses by its net assets.

F

FAC *See* face-amount certificate company.

face-amount certificate company (FAC) An investment company that issues certificates obligating it to pay an investor a stated amount of money (the face amount) on a specific future date. The investor pays into the certificate in periodic payments or in a lump sum.

face value *See* par.

Fannie Mae *See* Federal National Mortgage Association.

Farm Credit System (FCS) An organization of 37 privately owned banks that provide credit services to farmers and mortgages on farm property. Included in the system are the Federal Land Banks, Federal Intermediate Credit Banks and Banks for Cooperatives. *See also* Federal Intermediate Credit Bank.

FDIC *See* Federal Deposit Insurance Corporation.

Fed *See* Federal Reserve System.

Federal Deposit Insurance Corporation (FDIC) The government agency that provides deposit insurance for member banks and prevents bank and thrift failures.

Federal Home Loan Bank (FHLB) A government-regulated organization that operates a credit reserve system for the nation's savings and loan institutions.

Federal Home Loan Mortgage Corporation (FHLMC) A publicly traded corporation that promotes the nationwide secondary market in mortgages by issuing mortgage-backed pass-through debt certificates. *Syn.* Freddie Mac.

Federal Intermediate Credit Bank (FICB) One of 12 banks that provide short-term financing to farmers as part of the Farm Credit System.

Federal National Mortgage Association (FNMA) A publicly held corporation that purchases conventional mortgages and mortgages from government agencies, including the Federal Housing Administration, Department of Veterans Affairs and Farmers Home Administration. *Syn.* Fannie Mae.

Federal Open Market Committee (FOMC) A committee that makes decisions concerning the Fed's operations to control the money supply.

Federal Reserve Board (FRB) A seven-member group that directs the operations of the Federal Reserve System. The President appoints board members, subject to Congressional approval.

Federal Reserve System The central bank system of the United States. Its primary responsibility is to regulate the flow of money and credit. The system includes 12 regional banks, 24 branch banks and hundreds of national and state banks. *Syn.* Fed.

FHLB *See* Federal Home Loan Bank.

FHLMC *See* Federal Home Loan Mortgage Corporation.

FICB *See* Federal Intermediate Credit Bank.

fictitious quotation A bid or an offer published before being identified by source and verified as legitimate. A fictitious quote may create the appearance of trading activity where none exists; this violates the NASD Rules of Fair Practice.

fiduciary A person legally appointed and authorized to hold assets in trust for another person and manage those assets for that person's benefit.

filing *See* registration by filing.

filing date The day on which an issuer submits to the SEC the registration statement for a new securities issue.

final prospectus The legal document that states a new issue security's price, delivery date and underwriting spread, as well as other material information. It must be given to every investor who purchases a new issue of registered securities. *Syn.* prospectus.

firm quote The actual price at which a trading unit of a security (such as 100 shares of stock or five bonds) may be bought or sold. All quotes are firm quotes unless otherwise indicated. *See also* bona fide quote; nominal quote.

fiscal policy The federal tax and spending policies set by Congress or the President. These policies affect tax rates, interest rates and government spending in an effort to control the economy. *See also* monetary policy.

5 percent markup policy The NASD's general guideline for the percentage markups, markdowns and commissions on OTC securities transactions. The policy is intended to ensure fair and reasonable treatment of the investing public.

fixed annuity An insurance contract in which the insurance company makes fixed dollar payments to the annuitant for the term of the contract, usually until the annuitant dies. The insurance company guarantees both earnings and principal. *Syn.* fixed dollar annuity; guaranteed dollar annuity. *See also* annuity; variable annuity.

fixed dollar annuity *See* fixed annuity.

fixed unit investment trust An investment company that invests in a portfolio of securities in which no changes are permissible. *See also* nonfixed unit investment trust; unit investment trust.

flat A term used to describe bonds traded without accrued interest. They are traded at the agreed-upon market price only. *See also* accrued interest.

flexible premium policy A variable or whole life insurance contract that permits the holder to adjust the premium payments and death benefit according to changing needs.

FNMA *See* Federal National Mortgage Association.

FOMC *See* Federal Open Market Committee.

foreign fund *See* specialized fund.

form letter A sales letter sent to more than 25 persons within a 90-day period and, therefore, subject to the NASD's approval and filing requirements for sales literature. *See also* sales literature.

45-day letter *See* free-look letter.

forward pricing The valuation process for mutual fund shares, whereby an order to purchase or redeem shares is executed at the price determined by the portfolio valuation calculated after the order is received. Portfolio valuations occur at least once per business day.

401(k) plan A tax-deferred defined contribution retirement plan offered by an employer.

403(b) plan A tax-deferred annuity retirement plan available to employees of public schools and certain nonprofit organizations.

fourth market The exchange where securities are traded directly from one institutional investor to another without a brokerage firm's services, primarily through the use of INSTINET.

fractional share A portion of a whole share of stock. Mutual fund shares are frequently issued in fractional amounts. Fractional shares used to be generated when corporations declared stock dividends, merged or voted to split stock, but today it is more common for corporations to issue the cash equivalent of fractional shares.

fraud The deliberate concealment, misrepresentation or omission of material information or the truth, so as to deceive or manipulate another party for unlawful or unfair gain.

FRB *See* Federal Reserve Board.

Freddie Mac *See* Federal Home Loan Mortgage Corporation.

free credit balance The cash funds in customer accounts. Broker-dealers must notify customers of their free credit balances at least quarterly.

free-look letter A letter to mutual fund investors explaining a contractual plan's sales charge and operation. The letter must be sent within 60 days of a sale. During the free-look period, the investor may terminate the plan without paying a sales charge. *Syn.* 45-day letter. *See also* contractual plan; right of withdrawal.

freeriding Buying and immediately selling securities without making payment. This practice violates the SEC's Regulation T.

freeriding and withholding The failure of a member participating in the distribution of a hot issue to make a bona fide public offering at the public offering price. This practice violates the NASD Rules of Fair Practice. *See also* hot issue.

front-end load (1) A mutual fund commission or sales fee that is charged at the time shares are purchased. The load is added to the share's net asset value when calculating the public offering price. *See also* back-end load. (2) A system of sales charge for contractual plans that permits up to 50 percent of the first year's payments to be deducted as a sales charge. Investors have a right to withdraw from such a plan, but some restrictions apply if this occurs. *See also* contractual plan; spread load.

frozen account An account requiring cash in advance before a buy order is executed and securities in hand before a sell order is executed. An account holder under such restrictions has violated the SEC's Regulation T.

Full Disclosure Act *See* Securities Act of 1933.

full power of attorney A written authorization for someone other than an account's beneficial owner to make deposits and withdrawals and to execute trades in the account. *See also* limited power of attorney.

full trading authorization An authorization, usually provided by a full power of attorney, for someone other than the customer to have full trading privileges in an account. *See also* limited trading authorization.

fully registered bond A debt issue that prints the bondholder's name on the certificate. The issuer's transfer agent maintains the records and sends principal and interest payments directly to the investor. *See also* registered; registered as to principal only.

funded debt All long-term debt financing of a corporation or municipality; that is, all outstanding bonds maturing in five years or longer.

funding An ERISA guideline stipulating that retirement plan assets must be segregated from other corporate assets.

fund manager *See* portfolio manager.

fungible Interchangeable, owing to identical characteristics or value. A security is fungible if it can be substituted or exchanged for another security.

G

general account The account that holds all of an insurer's assets other than those in separate accounts. The general account holds the contributions paid for traditional life insurance contracts. *See also* separate account.

General Securities Representative *See* Series 7.

generic advertising Communications with the public that promote securities as investments, but that do not refer to particular securities. *Syn.* institutional advertising.

Ginnie Mae *See* Government National Mortgage Association.

Glass-Steagall Act of 1933 Federal legislation that forbids commercial banks to underwrite securities and forbids investment bankers to open deposit accounts or make commercial loans. *Syn.* banking act.

GNMA *See* Government National Mortgage Association.

Government National Mortgage Association (GNMA) A wholly government-owned corporation that issues pass-through mortgage debt certificates backed by the full faith and credit of the U.S. government. *Syn.* Ginnie Mae.

government security A debt obligation of the U.S. government, backed by its full faith, credit and taxing power, and regarded as having no risk of default. The government issues short-term Treasury bills, medium-term Treasury notes and long-term Treasury bonds. *See also* agency issue.

gross domestic product (GDP) The total value of goods and services produced in a country during one year. It includes consumption, government purchases, investments, and exports minus imports.

gross income All income of a taxpayer, from whatever source derived.

growth fund A diversified common stock fund that has capital appreciation as its primary goal. It invests in companies that reinvest most of their earnings for expansion, research or development. *See also* diversified common stock fund; mutual fund.

growth industry An industry that is growing faster than the economy as a whole as a result of technological changes, new products or changing consumer tastes.

growth stock A relatively speculative issue that is believed to offer significant potential for capital gains. It often pays low dividends and sells at a high price-earnings ratio.

guaranteed dollar annuity *See* fixed annuity.

guaranteed stock An equity security, generally a preferred stock, issued with a promise from a corporation other than the issuing corporation to maintain dividend payments. The stock still represents ownership in the issuing corporation, but it is considered a dual security.

guardian A fiduciary who manages the assets of a minor or an incompetent for that person's benefit. *See also* fiduciary.

H

HH savings bond *See* Series HH bond.

high The highest price a security or commodity reaches during a specified period of time. *See also* low.

holder The owner of a security. *See also* long.

holding company A company organized to invest in and manage other corporations.

holding period A time period signifying how long the owner possesses a security. It starts the day after a purchase and ends on the day of the sale.

hold in street name A securities transaction settlement and delivery procedure whereby a customer's securities are transferred into the broker-dealer's name and held by the broker-dealer. Although the broker-dealer is the nominal owner, the customer is the beneficial owner. *See also* transfer and hold in safekeeping; transfer and ship.

hot issue A new issue that sells or is anticipated to sell at a premium over the public offering price. *See also* freeriding and withholding.

HR-10 plan *See* Keogh plan.

I

identified security The particular security designated for sale by an investor holding identical securities with different acquisition dates and cost bases. This allows the investor to control the amount of capital gain or loss incurred through the sale.

immediate annuity An insurance contract purchased for a single premium that starts to pay the annuitant immediately following its purchase. *See also* annuity.

immediate family A parent, mother-in-law or father-in-law, husband or wife, or child or another relative supported financially by a person associated with the securities industry.

incidental insurance benefit A payment received from a variable life insurance policy, other than the variable death benefit and the minimum death benefit, and including but not limited to any accidental death and dismemberment benefit, disability income benefit, guaranteed insurability option, family income benefit or fixed-benefit term rider.

income bond A debt obligation that promises to repay principal in full at maturity. Interest is paid only if the corporation's earnings are sufficient to meet the interest payment and if the board of directors declares the interest payment. Income bonds are usually traded flat. *Syn.* adjustment bond. *See also* flat.

income fund A mutual fund that seeks to provide stable current income by investing in securities that pay interest or dividends. *See also* mutual fund.

income statement The summary of a corporation's revenues and expenses for a specific fiscal period.

indefeasible title Ownership that cannot be declared null or void.

index A comparison of current prices to some baseline, such as prices on a particular date. Indexes are frequently used in technical analysis. *See also* average.

indication of interest (IOI) An investor's expression of conditional interest in buying an upcoming securities issue after the investor has reviewed a preliminary prospectus. An indication of interest is not a commitment to buy.

individual retirement account (IRA) A retirement investing tool for employed individuals that allows an annual contribution of 100 percent of earned income up to a maximum of $2,000. Some or all of the contribution may be deductible from current taxes, depending on the individual's adjusted gross income and coverage by employer-sponsored qualified retirement plans. *See also* Keogh plan; nonqualified retirement plan; qualified retirement plan; simplified employee pension plan.

industry fund *See* sector fund.

inflation A persistent and measurable rise in the general level of prices. *See also* deflation.

initial public offering (IPO) A corporation's first sale of common stock to the public. *See also* new issue market; public offering.

inside information Material information that has not been disseminated to, or is not readily available to, the general public.

insider Any person who possesses or has access to material nonpublic information about a corporation. Insiders include directors, officers and stockholders who own more than 10 percent of any class of equity security of a corporation.

Insider Trading Act *See* Insider Trading and Securities Fraud Enforcement Act of 1988.

Insider Trading and Securities Fraud Enforcement Act of 1988 Legislation that defines what constitutes the illicit use of nonpublic information in making securities trades and the liabilities and penalties that apply. *Syn.* Insider Trading Act. *See also* Chinese wall; insider.

institutional account An account held for the benefit of others. Examples of institutional accounts include banks, trusts, pension and profit-sharing plans, mutual funds and insurance companies.

institutional investor A person or an organization that trades securities in large enough share quantities or dollar amounts that it qualifies for preferential treatment and lower commissions. An institutional order can be of any size. Institutional investors are covered by fewer protective regulations because it is assumed that they are more knowledgeable and better able to protect themselves.

interest The charge for the privilege of borrowing money, usually expressed as an annual percentage rate.

interest rate risk The risk associated with investments relating to the sensitivity of price or value to fluctuation in the current level of interest rates; also, the risk that involves the competitive cost of money. This term is generally associated with bond prices, but it applies to all investments. In bonds, prices carry interest risk because if bond prices rise, outstanding bonds will not remain competitive unless their yields and prices adjust to reflect the current market.

interlocking directorate Two or more corporate boards of directors that have individual directors who serve simultaneously on both boards. The concept is invoked in the Investment Company Act of 1940, which states that at least 40 percent of an investment company's board must remain independent from the investment company's operations, and no more than 60 percent of the directors may be affiliated persons, such as investment advisers, custodians or accountants.

Internal Revenue Code (IRC) The legislation that defines tax liabilities and deductions for U.S. taxpayers.

interstate offering An issue of securities registered with the SEC sold to residents of states other than the state in which the issuer does business.

investment adviser (1) Any person who makes investment recommendations in return for a flat fee or a percentage of assets managed. (2) For an investment company, the individual who bears the day-to-day responsibility of investing the cash and securities held in the fund's portfolio in accordance with objectives stated in the fund's prospectus.

Investment Advisers Act of 1940 Legislation governing who must register with the SEC as an investment adviser. *See also* investment adviser.

investment banker An institution in the business of raising capital for corporations and municipalities. An investment banker may not accept deposits or make commercial loans. *Syn.* investment bank.

investment banking business A broker, dealer or municipal or government securities dealer that underwrites or distributes new issues of securities as a dealer or that buys and sells securities for the accounts of others as a broker. *Syn.* investment securities business.

investment company A company engaged in the business of pooling investors' money and trading in securities for them. Examples include face-amount certificate companies, unit investment trusts and management companies.

Investment Company Act Amendments of 1970 Amendments to the Investment Company Act of 1940 requiring a registered investment company that issues contractual plans to offer all purchasers withdrawal rights and purchasers of front-end load plans surrender rights. *See also* Investment Company Act of 1940.

Investment Company Act of 1940 Congressional legislation regulating companies that invest and reinvest in securities. The act requires an investment company engaged in interstate commerce to register with the SEC.

Investment Company/Variable Contract Products Limited Principal *See* Series 26.

Investment Company/Variable Contract Products Limited Representative *See* Series 6.

investment grade security A security to which the rating services (Standard & Poor's, Moody's, etc.) have assigned a rating of BBB/Baa or above.

investment objective Any goal a client hopes to achieve through investing. Examples include current income, capital growth and preservation of capital.

investment pyramid A portfolio strategy that allocates investable assets according to an investment's relative safety. The pyramid base is composed of low-risk investments, the mid portion is composed of growth investments and the pyramid top is composed of speculative investments.

investor An individual who purchases an asset or a security with the intent of profiting from the transaction.

IPO *See* initial public offering.

IRA *See* individual retirement account.

IRA rollover The reinvestment of assets that an individual receives as a distribution from a qualified tax-deferred retirement plan into an individual retirement account within 60 days of receiving the distribution. The individual may reinvest either the entire sum or a portion of the sum, although any portion not reinvested is taxed as ordinary income. *See also* individual retirement account; IRA transfer.

IRA transfer The direct reinvestment of retirement assets from one qualified tax-deferred retirement plan to an individual retirement account. The account owner never takes possession of the assets, but directs that they be transferred directly from the existing plan custodian to the new plan custodian. *See also* individual retirement account; IRA rollover.

IRC *See* Internal Revenue Code.

irrevocable stock power *See* stock power.

issued stock Equity securities authorized by the issuer's registration statement and distributed to the public. *See also* outstanding stock; treasury stock.

issuer The entity, such as a corporation or municipality, that offers or proposes to offer its securities for sale.

J

joint account An account in which two or more individuals possess some form of control over the account and may transact business in the account. The account must be designated as either joint tenants in common or joint tenants with right of survivorship. *See also* joint tenants in common; joint tenants with right of survivorship.

joint life with last survivor An annuity payout option that covers two or more people, with annuity payments continuing as long as one of the annuitants remains alive.

joint tenants in common (JTIC) A form of joint ownership of an account whereby a deceased tenant's fractional interest in the account is retained by his estate. *Syn.* tenants in common. *See also* joint tenants with right of survivorship.

joint tenants with right of survivorship (JTWROS) A form of joint ownership of an account whereby a deceased tenant's fractional interest in the account passes to the surviving tenant(s). It is used almost exclusively by husbands and wives. *See also* joint tenants in common.

JTIC *See* joint tenants in common.

JTWROS *See* joint tenants with right of survivorship.

K

Keogh plan A qualified tax-deferred retirement plan for persons who are self-employed and unincorporated or who earn extra income through personal services aside from their regular employment. *Syn.* HR-10 plan. *See also* individual retirement account; nonqualified retirement plan; qualified retirement plan; top-heavy rule.

know your customer rule *See* Rule 405.

L

lagging indicator A measurable economic factor that changes after the economy has started to follow a particular pattern or trend. Lagging indicators are believed to confirm long-term trends. Examples include average duration of unemployment, corporate profits and labor cost per unit of output. *See also* coincident indicator; leading indicator.

leading indicator A measurable economic factor that changes before the economy starts to follow a particular pattern or trend. Leading indicators are believed to predict changes in the economy. Examples include new orders for durable goods, slowdowns in deliveries by vendors and numbers of building permits issued. *See also* coincident indicator; lagging indicator.

legal list The selection of securities a state agency (usually a state banking or insurance commission) determines to be appropriate investments for fiduciary accounts such as mutual savings banks, pension funds and insurance companies.

letter of intent (LOI) A signed agreement allowing an investor to buy mutual fund shares at a lower overall sales charge, based on the total dollar amount of the intended investment. A letter of intent is valid only if the investor completes the terms of the agreement within 13 months of signing the agreement. A letter of intent may be backdated 90 days. *Syn.* statement of intention.

leverage Using borrowed capital to increase investment return. *Syn.* trading on the equity.

liability A legal obligation to pay a debt owed. Current liabilities are debts payable within 12 months. Long-term liabilities are debts payable over a period of more than 12 months.

license *See* Series 6; Series 7; Series 26; Series 63; Series 65.

life annuity/straight life An annuity payout option that pays a monthly check over the annuitant's lifetime.

life annuity with period certain An annuity payout option that guarantees the annuitant a monthly check for a certain time period and thereafter until the annuitant's death. If the annuitant dies before the time period expires, the payments go to the annuitant's named beneficiary.

life contingency An annuity payout option that provides a death benefit during the accumulation stage. If the annuitant dies during this period, a full contribution is made to the account, which is paid to the annuitant's named beneficiary.

limited liability An investor's right to limit potential losses to no more than the amount invested. Equity shareholders, such as corporate stockholders and limited partners, have limited liability.

limited power of attorney A written authorization for someone other than an account's beneficial owner to make certain investment decisions regarding transactions in the account. *See also* discretion; full power of attorney.

limited principal A person who has passed an examination attesting to the knowledge and qualifications necessary to supervise a broker-dealer's business in a limited area of expertise. A limited principal is not qualified in the general fields of expertise reserved for a general securities principal; these include supervision of underwriting and market making and approval of advertising. *See also* Series 26.

limited representative A person who has passed an examination attesting to the knowledge and qualifications necessary to sell certain specified investment products. *See also* Series 6.

limited trading authorization An authorization, usually provided by a limited power of attorney, for someone other than the customer to have trading privileges in an account. These privileges are limited to purchases and sales; withdrawal of assets is not authorized. *See also* full trading authorization.

liquidity The ease with which an asset can be converted to cash in the marketplace. A large number of buyers and sellers and a high volume of trading activity provide high liquidity.

listed security A stock, a bond or another security that satisfies certain minimum requirements and is traded on a regional or national securities exchange such as the New York Stock Exchange. *See also* over the counter.

LOI *See* letter of intent.

long The term used to describe the owning of a security, contract or commodity. For example, a common stock owner is said to have a long position in the stock. *See also* short.

long-term gain The profit earned on the sale of a capital asset that has been owned for more than 12 months. *See also* capital gain; capital loss; long-term loss.

long-term loss The loss realized on the sale of a capital asset that has been owned for more than 12 months. *See also* capital gain; capital loss; long-term gain.

loss carryover A capital loss incurred in one tax year that is carried over to the next year or later years for use as a capital loss deduction. *See also* capital loss.

low The lowest price a security or commodity reaches during a specified time period. *See also* high.

M

M1 A category of the money supply that includes all coins, currency and demand deposits—that is, checking accounts and NOW accounts. *See also* M2; M3; money supply.

M2 A category of the money supply that includes M1 in addition to all time deposits, savings deposits and noninstitutional money-market funds. *See also* M1; M3; money supply.

M3 A category of the money supply that includes M2 in addition to all large time deposits, institutional money-market funds, short-term repurchase agreements and certain other large liquid assets. *See also* M1; M2; money supply.

Maloney Act An amendment enacted in 1938 to broaden Section 15 of the Securities Exchange Act of 1934. Named for its sponsor, the late Sen. Francis Maloney of Connecticut, the amendment provided for the creation of a self-regulatory organization for the specific purpose of supervising the over-the-counter securities market. *See also* National Association of Securities Dealers, Inc.

management company An investment company that trades various types of securities in a portfolio in accordance with specific objectives stated in the prospectus. *See also* closed-end management company; diversified management company; mutual fund; nondiversified management company.

marketability The ease with which a security can be bought or sold; having a readily available market for trading.

market letter A publication that comments on securities, investing, the economy or other related topics and is distributed to an organization's clients or to the public. *See also* sales literature.

market order An order to be executed immediately at the best available price. A market order is the only order that guarantees execution. *Syn.* unrestricted order.

market value The price at which investors buy or sell a share of common stock or a bond at a given time. Market value is determined by buyers' and sellers' interaction. *See also* current market value.

markup The difference between the lowest current offering price among dealers and the higher price a dealer charges a customer.

markup policy *See* NASD 5 percent markup policy.

material information Any fact that could affect an investor's decision to trade a security.

maturity date The date on which a bond's principal is repaid to the investor and interest payments cease. *See also* par; principal.

member (1) Of the New York Stock Exchange: one of the 1,366 individuals owning a seat on the Exchange. (2) Of the National Association of Securities Dealers: any broker or dealer admitted to membership in the Association.

member firm A broker-dealer in which at least one of the principal officers is a member of the New York Stock Exchange, another exchange, a self-regulatory organization or a clearing corporation.

membership The members of the New York Stock Exchange, another exchange, a self-regulatory organization or a clearing corporation.

minimum death benefit The amount payable under a variable life insurance policy upon the policy owner's death, regardless of the separate account's investment performance. The insurance company guarantees the minimum amount.

monetary policy The Federal Reserve Board's actions that determine the size and rate of the money supply's growth, which in turn affect interest rates. *See also* fiscal policy.

money market The securities market that deals in short-term debt. Money-market instruments are very liquid forms of debt that mature in less than one year. Treasury bills make up the bulk of money-market instruments.

money-market fund A mutual fund that invests in short-term debt instruments. The fund's objective is to earn interest while maintaining a stable net asset value of $1 per share. Generally sold with no load, the fund may also offer draft-writing privileges and low opening investments. *See also* mutual fund.

money supply The total stock of bills, coins, loans, credit and other liquid instruments in the economy. It is divided into four categories—L, M1, M2 and M3—according to the type of account in which the instrument is kept. *See also* M1; M2; M3.

MSRB *See* Municipal Securities Rulemaking Board.

multiplier effect The expansion of the money supply that results from a Federal Reserve System member bank's being able to lend more money than it takes in. A small increase in bank deposits generates a far larger increase in available credit.

municipal bond A debt security issued by a state, a municipality or another subdivision (such as a school, a park, a sanitation or another local taxing district) to finance its capital expenditures. Such expenditures might include the construction of highways, public works or school buildings. *Syn.* municipal security.

municipal bond fund A mutual fund that invests in municipal bonds and operates either as a unit investment trust or as an open-end fund. The fund's objective is to maximize federally tax-exempt income. *See also* mutual fund; unit investment trust.

Municipal Securities Rulemaking Board (MSRB) A self-regulatory organization that regulates the issuance and trading of municipal securities. The Board functions under the Securities and Exchange Commission's supervision; it has no enforcement powers. *See also* Securities Acts Amendments of 1975.

municipal security *See* municipal bond.

mutual fund An investment company that continuously offers new equity shares in an actively managed portfolio of securities. All shareholders participate in the fund's gains or losses. The shares are redeemable on any business day at the net asset value. Each mutual fund's portfolio is invested to match the objective stated in the prospectus. *Syn.* open-end investment company; open-end management company. *See also* asset allocation fund; balanced fund; contractual plan; net asset value.

mutual fund custodian A national bank, a stock exchange member firm, a trust company or another qualified institution that physically safeguards the securities a mutual fund holds. It does not manage the fund's investments; its function is solely clerical.

N

NASD *See* National Association of Securities Dealers, Inc.

NASD Bylaws The body of rules that describes how the NASD functions, defines its powers and determines the qualifications and registration requirements for brokers.

NASD District Business Conduct Committee (DBCC) A committee composed of up to 12 NASD members who each serves as administrator for one of the 13 local NASD districts. The DBCC has original jurisdiction for hearing and judging complaints.

NASD 5 percent markup policy A guideline for reasonable markups, markdowns and commissions for secondary over-the-counter transactions. According to the policy, all commissions on broker transactions and all markups or markdowns on principal transactions

should equal 5 percent or should be fair and reasonable for a particular transaction. *Syn.* markup policy.

NASD Manual A publication that outlines NASD policies for regulating the over-the-counter market. Included are the Rules of Fair Practice, the Uniform Practice Code, the Code of Procedure and the Code of Arbitration Procedure.

NASD Rules of Fair Practice (Conduct Rules) Regulations designed to ensure that NASD member firms and their representatives follow fair and ethical trade practices when dealing with the public. The rules complement and broaden the Securities Act of 1933, the Securities Exchange Act of 1934 and the Investment Company Act of 1940.

National Association of Securities Dealers, Inc. (NASD) The self-regulatory organization for the over-the-counter market. The NASD was organized under the provisions of the 1938 Maloney Act. *See also* Maloney Act.

NAV *See* net asset value.

NAV of fund The net total of a mutual fund's assets and liabilities; used to calculate the price of new fund shares.

NAV per share The value of a mutual fund share, calculated by dividing the fund's total net asset value by the number of shares outstanding.

negotiability A characteristic of a security that permits the owner to assign, give, transfer or sell it to another person without a third party's permission.

negotiable certificate of deposit (CD) An unsecured promissory note issued with a minimum face value of $100,000. It evidences a time deposit of funds with the issuing bank and is guaranteed by the bank.

negotiable order of withdrawal (NOW) account A bank account through which the customer can write drafts against money held on deposit; an interest-bearing checking account. *See also* M1.

net asset value (NAV) A mutual fund share's value, calculated once a day, based on the closing market price for each security in the fund's portfolio. It is computed by deducting the fund's liabilities from the portfolio's total assets and dividing this amount by the number of shares outstanding. *See also* mutual fund.

net change The difference between a security's closing price on the trading day reported and the previous day's closing price. In over-the-counter transactions, the term refers to the difference between the closing bids.

net investment income The source of an investment company's dividend payments. It is calculated by subtracting the company's operating expenses from the total dividends and interest the company receives from the securities in its portfolio.

net investment return The rate of return from a variable life insurance separate account. The cumulative return for all years is applied to the benefit base when calculating the death benefit.

net worth The amount by which assets exceed liabilities. *Syn.* owners' equity; shareholders' equity; stockholders' equity.

new account form The form that must be filled out for each new account opened with a brokerage firm. The form specifies, at a minimum, the account owner, trading authorization, payment method and types of securities appropriate for the customer.

new issue market The securities market for shares in privately owned businesses that are raising capital by selling common stock to the public for the first time. *Syn.* primary market. *See also* initial public offering; secondary market.

New Issues Act *See* Securities Act of 1933.

New York Stock Exchange (NYSE) The largest stock exchange in the United States. It is a corporation, operated by a board of directors, responsible for setting policy, supervising Exchange and member activities, listing securities, overseeing the transfer of members' seats on the Exchange and judging whether an applicant is qualified to be a specialist.

no-load fund A mutual fund whose shares are sold without a commission or sales charge. The investment company distributes the shares directly. *See also* mutual fund; net asset value; sales load.

nominal owner The person in whose name securities are registered if that person is other than the beneficial owner. This is a brokerage firm's role when customer securities are registered in street name.

nominal quote A quotation on an inactively traded security that does not represent an actual offer to buy or sell, but is given for informational purposes only. *See also* bona fide quote; firm quote.

nominal yield The interest rate stated on the face of a bond that represents the percentage of interest the issuer pays on the bond's face value. *Syn.* coupon rate; stated yield. *See also* bond yield.

noncumulative preferred stock An equity security that does not have to pay any dividends in arrears to the holder. *See also* convertible preferred stock; cumulative preferred stock; preferred stock.

nondiscrimination In a qualified retirement plan, a formula for calculating contributions and benefits that must be applied uniformly so as to ensure that all employees receive fair and equitable treatment. *See also* qualified retirement plan.

nondiversification A portfolio management strategy that seeks to concentrate investments in a particular industry or geographic area in hopes of achieving higher returns. *See also* diversification.

nondiversified management company A management company that does not meet the diversification requirements of the Investment Company Act of 1940. Such a company is not restricted in the choice of securities or by the concentration of interest it has in those securities. *See also* diversified management company; management company; mutual fund.

nonfixed unit investment trust An investment company that invests in a portfolio of securities and permits changes in the portfolio's makeup. *See also* fixed unit investment trust; unit investment trust.

nonqualified retirement plan A corporate retirement plan that does not meet the standards set by the Employee Retirement Income Security Act of 1974. Contributions to a nonqualified plan are not tax deductible. *See also* qualified retirement plan.

note A short-term debt security, usually maturing in five years or less. *See also* Treasury note.

notification *See* registration by filing.

NOW account *See* negotiable order of withdrawal account.

numbered account An account titled with something other than the customer's name. The title might be a number, symbol or special title. The customer must sign a form designating account ownership.

NYSE *See* New York Stock Exchange.

O

odd lot An amount of a security that is less than the normal unit of trading for that security. Generally, an odd lot is fewer than 100 shares of stock or five bonds. *See also* round lot.

offer (1) *See* ask. (2) Under the Uniform Securities Act, any attempt to solicit a purchase or sale in a security for value. *See also* bid; public offering price; quotation.

open-end investment company *See* mutual fund.

option A security that represents the right to buy or sell a specified amount of an underlying security—a stock, bond, futures contract, etc.—at a specified price within a specified time. The purchaser acquires a right, and the seller assumes an obligation.

order memorandum The form completed by a registered rep that contains customer instructions regarding an order's placement. The memorandum contains such information as the customer's name and account number, a description of the security, the type of transaction (buy, sell, sell short, etc.) and any special instructions (such as time or price limits). *Syn.* order ticket.

order ticket *See* order memorandum.

ordinary income Earnings other than capital gain.

OTC *See* over the counter.

OTC market The security exchange system in which broker-dealers negotiate directly with one another rather than through an auction on an exchange floor. The trading takes place over computer and telephone networks that link brokers and dealers around the world. Both listed and OTC securities, as well as municipal and U.S. government securities, trade in the OTC market.

outstanding stock Equity securities issued by a corporation and in the hands of the public; issued stock that the issuer has not reacquired. *See also* treasury stock.

over the counter (OTC) The term used to describe a security traded through the telephone-linked and computer-connected OTC market rather than through an exchange. *See also* OTC market.

P

par The dollar amount the issuer assigns to a security. For an equity security, par is usually a small dollar amount that bears no relationship to the security's market price. For a debt security, par is the amount repaid to the investor when the bond matures, usually $1,000. *Syn.* face value; principal; stated value. *See also* capital surplus; maturity date.

participation The provision of the Employee Retirement Income Security Act of 1974 requiring that all employees in a qualified retirement plan be covered within a reasonable time of their dates of hire.

partnership A form of business organization in which two or more individuals manage the business and are equally and personally liable for its debts.

pass-through certificate A security representing an interest in a pool of conventional, VA, Farmers Home Administration or other agency mortgages. The pool receives the principal and interest payments, which it passes through to each certificate holder. Payments may or may not be guaranteed. *See also* Federal National Mortgage Association; Government National Mortgage Association.

payment date The day on which a declared dividend is paid to all stockholders owning shares on the record date.

payment period As defined by the Federal Reserve Board's Regulation T, the period of time corresponding to the regular way settlement period established by the NASD.

payout stage *See* distribution stage.

payroll deduction plan A retirement plan whereby an employee authorizes a deduction from his check on a regular basis. The plan may be qualified, such as a 401(k) plan, or nonqualified.

pension plan A contract between an individual and an employer, a labor union, a government entity or another institution that provides for the distribution of pension benefits at retirement.

Pension Reform Act *See* Employee Retirement Income Security Act of 1974.

periodic payment plan A mutual fund sales contract in which the customer commits to buying shares in the fund on a periodic basis over a long time period in exchange for a lower minimum investment.

person As defined in securities law, an individual, a corporation, a partnership, an association, a fund, a joint stock company, an unincorporated organization, a trust, a government or a political subdivision of a government.

personal income (PI) An individual's total earnings derived from wages, passive business enterprises and investments. *See also* disposable income.

pipeline theory *See* conduit theory.

point A measure of a bond's price; $10 or 1 percent of the par value of $1,000. *See also* basis point.

POP *See* public offering price.

portfolio income Earnings from interest, dividends and all nonbusiness investments. *See also* earned income; passive income; unearned income.

portfolio manager The entity responsible for investing a mutual fund's assets, implementing its investment strategy and managing day-to-day portfolio trading. *Syn.* fund manager.

possession of securities *See* control of securities.

position The amount of a security either owned (a long position) or owed (a short position) by an individual or a dealer. Dealers take long positions in specific securities to maintain inventories and thereby facilitate trading.

positive yield curve *See* normal yield curve.

power of substitution *See* stock power.

preemptive right A stockholder's legal right to maintain her proportionate ownership by purchasing newly issued shares before the new stock is offered to the public. *See also* right.

preferred stock An equity security that represents ownership in a corporation. It is issued with a stated dividend, which must be paid before dividends are paid to common stock holders. It generally carries no voting rights. *See also* callable preferred stock; convertible preferred stock; cumulative preferred stock.

preferred stock fund A mutual fund whose investment objective is to provide stable income with minimal capital risk. It invests in income-producing instruments such as preferred stock. *See also* bond fund.

preliminary prospectus An abbreviated prospectus that is distributed while the SEC is reviewing an issuer's registration statement. It contains all of the essential facts about the forthcoming offering except the underwriting spread, final public offering price and date on which the shares will be delivered. *Syn.* red herring.

prime rate The interest rate that commercial banks charge their prime or most creditworthy customers, generally large corporations.

principal (1) A person who trades for his own account in the primary or secondary market. (2) *See* dealer. (3) *See* par.

principal transaction A transaction in which a broker-dealer either buys securities from customers and takes them into its own inventory or sells securities to customers from its inventory. *See also* agency transaction; agent; broker; dealer; principal.

profit-sharing plan An employee benefit plan established and maintained by an employer whereby the employees receive a share of the business's profits. The money may be paid directly to the employees or deferred until retirement. A combination of both approaches is also possible.

progressive tax A tax that takes a larger percentage of the income of high-income earners than that of low-income earners. An example is the graduated income tax. *See also* regressive tax.

property dividend A distribution made by a corporation to its stockholders of securities it owns in other corporations or of its products. *See also* dividend.

prospectus *See* final prospectus.

Prospectus Act *See* Securities Act of 1933.

proxy A limited power of attorney from a stockholder authorizing another person to vote on stockholder issues according to the first stockholder's instructions. To vote on corporate matters, a stockholder must either attend the annual meeting or vote by proxy.

prudent man rule A legal maxim that restricts discretion in a fiduciary account to only those investments that a reasonable and prudent person might make.

public offering The sale of an issue of common stock, either by a corporation going public or by an offering of additional shares. *See also* initial public offering.

public offering price (POP) (1) The price of new shares that is established in the issuing corporation's prospectus. (2) The price to investors for mutual fund shares, equal to the net asset value plus the sales charge. *See also* ask; bid; mutual fund; net asset value.

put (1) An option contract giving the owner the right to sell a certain amount of an underlying security at a specified price within a specified time. (2) The act of exercising a put option. *See also* call.

put buyer An investor who pays a premium for an option contract and receives, for a specified time, the right to sell the underlying security at a specified price. *See also* call buyer; call writer; put writer.

put writer An investor who receives a premium and takes on, for a specified time, the obligation to buy the underlying security at a specified price at the put

buyer's discretion. *See also* call buyer; call writer; put buyer.

Q

qualification *See* registration by qualification.

qualified retirement plan A corporate retirement plan that meets the standards set by the Employee Retirement Income Security Act of 1974. Contributions to a qualified plan are tax deductible. *Syn.* approved plan. *See also* individual retirement account; Keogh plan; nonqualified retirement plan.

quotation The price or bid a market maker or broker-dealer offers for a particular security. *Syn.* quote. *See also* ask; bid; bond quote; stock quote.

quote *See* quotation.

quote machine A computer that provides representatives and market makers with the information that appears on the Consolidated Tape. The information on the screen is condensed into symbols and numbers.

R

rating An evaluation of a corporate or municipal bond's relative safety, according to the issuer's ability to repay principal and make interest payments. Bonds are rated by various organizations, such as Standard & Poor's and Moody's. Ratings range from AAA or Aaa (the highest) to C or D, which represents a company in default.

rating service A company, such as Moody's or Standard & Poor's, that rates various debt and preferred stock issues for safety of payment of principal, interest or dividends. The issuing company or municipality pays a fee for the rating. *See also* bond rating; rating.

real estate investment trust (REIT) A corporation or trust that uses the pooled capital of many investors to invest in direct ownership of either income property or mortgage loans. These investments offer tax benefits in addition to interest and capital gains distributions.

realized gain The amount a taxpayer earns when he sells an asset. *See also* unrealized gain.

recession A general economic decline lasting from 6 to 18 months.

record date The date a corporation's board of directors establishes that determines which of its stockholders are entitled to receive dividends or rights distributions.

recovery *See* expansion.

redeemable security A security that the issuer redeems upon the holder's request. Examples include shares in an open-end investment company and Treasury notes.

redemption The return of an investor's principal in a security, such as a bond, preferred stock or mutual fund shares. By law, redemption of mutual fund shares must occur within seven days of receiving the investor's request for redemption.

red herring *See* preliminary prospectus.

regional exchange A stock exchange that serves the financial community in a particular region of the country. These exchanges tend to focus on securities issued within their regions, but also offer trading in NYSE- and AMEX-listed securities.

regional fund *See* sector fund.

registered The term describing a security that prints the owner's name on the certificate. The owner's name is stored in records kept by the issuer or a transfer agent.

registered as to principal only The term describing a bond that prints the owner's name on the certificate, but that has unregistered coupons payable to the bearer. *Syn.* partially registered. *See also* coupon bond; fully registered bond; registered.

registered principal An associated person of a member firm who manages or supervises the firm's investment banking or securities business. This includes any individual who trains associated persons and who solicits business.
Unless the member firm is a sole proprietorship, it must employ at least two registered principals, one of whom must be registered as a general securities principal and one of whom must be registered as a financial and operations principal. If the firm does options business with

the public, it must employ at least one registered options principal.

registered representative (RR) An associated person engaged in the investment banking or securities business. According to the NASD, this includes any individual who supervises, solicits or conducts business in securities or who trains people to supervise, solicit or conduct business in securities.
Anyone employed by a brokerage firm who is not a principal and who is not engaged in clerical or brokerage administration is subject to registration and exam licensing as a registered representative. *Syn.* account executive; stockbroker. *See also* associated person of a member.

registrar The independent organization or part of a corporation responsible for accounting for all of the issuer's outstanding stock and certifying that its bonds constitute legal debt.

registration by coordination A process that allows a security to be sold in a state. It is available to an issuer that files for the security's registration under the Securities Act of 1933 and files duplicates of the registration documents with the state administrator. The state registration becomes effective at the same time the federal registration statement becomes effective.

registration by filing A process that allows a security to be sold in a state. Previously referred to as *registration by notification*, it is available to an issuer who files for the security's registration under the Securities Act of 1933, meets minimum net worth and certain other requirements, and notifies the state of this eligibility by filing certain documents with the state administrator. The state registration becomes effective at the same time the federal registration statement becomes effective.

registration by notification *See* registration by filing.

registration by qualification A process that allows a security to be sold in a state. It is available to an issuer who files for the security's registration with the state administrator, meets minimum net worth, disclosure and other requirements and files appropriate registration fees. The state registration becomes effective when the administrator so orders.

registration statement The legal document that discloses all pertinent information concerning an offering of a security and its issuer. It is submitted to the SEC in accordance with the requirements of the Securities Act of 1933, and it forms the basis of the final prospectus distributed to investors.

regressive tax A tax that takes a larger percentage of the income of low-income earners than that of high-income earners. Examples include gasoline tax and cigarette tax. *See also* progressive tax.

regular way A settlement contract that calls for delivery and payment within a standard payment period from the date of the trade. The NASD's Uniform Practice Code sets the standard payment period. The type of security being traded determines the amount of time allowed for regular way settlement. *See also* cash transaction; settlement date.

regulated investment company An investment company to which Subchapter M of the Internal Revenue Code grants special status that allows the flow-through of tax consequences on a distribution to shareholders. If 90 percent of its income is passed through to the shareholders, the company is not subject to tax on this income.

REIT *See* real estate investment trust.

retirement account A customer account established to provide retirement funds.

return on investment (ROI) The profit or loss resulting from a security transaction, often expressed as an annual percentage rate.

right A security representing a stockholder's entitlement to the first opportunity to purchase new shares issued by the corporation at a predetermined price (normally less than the current market price) in proportion to the number of shares already owned. Rights are issued for a short time only, after which they expire. *Syn.* subscription right; subscription right certificate. *See also* preemptive right; rights offering.

right of accumulation A benefit offered by a mutual fund that allows the investor to qualify for reduced sales loads on additional purchases according to the fund account's total dollar value.

right of withdrawal An Investment Company Act of 1940 provision that allows an investor in a mutual fund

contractual plan to terminate the plan within 45 days from the mailing date of the written notice detailing the sales charges that will apply over the plan's life. The investor is then entitled to a refund of all sales charges. *See also* free-look letter.

rights agent An issuing corporation's agent who is responsible for maintaining current records of the names of rights certificate owners.

rights offering An issue of new shares of stock accompanied by the opportunity for each stockholder to maintain a proportionate ownership by purchasing additional shares in the corporation before the shares are offered to the public. *See also* right.

right to refund A benefit of a mutual fund front-end load plan that entitles an investor who cancels the plan within 18 months to receive the investment's current value and a refund of sales charges exceeding 15 percent.

ROI *See* return on investment.

rollover The transfer of funds from one qualified retirement plan to another qualified retirement plan. If this is not done within a specified time period, the funds are taxed as ordinary income.

round lot A security's normal unit of trading, which is generally 100 shares of stock or five bonds. *See also* odd lot.

RR *See* registered representative.

Rule 405 NYSE rule requiring that each member organization exercise due diligence to learn the essential facts about every customer. *Syn.* know your customer rule.

S

sale *See* sell.

sales charge *See* commission.

sales literature Any written material a firm distributes to customers or the public in a controlled manner. Examples include circulars, research reports, form letters, market letters, performance reports and text used for seminars. *See also* advertisement; form letter; market letter.

sales load The amount added to a mutual fund share's net asset value to arrive at the offering price. *See also* mutual fund; net asset value; no-load fund.

savings bond A government debt security that is not negotiable or transferable and that may not be used as collateral. *See also* Series EE bond; Series HH bond.

scheduled premium policy A variable life insurance policy under which the insurer fixes both the amount and the timing of the premium payments.

SEC *See* Securities and Exchange Commission.

secondary market The market in which securities are bought and sold subsequent to their being sold to the public for the first time. *See also* new issue market.

sector fund A mutual fund whose investment objective is to capitalize on the return potential provided by investing primarily in a particular industry or sector of the economy. *Syn.* industry fund; specialized fund.

Securities Act of 1933 Federal legislation requiring the full and fair disclosure of all material information about the issuance of new securities. *Syn.* act of 1933; Full Disclosure Act; New Issues Act; Prospectus Act; Trust in Securities Act; Truth in Securities Act.

Securities Acts Amendments of 1975 Federal legislation that established the Municipal Securities Rulemaking Board. *See also* Municipal Securities Rulemaking Board.

Securities and Exchange Commission (SEC) Commission created by Congress to regulate the securities markets and protect investors. It is composed of five commissioners appointed by the President of the United States and approved by the Senate. The SEC enforces, among other acts, the Securities Act of 1933, the Securities Exchange Act of 1934, the Trust Indenture Act of 1939, the Investment Company Act of 1940 and the Investment Advisers Act of 1940.

Securities Exchange Act of 1934 Federal legislation that established the Securities and Exchange Commission. The act aims to protect investors by regulating the exchanges, the over-the-counter market, the extension of credit by the Federal Reserve Board, broker-dealers, insider transactions, trading activities, client accounts and net capital. *Syn.* act of 1934; Exchange Act.

Securities Investor Protection Corporation (SIPC) A nonprofit membership corporation created by an act of Congress to protect clients of brokerage firms that are forced into bankruptcy. Membership is composed of all brokers and dealers registered under the Securities Exchange Act of 1934, all members of national securities exchanges and most NASD members. SIPC provides brokerage firm customers up to $500,000 coverage for cash and securities held by the firms (although cash coverage is limited to $100,000).

security Other than an insurance policy or a fixed annuity, any piece of securitized paper that can be traded for value. Under the act of 1934, this includes any note, stock, bond, investment contract, debenture, certificate of interest in a profit-sharing or partnership agreement, certificate of deposit, collateral trust certificate, preorganization certificate, option on a security, or other instrument of investment commonly known as a *security*.

self-regulatory organization (SRO) One of eight organizations accountable to the SEC for the enforcement of federal securities laws and the supervision of securities practices within an assigned field of jurisdiction. For example, the National Association of Securities Dealers regulates the over-the-counter market; the Municipal Securities Rulemaking Board supervises state and municipal securities; and certain exchanges, such as the New York Stock Exchange and the Chicago Board Options Exchange, act as self-regulatory bodies to promote ethical conduct and standard trading practices.

sell To convey ownership of a security or another asset for money or value. This includes giving or delivering a security with or as a bonus for a purchase of securities, a gift of assessable stock, and selling or offering a warrant or right to purchase or subscribe to another security. Not included in the definition is a bona fide pledge or loan or a stock dividend if nothing of value is given by the stockholders for the dividend. *Syn.* sale.

selling away An associated person engaging in private securities transactions without the employing broker-dealer's knowledge and consent. This violates the NASD Rules of Fair Practice.

selling concession *See* concession.

selling dividends (1) Inducing customers to buy mutual fund shares by implying that an upcoming distribution will benefit them. This practice is illegal. (2) Combining dividend and gains distributions when calculating current yield.

SEP *See* simplified employee pension plan.

separate account The account that holds funds paid by variable annuity contract holders. The funds are kept separate from the insurer's general account and are invested in a portfolio of securities that match the contract holders' objectives. *See also* accumulation unit; annuity; general account.

Separate Trading of Registered Interest and Principal of Securities (STRIPS) A zero-coupon bond issued and backed by the Treasury Department. *See also* zero-coupon bond.

Series 6 The investment company/variable contract products limited representative license, which entitles the holder to sell mutual funds and variable annuities and is used by many firms that sell primarily insurance-related products. The Series 6 can serve as the prerequisite for the Series 26 license.

Series 7 The general securities registered representative license, which entitles the holder to sell all types of securities products, with the exception of commodities futures (which requires a Series 3 license). The Series 7 is the most comprehensive of the NASD representative licenses and serves as a prerequisite for most of the NASD's principals examinations.

Series 26 The investment company/variable contract products limited principal license, which entitles the holder to supervise the sale of investment company and variable annuity products. A Series 6 or a Series 7 qualification is a prerequisite for this license.

Series 63 The uniform securities agent state law exam, which entitles the successful candidate to sell securities and give investment advice in those states that require Series 63 registration. *See also* blue-sky laws; Uniform Securities Act.

Series 65 The uniform investment adviser law exam, which entitles the successful candidate to sell securities and give investment advice in those states that require Series 65 registration. *See also* blue-sky laws; Uniform Securities Act.

Series EE bond A nonmarketable, interest-bearing U.S. government savings bond issued at a discount from par. Interest on Series EE bonds is exempt from state and local taxes. *See also* savings bond; Series HH bond.

Series HH bond A nonmarketable, interest-bearing U.S. government savings bond issued at par and purchased only by trading in Series EE bonds at maturity. Interest on Series HH bonds is exempt from state and local taxes. *See also* savings bond; Series EE bond.

settlement The completion of a trade through the delivery of a security or commodity and the payment of cash or other consideration.

settlement date The date on which ownership changes between buyer and seller. The NASD's Uniform Practice Code standardizes settlement provisions. *See also* cash transaction; regular way.

75-5-10 test The standard for judging whether an investment company qualifies as diversified under the Investment Company Act of 1940. Under this act, a diversified investment company must invest at least 75 percent of its total assets in cash, receivables or invested securities and no more than 5 percent of its total assets in any one company's voting securities. In addition, no single investment may represent ownership of more than 10 percent of any one company's outstanding voting securities. *See also* diversified management company.

share identification An accounting method that identifies the specific shares selected for liquidation in the event that an investor wishes to liquidate shares. The difference between the buying and selling prices determines the investor's tax liability.

share of beneficial interest *See* unit of beneficial interest.

short The term used to describe the selling of a security, contract or commodity that the seller does not own. For example, an investor who borrows shares of stock from a broker-dealer and sells them on the open market is said to have a *short position* in the stock. *See also* long.

simplified employee pension plan (SEP) A non-qualified retirement plan designed for employers with 25 or fewer employees. Contributions made to each employee's individual retirement account grow tax deferred until retirement. *See also* individual retirement account.

single account An account in which only one individual has control over the investments and may transact business.

SIPC *See* Securities Investor Protection Corporation.

specialized fund *See* sector fund.

special situation fund A mutual fund whose objective is to capitalize on the profit potential of corporations in nonrecurring circumstances, such as those undergoing reorganizations or being considered as takeover candidates.

spousal account A separate individual retirement account established for a nonworking spouse. Contributions to the account made by the working spouse grow tax deferred until withdrawal. *See also* individual retirement account.

spread In a quotation, the difference between a security's bid and ask prices.

spread load A system of sales charges for a mutual fund contractual plan. It permits a decreasing scale of sales charges, with a maximum charge of 20 percent in any one year and of 9 percent over the life of the plan. Rights of withdrawal with no penalty exist for 45 days. *See also* contractual plan; front-end load.

SRO *See* self-regulatory organization.

stated yield *See* nominal yield.

statement of intention *See* letter of intent.

statutory disqualification Prohibiting a person from associating with a self-regulatory organization because the person has been expelled, barred or suspended from association with a member of an SRO; has had his registration suspended, denied or revoked by the SEC; has been the cause of someone else's suspension, barment or revocation; has been convicted of certain crimes; or has falsified an application or a report that he must file with or on behalf of a membership organization.

statutory voting A voting procedure that permits stockholders to cast one vote per share owned for each position. The procedure tends to benefit majority stockholders. *See also* cumulative voting.

stockbroker *See* registered representative.

stock certificate Written evidence of ownership in a corporation.

stock dividend *See* dividend.

stock power A standard form that duplicates the back of a stock certificate and is used for transferring the stock to the new owner's name. A separate stock power is used if a security's registered owner does not have the certificate available for signature endorsement. *Syn.* irrevocable stock power; power of substitution. *See also* assignment.

stock quote A list of representative prices bid and asked for a stock during a particular trading day. Stocks are quoted in points, where one point equals $1 and 1/8 of a point equals 12.5 cents. Stock quotes are listed in the financial press and most daily newspapers. *See also* bond quote.

stock split An increase in the number of a corporation's outstanding shares, which decreases its stock's par value. The market value of the total number of shares remains the same. The proportional reductions in orders held on the books for a split stock are calculated by dividing the stock's market price by the fraction that represents the split.

subscription right *See* right.

suitability A determination made by a registered representative as to whether a particular security matches a customer's objectives and financial capability. The rep must have enough information about the customer to make this judgment. *See also* Rule 405.

supervision A system implemented by a broker-dealer to ensure that its employees and associated persons comply with the applicable rules and regulations of the SEC, the exchanges and the SROs.

T

taxability The risk of the erosion of investment income through taxation.

taxable gain The portion of a sale or distribution of mutual fund shares subject to taxation.

tax-deferred annuity *See* tax-sheltered annuity.

tax-equivalent yield The rate of return a taxable bond must earn before taxes in order to equal the tax-exempt earnings on a municipal bond. This number varies with the investor's tax bracket.

tax-exempt bond fund A mutual fund whose investment objective is to provide maximum tax-free income. It invests primarily in municipal bonds and short-term debt. *Syn.* tax-free bond fund.

tax-free bond fund *See* tax-exempt bond fund.

tax liability The amount of tax payable on earnings, usually calculated by subtracting standard and itemized deductions and personal exemptions from adjusted gross income, then multiplying by the tax rate. *See also* adjusted gross income.

tax-sheltered annuity (TSA) An insurance contract that entitles the holder to exclude all contributions from gross income in the year they are made. Tax payable on the earnings is deferred until the holder withdraws funds at retirement. TSAs are available to employees of public schools, church organizations and other tax-exempt organizations. *Syn.* tax-deferred annuity.

T bill *See* Treasury bill.

T bond *See* Treasury bond.

TDA *See* tax-sheltered annuity.

tenants in common *See* joint tenants in common.

third-party account (1) A customer account for which the owner has given power of attorney to a third party. (2) A customer account opened by an adult naming a minor as beneficial owner. (3) A customer account opened for another adult. This type of account is prohibited.

time deposit A sum of money left with a bank (or borrowed from a bank and left on deposit) that the depositing customer has agreed not to withdraw for a specified time period or without a specified amount of notice. *See also* demand deposit.

tombstone A printed advertisement that solicits indications of interest in a securities offering. The text is limited to basic information about the offering, such as the name of the issuer, type of security, names of the underwriters and where a prospectus is available.

top-heavy rule The provision of a Keogh plan that sets the maximum salary on which employer contributions may be based. The rule prevents great disparities in the dollar amounts contributed for employees at different salary levels. *See also* Keogh plan.

trade confirmation A printed document that contains details of a transaction, including the settlement date and amount of money due from or owed to a customer. It must be sent to the customer on or before the settlement date.

trade date The date on which a securities transaction is executed.

trading authorization *See* full trading authorization; limited trading authorization.

transfer agent A person or corporation responsible for recording the names and holdings of registered security owners, seeing that certificates are signed by the appropriate corporate officers, affixing the corporate seal and delivering securities to the new owners.

transfer and hold in safekeeping A securities buy order settlement and delivery procedure whereby the securities bought are transferred to the customer's name, but are held by the broker-dealer. *See also* hold in street name; transfer and ship.

transfer and ship A securities buy order settlement and delivery procedure whereby the securities bought are transferred to the customer's name and sent to the customer. *See also* hold in street name; transfer and hold in safekeeping.

Treasury bill A marketable U.S. government debt security with a maturity of less than one year. Treasury bills are issued through a competitive bidding process

380

at a discount from par; they have no fixed interest rate. *Syn.* T bill.

Treasury bond A marketable, fixed-interest U.S. government debt security with a maturity of more than 10 years. *Syn.* T bond.

Treasury note A marketable, fixed-interest U.S. government debt security with a maturity of between 1 and 10 years. *Syn.* T note.

Treasury receipt The generic term for a zero-coupon bond issued by a brokerage firm and collateralized by the Treasury securities a custodian holds in escrow for the investor.

treasury stock Equity securities that the issuing corporation has issued and repurchased from the public at the current market price. *See also* issued stock; outstanding stock.

trustee A person legally appointed to act on a beneficiary's behalf.

Trust in Securities Act *See* Securities Act of 1933.

Truth in Securities Act *See* Securities Act of 1933.

TSA *See* tax-sheltered annuity.

12b-1 asset-based fees An Investment Company Act of 1940 provision that allows a mutual fund to collect a fee for the promotion or sale of or another activity connected with the distribution of its shares. The fee must be reasonable (typically ½ percent to 1 percent of net assets managed), up to a maximum of 8.5 percent of the offering price per share.

U

UGMA *See* Uniform Gifts to Minors Act.

UIT *See* unit investment trust.

underwriting The procedure by which investment bankers channel investment capital from investors to corporations and municipalities that are issuing securities.

unearned income Income derived from investments and other sources not related to employment services. Examples of unearned income include interest from a savings account, bond interest and dividends from stock. *See also* earned income; passive income; portfolio income.

Uniform Gifts to Minors Act (UGMA) Legislation that permits a gift of money or securities to be given to a minor and held in a custodial account that an adult manages for the minor's benefit. Income and capital gains transferred to a minor's name are taxed at a lower rate. *See also* Uniform Transfers to Minors Act.

Uniform Investment Adviser Law Exam *See* Series 65.

Uniform Practice Code (UPC) The NASD policy that establishes guidelines for a brokerage firm's dealings with other brokerage firms.

Uniform Securities Act (USA) Model legislation for securities industry regulation at the state level. Each state may adopt the legislation in its entirety or it may adapt it (within limits) to suit its needs. *See also* blue-sky laws; Series 63; Series 65.

Uniform Securities Agent State Law Exam (USASLE) *See* Series 63.

Uniform Transfers to Minors Act (UTMA) Legislation adopted in some states that permits a gift of money or securities to be given to a minor and held in a custodial account that an adult manages for the minor's benefit until the minor reaches a certain age (not necessarily the age of majority). *See also* Uniform Gifts to Minors Act.

unit investment trust (UIT) An investment company that sells redeemable shares in a professionally selected portfolio of securities. It is organized under a trust indenture, not a corporate charter. *See also* fixed unit investment trust; nonfixed unit investment trust; unit of beneficial interest.

unit of beneficial interest A redeemable share in a unit investment trust, representing ownership of an undivided interest in the underlying portfolio. *Syn.* share of beneficial interest. *See also* unit investment trust.

unit refund annuity An insurance contract in which the insurance company makes monthly payments to the annuitant over the annuitant's lifetime. If the annuitant dies before receiving an amount equal to the account's value, the money remaining in the account goes to the annuitant's named beneficiary.

unrealized gain The amount by which a security appreciates in value before it is sold. Until it is sold, the investor does not actually possess the sale proceeds. *See also* realized gain.

USA *See* Uniform Securities Act.

USASLE *See* Series 63.

U.S. government and agency bond fund A mutual fund whose investment objective is to provide current income while preserving safety of capital through investing in securities backed by the U.S. Treasury or issued by a government agency.

UTMA *See* Uniform Transfers to Minors Act.

V

variable annuity An insurance contract in which at the end of the accumulation stage, the insurance company guarantees a minimum total payment to the annuitant. The performance of a separate account, generally invested in equity securities, determines the amount of this total payment. *See also* accumulation stage; annuity; fixed annuity; separate account.

variable death benefit The amount paid to a decedent's beneficiary that depends on the investment performance of an insurance company's separate account. The amount is added to any guaranteed minimum death benefit.

variable life insurance policy An insurance contract that provides financial compensation to the insured's named beneficiary if the insured dies. The insurance company guarantees payment of a minimum amount plus an additional sum according to the performance of a separate account, usually invested in equities or other relatively high-yielding securities.

vesting (1) An ERISA guideline stipulating that an employee must be entitled to her entire retirement benefits within a certain period of time even if she no longer works for the employer. (2) The amount of time that an employee must work before retirement or before benefit plan contributions made by the employer become the employee's property without penalty. The IRS and the Employee Retirement Income Security Act of 1974 set minimum requirements for vesting in a qualified plan.

voluntary accumulation plan A mutual fund account into which the investor commits to depositing amounts on a regular basis in addition to the initial sum invested.

voluntary contribution An additional contribution an employee makes to a Keogh Plan to supplement plan benefits. The contribution amount is limited to 10 percent of the employee's compensation. Although the contribution is not tax deductible, the resultant earnings are not subject to tax until retirement.

voting right A stockholder's right to vote for members of the board of directors and on matters of corporate policy—particularly the issuance of senior securities, stock splits and substantial changes in the corporation's business. A variation of this right is extended to variable annuity contract holders and mutual fund shareholders, who may vote on material policy issues.

W

warrant A security that gives the holder the right to purchase securities from the warrant issuer at a stipulated subscription price. Warrants are usually long-term instruments, with expiration dates years in the future.

wash sale Selling a security at a loss for tax purposes and, within 30 days before or after, purchasing the same or a substantially identical security. The IRS disallows the claimed loss. *See also* bond swap.

withdrawal plan A benefit offered by a mutual fund whereby a customer receives the proceeds of periodic systematic liquidation of shares in the account. The amounts received may be based on a fixed dollar amount, a fixed number of shares, a fixed percentage or a fixed period of time.

writer The seller of an option contract. An option writer takes on the obligation to buy or sell the underlying security if and when the option buyer exercises the option. *Syn.* seller.

Y

yield The rate of return on an investment, usually expressed as an annual percentage rate. *See also* current yield; dividend yield; nominal yield.

yield curve A graphic representation of the actual or projected yields of fixed-income securities in relation to their maturities. *See also* flat yield curve; inverted yield curve; normal yield curve.

Z

zero-coupon bond A corporate or municipal debt security traded at a deep discount from face value. The bond pays no interest; rather, it may be redeemed at maturity for its full face value. It may be issued at a discount, or it may be stripped of its coupons and repackaged.

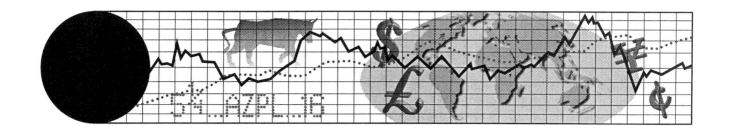

Index

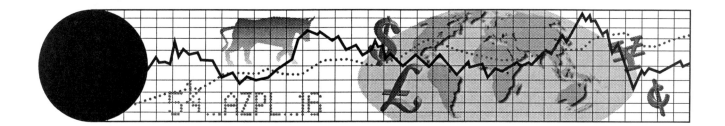

Equity Securities Hotsheet

Stock Classifications:
- Authorized—number of shares corporation is permitted to issue
- Issued—has been sold to the public
- Treasury—repurchased by corporation; no voting rights, receives no dividends
- Outstanding—Number of shares held by the public

- Treasury = Issued – Outstanding
- Outstanding = Issued – Treasury

Stock Valuations:
- Par—assigned accounting value
- Book—liquidation or net worth value
- Market—value determined by supply and demand

Preemptive Rights: Allow shareholders to maintain proportionate interest

Voting Rights: Directors, issuance of convertible bonds or preferred stock; *not* on dividend payment or amount

Stock Splits:
- Normal – More shares, less value per share, same total value before and after
- Reverse – Less shares, more value per share, same total value before and after

Preferred Stock:
- Par value = $100
- Stated (fixed) dividend rate
- Priority over common stock in liquidation and dividend payment
- Typically no voting rights

Current Yield: *Annual* dividends divided by current market price

Stock Points:

1 point = $1	⅛ = .125	¼ = .25	⅜ = .375
⅝ = .625	¾ = .75	⅞ = .875	½ = .5

Rights: 30–45 day duration

Strike price below market

Trade as a separate security

Available to existing shareholders only

One right per share outstanding

Warrants: Long term

Strike price above market

Trade as separate security

Offered as "sweeteners"

ADRs:
- No preemptive rights
- Dividends in dollars
- Investors have voting rights

Investment Grade: Baa or BBB and above, based on default risk, ability to pay interest and principal when due

Call Features:
- Called by issuer when interest rates are falling; no interest after call
- Issuer cannot call during call protection period

Refunding: Refinancing at a lower rate, done when interest rates are declining

Bond Yields: Current yield = annual interest ÷ current market price

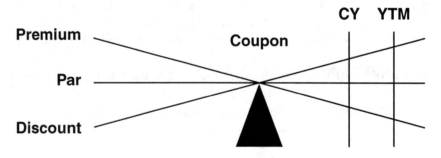

Corporate Bonds:
- Called funded debt
- Secured: Mortgage, collateral trust (backed by securities), equipment trust certificates
- Unsecured: backed by full faith and credit, debentures and subordinated debentures

Convertibles: Par ÷ conversion price = conversion ratio; new price/conversion ratio = parity price of common; conversion ratio × common stock price = parity price of bonds

Governments: Bills quoted at a discount, notes and bonds in 32nds; notes/bonds are callable, bills are not; Treasury STRIPS are backed in full by the U.S. government

Agencies: Ginnie Maes are backed in full by U.S. government

CMOs: Corporate instrument with tranches; taxable monthly interest

Money Markets:
- Commercial paper: most heavily traded; corporate issue; issued at a discount, 270-day max maturity
- Negotiable CD: minimum face of $100,000, issued by banks
- Bankers' Acceptances: Time draft, letter of credit for foreign trade; 270-day max maturity

Interest Rates: Fed funds rate most volatile, established by market; Discount rate set by FRB

Municipals:
- GOs backed by taxes, Revenues backed by user fees, IDRs may be taxable
- Interest is not taxable at the federal level

Underwriting:
- Firm commitment – underwriters act as principal, financial risk
- Best efforts – underwriters act as agent, no financial risk
- Corporate underwriters must be NASD members

Trading:
- Listed securities are exchange traded in auction market
- Unlisted securities trade OTC; price is negotiated
- Third market is listed securities trading OTC

Broker-Dealers:
- Agent = Broker = Commissions
- Dealer = Principals = Markups

Settlement Dates:
- Regular Way: Corps and Munis, T + 3; Governments, T + 1
- Cash settlement: same day
- Reg T settlement: T + 5

Frozen Accounts: If no extension granted from SRO, 90-day freeze, amounts of less than $1,000 can be ignored

Ex-dates:
- Two business days before record date (regular way)
- Business day after record date (cash settlement and mutual funds)
- *DERP*—order of dates is declaration, ex, record, payable
- *D, R and P* determined by Board of Directors, NASD determines ex-date
- Buy before the ex-date to get the dividend

Money Supply:
- Fiscal policy – set by government through taxes and spending
- Monetary policy – set by FRB through discount rate, FOMC (most used tool) and reserve requirement (most drastic)

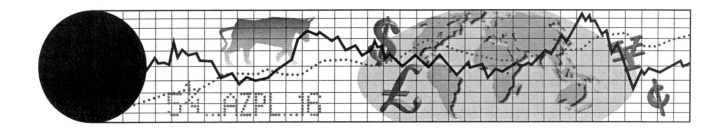

Investment Company Products Hotsheet

Inv. Co. Act of 1940:
- Defines and regulates investment companies
- Three types: face amount certificate, unit investment trust, management company

Open-End Company:
- Mutual fund; continuous primary offering, redemption in seven calendar days, price by formula in prospectus, fractional shares

Closed-end Company:
- Trades in secondary market, issues debt and equity, fixed number of shares, sold with prospectus in IPO only

Diversified Status:
- *75 percent* invested in other companies; max of *5 percent* in any one company; can own no more than *10 percent* of a target company's voting stock
- Status applies to open- and closed-end companies

Registration Requirements:
- Minimum $100,000 capital, 100 investors, clearly defined investment objective
- Asset to debt ratio not less than 3 to 1 (300 percent)

Prohibited Investing:
- No purchases on margin, no short sales, no naked options sold

Shareholder Votes:
- Change investment objective, change sales load policy, change fund classification

Shareholder Reports:
- Annual audited report, semiannual unaudited report (two per year)

Sector Funds:
- Minimum of 25 percent of assets in area of specialty; more aggressive

Money-market Funds:
- No load, fixed NAV, check-writing privileges, daily interest

Performance History:
- 1, 5, 10 years (or fund's life if less than 10 years)

Sales Charge %:	• (POP − NAV) ÷ POP (NASD maximum of 8.5 percent of POP)
POP Calculation:	• NAV ÷ (100% − SC%)
12b-1 Charges:	• Distribution fee approved annually and charged quarterly; cannot be described as no-load fund if exceeds .25 percent.
8½% Sales Charge:	• Only if fund offers reinvestment at NAV, rights of accumulation, breakpoints
Letter of Intent:	• Must be in writing, maximum 13 months, can be backdated 90 days
Conduit Theory:	• IRC subchapter M. Fund is "regulated investment company" if it distributes a minimum of 90 percent of net investment income; fund taxed only on retained earnings.
Ex-dividend Date:	• Determined by BOD, typically business day after record date
Calculating Yield:	• Annual dividends/POP; capital gains distributions are not included.
Dollar Cost Averaging:	• Produces an average cost per share that is lower than average price per share; no guarantees allowed
Contractual Plans:	• Refunds:

Front End Load Act	*Spread Load Act*
• Before 45 days: NAV + 100% SC	• Before 45 days: NAV + 100% SC
• After 45 days, before 18 months: NAV + SC exceeding 15% of investment	• After 45 days: NAV only
• After 18 months: NAV only	

- Objectives:
- *Growth* = stock funds
- *Income* = bond funds
- *Safety of principal* = government bond funds
- *Immediate liquidity* = money market funds
- *Aggressive growth* = technology stock funds or stock funds invested in new companies, small caps
- *Conservative growth* = blue chip stock funds
- *Highest possible income with little concern for risk* = corporate bond fund
- *High tax bracket seeking income* = municipal bond fund
- *Income-producing stock* = blue chip stock fund, preferred stock fund, utility stock fund
- *Mirror performance of the stock market overall* = index fund

New Account Forms:	• Required for all accounts • Birth date not required • Customer signature not required for cash accounts; needed for margin accounts • Signed by rep and approving principal
Account Approval:	• By principal, either prior to or promptly after the first transaction
Trading Authorization:	• Limited—third party can trade only • Full—third party can trade and withdraw cash and securities
Accounts for other Broker-Dealer Employees:	• NASD—prior written notification, duplicate confirms upon request only
Joint Accounts:	• All signatures required to open • Any party can trade • Distributions payable to all • Each owns undivided interest

JTWROS	*JTIC*
• equal ownership interest	• unequal interests OK
• Passes to survivor(s) at death; no probate	• Passes by will to heirs, probate

Discretionary:	• Authority from customer must be in writing • Account must be approved before the first trade • Principal must review discretionary accounts frequently for churning • Time and price not discretionary
UGMA:	• Cash accounts only • Minor is beneficial owner; minor's Social Security number on account • One minor, one custodian • No short sales, no options, no margins

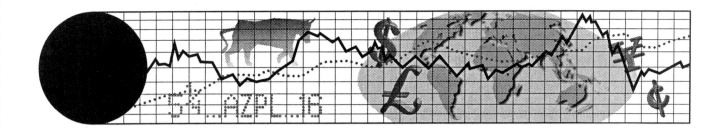

Variable Contracts and Retirement Plans Hotsheet

Variable Annuities

Fixed Annuity:
- Guaranteed rate of return
- Insurance company has investment risk
- Subject to purchasing power risk
- Fixed income guaranteed for life
- Not a security

Variable Annuity:
- Rate of return dependent on separate account performance
- Investor has investment risk
- Sold with prospectus
- Can keep pace with inflation
- Variable income guaranteed for life; principal is not guaranteed

Accumulation Phase:
- Investor pays money to insurer
- Units vary in number and in value

Annuity Phase:
- Investor receives payments from insurer
- Fixed number of units, vary in value

Purchase Methods:
- Periodic deferred—paid in installments, payouts taken later
- Single premium immediate—lump-sum payment, payouts begin immediately, no accumulation period
- Single premium deferred—lump-sum payment, payouts taken later

Payout Methods:
- Lump sum or random withdrawals
- Annuitization (monthly income guaranteed for life)
- Life Income—no beneficiary, largest monthly payment
- Life with Period Certain—minimum guaranteed period
- Joint Life with Last Survivor—annuity on two lives; smallest monthly payment

AIR:	• Used to determine monthly income • Income goes up from previous month if separate account performance is greater than AIR • Income stays the same as previous month if separate account performance is equal to AIR • Income falls from the previous month if separate account performance is less than the AIR
Taxation:	• Monthly income: part return of cost basis, part taxable; proportion determined by exclusion ratio • Lump sum/random withdrawals: LIFO applies; earnings withdrawn first, taxable as ordinary income; no tax on remainder because it is a return of cost basis
Regulated By:	• Act of 1933; Act of 1934; Investment Company Act of 1940; Investment Advisers Act of 1940 • State Insurance Departments; Federal insurance law

Variable Life Insurance

	WHOLE LIFE	VARIABLE LIFE
Premium	Fixed	Fixed
Cash Value	Guaranteed	No guarantee
Death Benefit	Guaranteed and fixed	Minimum guaranteed, variable
Loan Privilege	100 percent of cash value allowed	Usually up to 90 percent of cash value allowed
Investment of Premiums	General account	Separate account
Investment Risk	Insurer	Policyowner
Regulation	State insurance regulations; not a security	State insurance and security regulations; NASD, SEC

Contract Exchange:	• 24 months to exchange variable to fixed
Policy Refunds:	• Full refund within free-look period (45 days) • First year: Cash value plus 30 percent • Second year: Cash value plus 10 percent
Calculations:	• Death benefit—annually; cash value—monthly

| AIR: | • Death benefit fluctuates based on comparison of separate account performance to AIR |
| | • Cash value is not affected by AIR |

| Voting Rights: | • 1 vote per $100 of cash value |

| Loan Provision: | • Minimum of 75 percent available after three years; up to maximum of 90 percent |

Retirement Plans

Nonqualified plans:
- Nondeductible contributions, can be discriminatory
- Examples are payroll deduction, deferred compensation
- Risk of deferred compensation is employer failure

IRAs:
- Maximum contribution is $2,000, or 100 percent of earned income
- Spousal IRA allows $4,000 between two spouse filing joint returns, split between two accounts
- No life insurance or collectibles as contributions
- 10 percent penalty, plus applicable ordinary income tax, on withdrawals before age 59½
- 6 percent excess contribution penalty
- 50 percent insufficient distribution penalty (insufficient if after 70½)
- One rollover allowed each 12 months to be completed within 60 days
- Unlimited trustee to trustee transfers

SEPs:
- Qualified plan that allows employers to contribute money to employee IRAs
- Contribution max = 15 percent of employee salary up to $30,000
- Contributions immediately vested

Roth IRAs:
- New IRA that allows after-tax contributions, possible tax-free distributions
- Maximum contribution of $2,000 per individual, $4,000 per couple
- Does not require distributions to begin at age 70½

Education IRAs:
- New IRA that allows after-tax contributions for children under age 18
- Maximum contribution is $500 per year per child
- Tax-free distributions if funds are used for higher education

Keoghs (HR-10):
- Available to self-employed persons, owners of unincorporated businesses and professional practices

- Contribution max is lesser of 20 percent of gross for employer (25 percent for employee) or $30,000
- All employees must participate if age 21 or older, employed more than one year, work more than 1,000 hours per year
- Life insurance may be held within the plan
- Distributions in lump sums are eligible for five-year income averaging through 1999

TSAs (403(b) plans):
- Available to employees of non-profit organizations
- Typically funded by elective employee salary reductions, usually no cost basis

Pension Plans:
- Require annual contribution

Defined Benefit:
- Based on formula factoring age, salary years of service, calculated by actuary; favor older key employees

Defined Contribution:
- Simpler to administer, contribution is typically a percent of salary
- Five-year income averaging available on distributions through 1999

Profit-Sharing Plans:
- Annual contribution not required, great investment and contribution flexibility

Withholding Rule:
- 20 percent withholding applied to distributions from qualified plans made payable to participant

ERISA:
- Protects participants in corporate (private) plans, not public plans
- Rules for funding, vesting, nondiscrimination, participation, communication

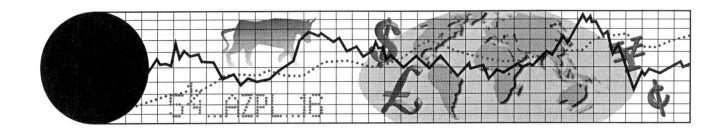

Securities Industry
Regulations Hotsheet

Act of 1933:
- The Paper Act
- Nonexempt issuers must file registration statements with the SEC
- Requires use of prospectus when selling new issues
- Requires full and fair disclosure of new issues
- Regulates primary market activity (issuing and underwriting)

Act of 1934:
- The People Act
- Regulates secondary market activity
- Created the SEC
- Requires registration of all reps and firms that trade securities for the public
- Oversees exchanges and OTC market
- No security is exempt from antifraud provisions (even if exempt from 1933 registration)

Maloney Act:
- Chartered the NASD as the SRO of the OTC
- Investment Advisers Act of 1940
- Requires registration of persons who receive flat fees or percentages for giving investment advice

Insider Trading Act of 1988:
- Tippers and tippees are guilty
- Penalties are up to the greater of $1,000,000 or three times profits made/losses avoided
- Broker-dealers must have written supervisory procedures

Telephone Consumer Protection Act:
- Must call noncustomers at home between 8 A.M. and 9 P.M.
- Firms must maintain "do-not-call list" and written procedures
- Not applicable to nonprofit organizations

Principals:
- Minimum of two per firm; manage, train and supervise
- Approve all accounts and client transactions

Felony Conviction:
- May be disqualified for 10 years (also for cash/securities misdemeanor)

Private Transactions:	• Not allowed without broker-dealer's knowledge and consent. Prior written notice and disclosure of compensation required. Passive investments not subject to this requirement.
Gift Limit:	• No more than $100 cash per year to employees of other member firms from broker-dealer • No more than $50 cash per year from mutual fund underwriter
Selling Dividends:	• Prohibited practice due to tax liability
Breakpoint Sales:	• Encouraging customer to purchase below the opportunity for a discount; • Prohibited practice
Research Reports:	• Must disclose if prepared by someone outside firm
Shared Accounts:	• Allowable only if firm grants prior written approval; sharing only in proportion to contribution
Continuing Commissions:	• Allowed to rep or heirs with bona fide contract
Financial Disclosure:	• Customers entitled to most recent balance sheet upon written request
NASD Communications:	• Advertising = nontargeted communications • Sales literature = targeted communications • Both must be approved by principal before use, filed for three years, two years easily accessible • Investment company material must be filed with NASD within 10 days of use • First year firms must file with NASD 10 days before first use • Generic advertising is OK if product or service offered is available • Name of member required except on recruitment ads • Testimonials OK with disclosure of compensation
Recommendations:	• Must be suitable; disclose current price; potential conflicts of interest • "Past performance does not guarantee future results"
Investment Company Recommendations:	• Advertising/sales literature must disclose 10-year period unless new fund • Advertise based on highest charge; no breakpoint
COP:	• Respond to Department of Enforcement notice within 25 days • DOE can administer any penalty other than jail • Appeal from DOE to National Adjudicatory Council within 25 days • Decision final after 45 days

Summary Complaint: • Maximum fine $2,500 and/or censure

Code of Arbitration:
- Between members, with public only with written consent
- Decisions are final and binding on all parties
- Awards after 30 days
- Simplified is $25,000 for public and industry